I0754866

MICK ROCK
ROCKY HORROR

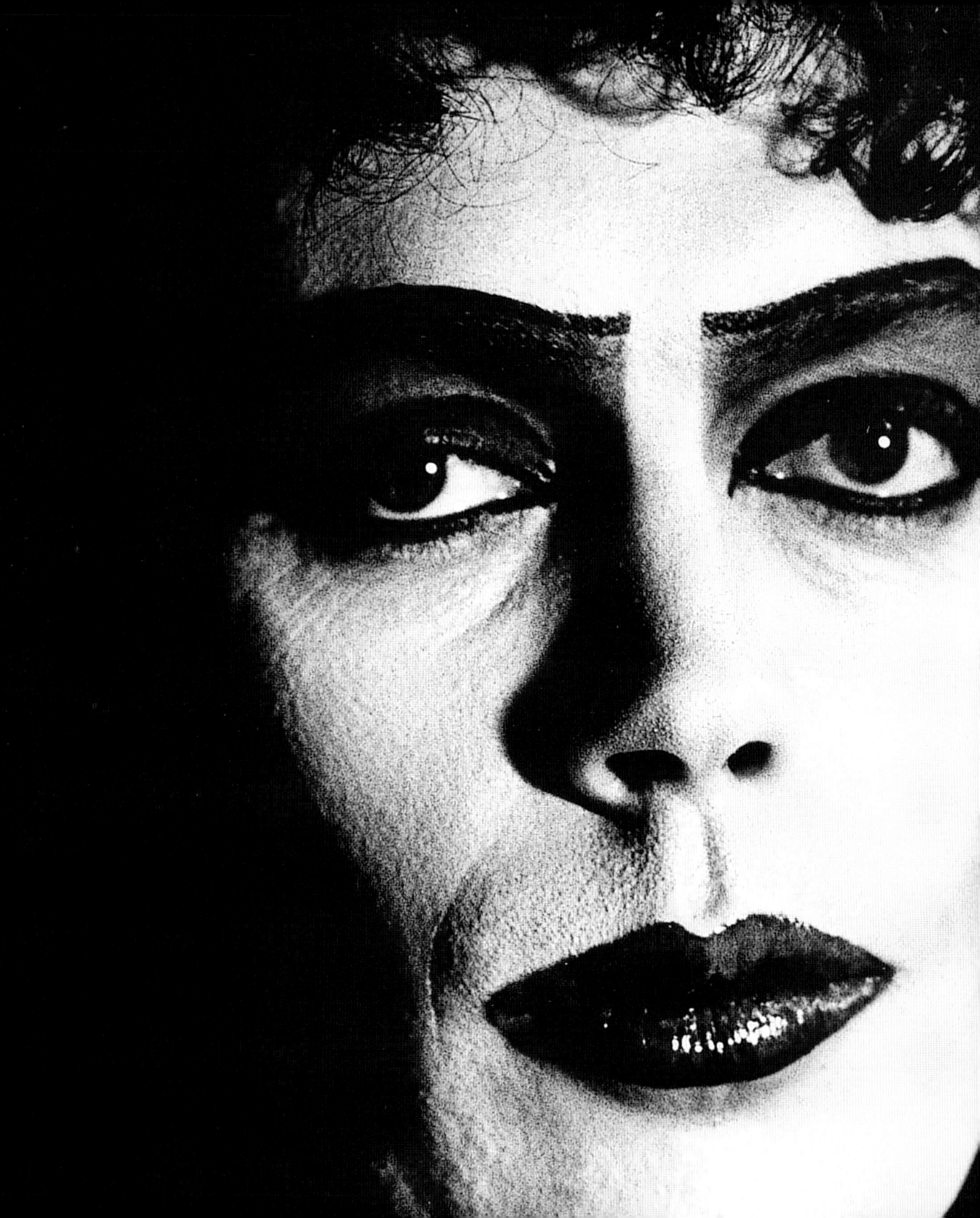

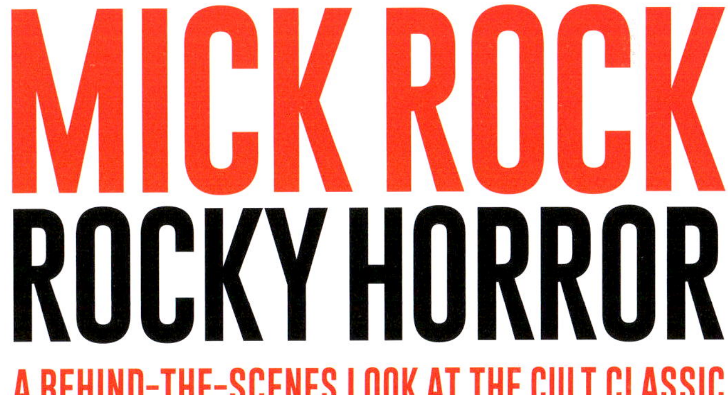

WITH **Tim Mohr**
FOREWORD BY **Richard O'Brien**
AFTERWORD BY **Pati Rock**

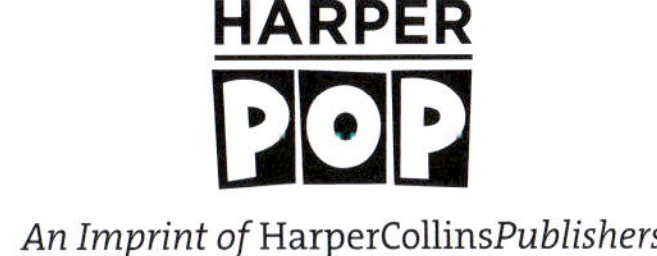

An Imprint of Harper Collins*Publishers*

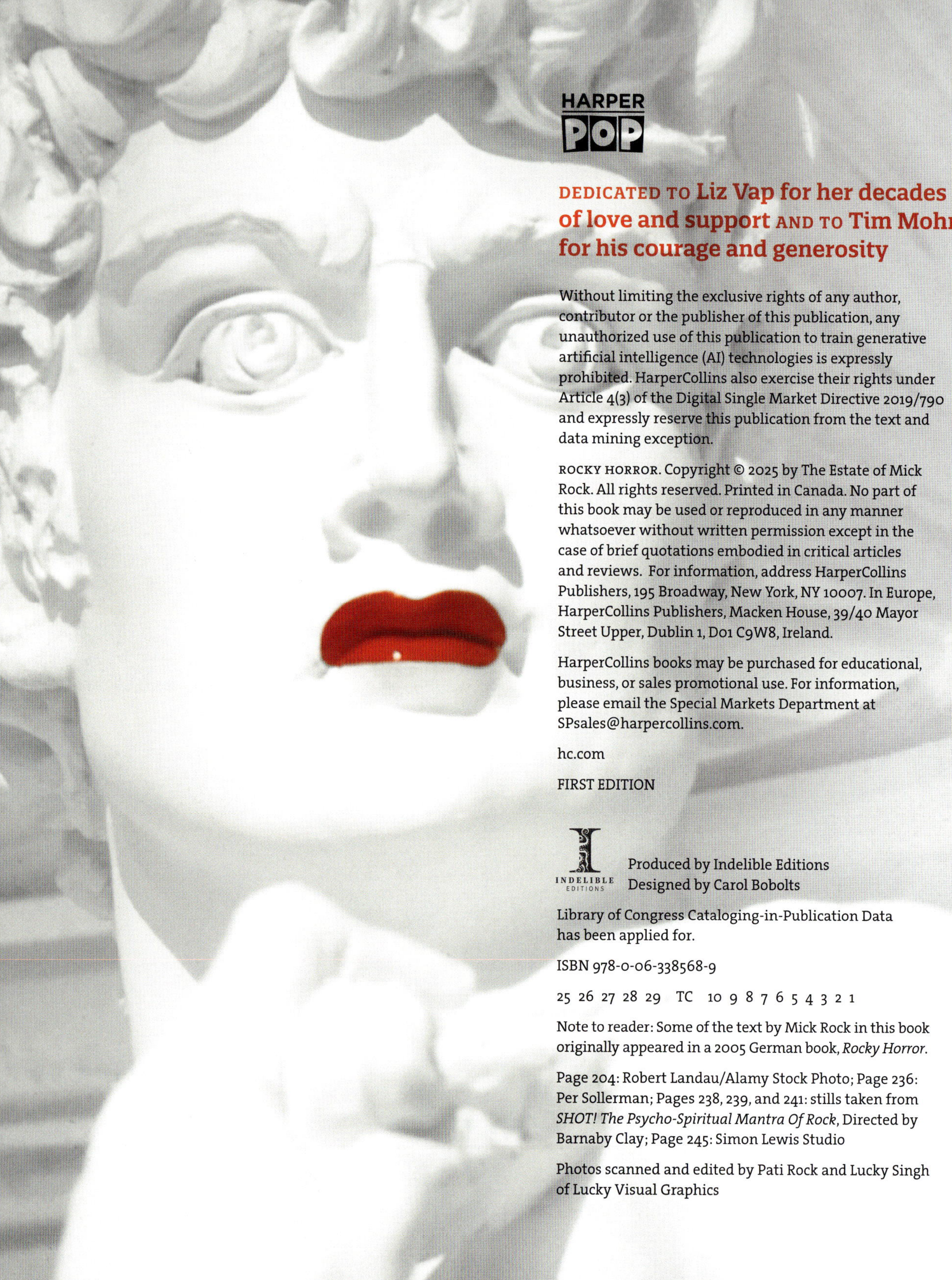

DEDICATED TO **Liz Vap for her decades of love and support** AND TO **Tim Mohr for his courage and generosity**

 For information, address HarperCollins Publishers, 195 Broadway, New York, NY 10007. In Europe, HarperCollins Publishers, Macken House, 39/40 Mayor Street Upper, Dublin 1, D01 C9W8, Ireland.

HarperCollins books may be purchased for educational, business, or sales promotional use. For information, please email the Special Markets Department at SPsales@harpercollins.com.

hc.com

FIRST EDITION

INDELIBLE EDITIONS

Produced by Indelible Editions
Designed by Carol Bobolts

Library of Congress Cataloging-in-Publication Data has been applied for.

ISBN 978-0-06-338568-9

25 26 27 28 29 TC 10 9 8 7 6 5 4 3 2 1

Note to reader: Some of the text by Mick Rock in this book originally appeared in a 2005 German book, *Rocky Horror*.

Page 204: Robert Landau/Alamy Stock Photo; Page 236: Per Sollerman; Pages 238, 239, and 241: stills taken from *SHOT! The Psycho-Spiritual Mantra Of Rock*, Directed by Barnaby Clay; Page 245: Simon Lewis Studio

Photos scanned and edited by Pati Rock and Lucky Singh of Lucky Visual Graphics

CONTENTS

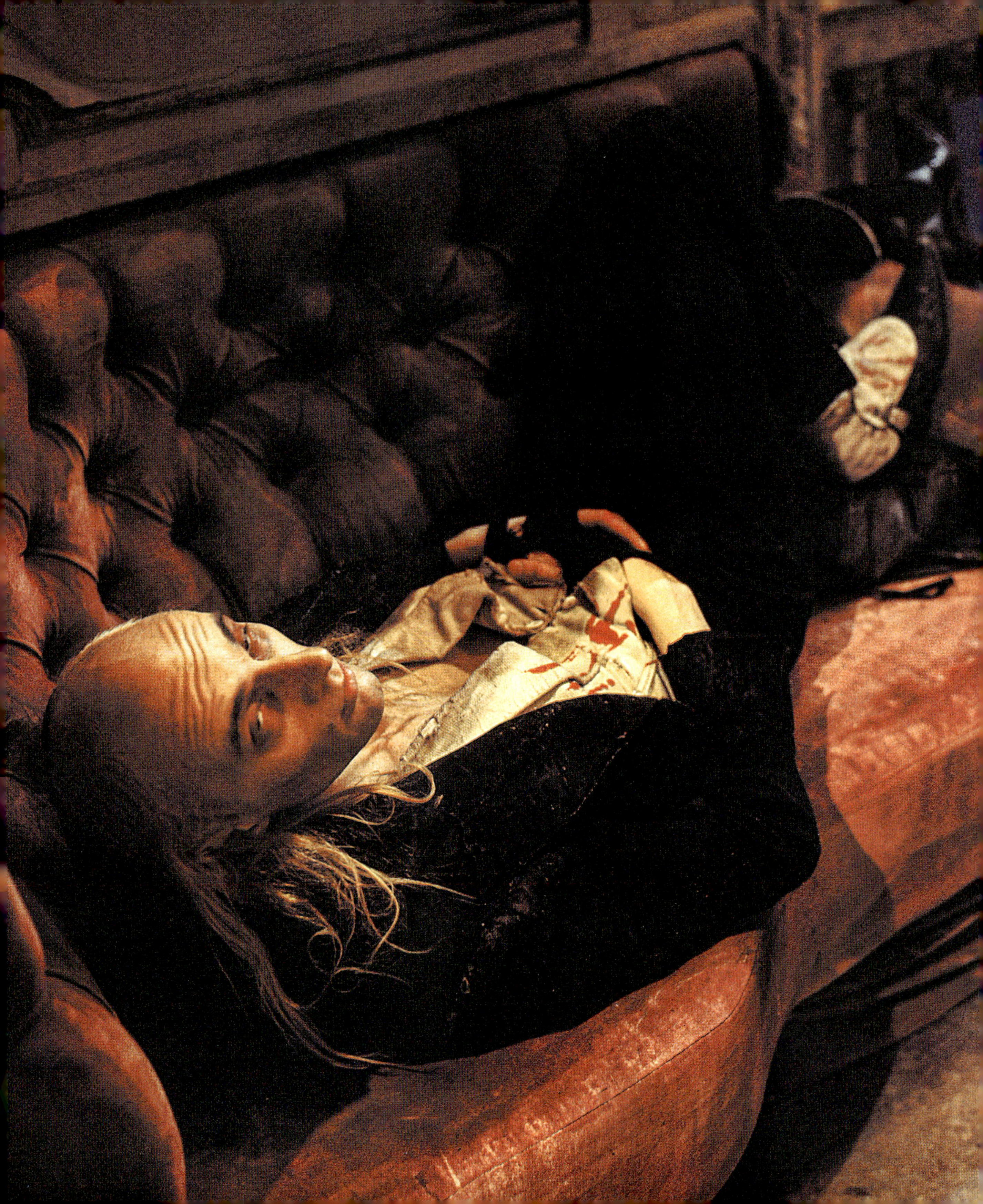

FOREWORD BY RICHARD O'BRIEN

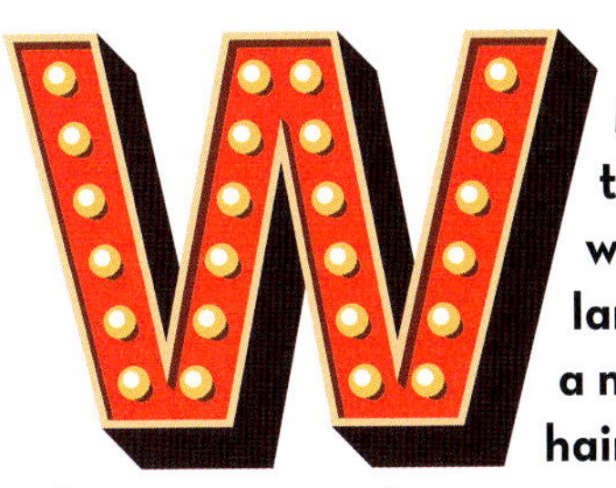

When I first met Mick Rock in the 1970s, he was a barefoot, lanky chap with a mop of unruly hair, the smile of a buccaneer, and a camera welded to his hand. (Later he wore shoes.)

Mick's "frozen moments" of an extremely childish and self-obsessed period in Western civilization's decline are self-evidential and, although it is on occasion rather embarrassing to see oneself as a major perp of vanity crimes, it also comes as something of a relief to see that we appeared to be enjoying ourselves.

Frank-N-Furter, mad scientist, self-obsessed, narcissistic exhibitionist, obviously adores to be admired, and for him the seductive clicking shutter of a Hasselblad camera was like a bell to Pavlov's dogs come chow time on the last day of Lent.

How much bigger and better champions appear to become when they are immortalized in portraiture, for they metamorphose into "icons." The meeting of Frank-N-Furter and Mick Rock was that of two people hungry for a symbiotic relationship or experience, with each of them taking as much as they could from one another, and willingly so. Tim Curry's marvelous Frank was a monster of self-regard, and Tim knew exactly how to give this evil genius his head and Mick served it up on a photographic plate.

Staunch *Rocky Horror* fans will be familiar with some of the pictures in this book, though there are many here that I had never seen before. How glad I am that director Jim Sharman felt moved to invite Mick down to Bray Studios during filming, and how grateful I am that he accepted.

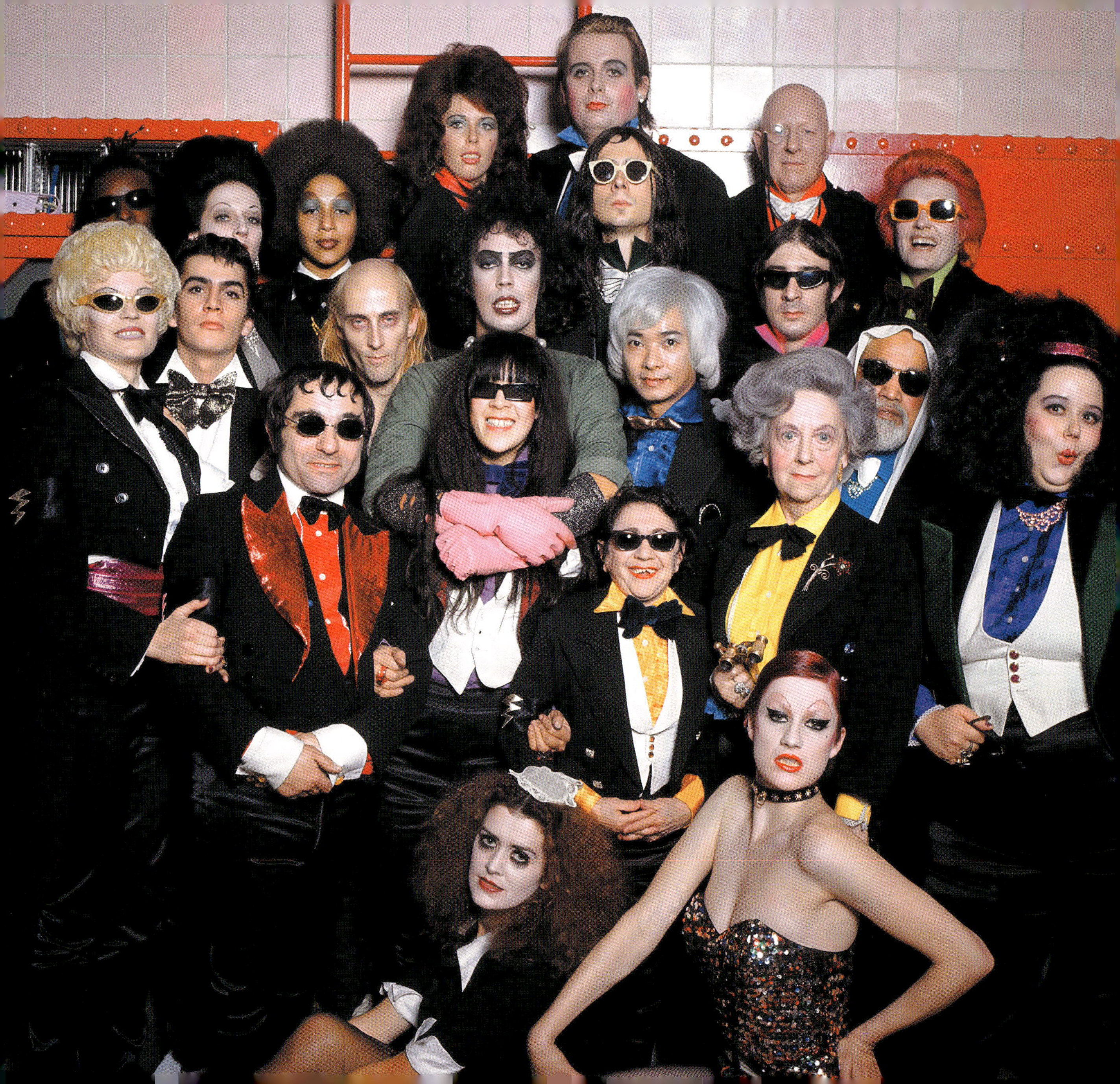

AS PURE AS CULT GETS
BY MICK ROCK

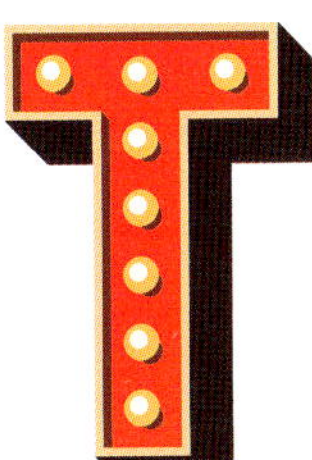

***he Rocky Horror Picture Show* is a totally unique phenomenon; there's nothing even to compare it to.** It occupies its own unchallenged space in the history of modern popular culture, for this is a special movie, a very special work of popular art, drummed up from the recesses of my friend Richard O'Brien's mobile imagination. It has weathered all the shifts in fashion and taste of postmodern distraction, and is now as embedded in the modern Western psyche as veggie burgers and the Rolling Stones.

It has long been the king of the midnight movie circuit, grossing, by some estimation, over $200 million to date—that's a lot of popcorn and cola! Of course, it stumbled out of the box office gate so limply that it looked to be destined for the celluloid knacker's yard. One early critic of the film deemed it "a piece of kitsch trash." For him that was a must-to-avoid dismissal; he meant "stick in the garbage can and whistle."

For those of more supple and eclectic taste (like us, dear reader), such a label promised something delicious, a call to illicit revelry. I don't get critics anyway—why not just ignore what you don't like and put your powers of discrimination into celebrating something you admire? I barely register what I don't like. There's too little time. I'd rather gnaw on a sweeter bone. And *The Rocky Horror Picture Show* provides a very succulent bone for the young at heart.

Back then we were all so very young in heart and even years. Somehow I had

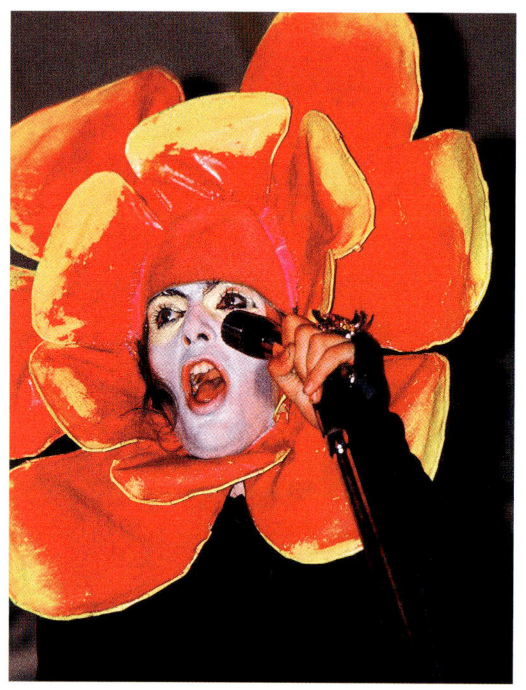

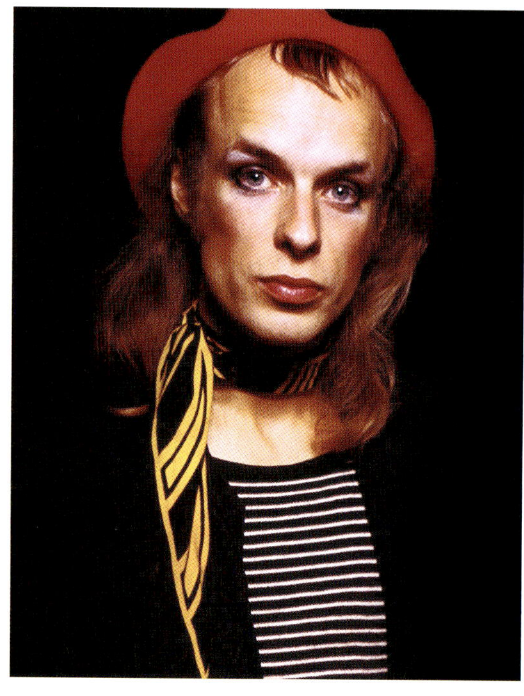

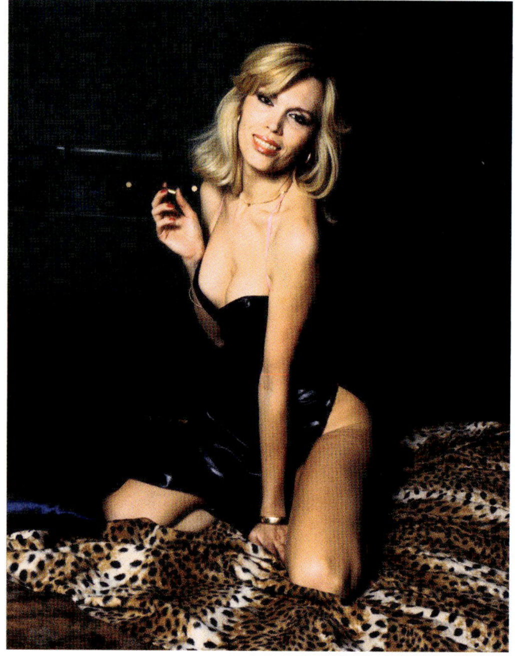

connected with the zeitgeist and was sitting right in the eye of a colorful cultural storm, and I didn't even really know it. Well, I had suspicions, but I had no firm frame of reference, so I just kept on doing what I had been doing, trusting my instincts, knowing what I liked, tripping shutters, exposing my times—for I had learned that my pictures spoke louder than my words.

Nineteen seventy-three was a very good-looking year in London from where I was perched. My retina blinked more often than most. I sucked on film like it was manna. I was hungry for imagery and bold in my grab. Androgyny and women's lib were flooding the ether. Bowie, Roxy Music, Queen, and

Peter Gabriel, Brian Eno, and Amanda Lear, 1974.

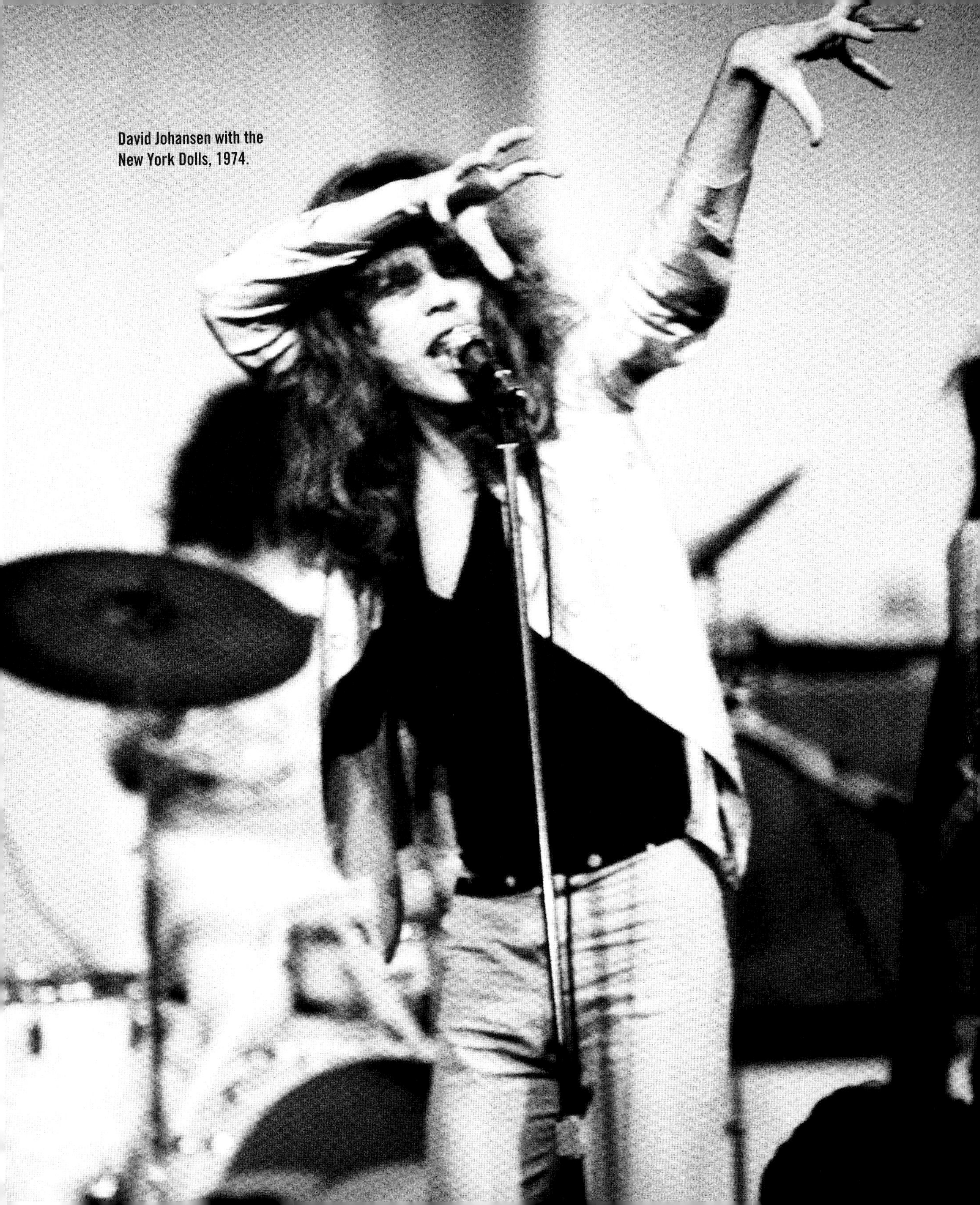

David Johansen with the
New York Dolls, 1974.

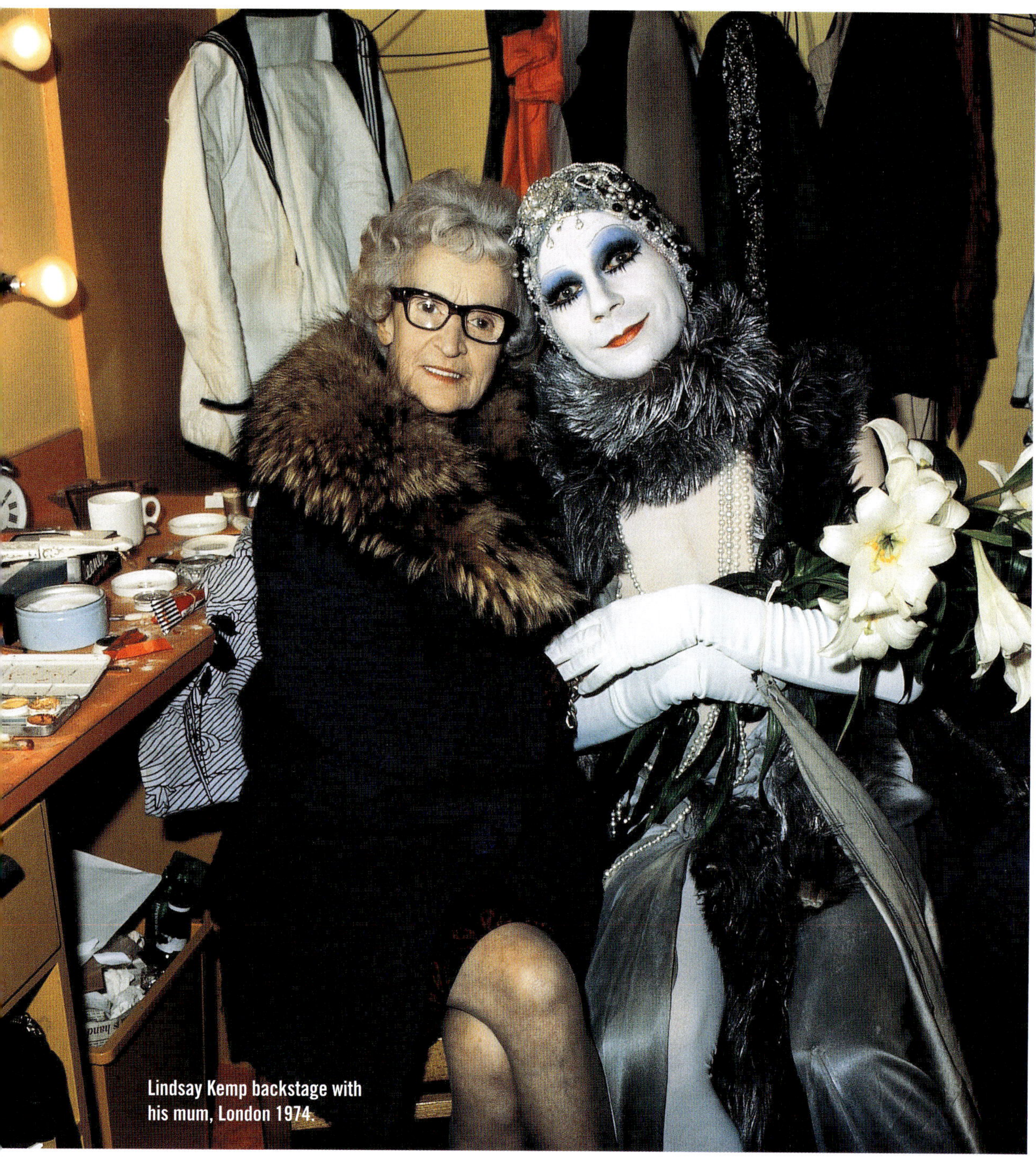

Lindsay Kemp backstage with his mum, London 1974.

Lou Reed were proving that style could also be rock 'n' roll substance, and that boys in makeup could be more than just sissies and narcissists. And Lindsay Kemp, mime and choreographer extraordinaire, the resident godfather of camp and glam, was finally parading drag as art to an eager young audience. I was having a good time.

Then snap, crackle, and rock right in the middle of it all—a rock 'n' roll musical that so perfectly summed up our obsessions bubbled hilariously into view and some rare wind blew me in a ticket for the play's premiere. I loved the title *The Rocky Horror Show*. I didn't have a clue what it was about, but I knew I should go. And I was entranced. It was so wild, energetic, camp, and colorful. Like a pop collage, an all singing and swinging Rauschenberg. It was sexy and draggy and toon-y and retro and futuristic and funny and fiddled with references to old horror movies: *Frankenstein*, *Nosferatu*, *Frankenstein's Bride*,

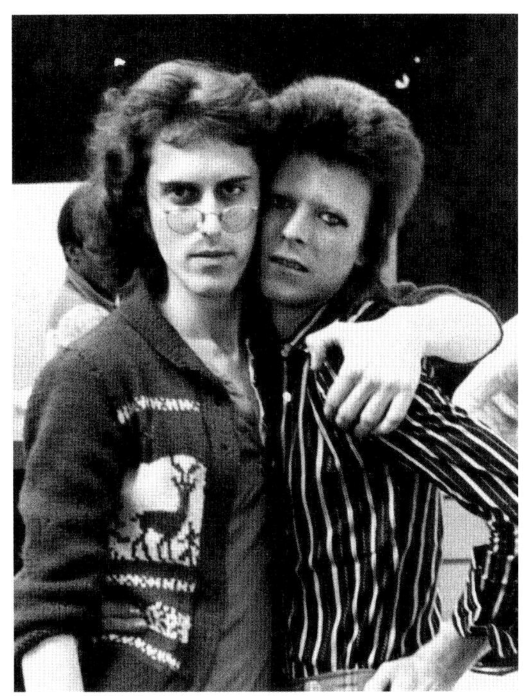

David Bowie with Mick during the *Pin Ups* recordings at the Chateau d'Hérouville in France, 1973.
Bowie backstage with mentor Lindsay Kemp, 1973.

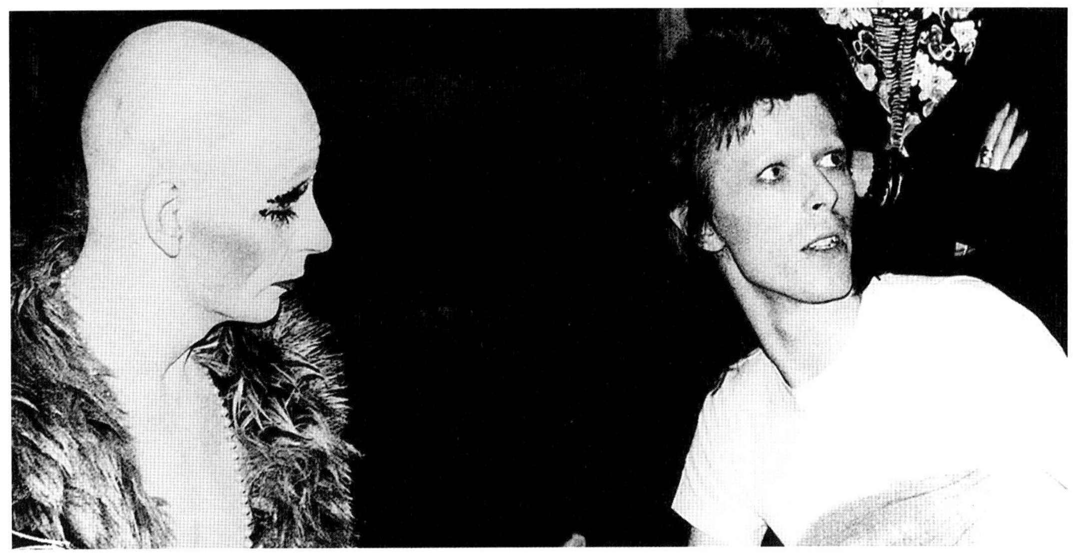

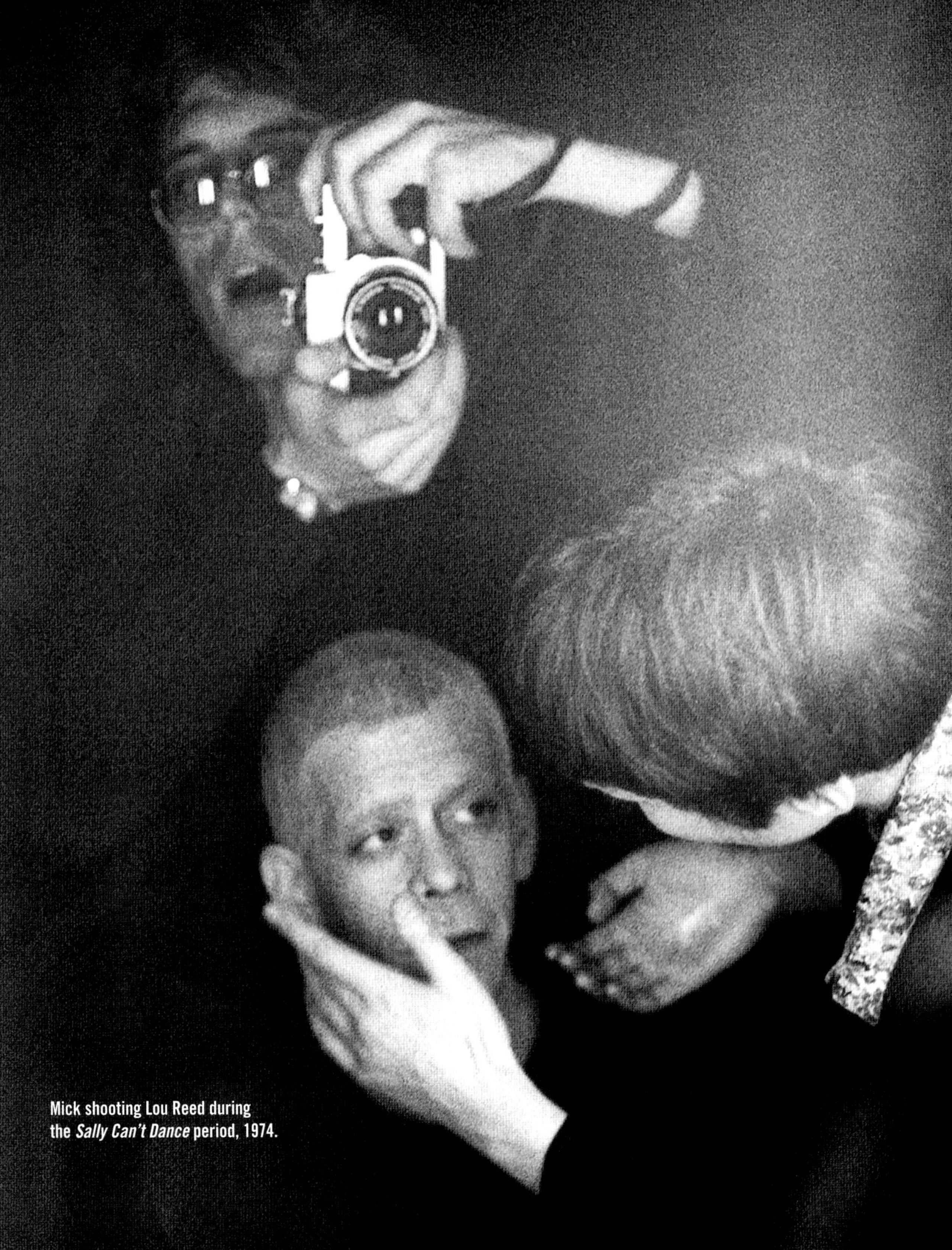

Mick shooting Lou Reed during the *Sally Can't Dance* period, 1974.

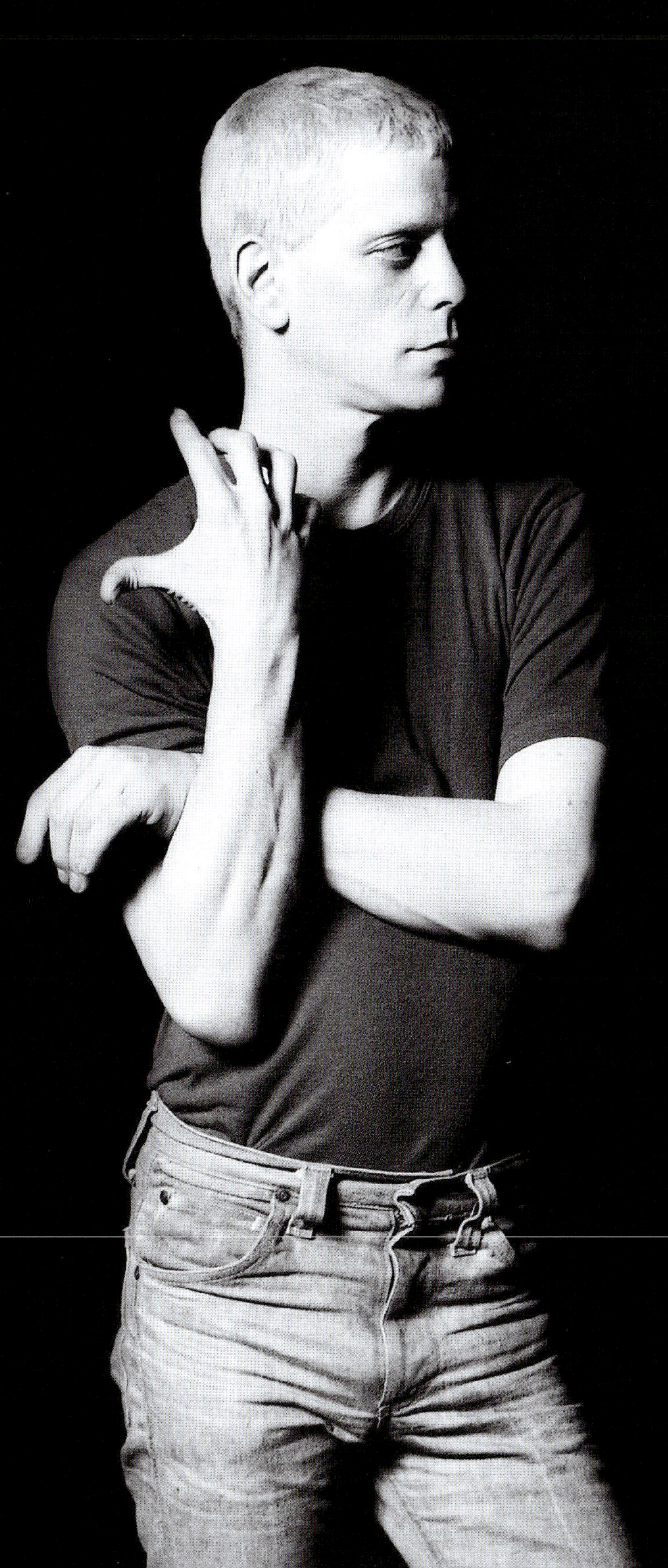

ANDREW WATT, MUSICIAN AND MUSIC PRODUCER: "Mick had the ability to look into someone and see their potential and see what he felt could be their place within popular culture. He was kind of the first person to serve blown-out images, larger-than-life images of people. He had a magic touch and ability to create images that would stand the test of time."

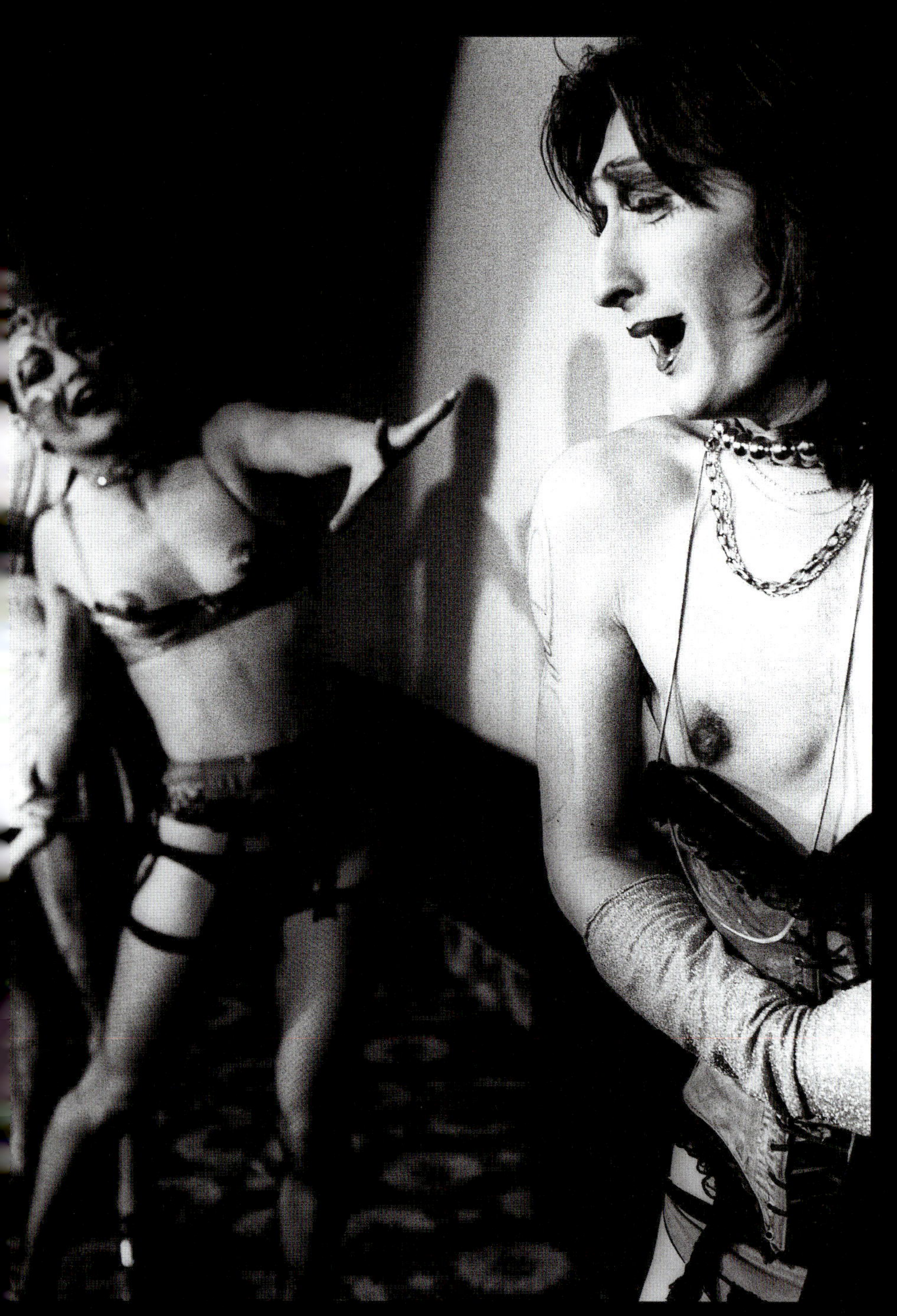

ANNA SUI, DESIGNER:

"I saw *Rocky Horror Show* on Broadway and also in the movie theater on 8th street in 1975. This is just after The New York Dolls and Bowie's *Diamond Dogs*, so glam rock was in the air. Mick Rock captured so many iconic moments during that period. He came over to my place for dinner, Anita [Palenberg] cooked, and we looked at all his photos from that period. I especially loved how intimate Mick's photos of Bowie were."

and 1960s English Hammer Film Productions. It was all there. It was a riot and irresistible.

I wondered how anyone could hold all these disparate elements in their head, wondered how anyone could meld them together so deliciously. Like a master cook with a brand-new recipe, guaranteed to awaken even the most jaded taste buds. I wished I could have a talent like that; so totally zany and timely. I wanted very much to meet with the author, to smell what he smelled, to dip a little into his well of fun. He clearly understood the power of pure, rollicking fun. He had a sticky mind with many tentacles and a sly heart that wanted to hold your hand and never let go. I knew we could be friends. It was a hot time in old King's Road that night but I wasn't yet destined to meet the man. That would come a little later.

I absolutely wanted to photograph the show but I was busy as hell and the stars wouldn't line up right. By the time I was asked to poke my lens at it, the original cast had gone to launch the show in Los Angeles and I was left with *The Rocky Horror Show* Mark II. It had moved to a second theater farther down the King's Road—closer to the World's End, where Malcolm McLaren and Vivienne Westwood had a rockabilly fashion store called Too Fast To Live, Too Young To Die, and which, within a year or so, would morph into the subversive SEX shop and by late-1975 foist the Sex Pistols and the punk movement onto young England's fashion-hungry and anarchic psyche.

A very handsome and friendly young Aussie called Phil Sayer was now cast in the role of Frank-N-Furter, of whom Richard declared: "It was a big job trying to replace Tim Curry, but I thought he did an excellent job."

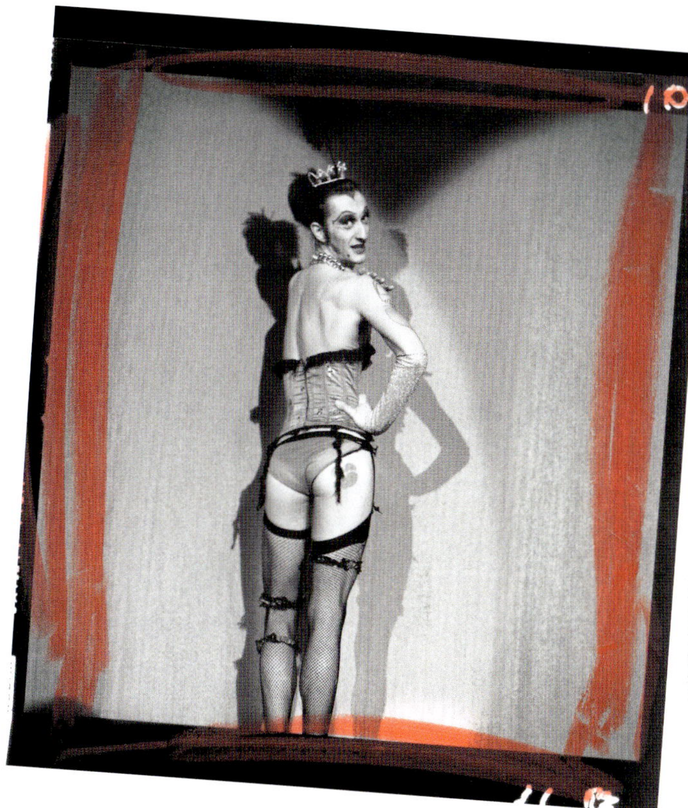

Phil Sayer as Frank-N-Furter for the London production of *The Rocky Horror Show*, Royal Court Theatre, 1973.

I was asked to shoot the publicity/production stills and it was a hoot. Tim and Richard and Little Nell and company—the backbone of the original cast—had already created such a strong impression that Mark II suffered by contrast, but it still had plenty of bite and energy, and had a good run. So I shot the rehearsals, had fun, got paid; probably not much because photographers never got paid well for such services in those days. But I still had shot a *Rocky Horror* production and I was happy with the images.

Around this time, I had connected with the then-unknown band Queen, and had shot their now-legendary *Queen II* album session, which would be faithfully copied in pose and lighting the following year for their "Bohemian Rhapsody" promo film. I remember the fabulous Freddie Mercury inquiring about the show. He had missed the original lineup and wanted to know if Mark II was worth the price of entry. Of course it was, I assured him. As time has proven with numerous worldwide productions over the past thirty-plus years, the basic script and musical material are so sharp, so tight, so brilliantly conceived, just about any production always works. I personally have viewed seven or eight

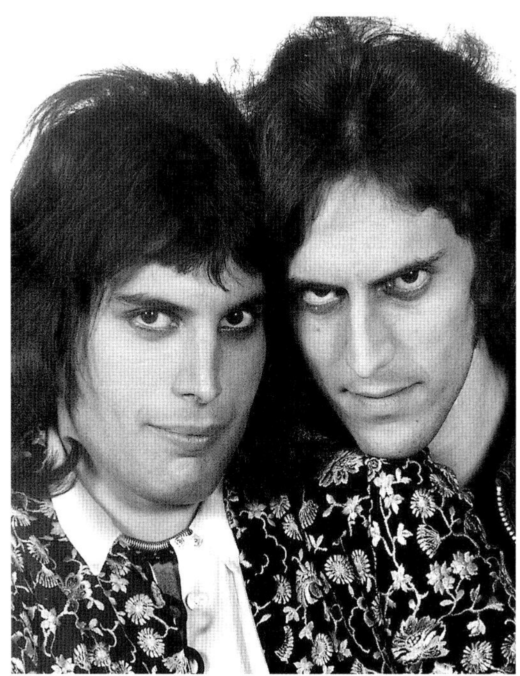

Mick and pal Freddie Mercury in London, 1974.

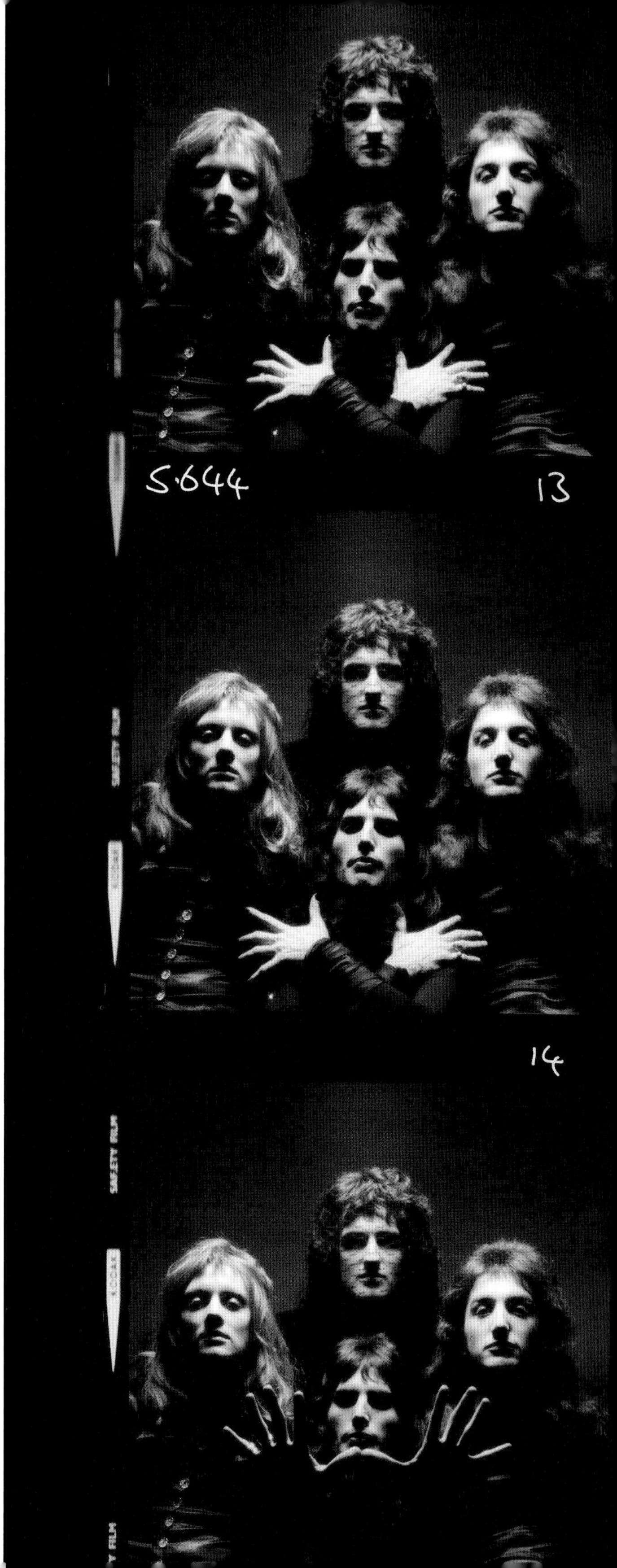

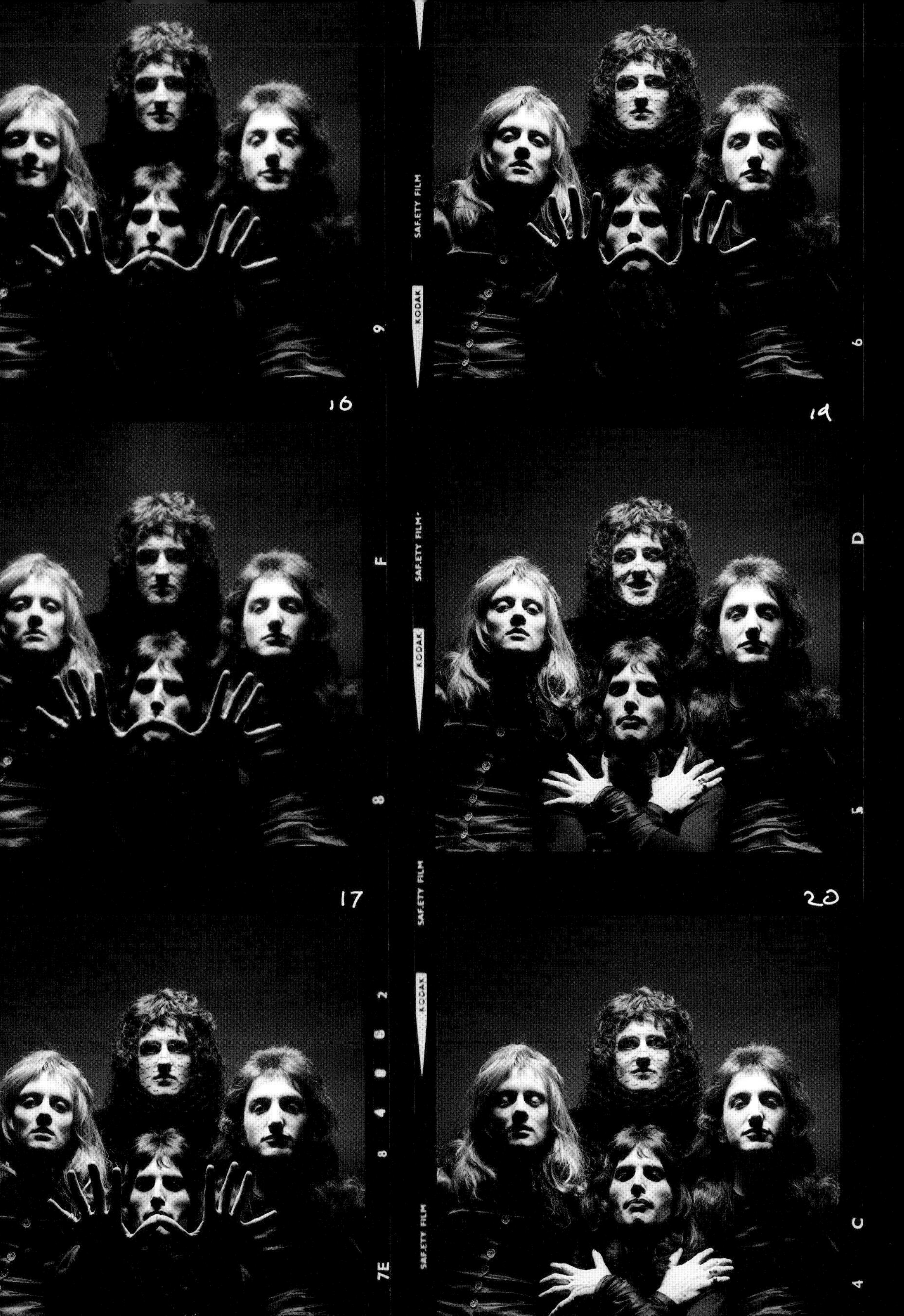

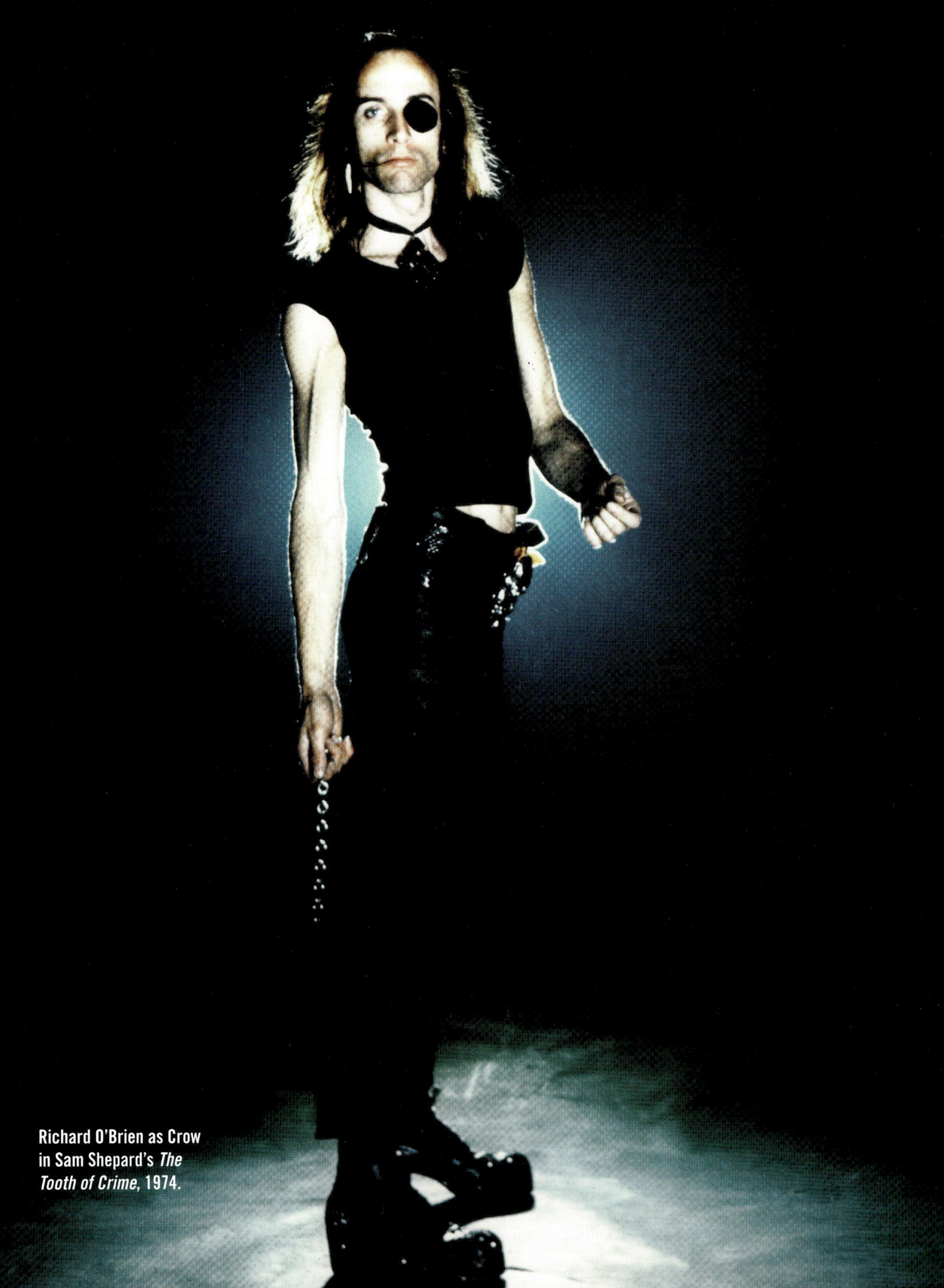

Richard O'Brien as Crow in Sam Shepard's *The Tooth of Crime*, 1974.

different renditions, and I have been well entertained each and every time. Freddie did love it. He thought Phil Sayer was handsome and sexy.

"He has such marvelous legs and a very attractive bottom," Freddie opined.

Fast-forward a few months to the spring of 1974, and I received a call from the press lady at the Royal Court Theatre, Sloane Square. Jim Sharman (who I was aware had directed *Rocky Horror*) had requested my skills to shoot a new production of Sam Shepard's *The Tooth of Crime*, a play with some music (as opposed to a musical). Jim was a fan of my work with David Bowie, Iggy Pop, and especially Lou Reed. He considered *Transformer* the finest of all album covers—and amongst the finest albums. I was understandably flattered and accepted.

When the time came to shoot the final dress rehearsal, I scooted over to the theater, where I met not only Jim and Sam, but also, to my pleasant surprise, the man who had played Riff Raff in the premiere production of *The Rocky Horror Show*—Richard O'Brien.

At this meeting I learned that Richard had also written the dialogue, music, and lyrics of *Rocky Horror*. And I was, to say the least, impressed. Dressed in character, he had on an eye patch, full leather attire, a swastika round his neck—he was playing an upstart rocker named Crow, battling an outlaw king of rock called Hoss for his throne. At the dramatic climax of *The Tooth of Crime*, the two rockers lock vocal horns in an orgy of rock 'n' roll attack and counterattack, and the aging king gives ground: a superb piece of rock theater loaded with gambling, outlaws, and rock 'n' roll imagery. It was written by Sam while he was living in New York's East Village with Patti Smith in the late 1960s. He originally wrote the role played by Richard with Patti in mind, and she performed it in its first-ever production.

I also shot both protagonists—Crow and Hoss—in my recently acquired (and first) photo studio on Great Newport Street, just off Leicester Square. I found Richard particularly photogenic and the likes of early subjects such as Syd Barrett, Bowie, Iggy, Lou, and Freddie, and we would do several sessions for different projects over the ensuing two or three years.

The most significant, of course, came a few months later when Jim Sharman personally called to invite me to be the "special photographer" on the set of the upcoming film production of what was now called *The Rocky Horror Picture Show*. I couldn't be the regular set photographer because I wasn't in the union; nor in fact would I have had the time because I was very much in demand by then for other projects. It would also have been totally against my philosophical regimen to be up early every morning for weeks at a time. I was essentially a bohemian spirit in those days with little interest in any form of creative activity before noon.

The film company wouldn't pay me, but that was no problem, because I was the only lensman outside of the unit pro that Jim would allow on the set, so there would be no competition for magazine sales when the film was released. More important to me, I would own and control the photos.

I was given the freedom to come and go

exactly as I wished, on my own time. I could snap whatever caught my eye, stirred my imagination. It was to be filmed just outside London at Bray Studios. This was a decision made to enhance the aura of the shoot, because this was where many of the 1960s Hammer low-budget horror films were incubated: movies that now show up on late-night TV, many of them featuring those master British actors of the genre Peter Cushing and Christopher Lee. To younger audiences, the extraordinary Lee is better known as the big bad wizard in *The Lord of the Rings*, Saruman. He wouldn't have known what to make of the bunch of eccentrics, changelings, and glamsters who frolicked on his hallowed turf during the frantic month it took to shoot *Rocky Horror*. Later I found out he had in fact seen the movie and loved it. He had a keener sense of camp than any of us suspected.

My nervous system always goes through some interesting changes when I have to roll back the years as I contemplate my early images, especially when I have to apply words to paper. The 1970s, as embodied by glam and punk, do hold a particular fascination for a modern audience. Perhaps because they conjure up a time when material control and acquisition were completely subsidiary to sensory exploration and creativity.

It was a time of colorful exploration in sex, music, fashion, and chemistry. Certainly, in our naïveté, we were a bold and adventurous brigade. Maybe it's a nostalgia for a time when so many doors were opening for young, creative people, whereas today the constant scrutiny of the media and the far greater awareness of sensory overload make us all the more alert to the dangers of which we were all so blissfully and willfully ignorant.

Richard has said that *Rocky Horror* was a reflection of the self-indulgence of that faraway world of satin, mascara, and chains, but it's worth pointing out that the extremely short shooting schedule and the tightness of the budget ensured that there was less time for self-indulgence than the work itself might imply. The cast and crew had to deliver the goods at breakneck speed. Everyone had to be on their toes. Performances had to be delivered on demand. There was no time for multiple retakes and rampant frivolity. Of course, once the shooting was over . . . I leave it to your fervent imagination, most honorable reader.

Maybe the strongest impression that these modest stills project is that, as Richard points out, everyone appears to be having such a good time. That also may partly account for the delightful potency of this celluloid classic. It's a privilege to have been of service to such a legendary piece of art. For although these may be my images, they are extrapolated from the gestation of Richard's art, and physically I needed his nod to proceed.

Richard, Jim, and Tim especially, I want to thank you for allowing me to witness and record a process the result of which just keeps on giving.

Mick Rock

(1948–2021)

Mick in London, photographed by Lou Reed.

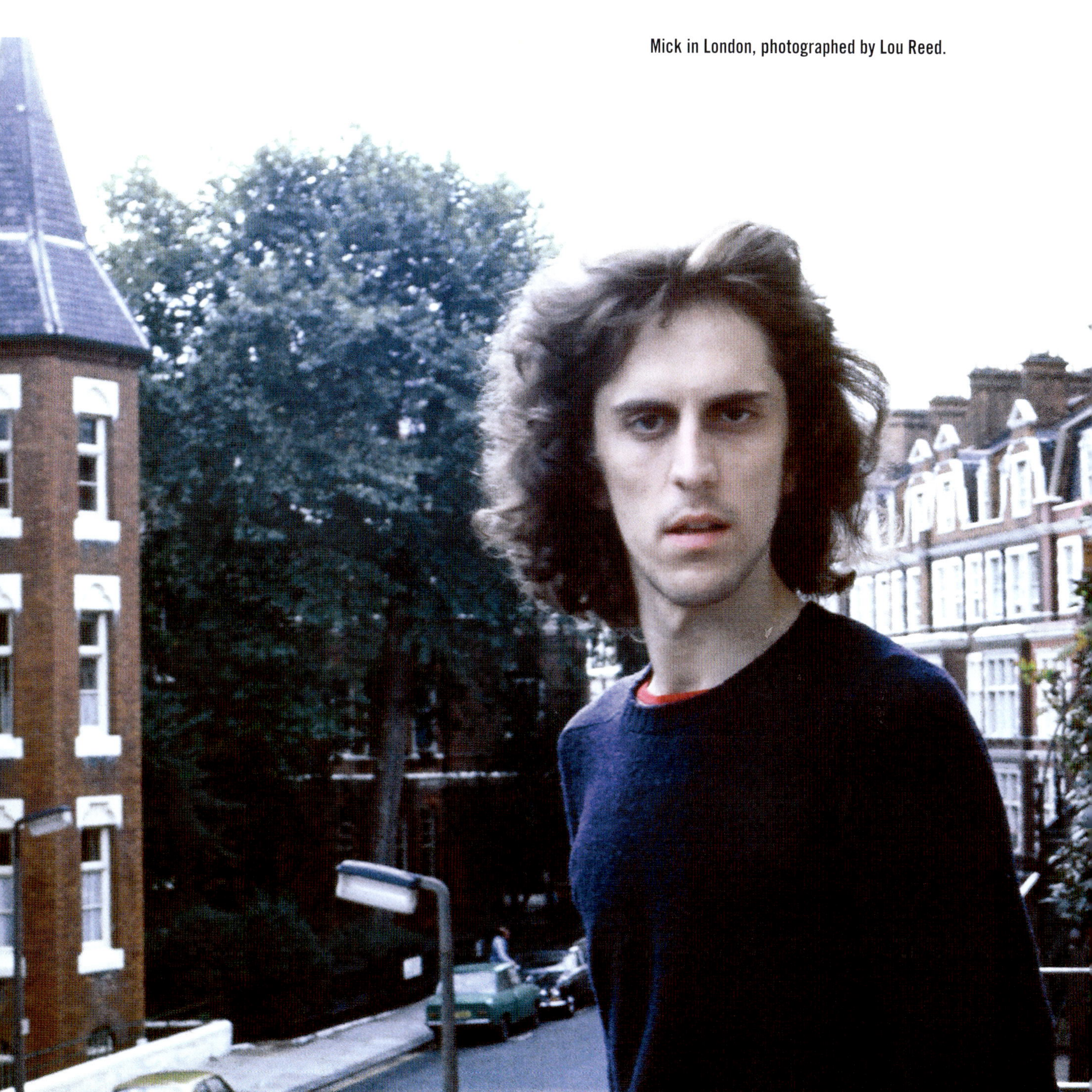

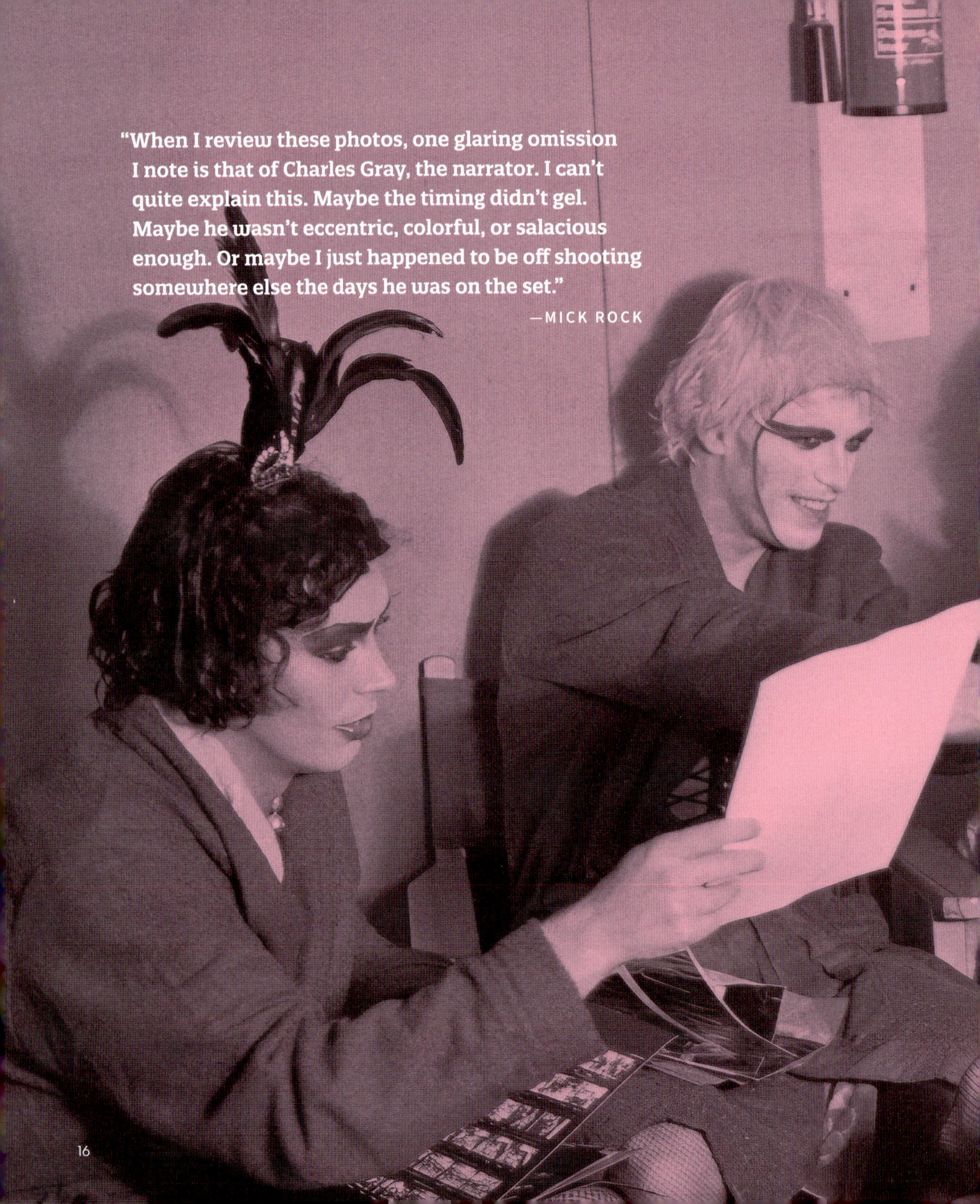

"When I review these photos, one glaring omission I note is that of Charles Gray, the narrator. I can't quite explain this. Maybe the timing didn't gel. Maybe he wasn't eccentric, colorful, or salacious enough. Or maybe I just happened to be off shooting somewhere else the days he was on the set."

—MICK ROCK

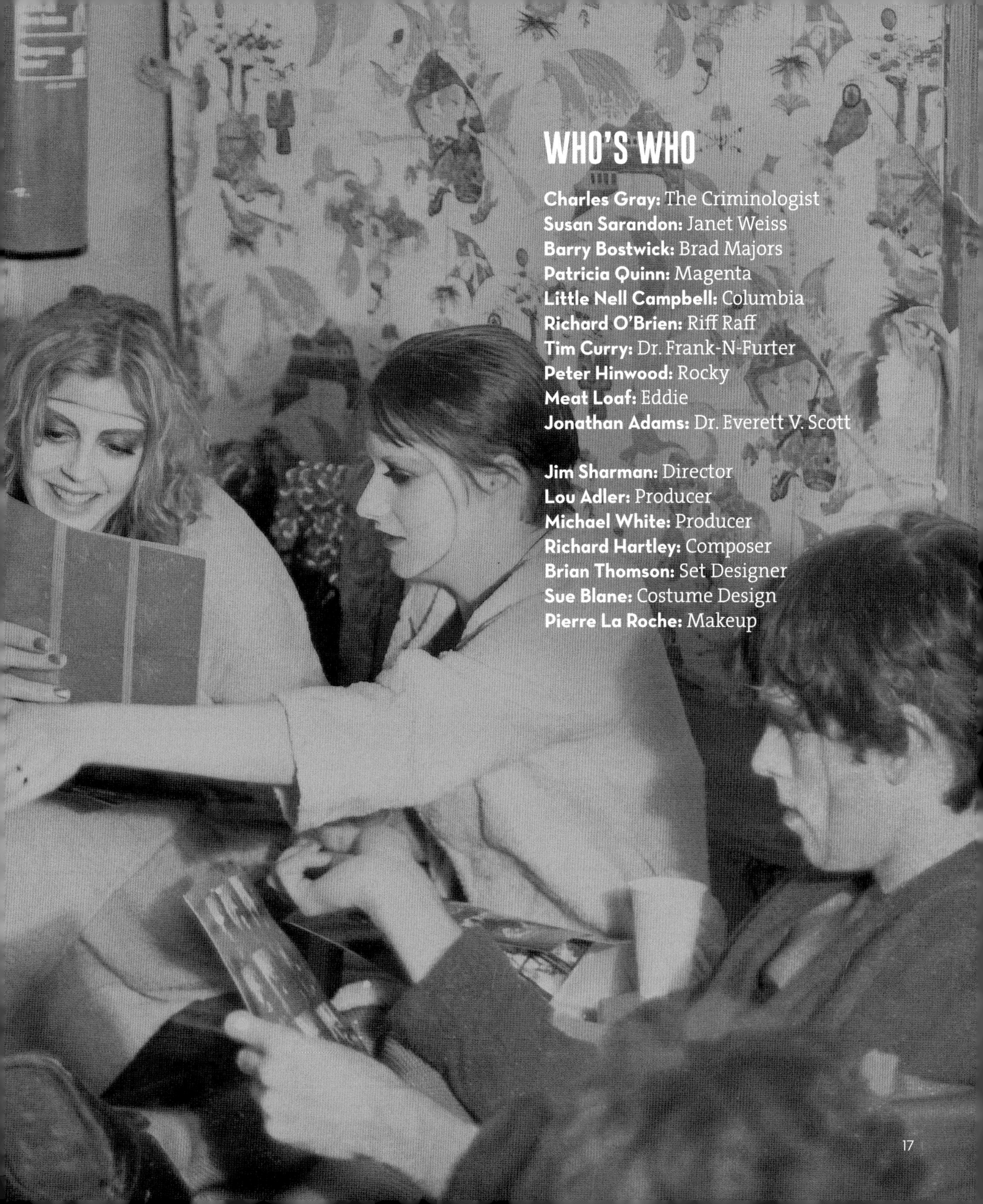

WHO'S WHO

Charles Gray: The Criminologist
Susan Sarandon: Janet Weiss
Barry Bostwick: Brad Majors
Patricia Quinn: Magenta
Little Nell Campbell: Columbia
Richard O'Brien: Riff Raff
Tim Curry: Dr. Frank-N-Furter
Peter Hinwood: Rocky
Meat Loaf: Eddie
Jonathan Adams: Dr. Everett V. Scott

Jim Sharman: Director
Lou Adler: Producer
Michael White: Producer
Richard Hartley: Composer
Brian Thomson: Set Designer
Sue Blane: Costume Design
Pierre La Roche: Makeup

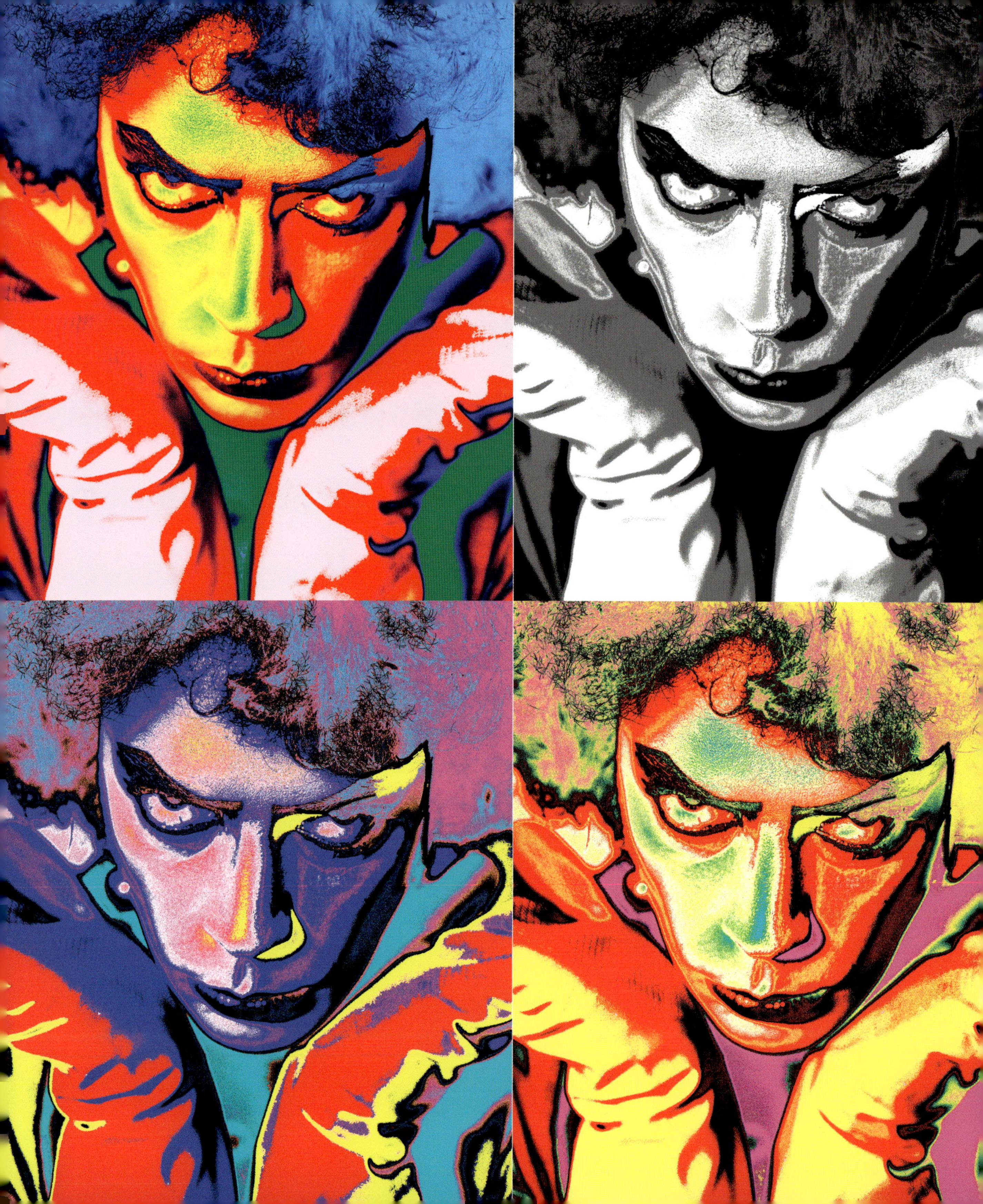

I WOULD LIKE, IF I MAY, TO TAKE YOU ON A STRANGE JOURNEY

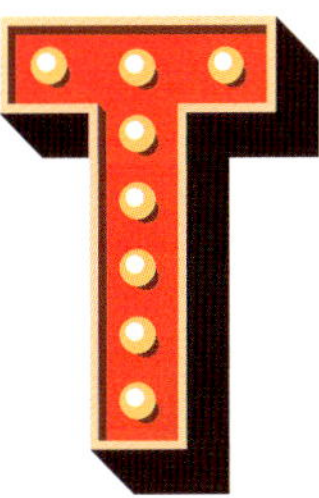

hrough his friendship with Chrissie Shrimpton—model, girlfriend of Mick Jagger for several years, and sister of the face of Swinging London, Jean Shrimpton—actor and composer Richard O'Brien was already ensconced in the royal court of 1960s rock 'n' roll.

"She introduced me to the rockocracy," O'Brien told *The Guardian* in 2020. "England was swinging like a pendulum. There was nowhere better to be on the planet, and I went for it."

And though he had appeared in of-the-moment musicals like *Jesus Christ Superstar* and *Hair*, he began looking for something else: "I was starting to think I wouldn't mind seeing a musical that appealed to me, an eternal adolescent. I loved B-movies, rock 'n' roll, and glam, so I thought I'd do a parody—or homage—to all those things," as he told *The Guardian* in 2013.

By the early 1970s, some of what would become the key material for *The Rocky Horror Show* was already gestating in O'Brien's head. Asked to perform at the 1972 staff Christmas party thrown by EMI Records, he had composed "Science Fiction/Double Feature," an ode to B movies that would serve as the introductory tune of *Rocky Horror*.

O'Brien already knew director Jim Sharman too. Originally from Australia, Sharman had enjoyed a spectacular rise from origins in experimental theater productions in Sydney. At just twenty-one, he had directed a controversial version of Mozart's *Don Giovanni* for Sydney's main opera company;

he went on to direct *Hair* and *Jesus Christ Superstar*. It was the latter production that took him—and set designer Brian Thomson, who would also work on *Rocky Horror*—from Sydney to London, where in 1972 he cast O'Brien in the UK version of *Superstar*.

One night in early 1973, Sharman stopped by O'Brien's place with musical director Richard Hartley, who was working on music for another Sharman project. O'Brien sang them "Science Fiction" and "Hot Patootie," and Sharman instantly realized these songs deserved to be part of something larger. Soon Sharman negotiated three weeks' use of the Theatre Upstairs at the Royal Court Theatre in the summer of 1973 in exchange for directing something in the main theater, and O'Brien, who was between acting gigs, set to work on what would become *The Rocky Horror Show*.

"Writing *Rocky Horror* was almost like working on a jigsaw puzzle," O'Brien explained for the film's Blu-ray edition. "I had written several of the songs before and all I had to do was slot them in. I didn't start at the beginning and develop the plot from there. I started at both ends and then filled in the middle."

Still, even after he had written the bulk of *Rocky Horror*, O'Brien didn't envision a hit: "I thought we'd have our three weeks of fun . . . then move on."

Richard Hartley, who served as musical director and arranger, explained to *The Guardian* that "Richard and I listened to the same records when we were growing up, so we just put all the things we loved in. It's self-indulgent, but the songs aren't pastiche like the ones in *Grease*," which, already a hit on Broadway for two years at that point, opened in London at almost the same time as *Rocky Horror*. "'Time Warp' was added during rehearsals because you need a dance number in a musical. Plus we had to pad it out: the show was only about 40 minutes. It evolved on the fly, all within three weeks. I'd dream up musical arrangements as we rehearsed and, though half the cast were vocally challenged, somehow it fell into place."

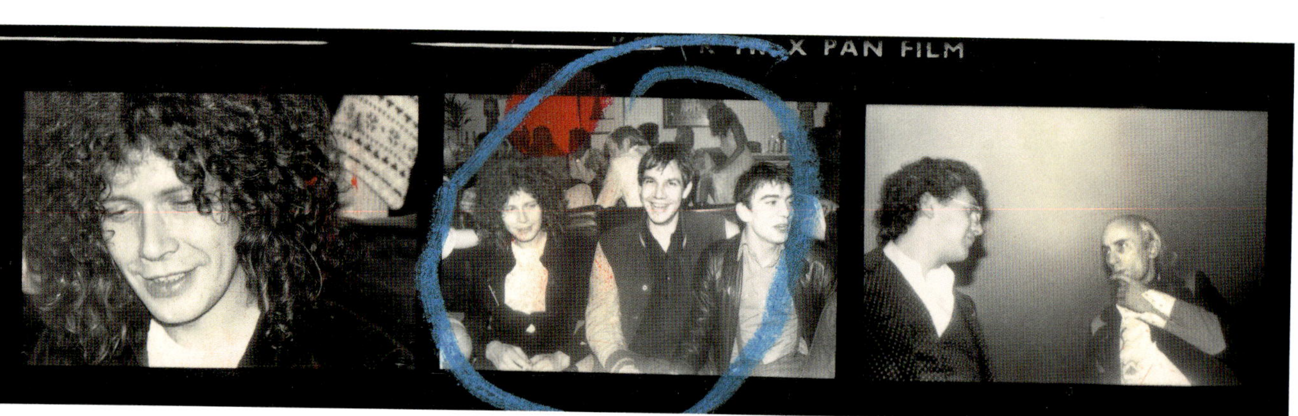

Composer Richard Hartley. Hartley, set designer Brian Thompson, and his friend. Producer Michael White and Richard O'Brien.

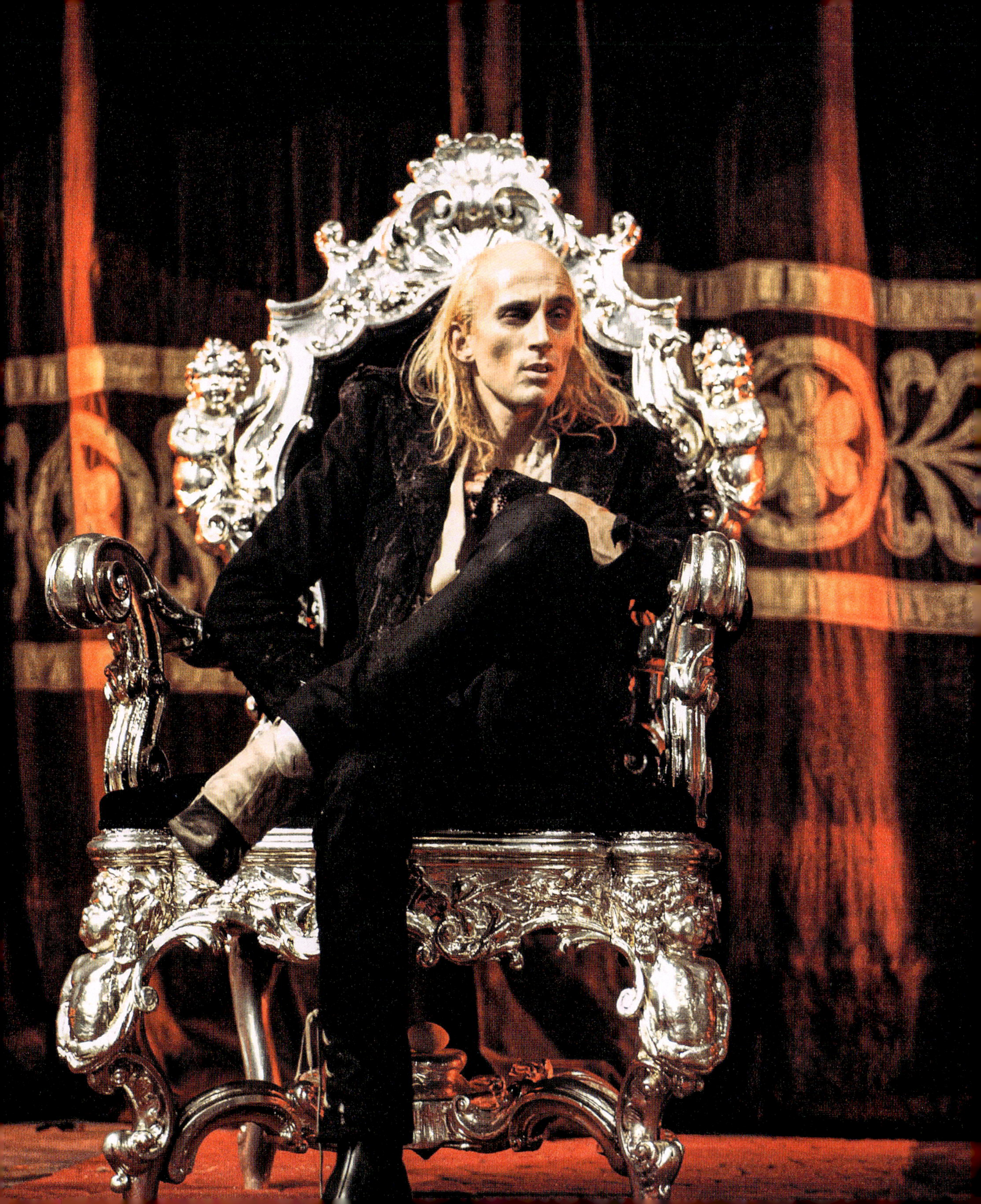

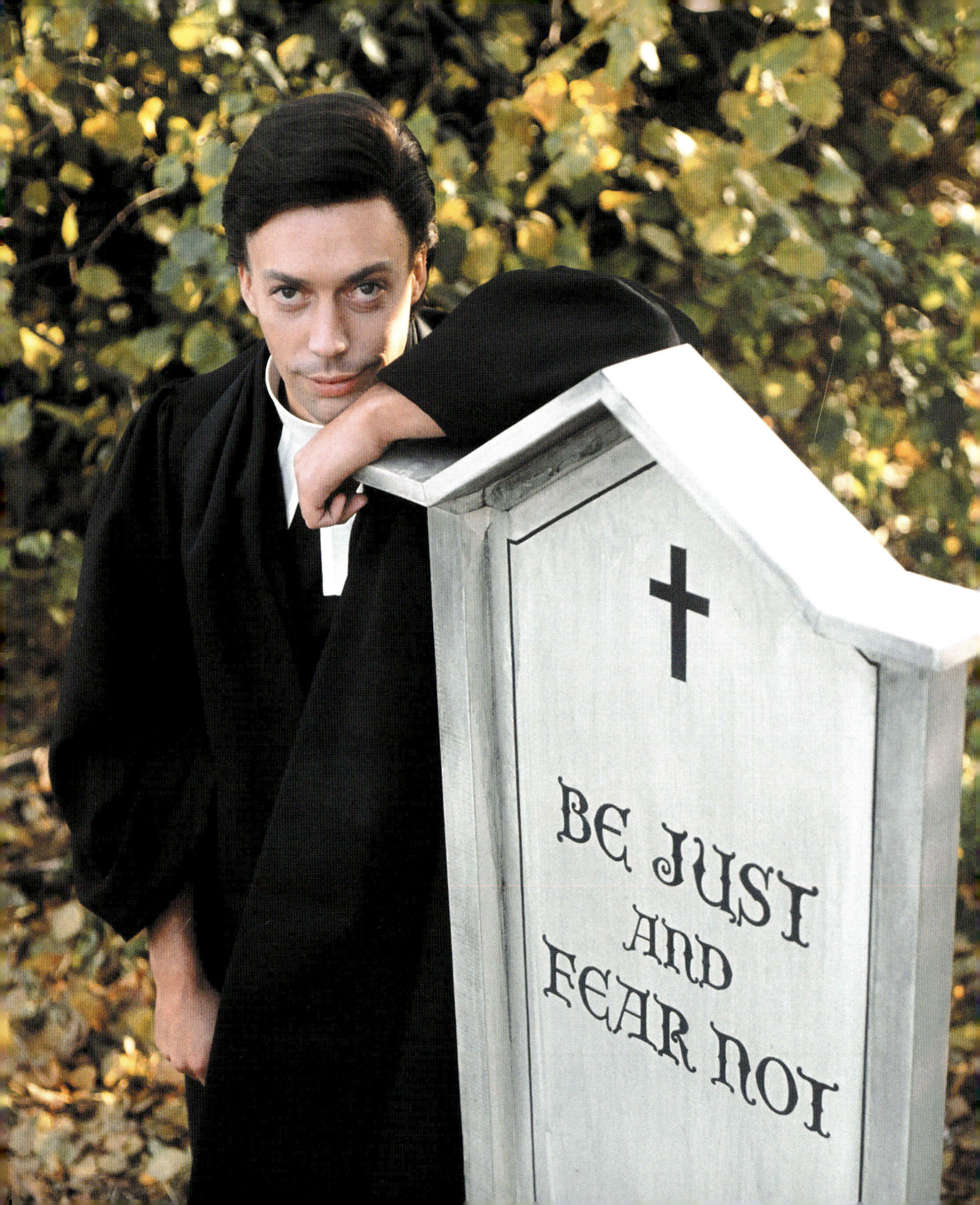
BE JUST
AND
FEAR NOT

Actor Tim Curry lived on Paddington Street at the time, a few doors down from a gym. Walking near his home one day, he ran into O'Brien—whom he'd befriended while working together in the original London production of *Hair*. As Curry explained in a 1992 interview, O'Brien told him he had just visited the gym "to see if he could find a muscleman who could sing. I said, 'Why do you need him to sing?' And he told me that his musical was going to be done, and I should talk to Jim Sharman. He gave me the script, and I thought, *Boy, if this works, it's going to be a smash*."

According to O'Brien, the basic plot is simple. "It taps into the most primal story of western civilization: the fall of man. Brad and Janet are Adam and Eve, and Frank-N-Furter is the serpent," as he told *The Guardian* in 2009.

Yet despite the ostensibly classic plot, the musical earworms, the innovative costuming and set design, and the involvement of producer Michael White—who had already mounted West End productions such as *Oh! Calcutta!* and *Joseph and the Amazing Technicolor Dreamcoat*—it took unique chemistry and belief among everyone involved in order to pull it off. And it took Curry morphing into and inhabiting the role of Frank-N-Furter, moving from a lab coat–wearing mad scientist with an Eastern European accent to a corset-wearing Ziggy scientist with a patrician English accent. Curry credits shoe designer Terry de Havilland's towering platform shoes as the final catalyst for the tour de force performance that would be as indelible as any ever to grace the stage or screen.

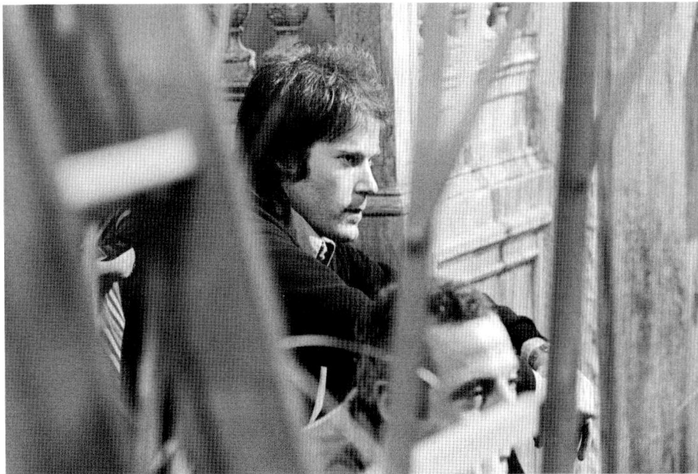

Director Jim Sharman on set.

Richard O'Brien remembers the view from the stage on opening night, June 19, 1973. "There was a big electrical storm and Vincent Price was sitting in the audience under the skylight. The lightning flashed and lit him up. I thought: *Fuck me, that's a good omen!*"

Director Jim Sharman recalls that same moment: "On the opening chord on the opening night of the original stage version at the Royal Court, an electrical storm broke over London, and that lightning has been chasing it ever since."

"There was a life to this piece that we hadn't anticipated," Richard O'Brien told *The Guardian*. "I was dispassionate about it. I was one of those people who held off getting too excited about things in case they got taken away."

Instead, the opposite happened: *Rocky Horror* became the talk of the town.

JOHN VARVATOS, FASHION DESIGNER:

"When I first got to know Mick, I was so interested in what it was like to be on the set and behind the scenes at *The Rocky Horror Picture Show*. Mick found a way to have a connection with every artist he shot. He would put himself in the right mental zone to truly understand the talent he was shooting and bring out their true aura."

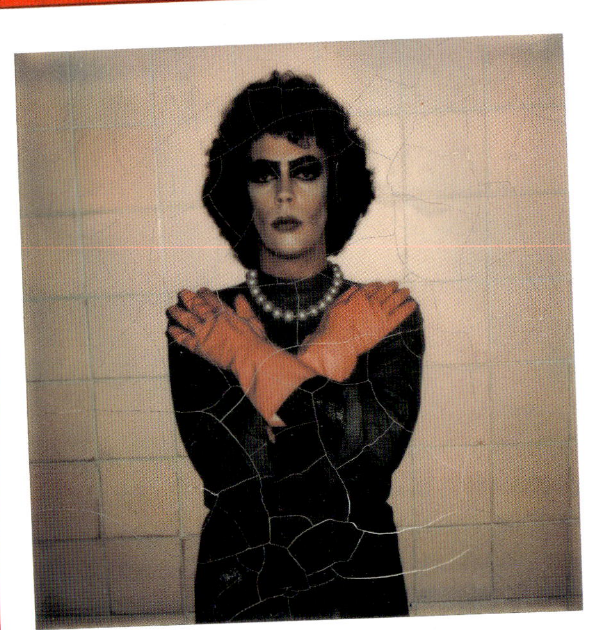

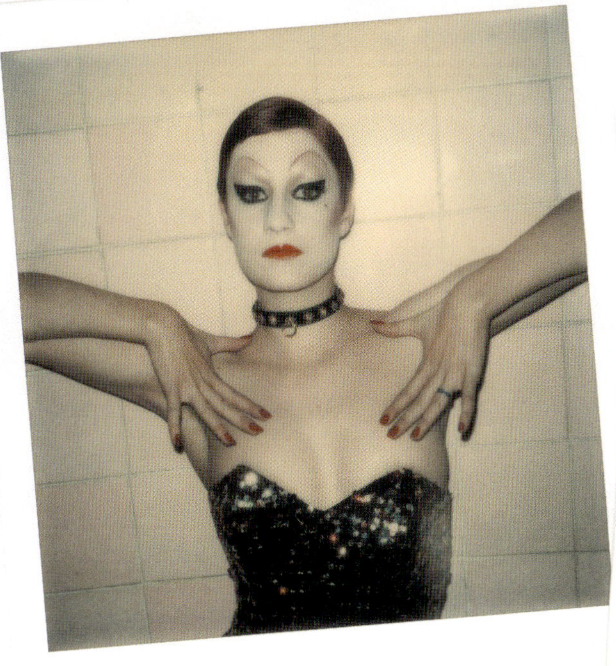
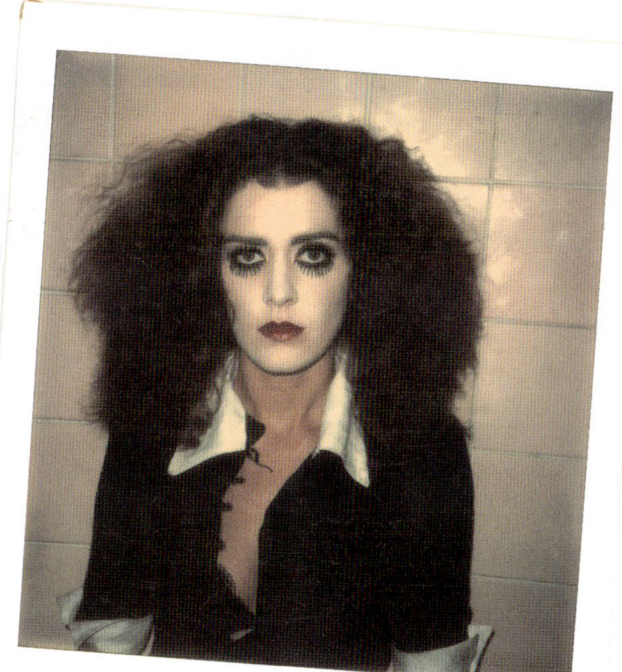
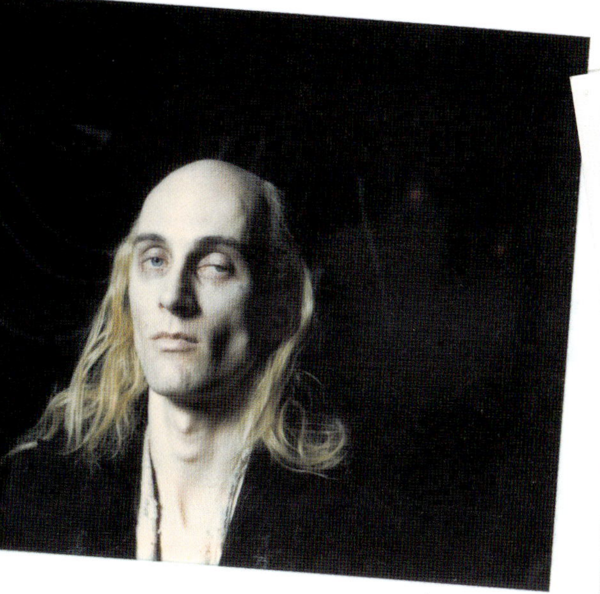
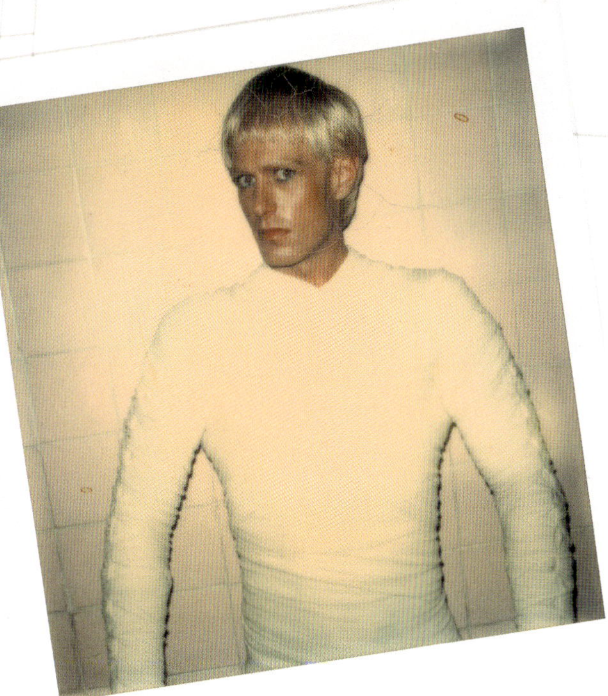

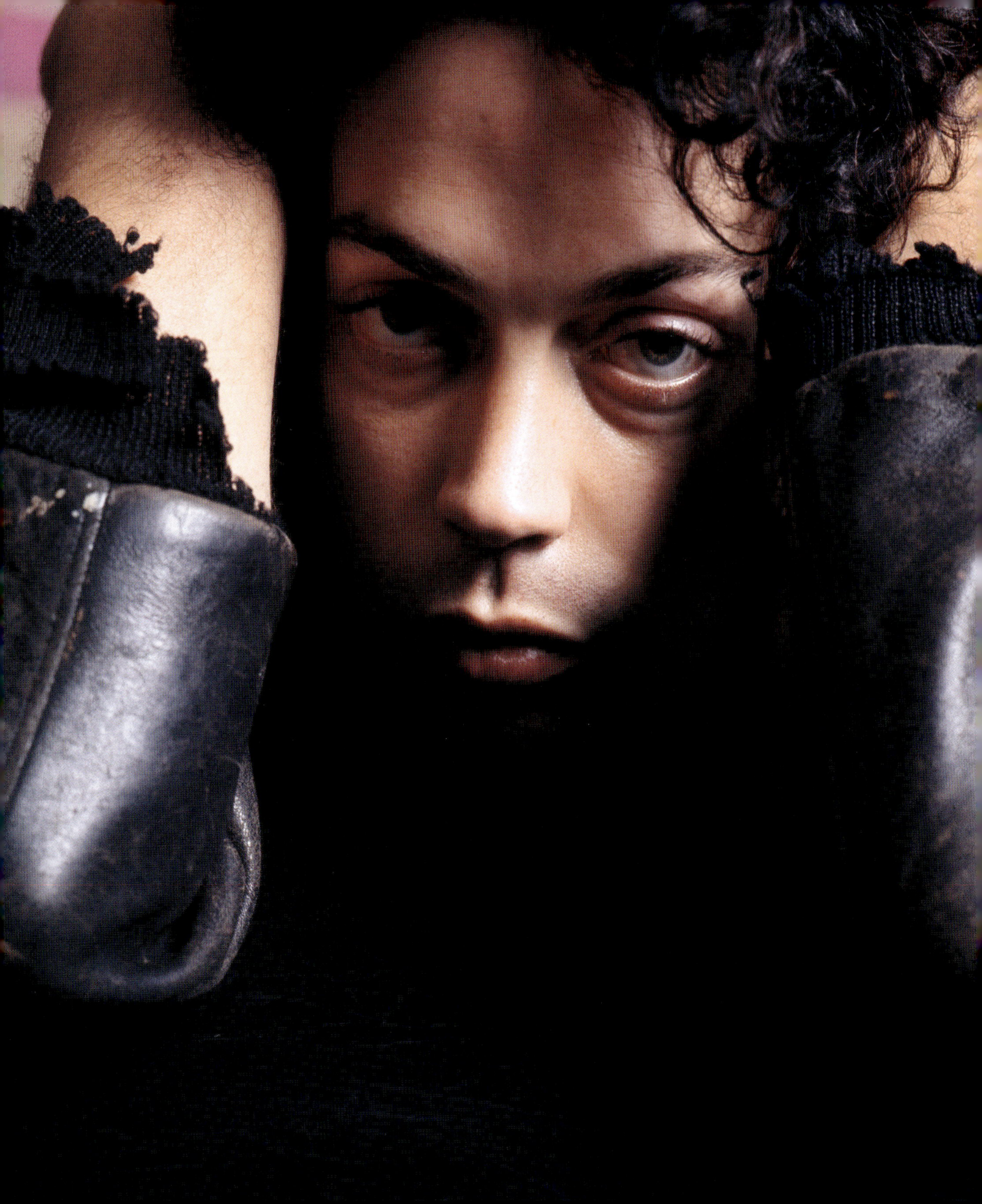

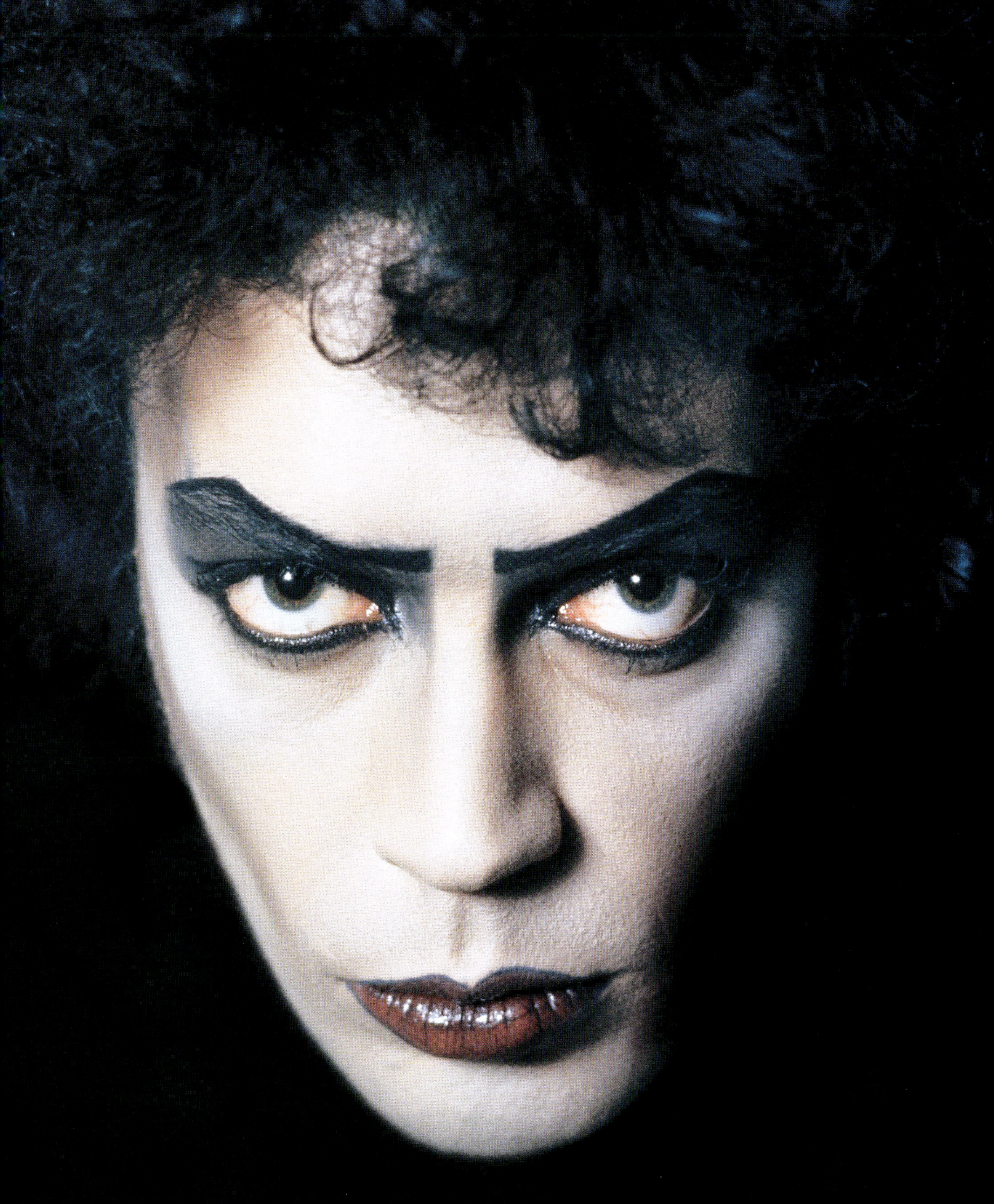

At the second night's performance, Jonathan King, a songwriter and producer associated with Genesis, 10cc, and the early Bay City Rollers, pushed O'Brien to let him invest in the show and record it for release as an album.

Twiggy and her then-boyfriend, Lou Adler—the music impresario behind Carole King, The Mamas & the Papas, and the Monterey Pop Festival and its accompanying film—also attended a performance. Adler had an instant and powerful reaction to the show.

"Bam! *The Rocky Horror Show*. It cut like a knife. From the moment I entered the theater: cobwebs, flashlights, white-faced ushers, and the opening chord of 'Science Fiction,'" Adler recalled for the fifteenth-anniversary CD box set. In an exclusive interview in 2024, he further explained, "I also connected with the songs—they had a 1950s feel, which was the era when I started my career. It fit everything that had in some way touched my musical life and career. But Tim Curry was also very important. In his own way he reminded me of what critic Jon Landau said about Springsteen the first time he saw him: 'I saw rock 'n' roll's future.' In Curry, I saw the future of what a star would look like in theater. He had unique charisma, loved by men, women, any gender. Not only could he act but he could also really sing. And he had nice legs."

Adler refused to leave without securing the rights to mount the production in the Roxy, a nightclub he owned on the Sunset Strip in Los Angeles.

Both Susan Sarandon and Barry Bostwick, who would later play Janet and Brad in the film, saw the stage production in Los Angeles.

JULIETTE LEWIS, ACTOR AND MUSICIAN: "I saw *The Rocky Horror Picture Show* when I was eleven years old—my brother snuck me into the theatre. I felt like I had entered the world of my own people: the otherworldly rock 'n' roll freaks. The movie, the costumes, and the imagery took me on a deeper journey. It became more than a film. It became like a cosmic family, part of my creative DNA, an everlasting imprint that runs through my cells. It makes you feel seen and able to live louder and larger in your own self."

As Sarandon recalled in an exclusive 2024 interview, "Tim Curry's entrance at the Roxy remains the most theatrical moment in my memory. The audience audibly gasped. At that moment, he owned the stage and everybody in the house. For me it was the beginning of a friendship, facilitated by a friend of mine named Jamie Donnelly, who played Magenta in that production."

The experience was equally intense for Bostwick, as he also explained in an exclusive interview in 2024: "It exploded at the Roxy, and Tim and the cast ruled the town. I fell in love with Tim. If you didn't feel hip before you saw it, you were the *hippest* after the experience."

After the successful run at the Roxy and all the buzz it generated around LA, Adler,

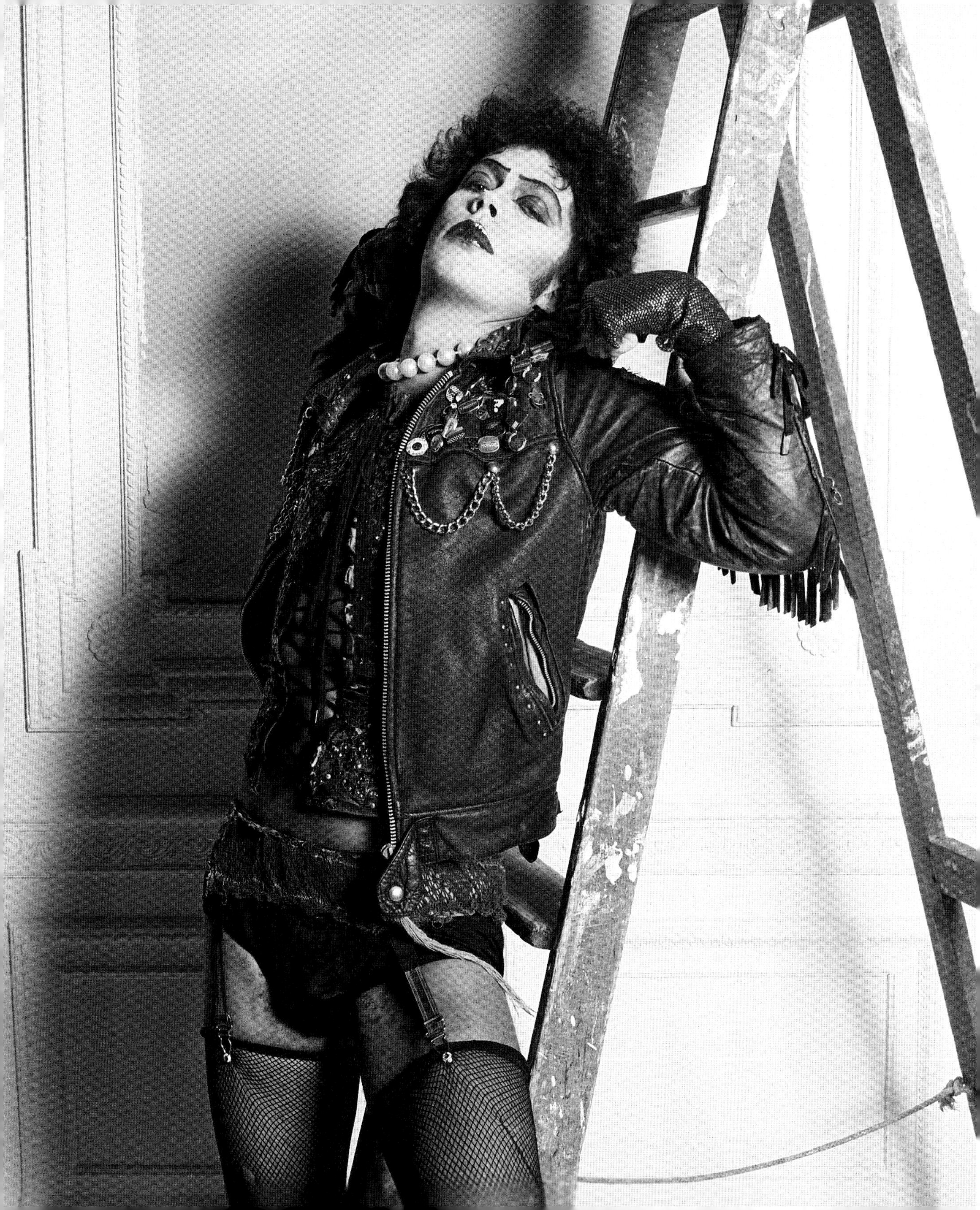

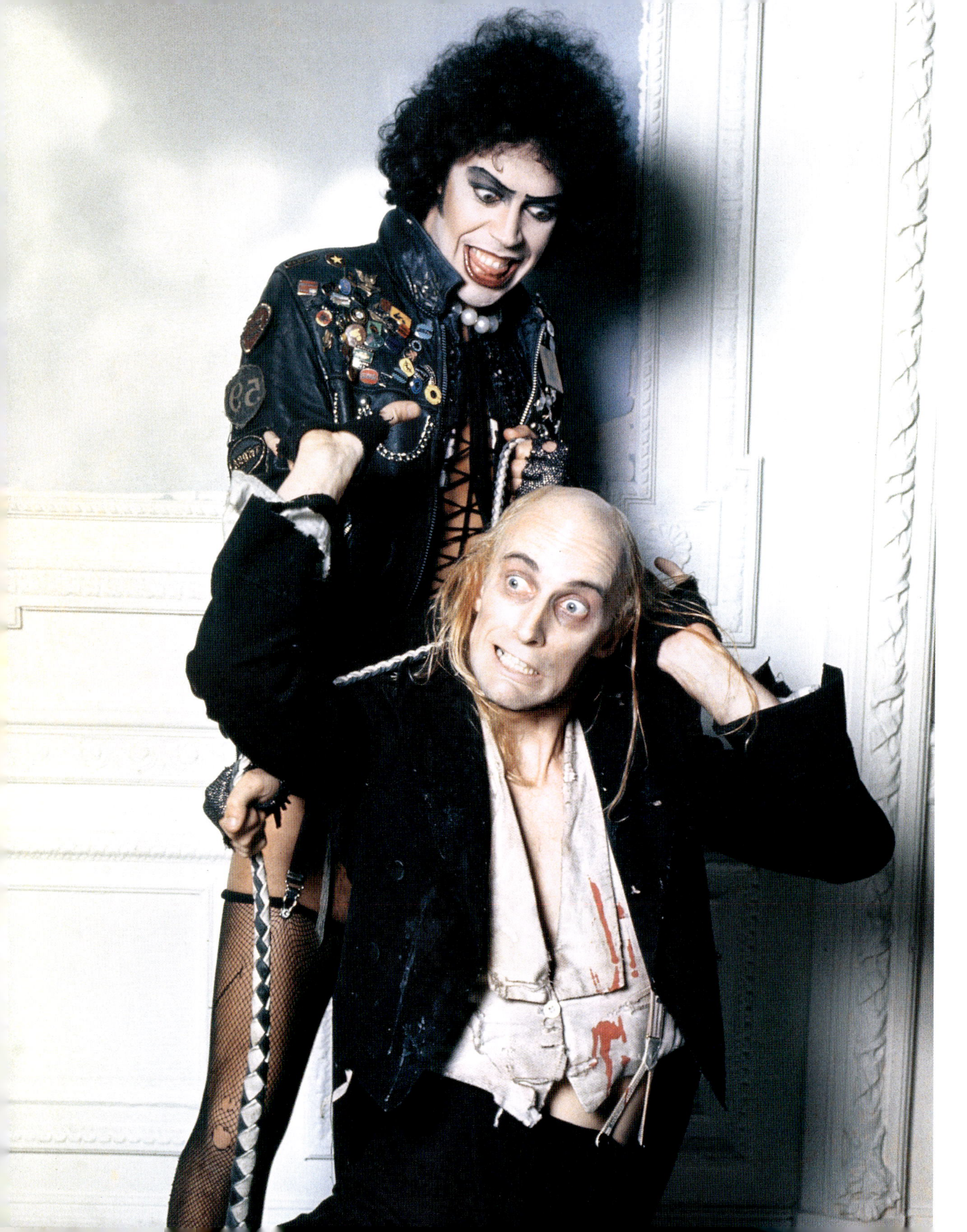

PEACHES, MUSICIAN: "Three movies were a direct line to everything I did after that: *The Rocky Horror Picture Show*, *Phantom of the Paradise*, and *Tommy*. I was very interested in rock musicals. I didn't like other musicals. I was also obsessed with the interactive quality of *Rocky Horror*. That you would go to the theater and you would take these objects, and act out your fantasies. I ended up going to theater school because I wanted to make cool musicals. I didn't know I was a musician; I only knew about theater. *Rocky Horror* made me understand music as a very theatrical, performative, and subversive action."

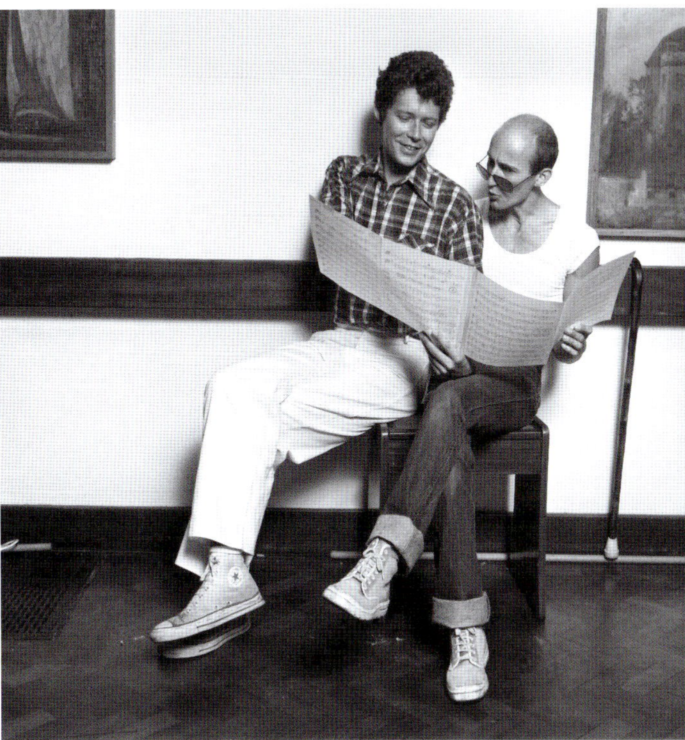

Michael White and Richard O'Brien.

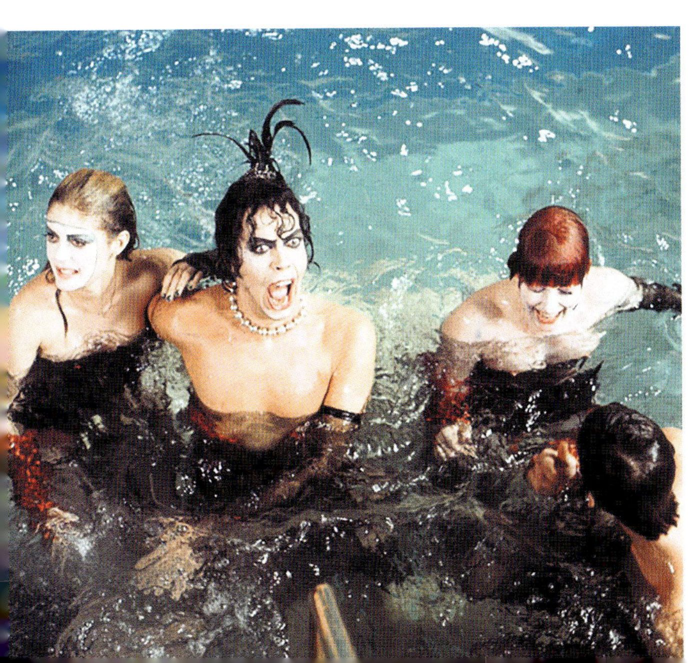

together with Michael White, who by then had co-produced *Monty Python and the Holy Grail*, secured a deal with Fox to shoot a movie version. Though the film adaptation would—slowly, of course—go on to overshadow the musical, the stage production has also remained a perennial favorite, having been performed in nearly two dozen languages and seen by thirty million people.

"It's astonishing that the U.S. movie industry bought into it," O'Brien told *The Guardian*. "There we were with a fringe theatre event that hadn't even gone to the West End, and not only were we allowed to make it into a film, we also all got to star in

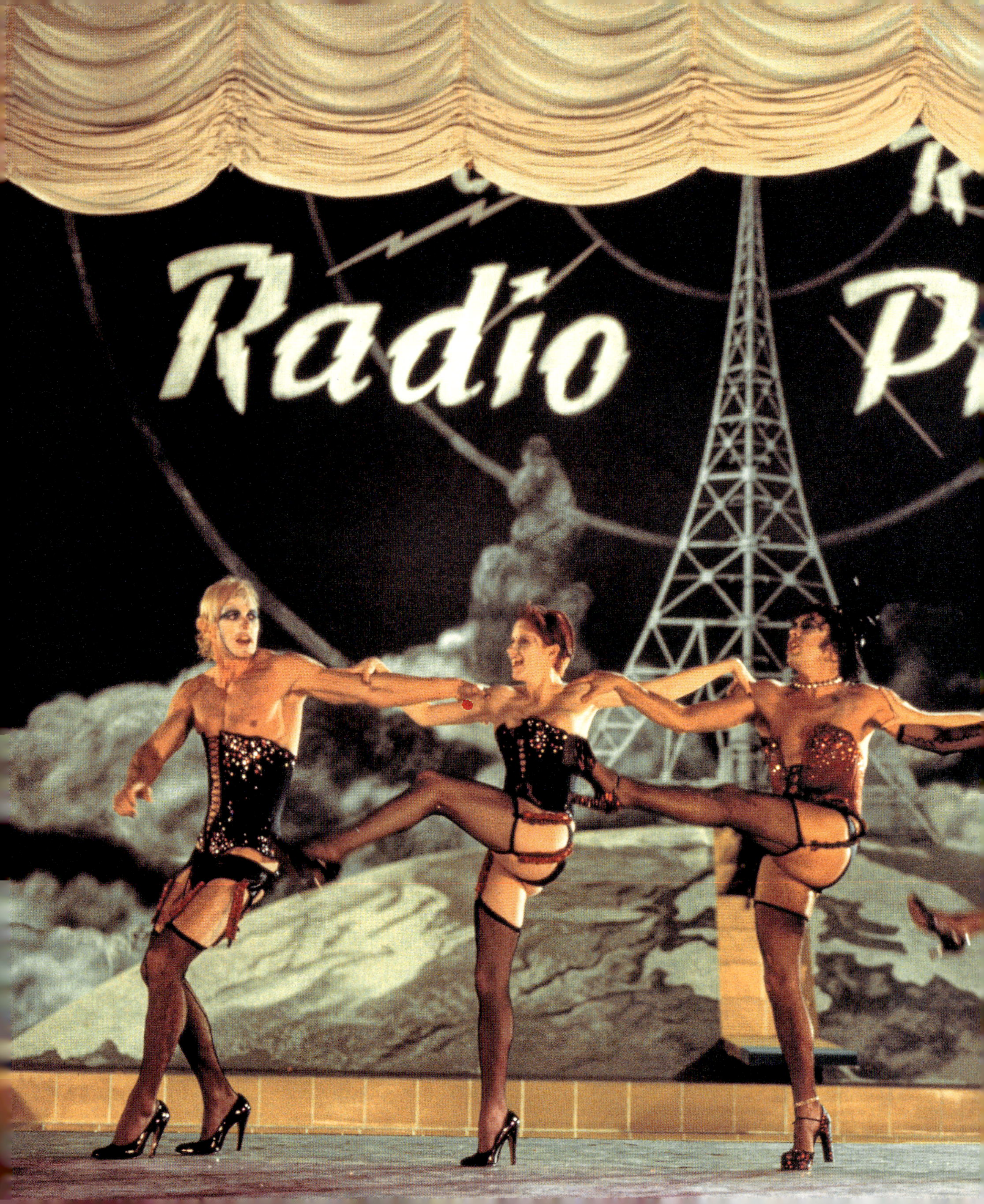
Radio

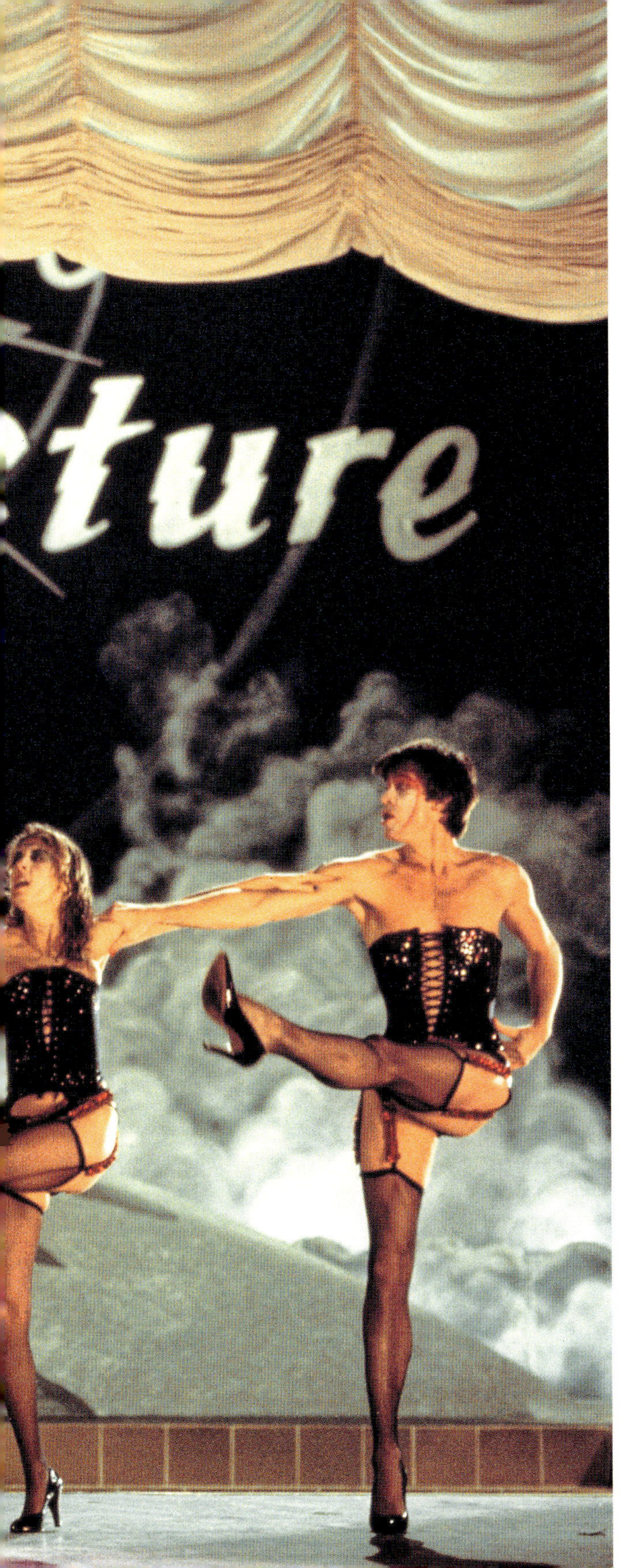

it—with Jim directing." The only stipulation from Fox was that they cast some American actors, which is how Barry Bostwick and Susan Sarandon ended up playing Brad and Janet.

The *Rocky Horror* gang reconvened back in England at Bray Studios and the adjacent Oakley Court, a nineteenth-century country manor vaguely recognizable from its use in British horror films made by Hammer Film Productions, the iconic studio behind 1950s and 1960s franchises *Frankenstein*, *Dracula*, and *The Mummy*, among countless other horror flicks. "Listed, gloomy, and semi-derelict, with its owner living abroad, it was perfect for us—even if we did have to carry all our lights and technical stuff across the paddock to get to it," as O'Brien explained.

Set designer Brian Thomson told *Mental Floss* in 2020 that the crumbling, unheated manor was the perfect location. "The minute we saw it, we realized that this gave us the basis for the whole look of the movie."

After a mere two months of pre-production and rehearsals, shooting began on October 21, 1974.

"It was so low-budget I think it was always considered an oddity by the studio," said Sharman. "They would never have imagined it as a potential blockbuster, more like a sleeper—which it turned out to be. It was the low budget that restricted us, yet also liberated us. With stars and big budgets, there would have been much more interference, but it was considered so cheap and quirky that, mercifully, we were left to our own devices to make the film we wanted to make—ironically, every other Fox release of that year is now forgotten, while the quirky one is still enjoyed today. There's a lesson in that somewhere."

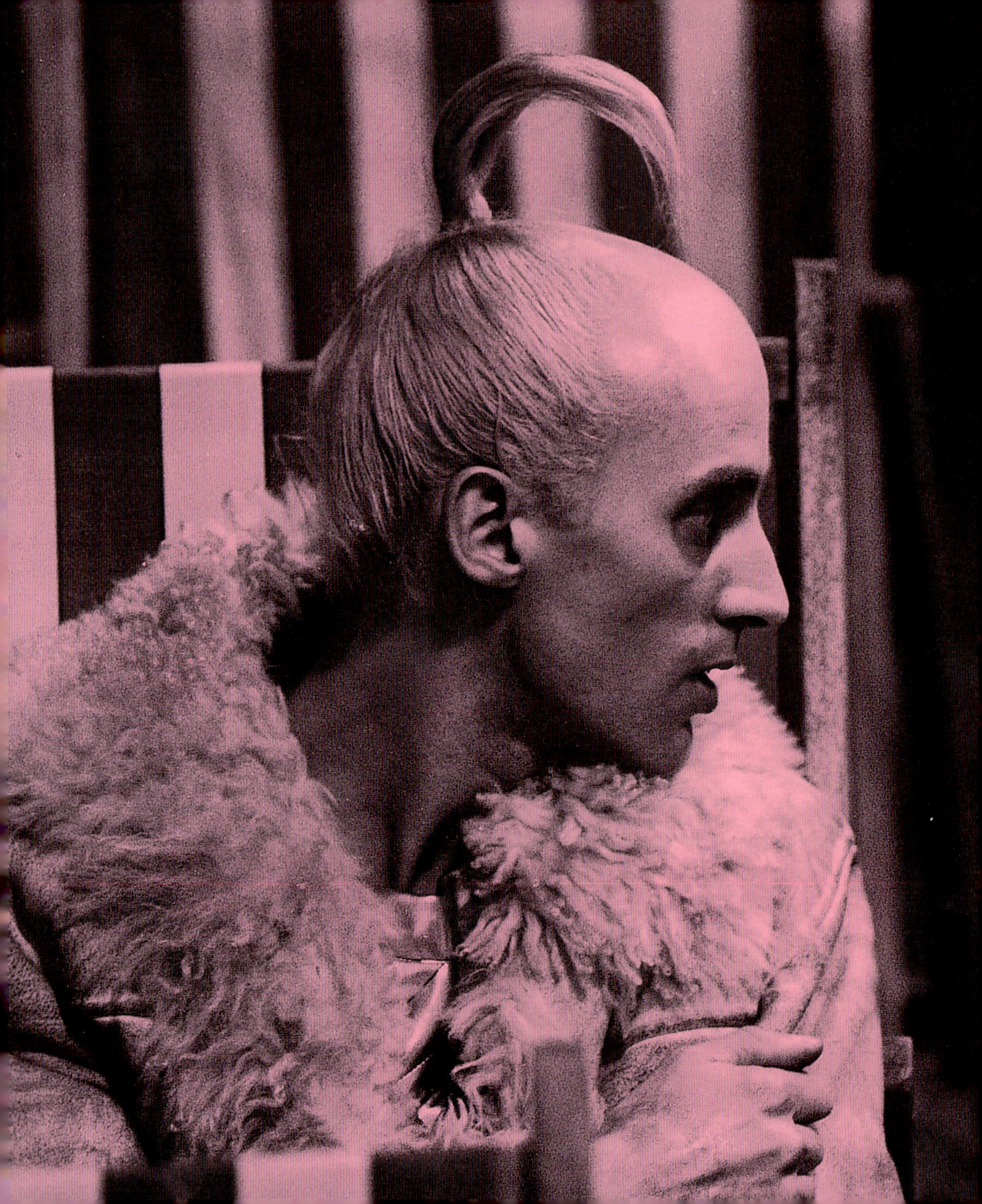

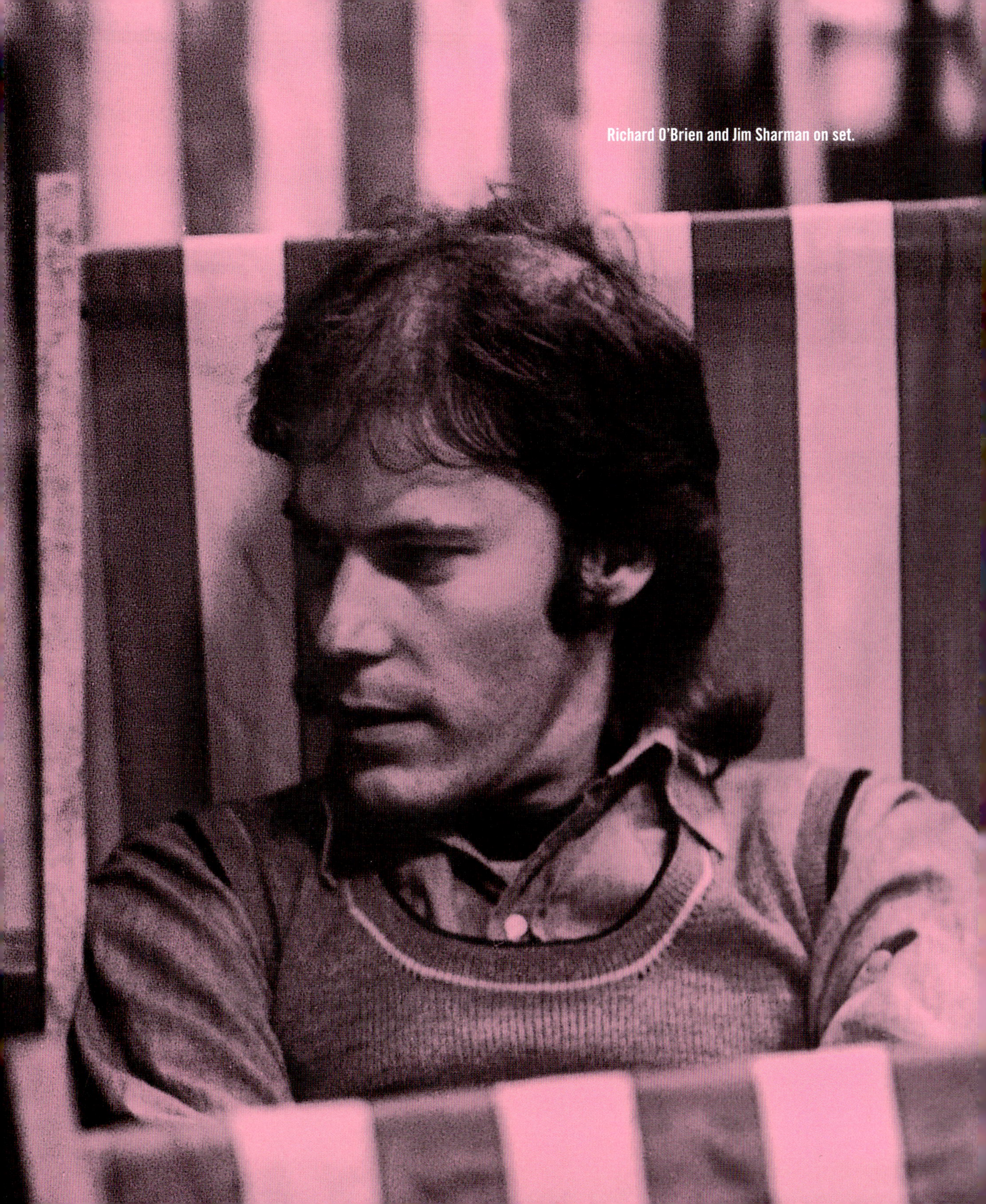
Richard O'Brien and Jim Sharman on set.

CASSANDRA PETERSON, AKA ELVIRA, MISTRESS OF THE DARK: "I went to the Roxy all the time because it was across the street from where I was working at the time, *Don Kirshner's Rock Concert*. So when a musical called the *The Rocky Horror Show* popped up in 1974, and me being seriously into horror already, I had to go. The Roxy was a tiny little theater, and for the production, the stage jutted almost the entire length of the room—and Tim Curry would come down that runway. You had a really intimate experience of the show. The music was amazing, and I was just blown away. I became a complete fanatic. I was madly in love with Tim Curry; I was madly in love with Kim Milford, too, the person playing Rocky at the Roxy—whew, he was hot. I went to that show so many times I lost count.

I have a picture of me at Halloween that same year, 1974, dressed as a female version of Frank-N-Furter. The same kind of makeup, hair standing on end, black fishnet stockings, and garter belt, really sexy. And later, when I became Elvira, Robert Redding, who had done my hair and makeup when we went out for Halloween that night took elements of that look."

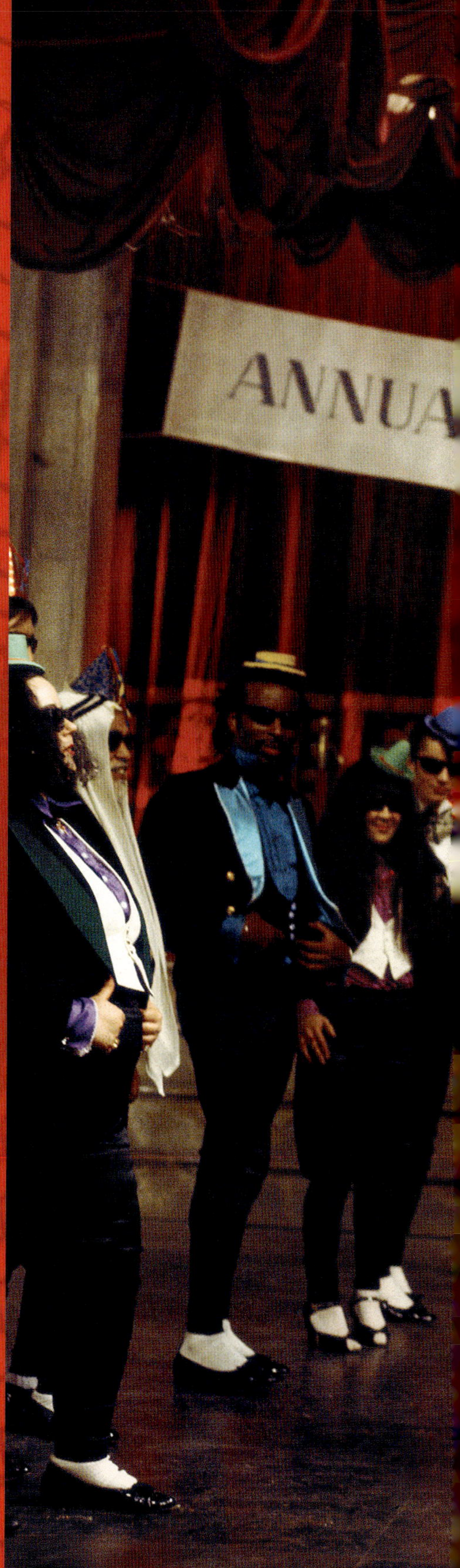

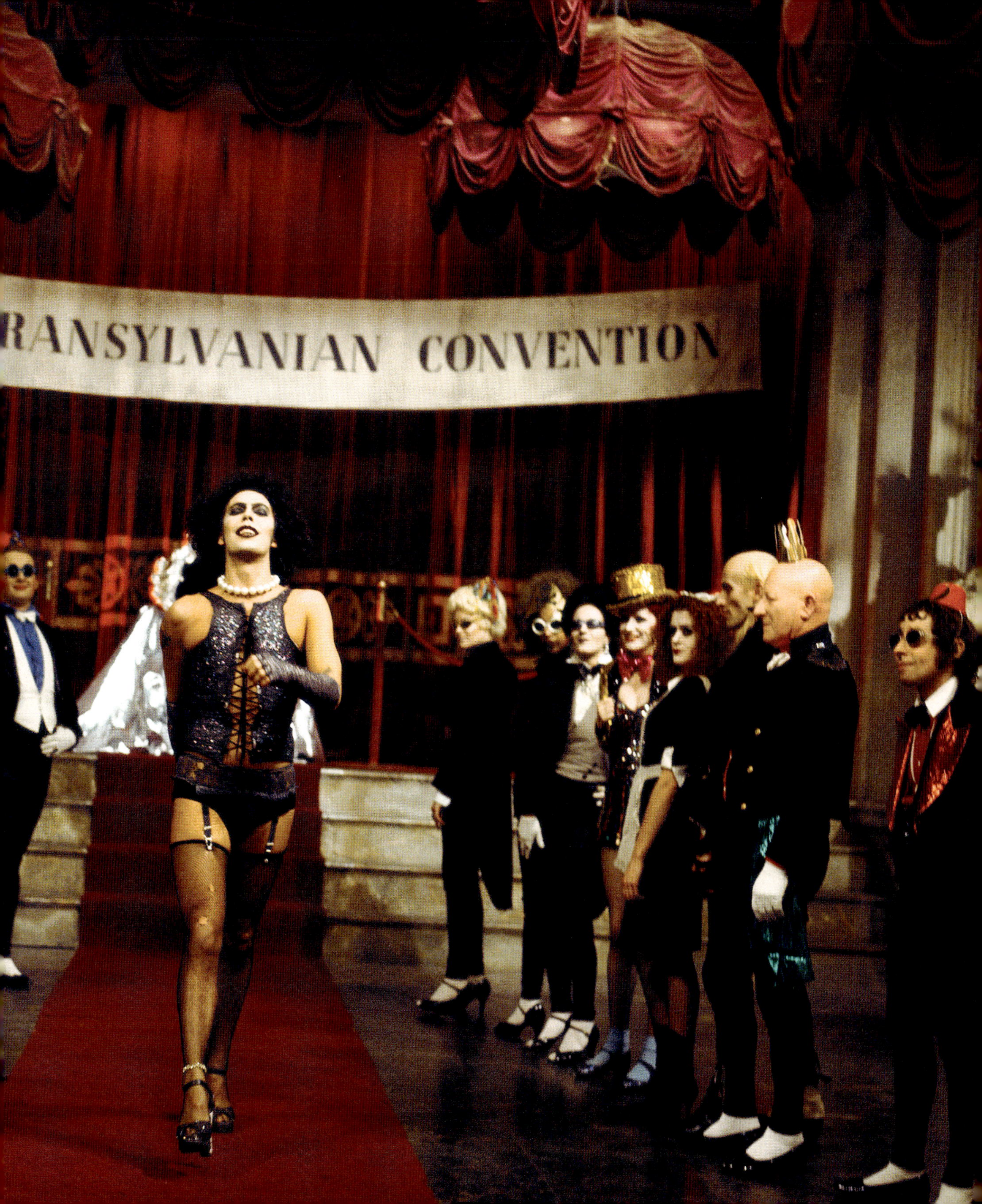
RANSYLVANIAN CONVENTION

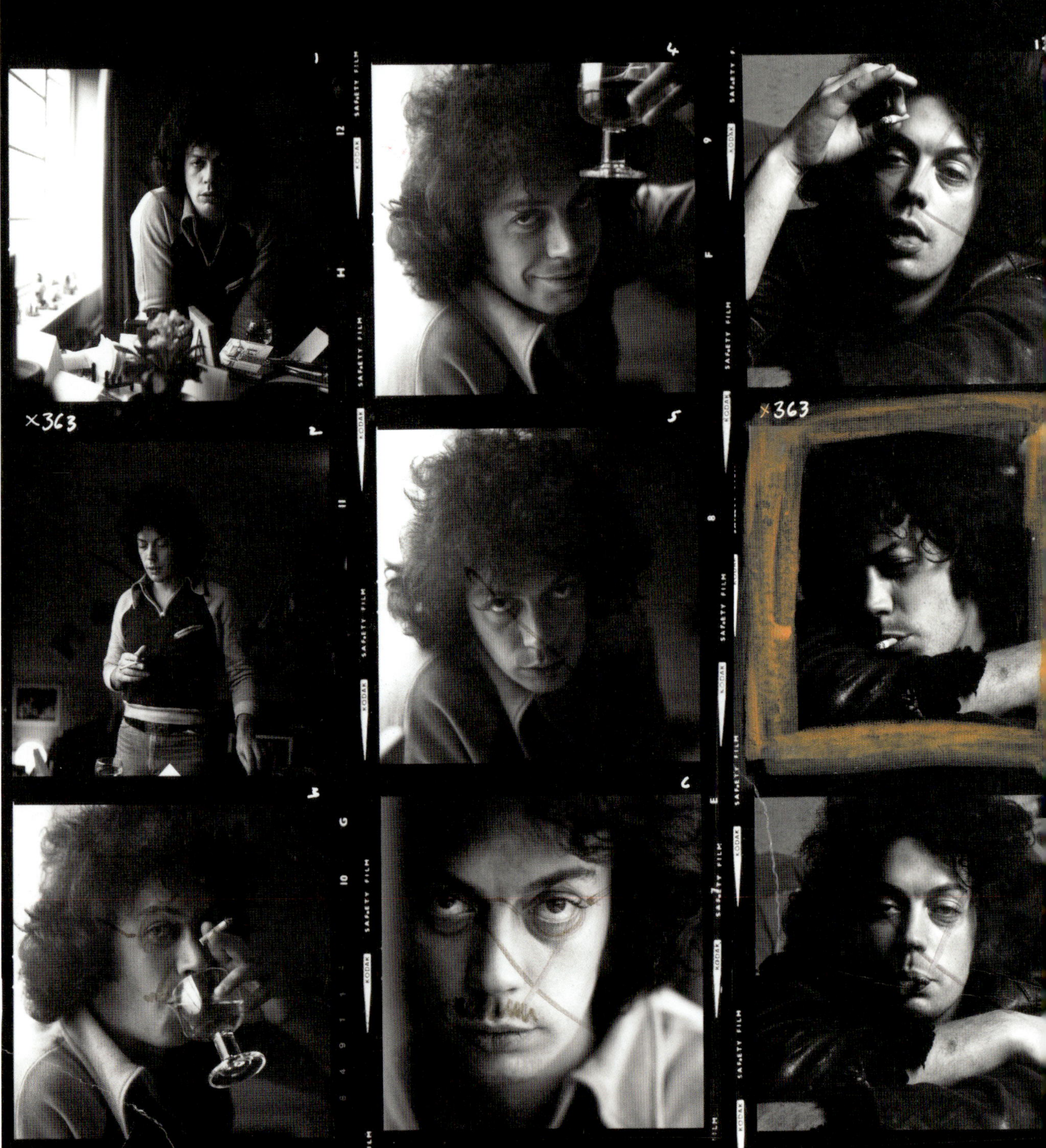

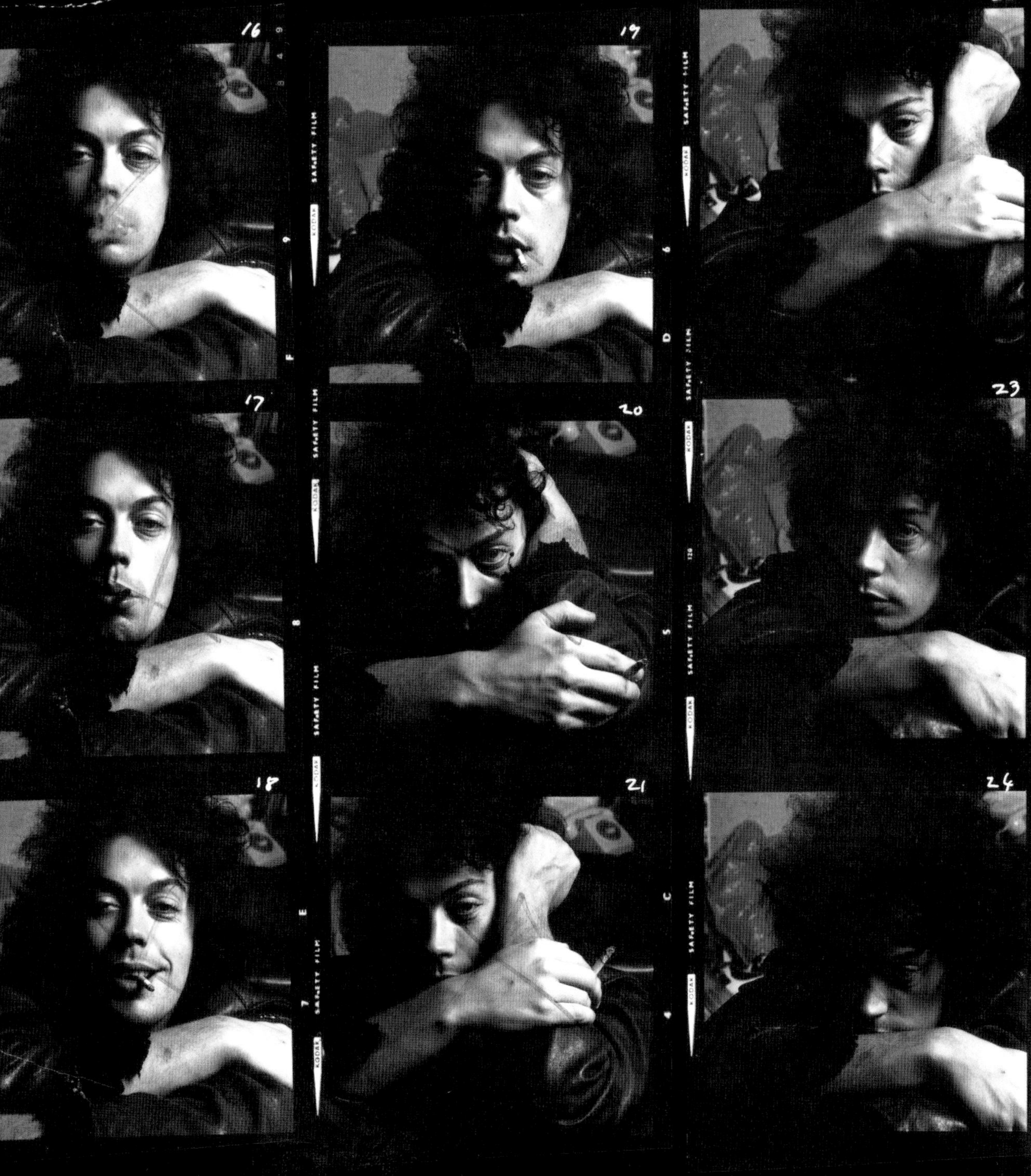

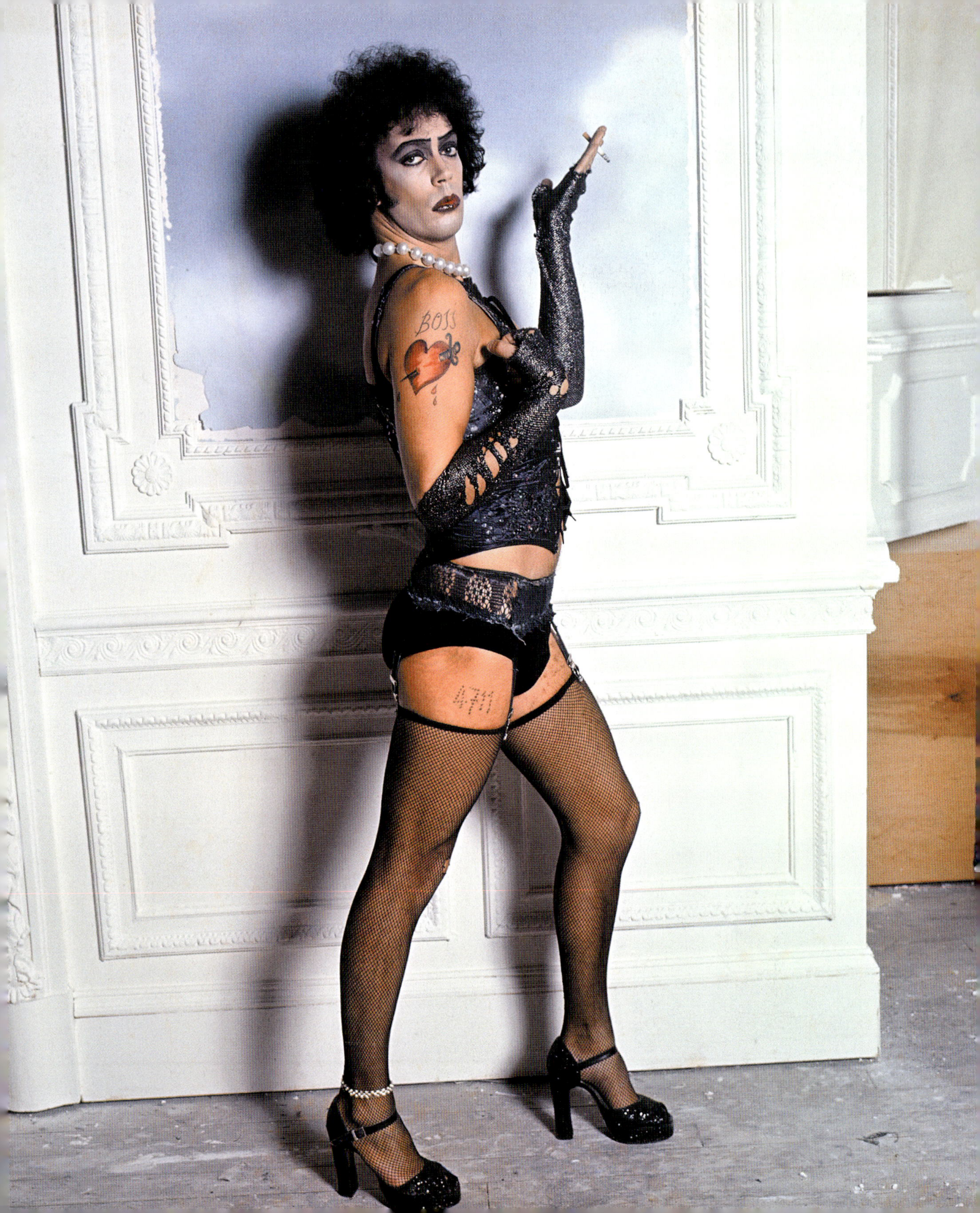
BOSS
4711

GIVE YOURSELF OVER TO ABSOLUTE PLEASURE: FRANK-N-FURTER

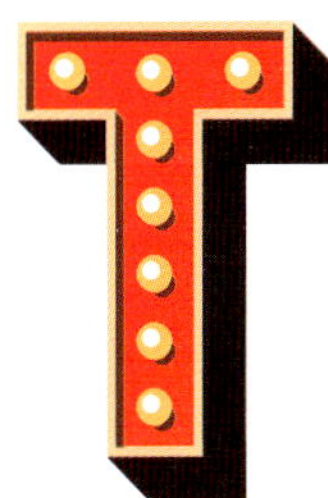

im Curry remains and always will be THE definitive Frank-N-Furter," said Mick. "It's unquestionably a brilliant and unique bravura performance. He played the character to the hilt and provided a performance for the ages. He is so strong that his blueprint of the role is the one that every successive stage Frank has tried to copy. It's as if he's precluded any other way of interpreting it."

For Curry, there were two keys to the invention of his iconic role: the accent—which migrated from Transylvania to an English country manor over the course of rehearsals—and the towering Terry de Havilland–designed platform heels.

"The shoes were very important," he told *The Rocky Horror Picture Show* magazine. "I didn't get near the part until very late in rehearsal and I said I must have the shoes. Then it all happened. I tend to work from the feet upwards. It's a question of balance, of dynamics."

The rest is history.

"It takes a certain amount of courage to play Frank. But the only thing I'm sure about as a performer is that you have to be dangerous. He's the dynamics of the show—he's the one who makes things happen," said Curry. "It's such a witty part that the bizarre aspects don't bother me. He's just another variation of the mad scientist really—and he is *funny*. The odd thing about Frank-N-Furter is that he can go from doing something really outrageous and horrific to being deeply endearing, sort of jolly. I think that's why he has worked the way he has."

Frank-N-Furter—and the music of *Rocky Horror*—was perfect for Curry for another reason too. "I couldn't make up my mind whether to be a singer or an actor," he says. "Although in *Hair* they never let me sing that much, because the score was fairly high and I didn't have a high enough voice. I treated *Hair* like a drama school. You were always able to rewrite your part. You built up your physical presence. And because everyone was competing for attention, you learned quite quickly to make your presence felt."

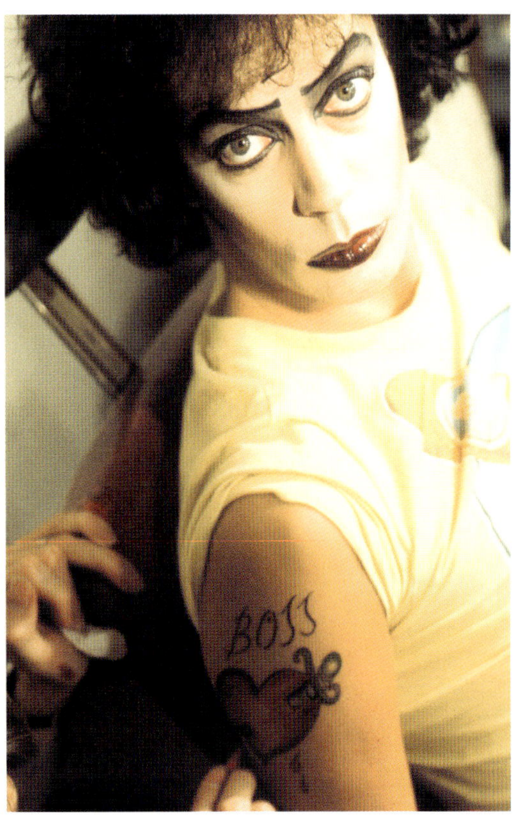

Richard O'Brien says, "I've always thought of Frank as a cross between Ivan the Terrible and Cruella de Vil of *101 Dalmatians*. It's that sort of evil beauty that's attractive. And Tim is a great performer. I much prefer to see him singing, dancing, and acting—the three things together, rather than when he limits himself to just straight acting."

As Curry explained to the *New York Times* in 2015, O'Brien had "reached up into the zeitgeist and brought down the most salient ingredients." Those ingredients were, of course, right in Mick Rock's wheelhouse. And as with so much of Mick's work, the authenticity of his *Rocky Horror* oeuvre pops off the page when his photos are printed. As Larry Viezel, president of the official Rocky Horror Picture Show Fan Club, puts it: "You can almost smell the makeup on Tim Curry's face just by looking at some of Mick's pictures."

"Tim's campiness in the role wasn't a fey camp," Mick himself explained. "It was a potent, quite masculine camp. There's an aggressive power-hungry twist to his projection. Frank was definitely in charge even in the shots where he's half in and half out of character, hanging about on the set, being made up, chatting with the other actors, with the crew, or with Jim. His presence is potent. Tim looked like a boss, and his voice was like a fantastic mixture of Queen Elizabeth and his own mother. And he rocked the corset too."

Mick also raved about how much fun it was to shoot Curry. "In many ways, our special setups with his over-the-top projections have become the definitive stills

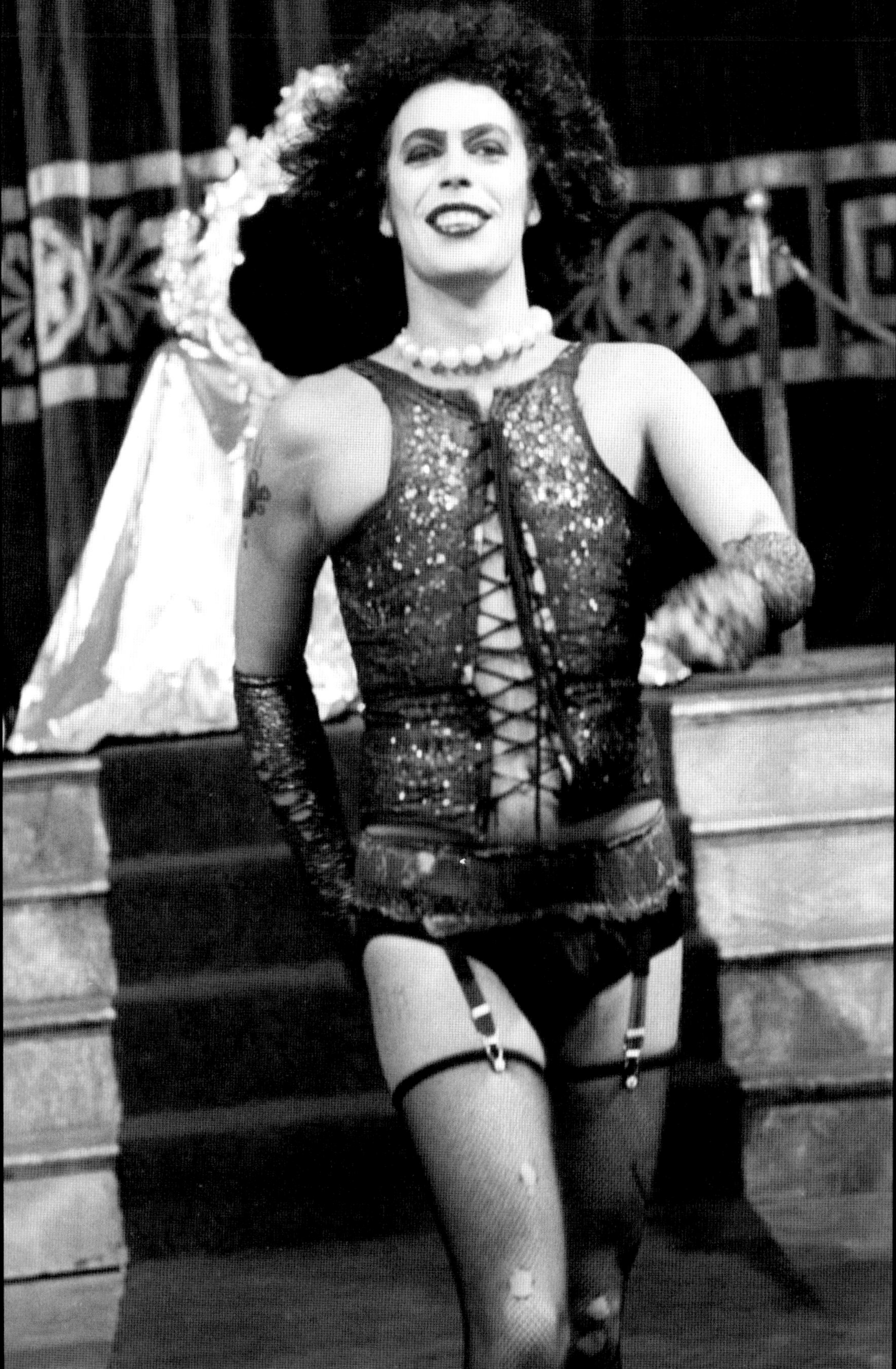

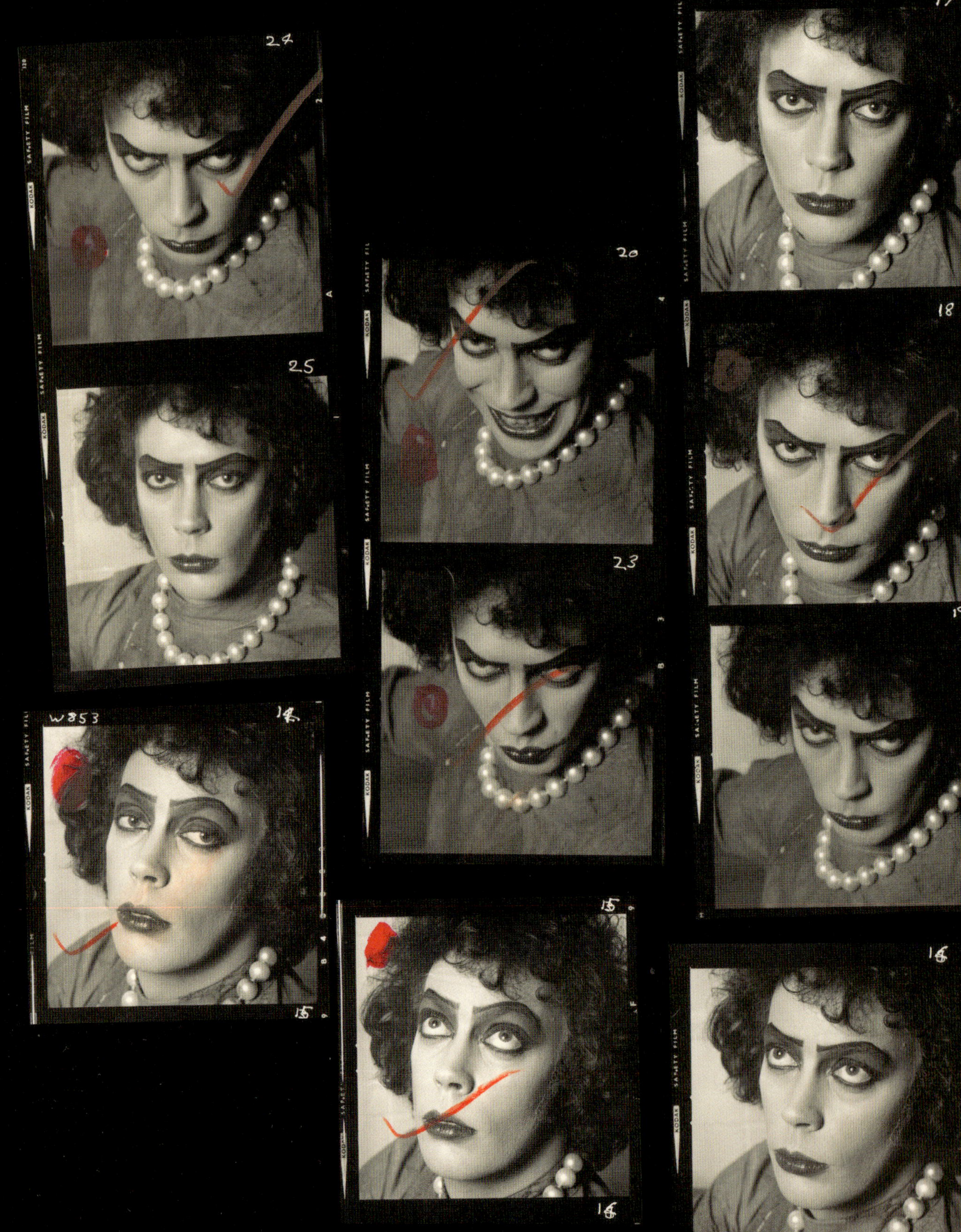

of the movie. He was just a stunning photo subject and was totally responsive to my mildest prodding. He's completely in playful character in every frame of my special setups, whether solo or with Riff Raff or with Magenta and Columbia. The solo images of Tim rank up there with my signature images of Bowie, Iggy, Lou Reed, Freddie, Johnny Rotten, etcetera. Together, we captured his iconic energy forever in still form."

At the time, as Curry explained in an exclusive interview in 2024, he didn't necessarily foresee the earth-shaking implications his performance would have: "I wasn't aware of any epochal moment. I had no intention of influencing the prevailing culture. I just wanted to entertain and amuse."

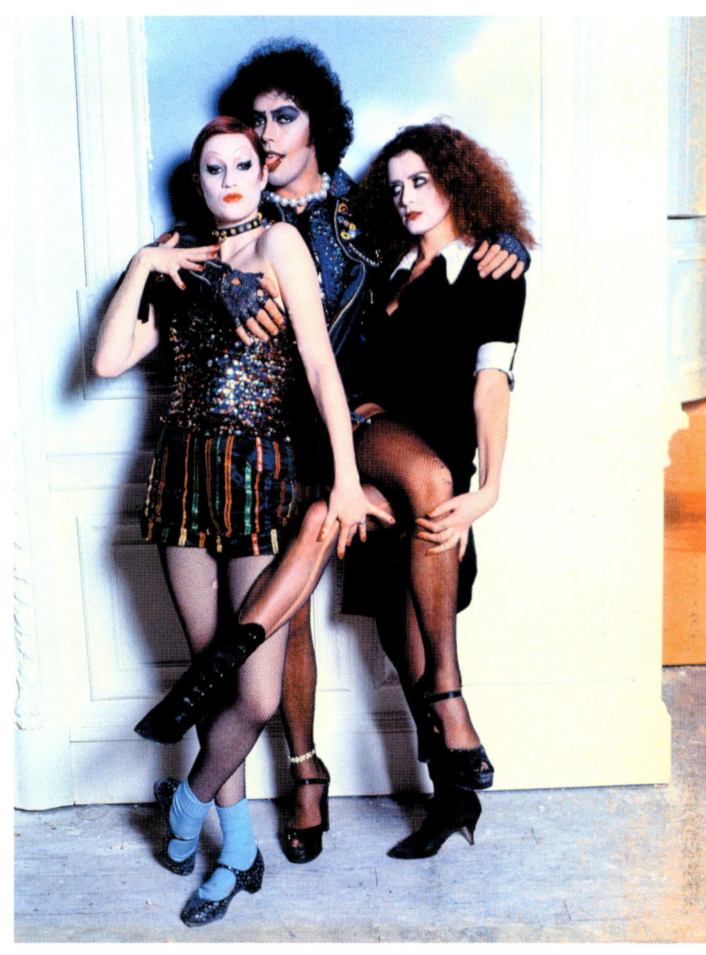

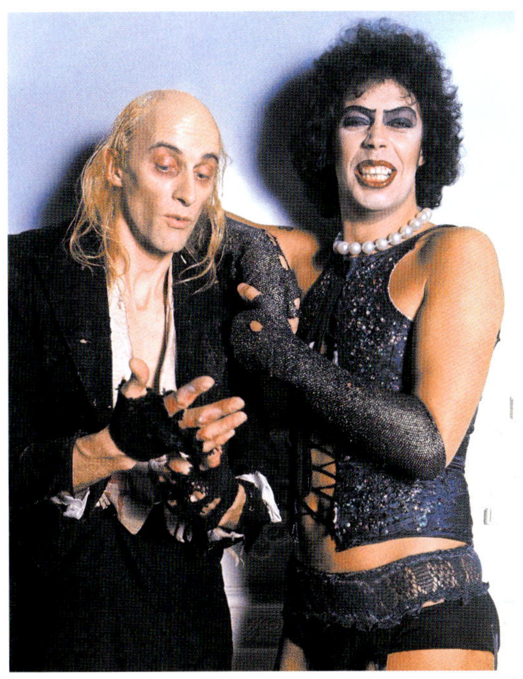

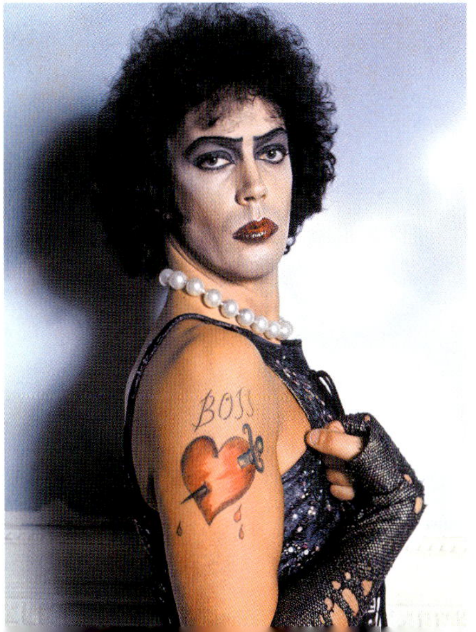

KAREN O, THE YEAH YEAH YEAHS: "*Rocky Horror* found its way to my VCR when I was twelve. I was living in a suburban New Jersey McMansion, sporting a perm, braces, and zits—so, in short, it changed my life. Living so close to New York City, I grew up going to Broadway musicals, but it wasn't until the rock opera entered my life that something clicked. Rock operas as I know them are at their core GLAM. Kids respond to glam—like, why does it have to be a princess or a caped superhero, aren't we all a bit nonbinary? Cross-dressing aliens, depraved newlyweds, S&M vaudeville . . . obsessed! And all in the safe container of really good music. I might have seen men cross-dressing on *Saturday Night Live*, but it was silly, crude; Frank-N-Furter—that look—was art. I recall pictures of me and my best friend Veronica reenacting scenes, decked out in our best Transylvanian Transvestite. PVC hadn't made it into my Jersey wardrobe at that point, so it was red lips and anything black 'n' clingy with a goth texture, like crushed velvet or lace. Our looks really popped against the light beige earth tones of my carpeted hallways! *Rocky Horror* felt like a love letter to us weirdos-in-the-making. Once it came into my life, it was mine, all mine! And I didn't have to worry about whether other kids in my class would like it too. If anything, it was better if they didn't. It was confirmation that there was the you that most people know at face value, and then there was the other you that was Tim Curry in pumps, yeah!"

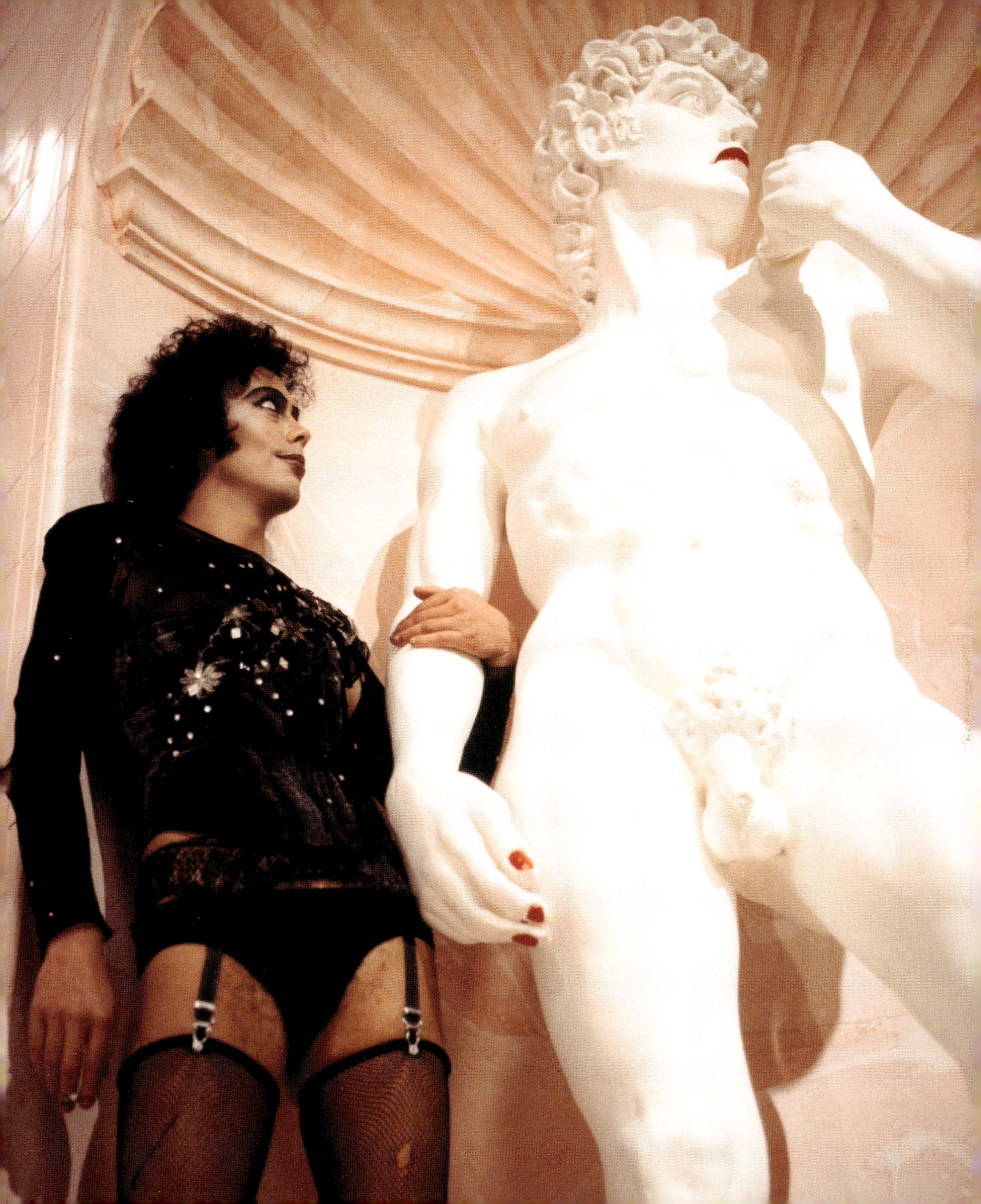

I didn't get the part until very late in the rehearsal and I said I must have the shoes . . . then it all happened." —TIM CURRY

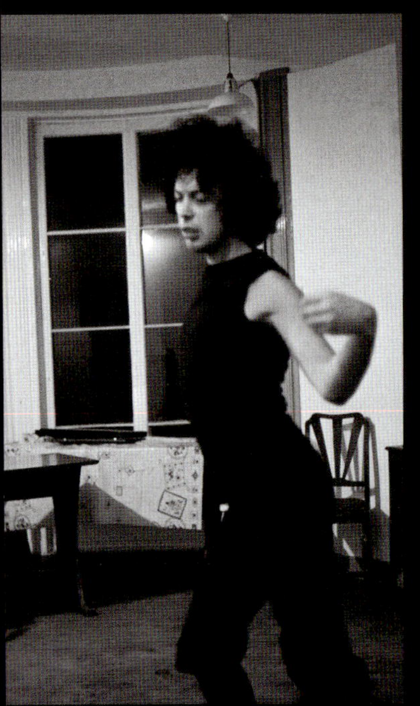

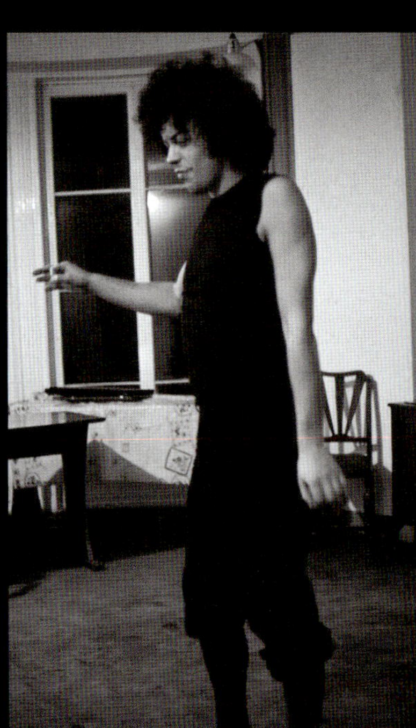

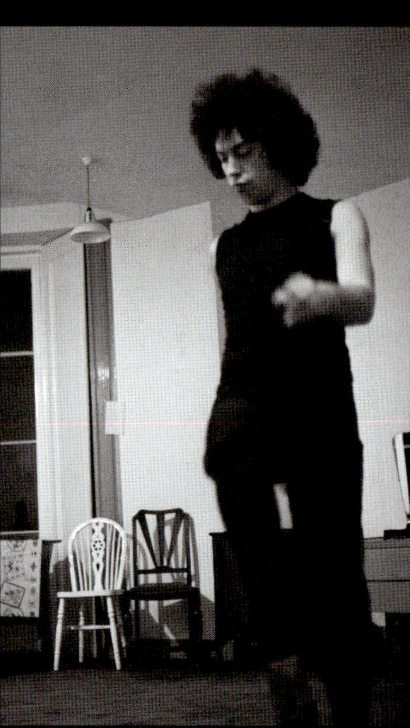

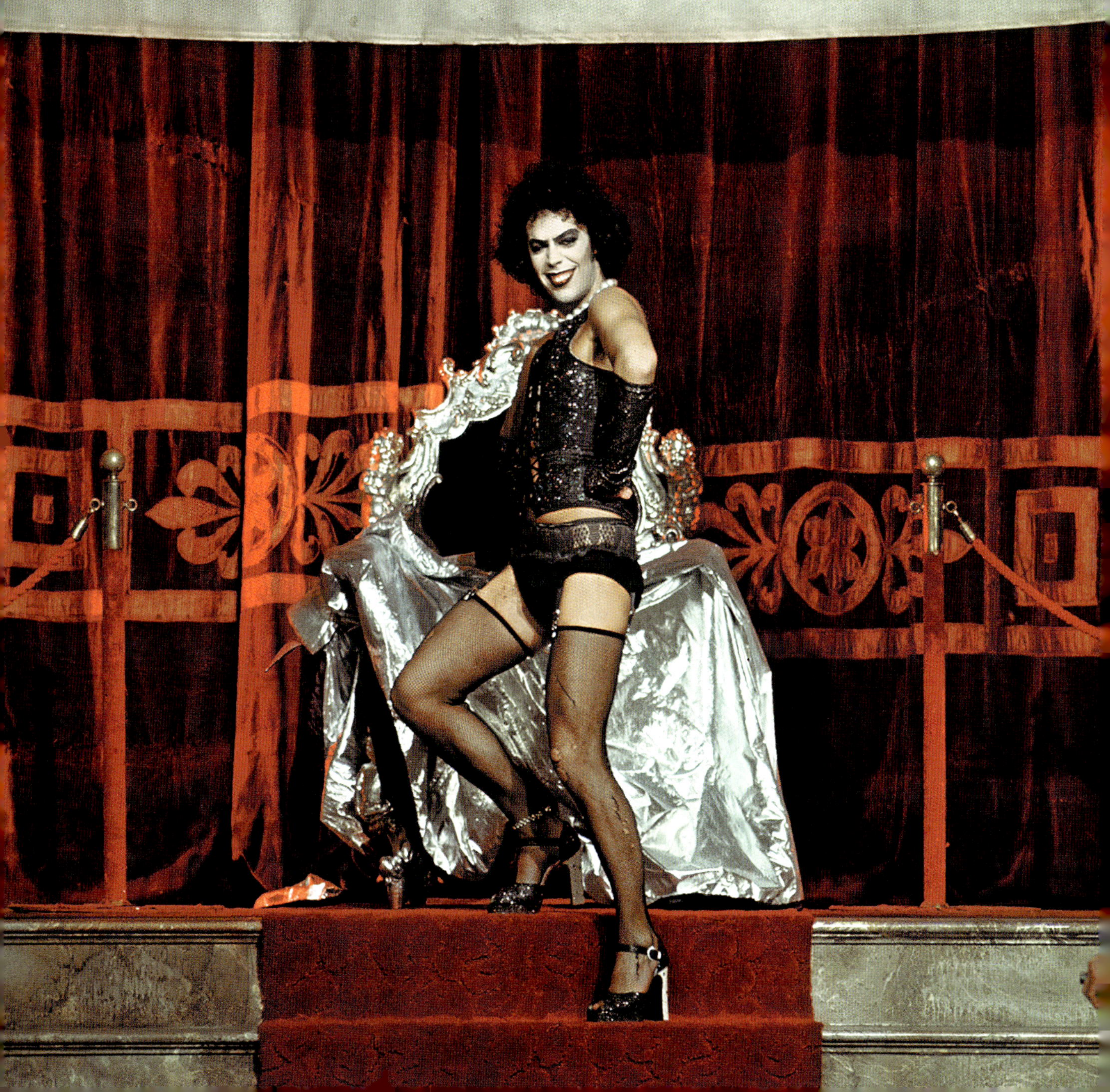
RANSYLVANIAN CO

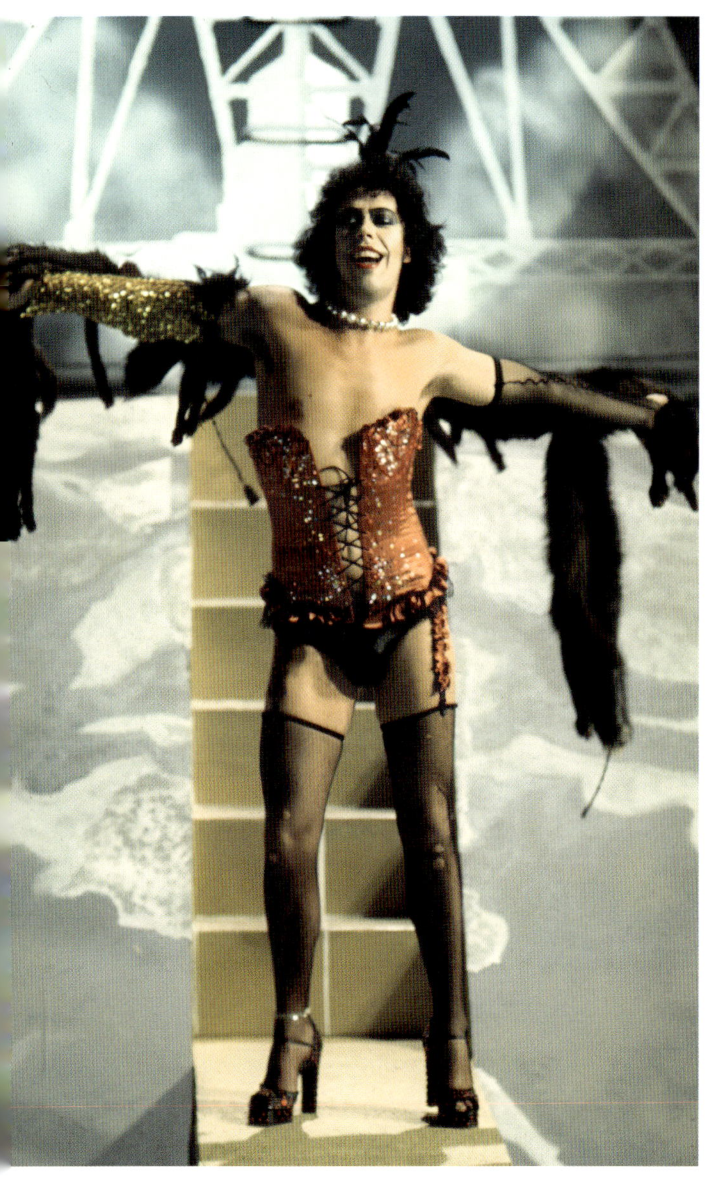

MARK MOTHERSBAUGH, DEVO:

"While some of the best music came out of the fifties, it was also a time when social and political tension rose, forcing people to wake up to what was happening around them. By the time the 1970s came around, much of rock 'n' roll had become maximalized in an unclever, misogynistic, and flaccid way, urging some people to respond by deconstructing and subverting common expectations of music and message. *Rocky Horror* and DEVO developed at the same time, along with Roxy Music, David Bowie, David Lynch, John Waters, and others who were all seeing pop culture through cynical yet humorous lenses. Richard O'Brien was a genius, that's for sure. The music and score blended perfectly together, and he set a new standard for both Broadway and pop music of the time."

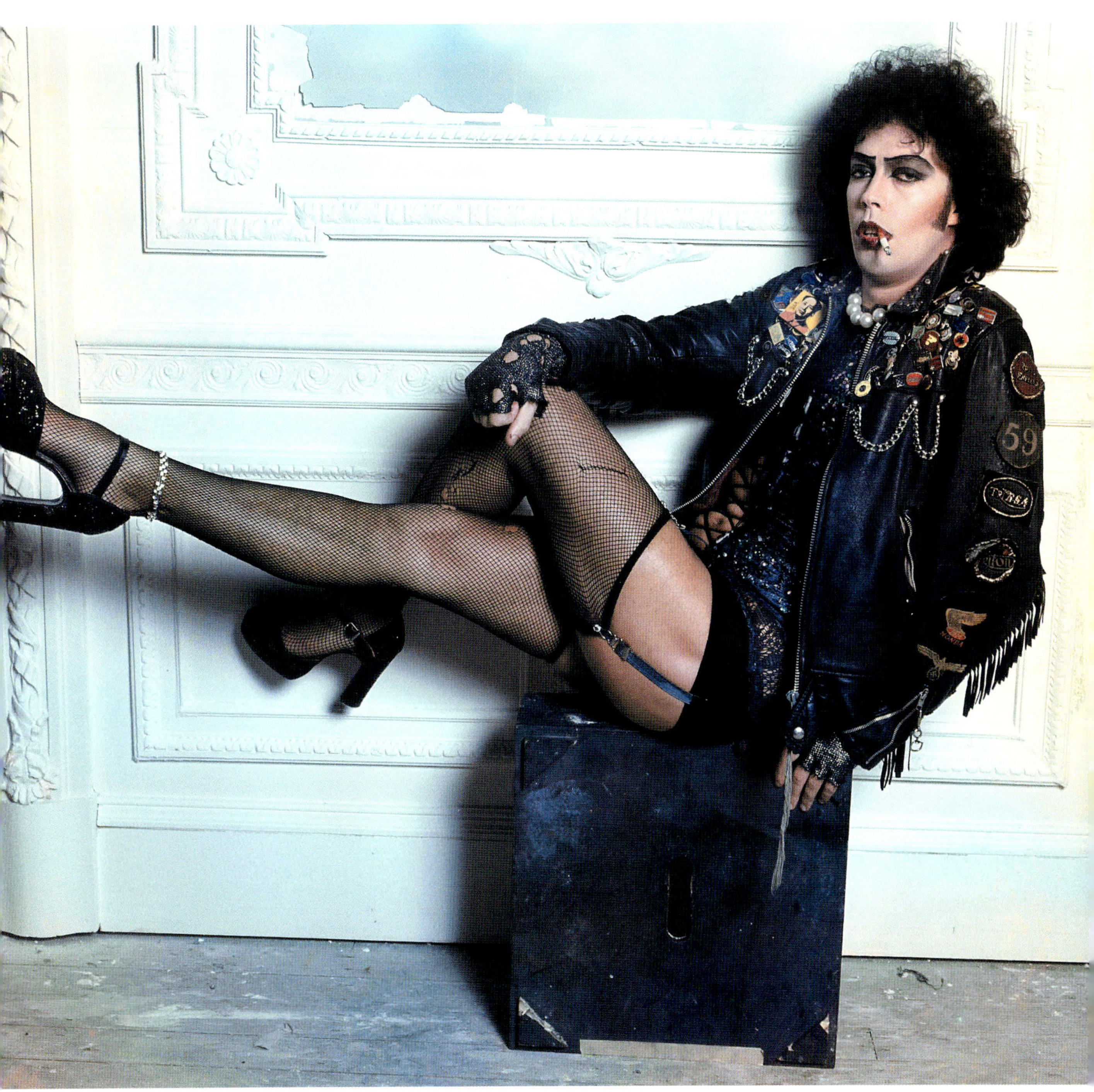
59

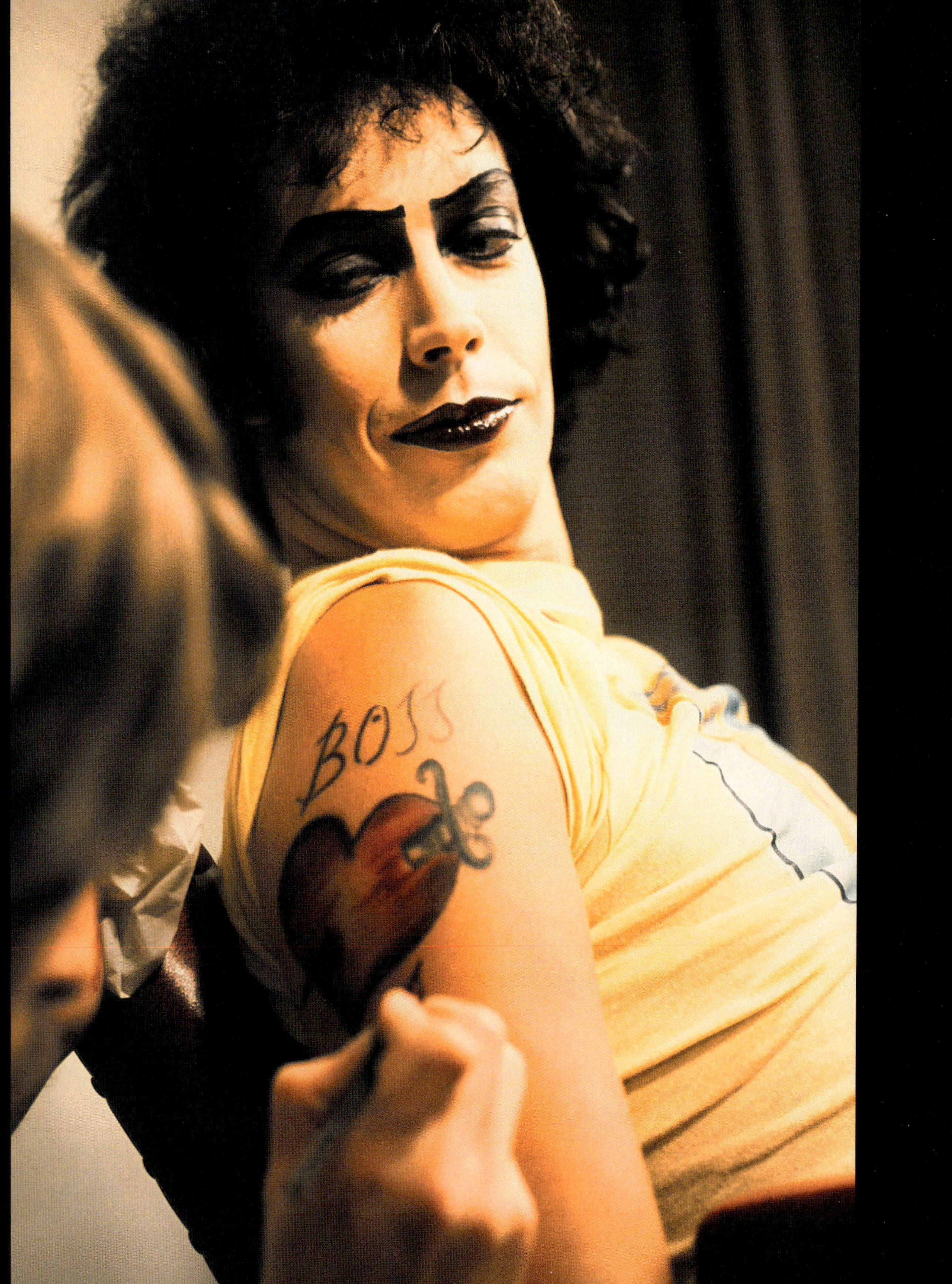
BOSS

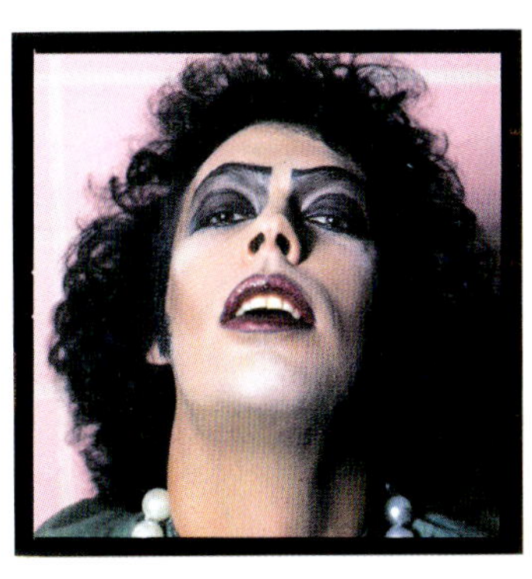
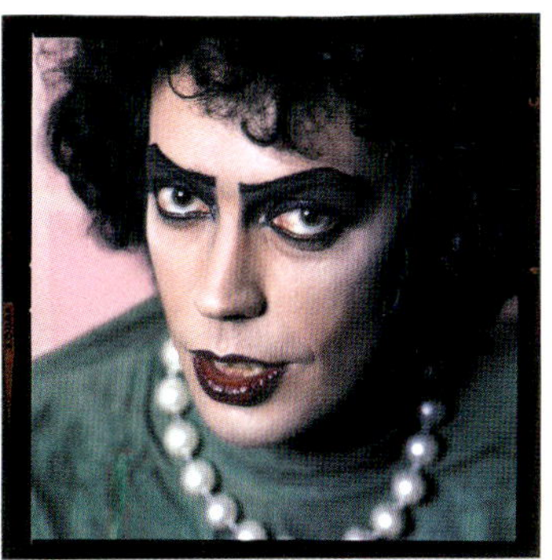
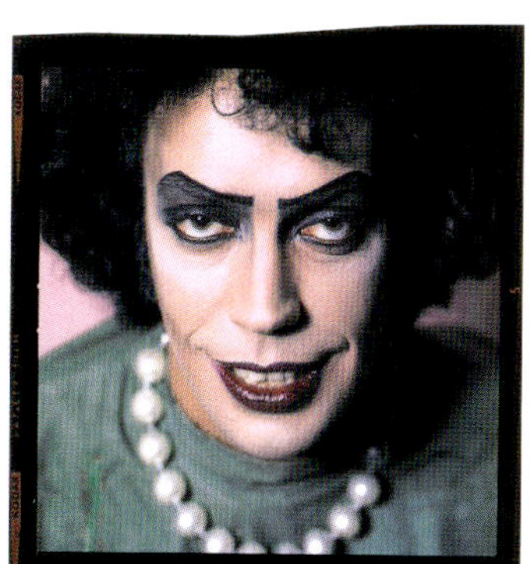
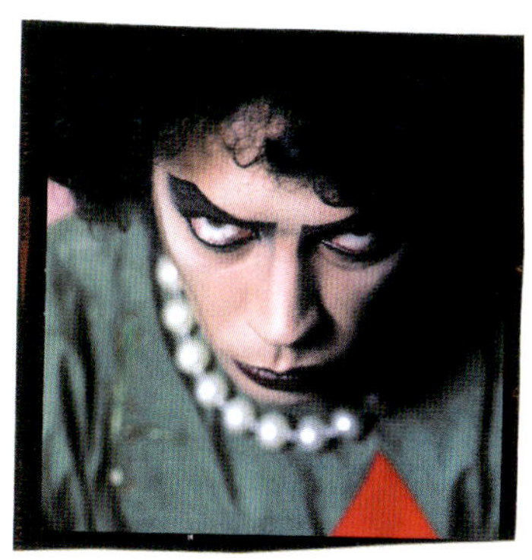
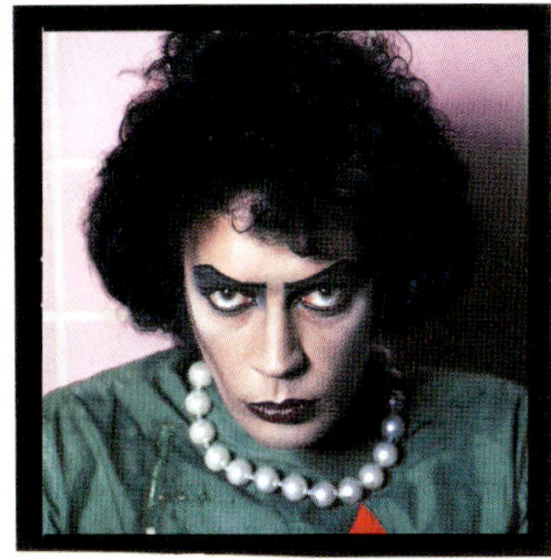
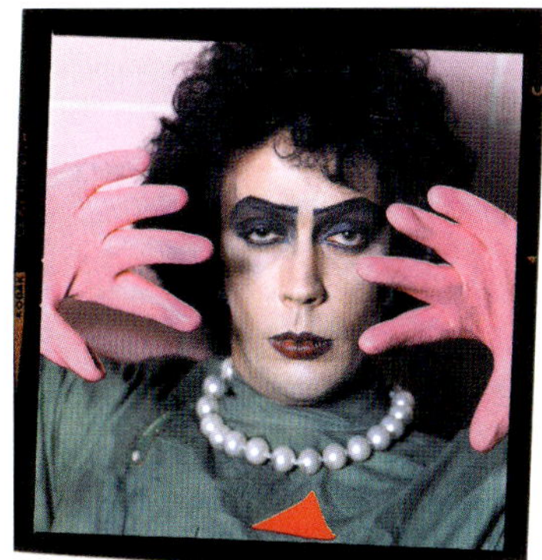
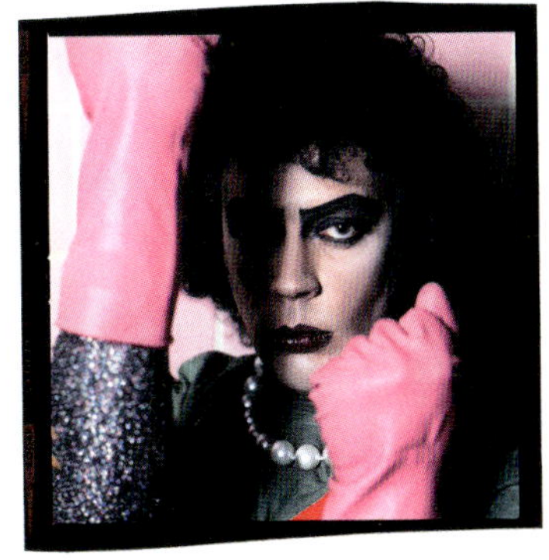
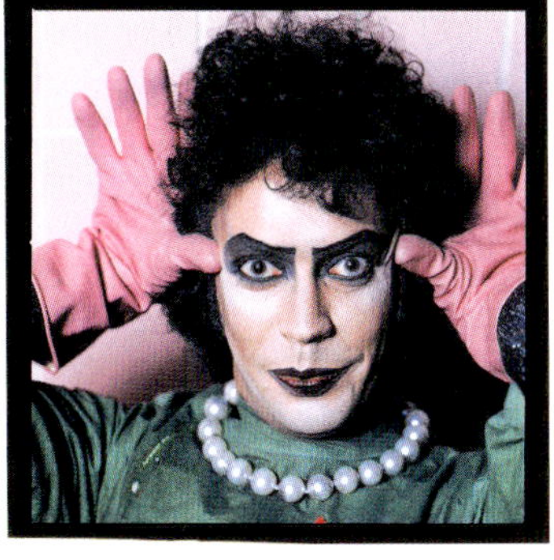
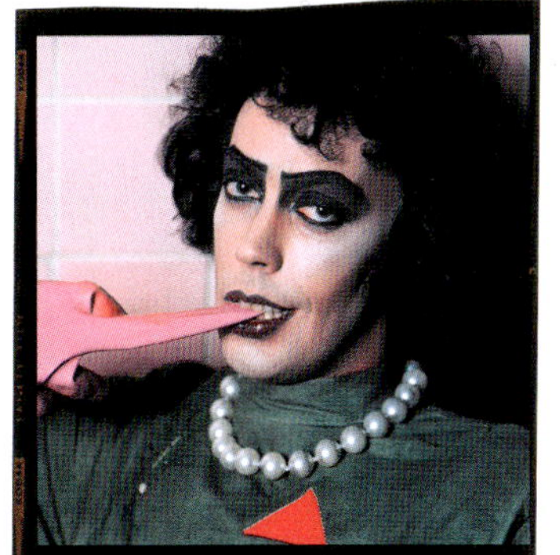

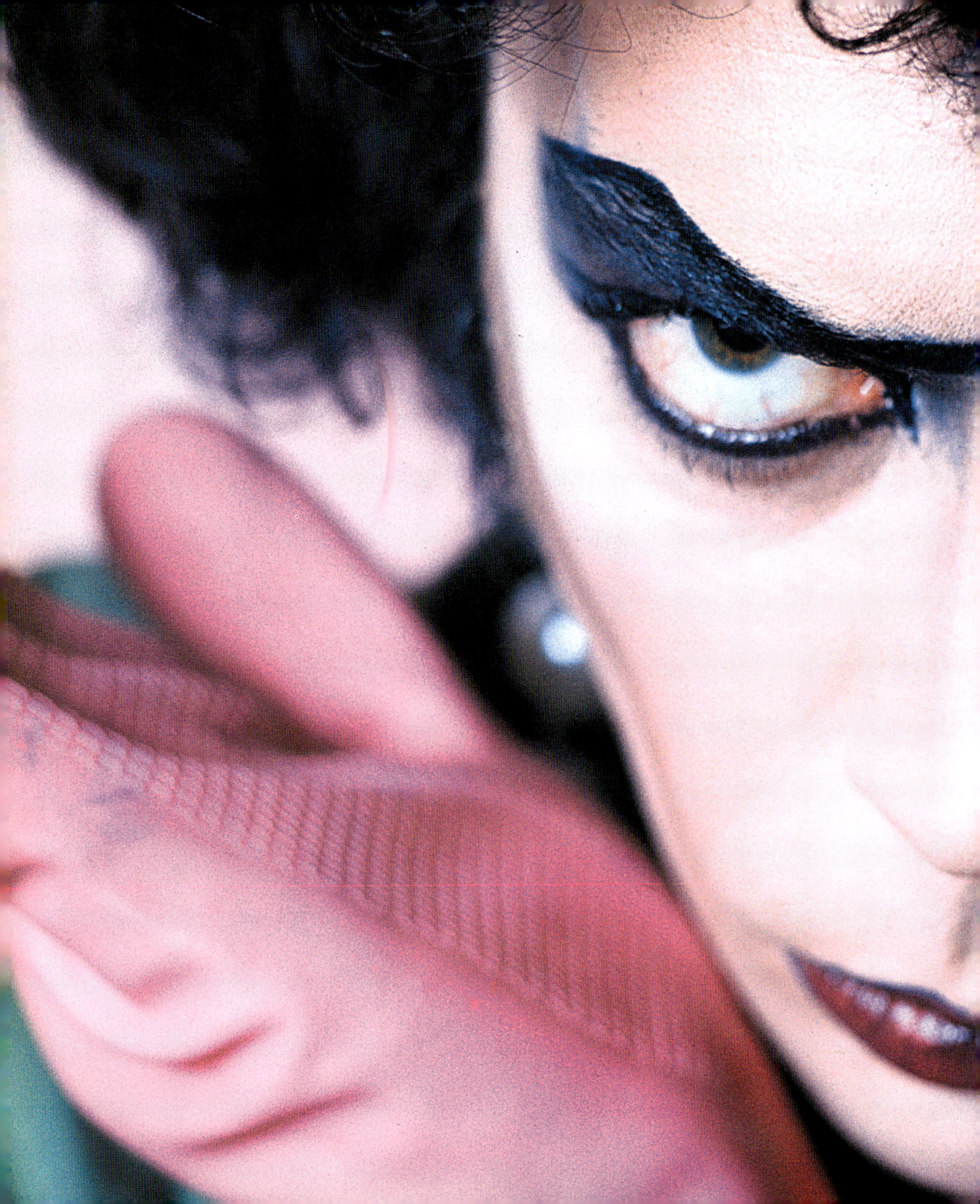

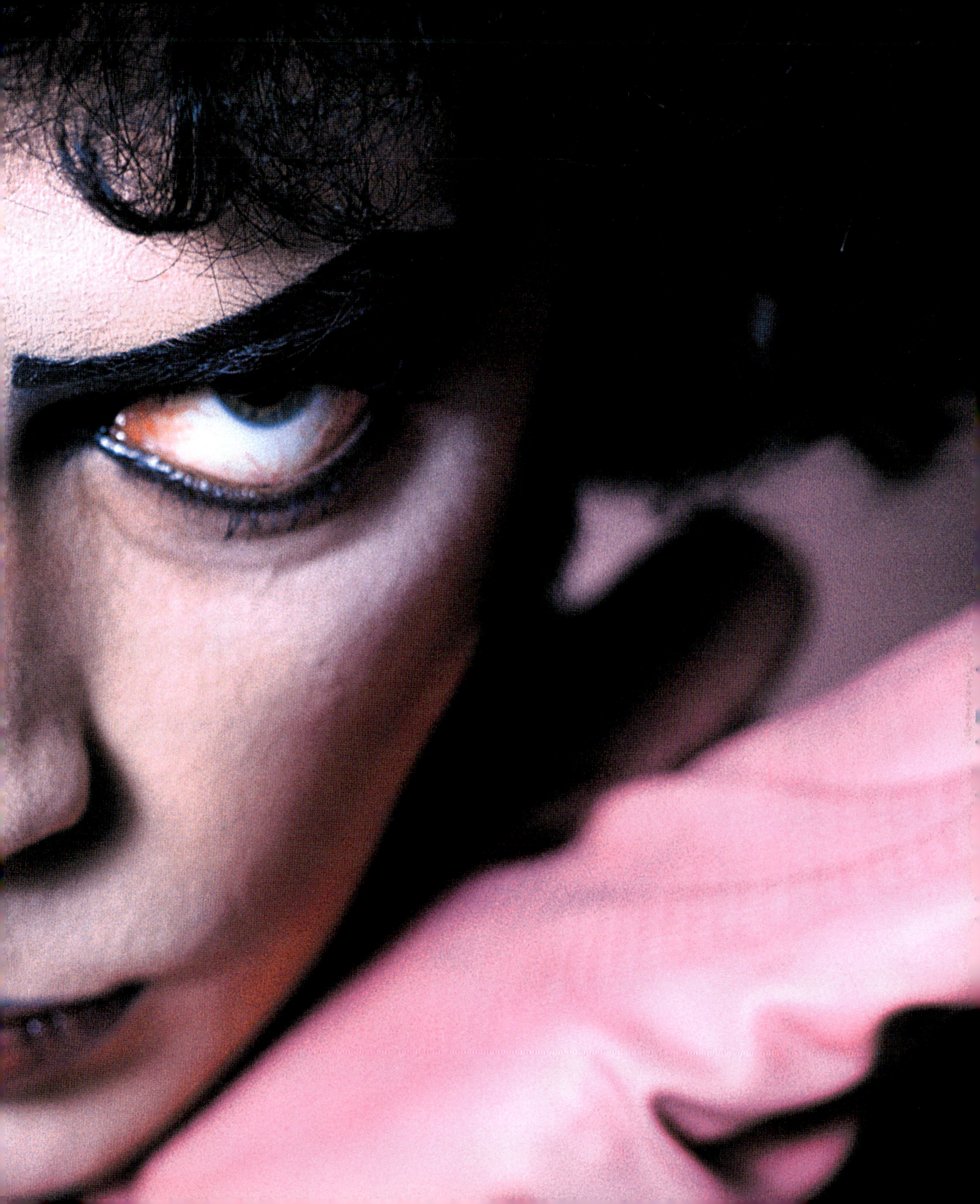

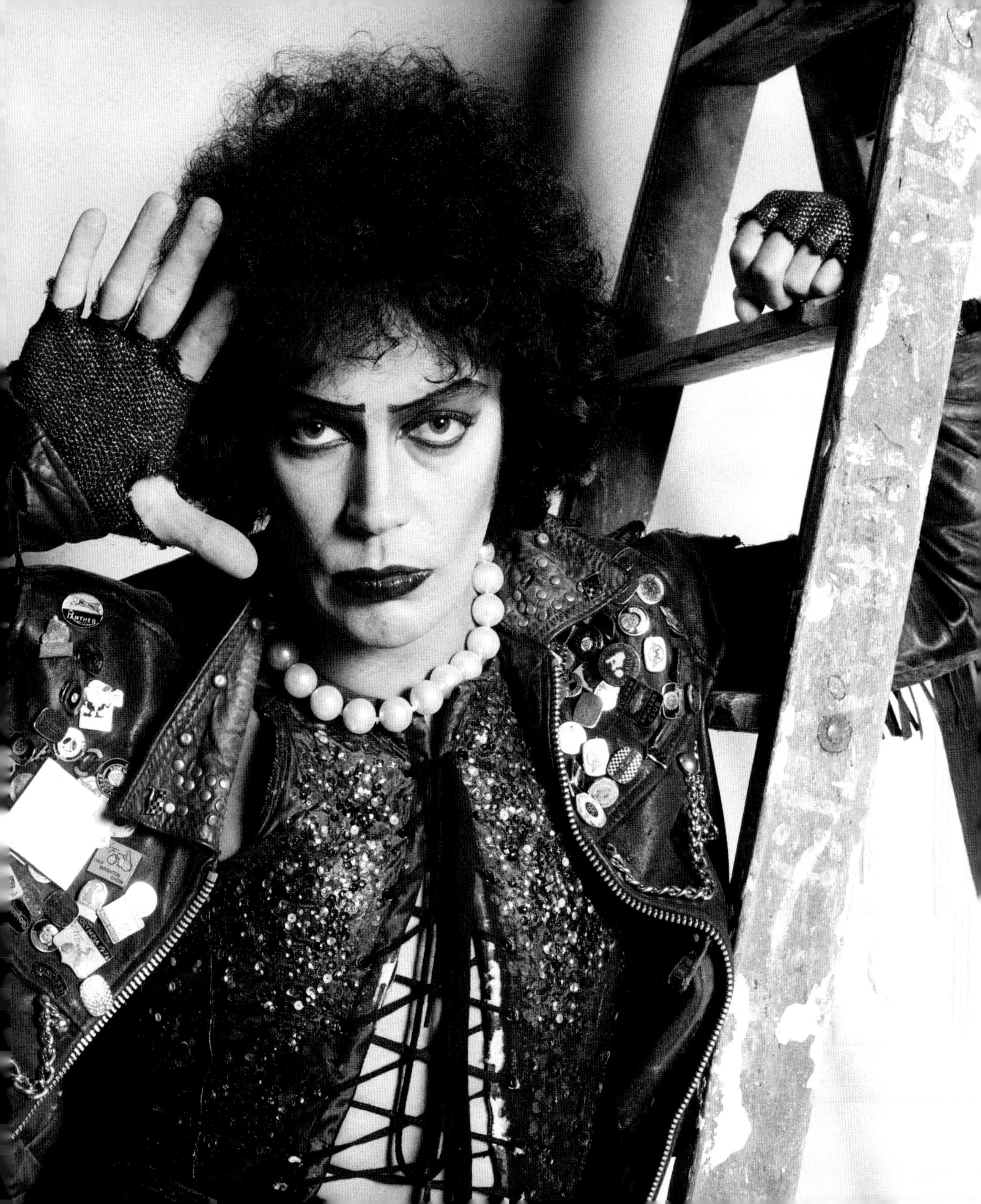

DON'T GET STRUNG OUT BY THE WAY THAT I LOOK

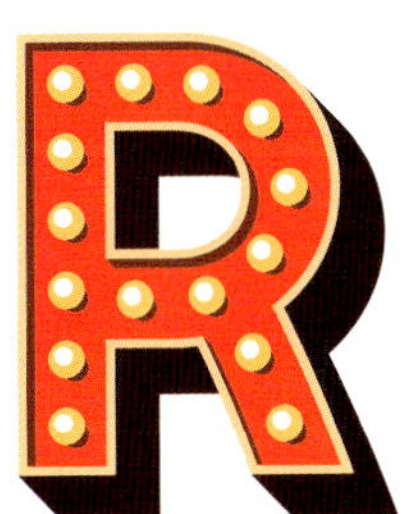

ocky *Horror* was probably not the first example of gender-bending on film, but it was the most in-your-face," said Richard O'Brien to *The Guardian*. "When Dr. Frank-N-Furter sings 'I'm just a sweet transvestite' without any apology, it was empowering for many people. And Janet singing 'Touch-a Touch-a Touch Me' was controversial too—a girl wanting to be sexual in a let's-get-down-and-do-it way. I'm grateful it's helped other people feel less isolated or lonely."

As O'Brien told the Australian Broadcasting Corporation in 2019, "The transsexual nature of *Rocky Horror* is driven from my own transsexual nature, but I didn't see it as a vehicle for that or a cathartic piece of work for myself. The driving force behind it was me watching those old movies late at night on the television, when everyone else had gone to bed, and getting such pleasure from the creaky plots and the pretentious dialogue, the unintended comedy. My first love was always populist themes. I loved the sci-fi movies, I loved the late-night double features. All my interests were low-brow, populist interests: rock 'n' roll, comics, and that kind of stuff. Much frowned upon by the older generation at the time, but now turned into high art."

As for the personal impact of his most famous creation, he told the *Daily Mail* in 2015 that *Rocky Horror* "changed the way a lot of people thought about themselves and their sexuality. It made it OK for men to dress up as women, but it didn't make it OK for

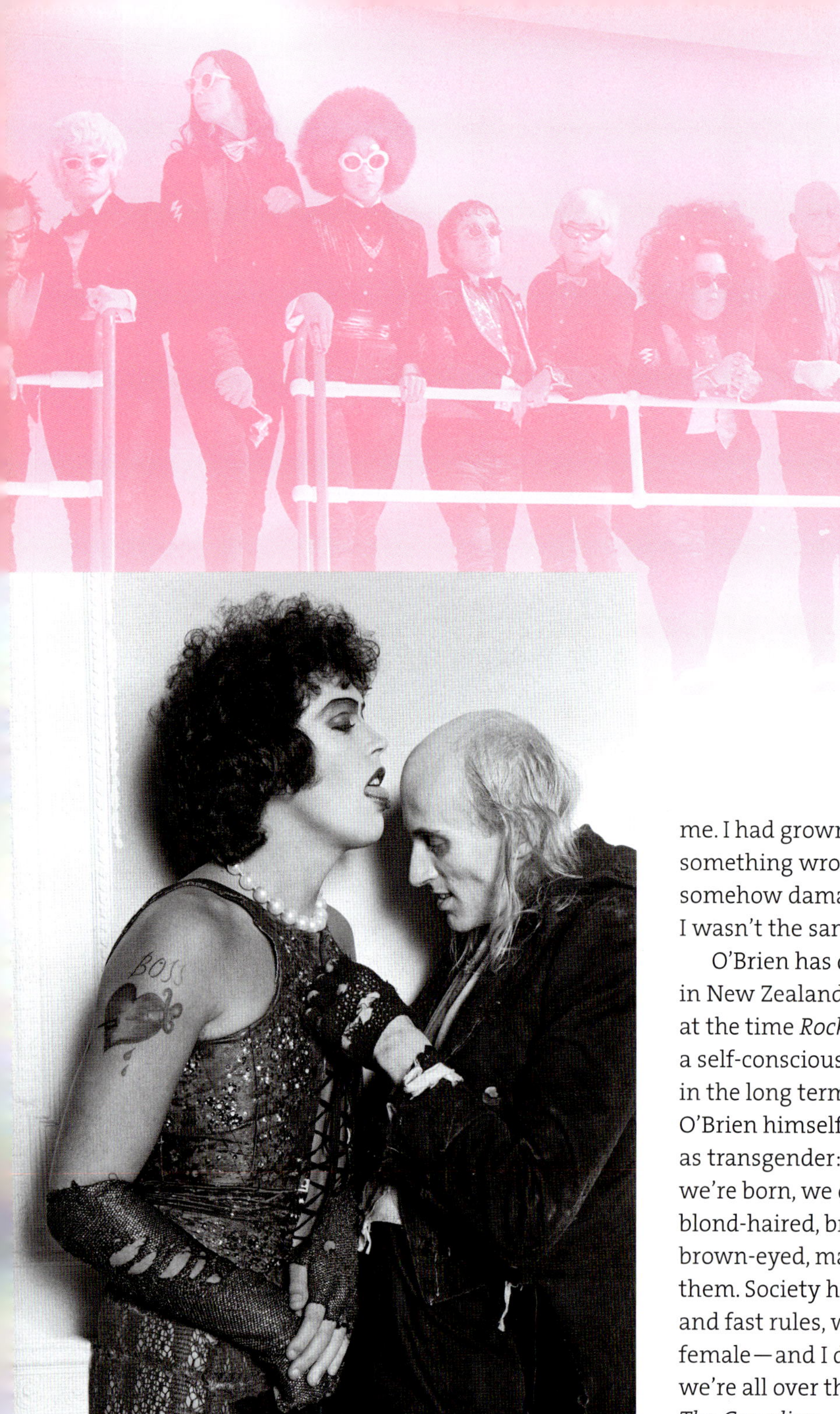

me. I had grown up believing there was something wrong with me and that I was somehow damaged and dirty because I wasn't the same as everyone else."

O'Brien has described his adolescence in New Zealand as oppressive. And though at the time *Rocky Horror* may not have been a self-conscious work of personal catharsis, in the long term the project empowered O'Brien himself, too, who now identifies as transgender: "We get dealt cards when we're born, we don't ask for them: tall, short, blond-haired, brown-haired, blue-eyed, brown-eyed, male, female. We don't ask for them. Society has decided there are hard and fast rules, we're hardwired male or female—and I don't think it's true, I think we're all over the fucking place," he told *The Guardian*.

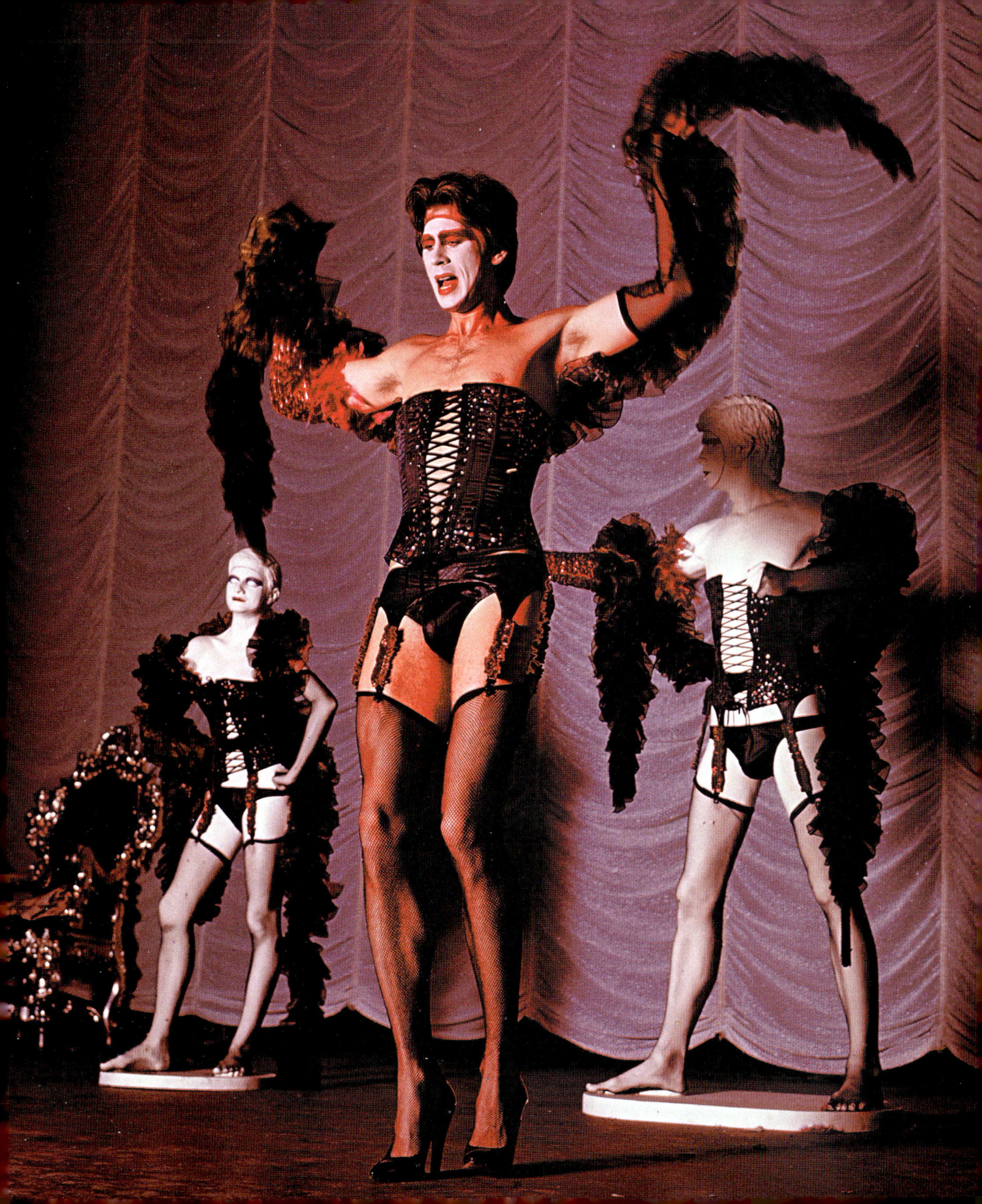

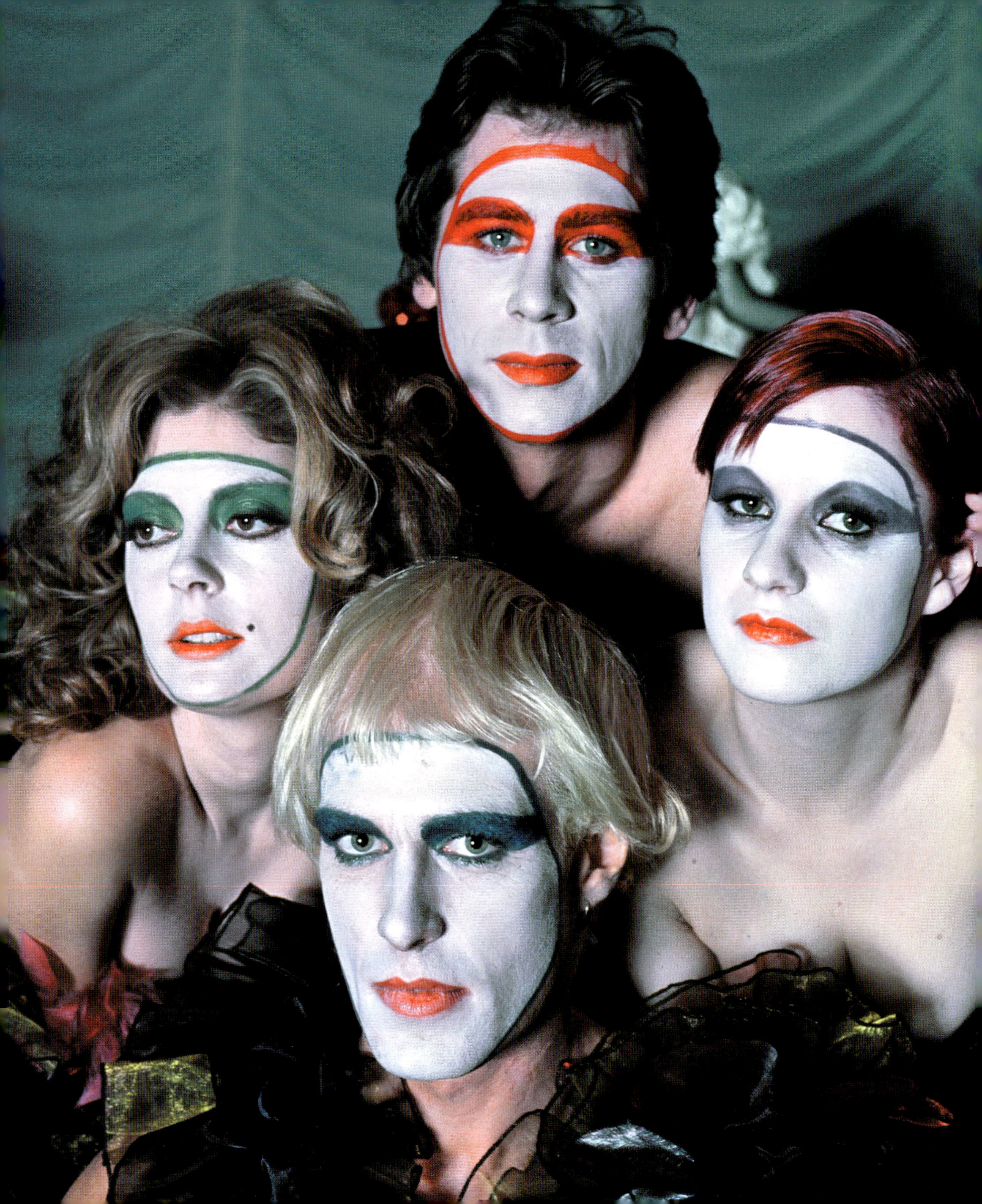

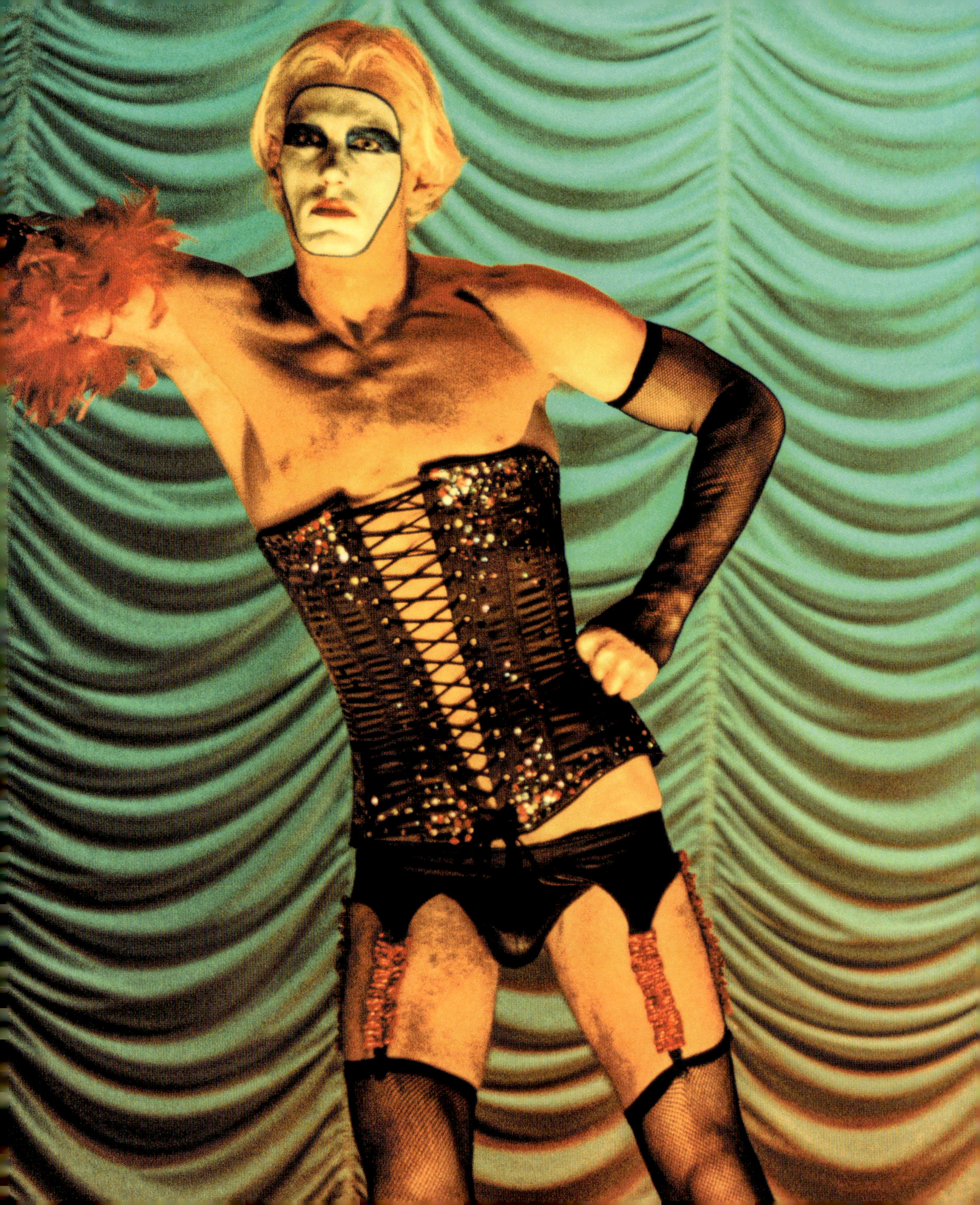

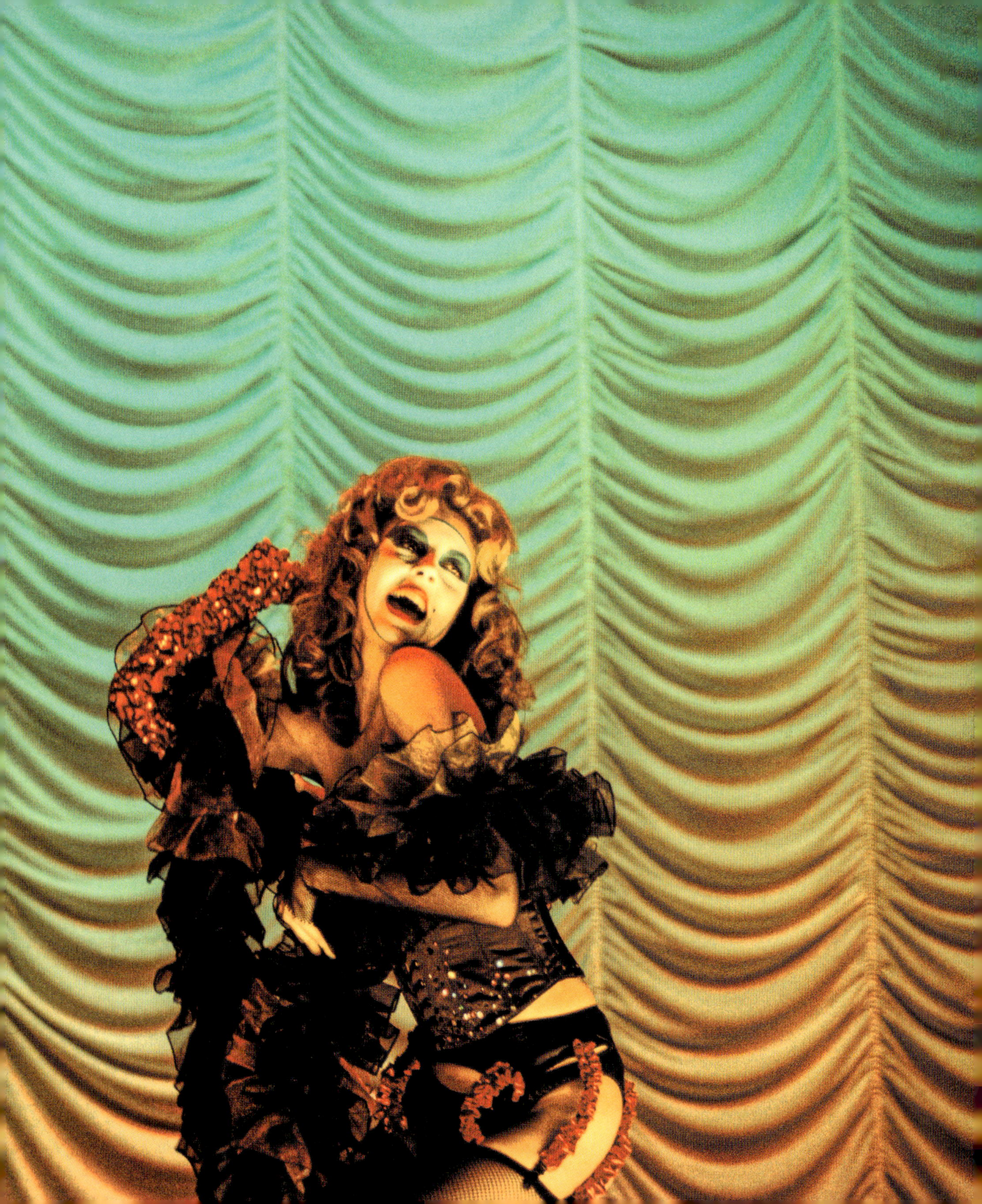

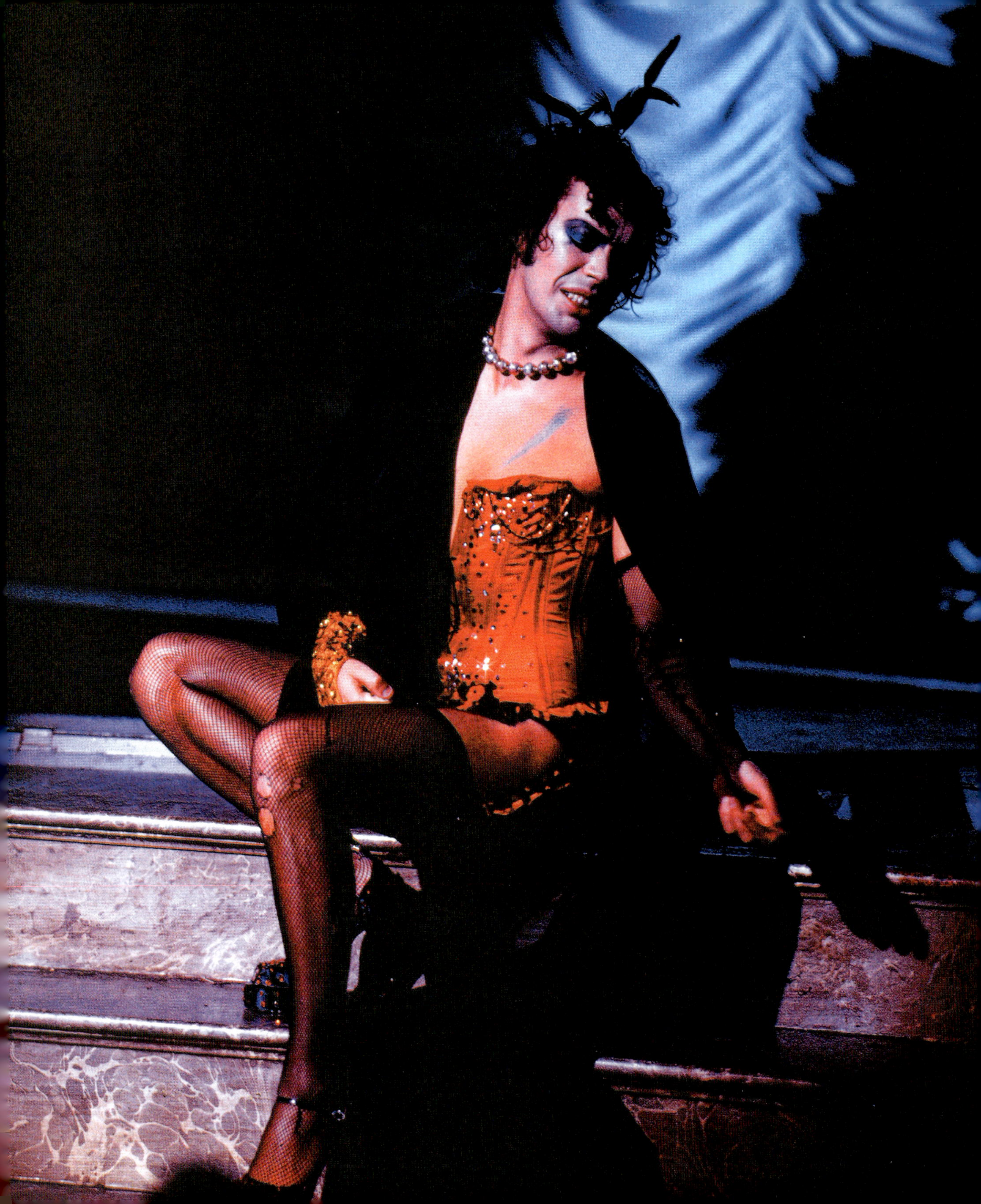

COURTNEY LOVE, HOLE: "In 1979 my stepfather exited the chat, went down to San Francisco, and had a fabulous gay summer. I visited him down there. He had all this knowledge about fluidity, and sexuality, and masculinity, and took me to a midnight showing of *The Rocky Horror Picture Show*. I thought, I've found my people. I didn't know any of these people; I wasn't dressed up. But people were dressed as Little Nell, and there were men in corsets. They had toast and they had toilet paper, and I didn't understand. We went in and watched this crazy movie. And Tim Curry appeared, and it just blew my mind—'I'm just a sweet transvestite from Transsexual, Transylvania.' This was the moment the borders of gender opened up for me in a beautiful way."

EUGENE HÜTZ, SINGER AND COMPOSER OF GOGOL BORDELLO: "Even though I discovered *The Rocky Horror Picture Show* through my own digging in the '90s, when I first came to the U.S., I instantly recognized something in it that was perhaps a portal into a whole other way of life for an entire generation of the right kind of freaks. Then I asked around, and yes, it was."

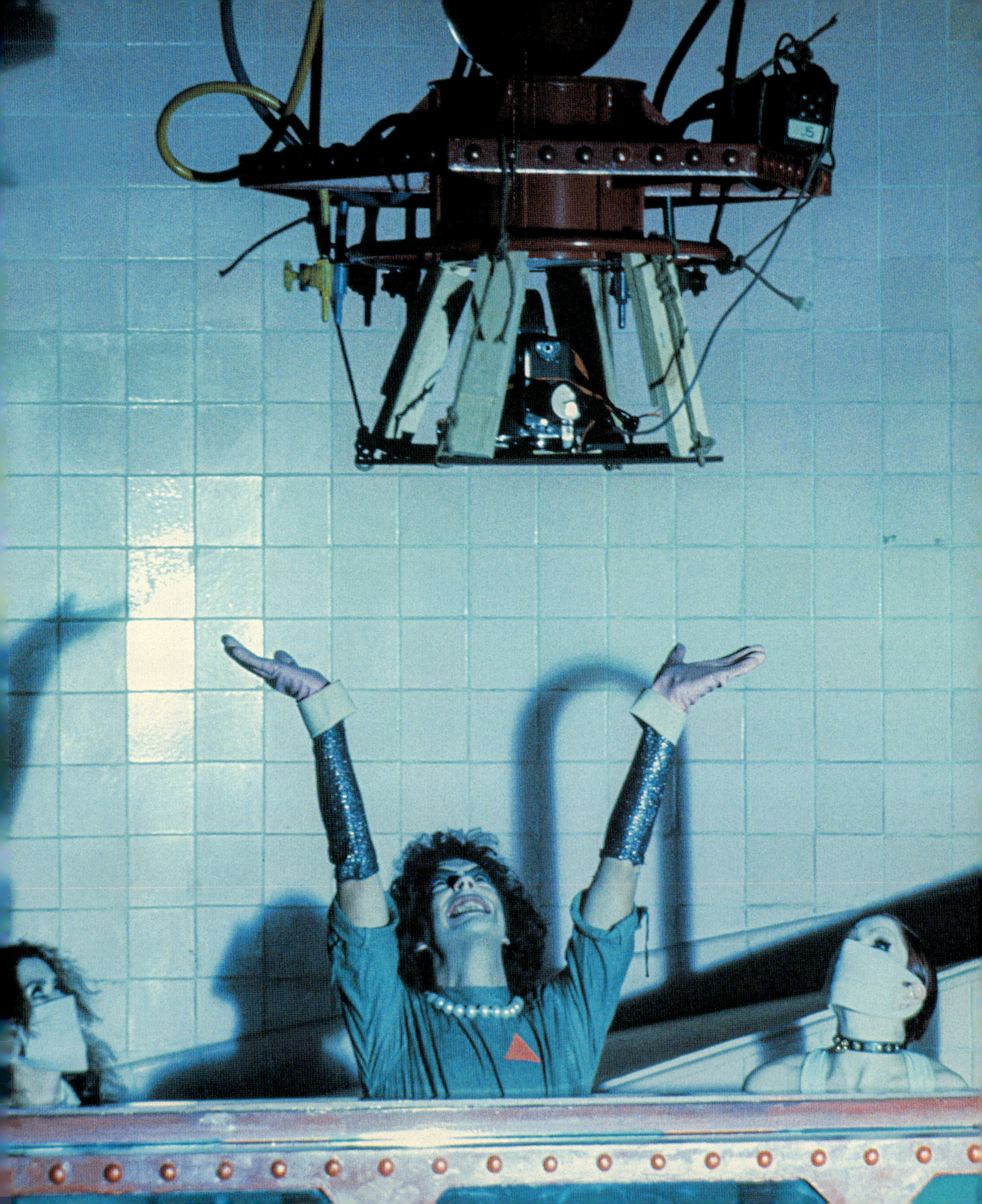

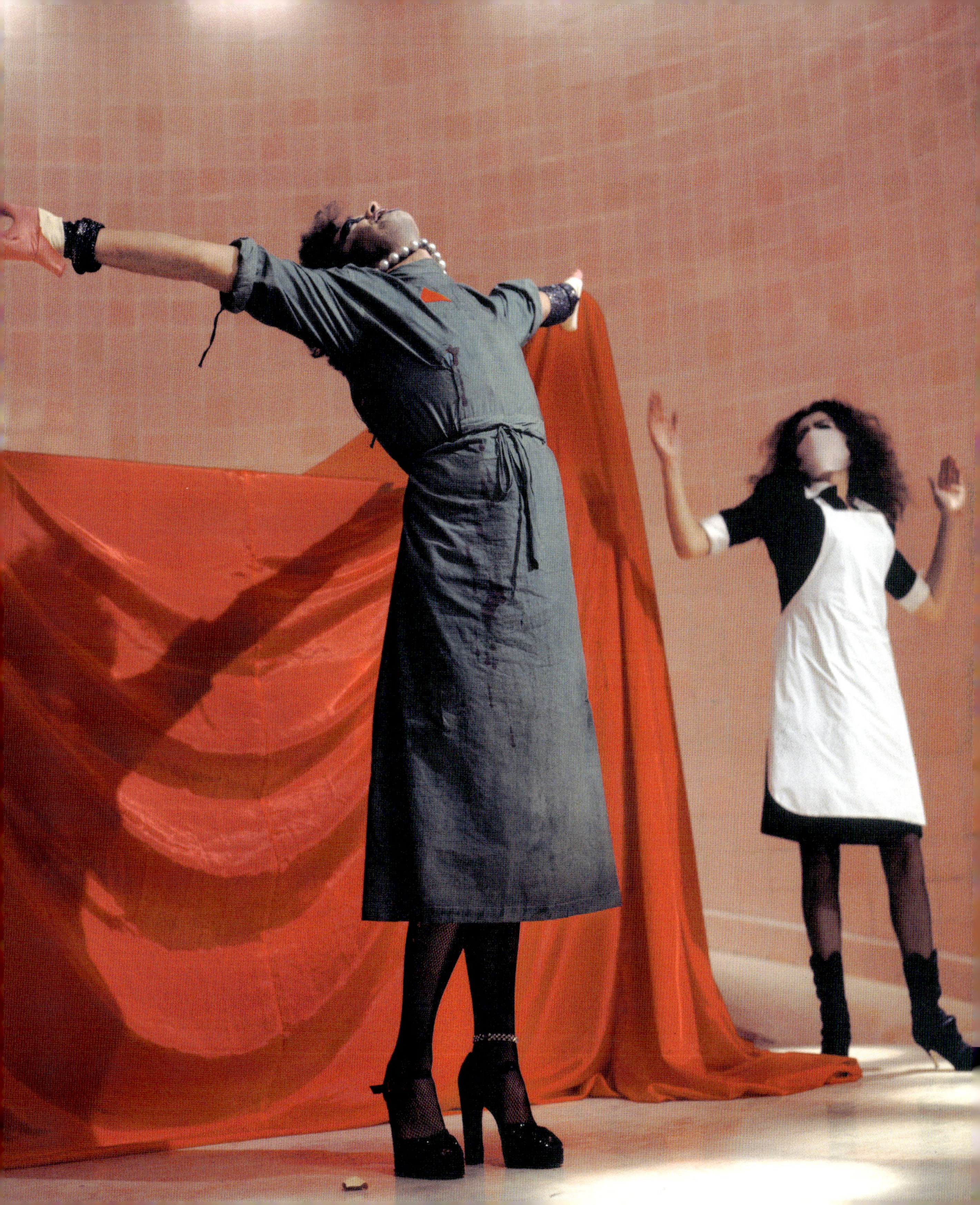

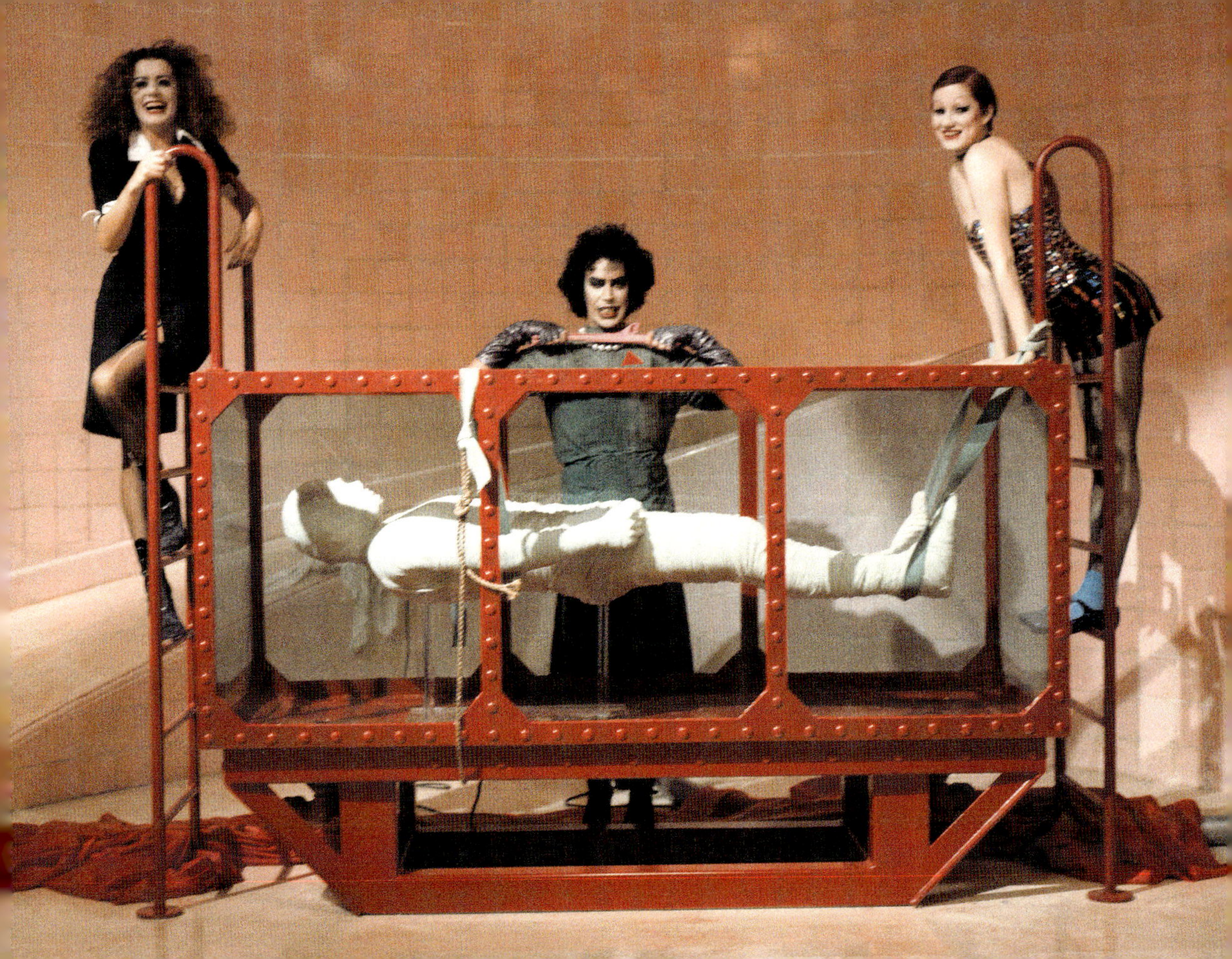

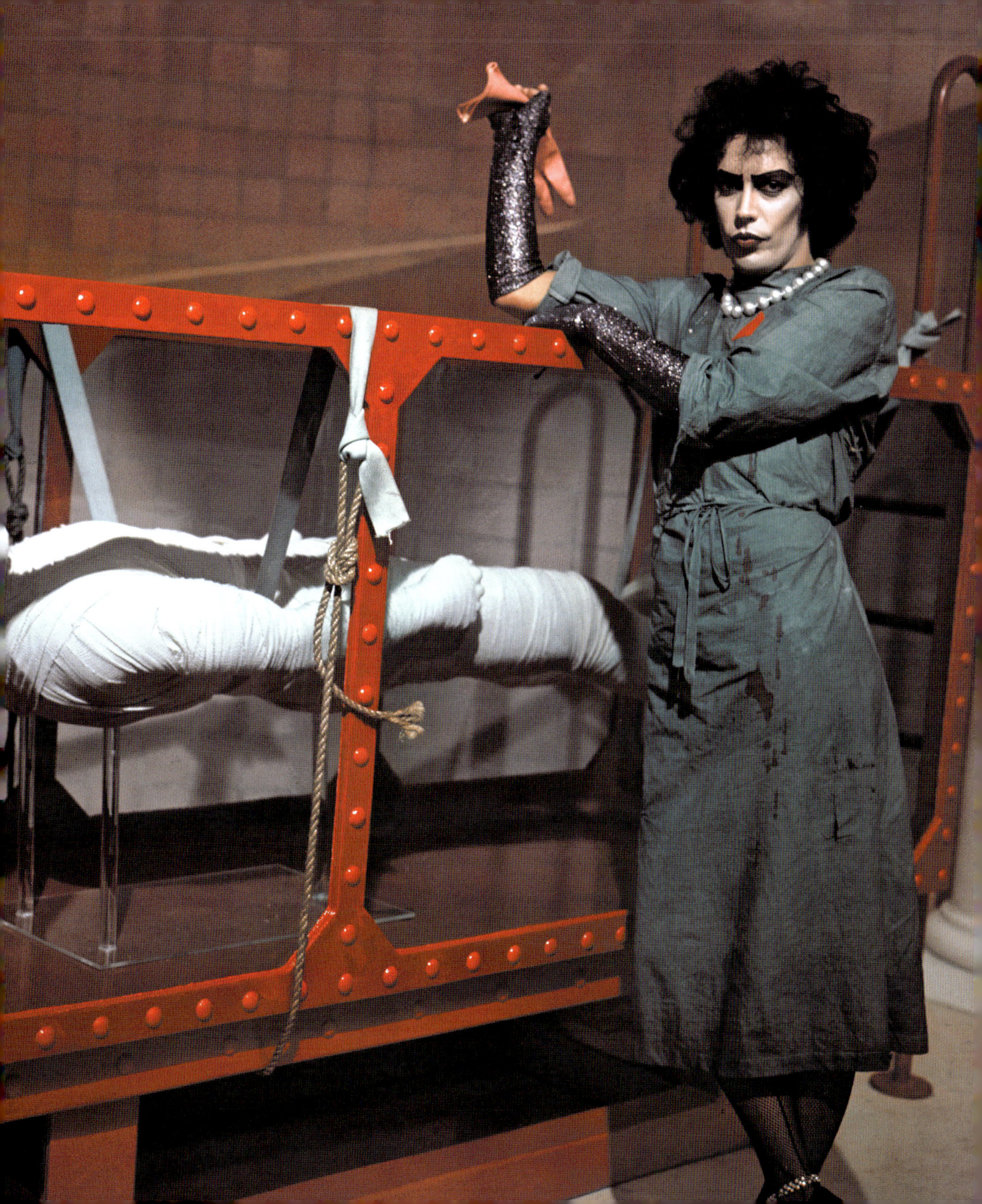

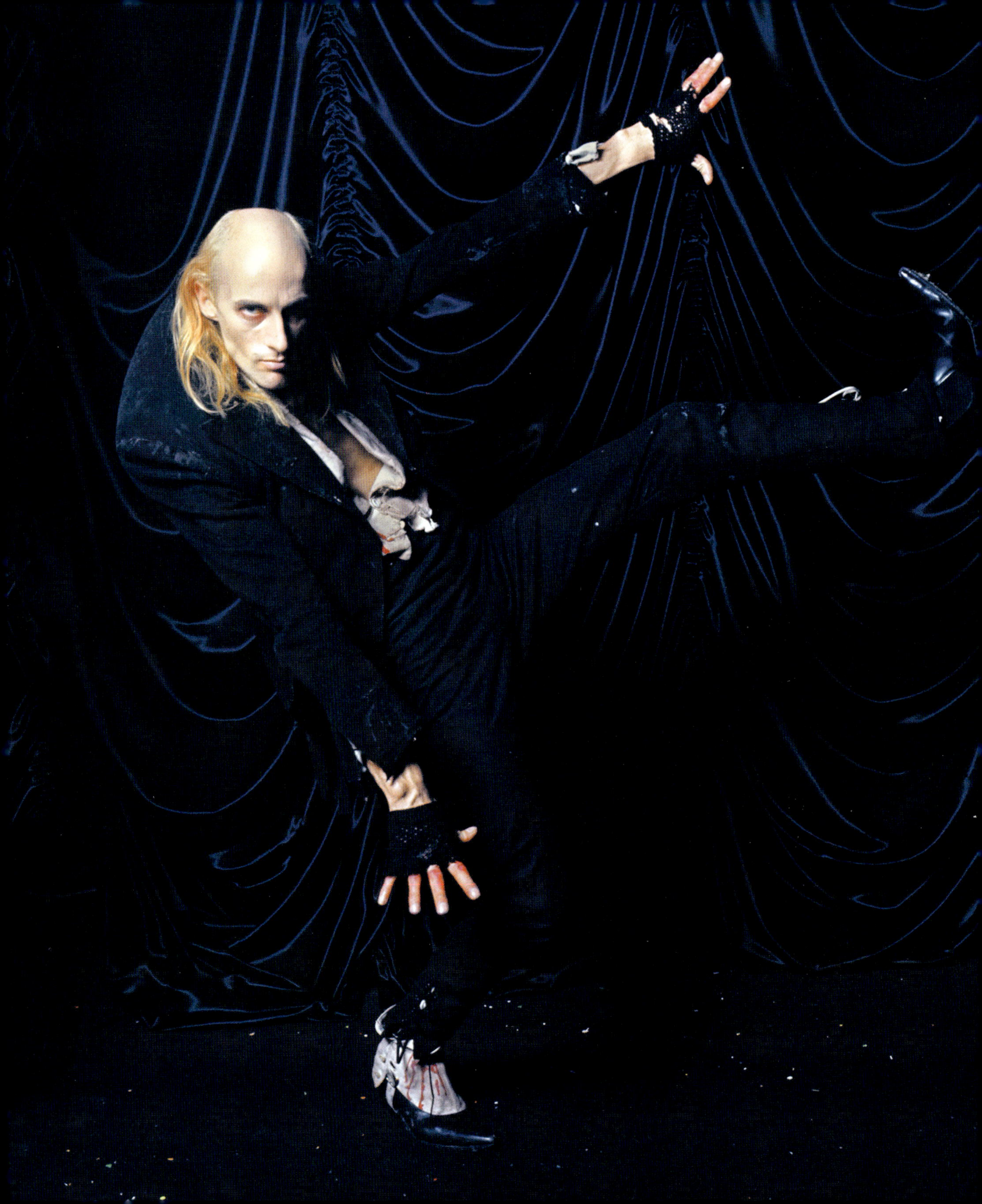

I'M YOUR NEW COMMANDER: RIFF RAFF

"Ah, Mr. Wonderful," says O'Brien. "I was the love interest in the movie."

As O'Brien told *Theatre Scenes* magazine in 2011, "All the characters are stereotypes, that's why the actors have to play them as if they are incredibly serious and deeply written characters. Because the more seriously they play them, the funnier it all becomes. Riff Raff is the hunchback, the Igor figure that we have known and loved from various B-movies, the resentful butler. It is enjoyable to play someone who is so resentful, such a misery guts, and so resentful of the other, harboring all that discontent and loathing. It's a good role to feast on."

O'Brien had originally envisioned himself in another role. "I didn't see myself as playing Riff Raff. I wanted to play Eddie. I just wanted to get out of the fridge, sing a song, and get off. I didn't know that the show was going to be successful; I never thought that we'd be allowed to have the luxury of casting someone just to sing one song. But I was young and naïve, and I thought if the show wasn't doing very well, and the audiences were sitting there just saying oh-my-god, if I just sang one song and got off then I wouldn't have to carry the can, that everyone else would be getting hit with the rotten tomatoes and what not being thrown at them, and I would have escaped into the wings.

"Jim Sharman, it was him that suggested I should play Riff Raff. And I thought, *Well, if I hadn't written the show, if I had nothing*

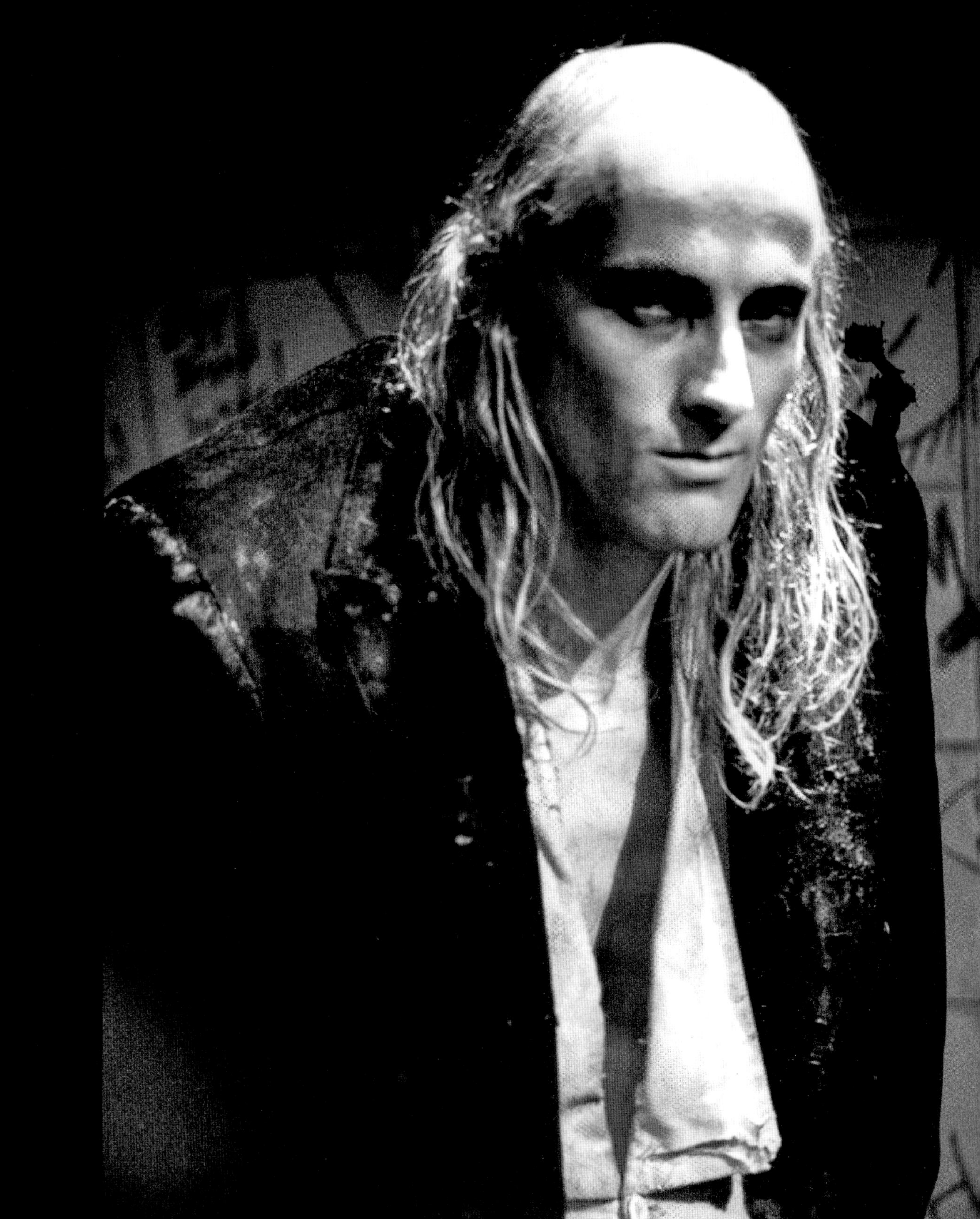

to do with the show, and I got a phone call from Jim saying I've got this show and there is a character who I would like you to play, I would have been there with bells on. And he was quite right: I think Riff Raff was a perfect role for me to play, being a strange, peculiar, skinny kind of person, it was good casting."

As Mick recalled, "Richard himself delivers a delightfully obsequious and subversive performance as Riff Raff. His presence is very spectral. Part Nosferatu, part Igor, and part Uriah Heep. I recall he had some reservations when he first saw the final cut of the film: 'It's not nearly as funny and energetic as the stage show. It's much darker than I thought it would be. But maybe I'm just too close to it.' So he didn't seem surprised at its initial failure."

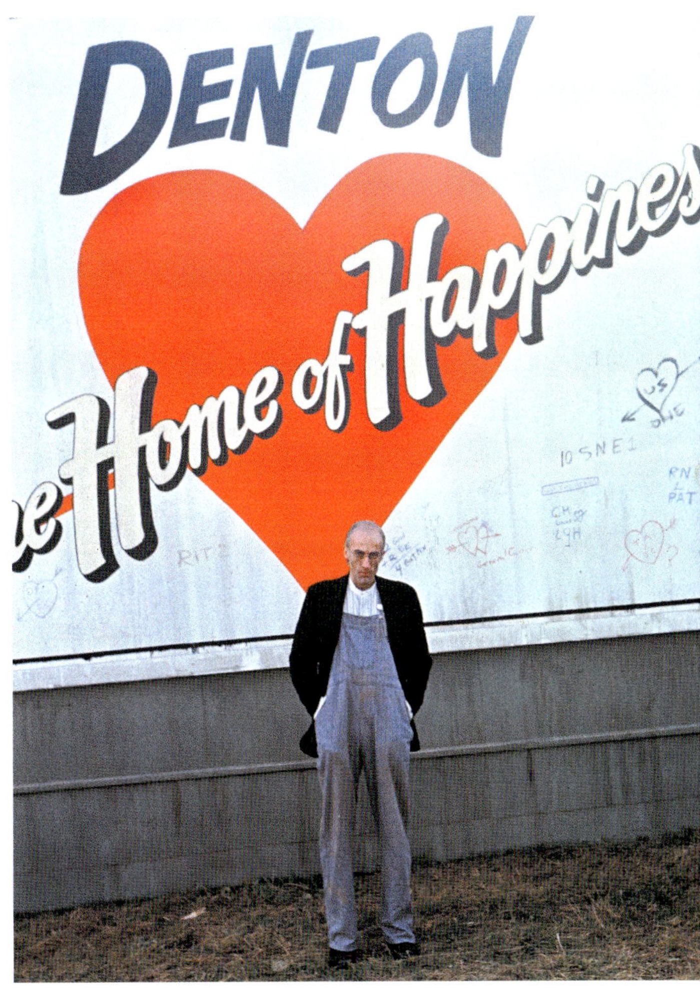

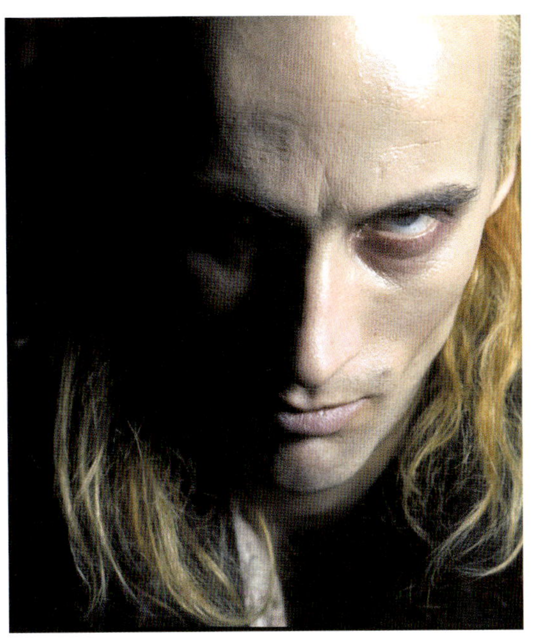

"It is enjoyable to play someone who is so resentful, such a misery guts, and so resentful of the other, harboring all that discontent and loathing. It's a good role to feast on."

—RICHARD O'BRIEN

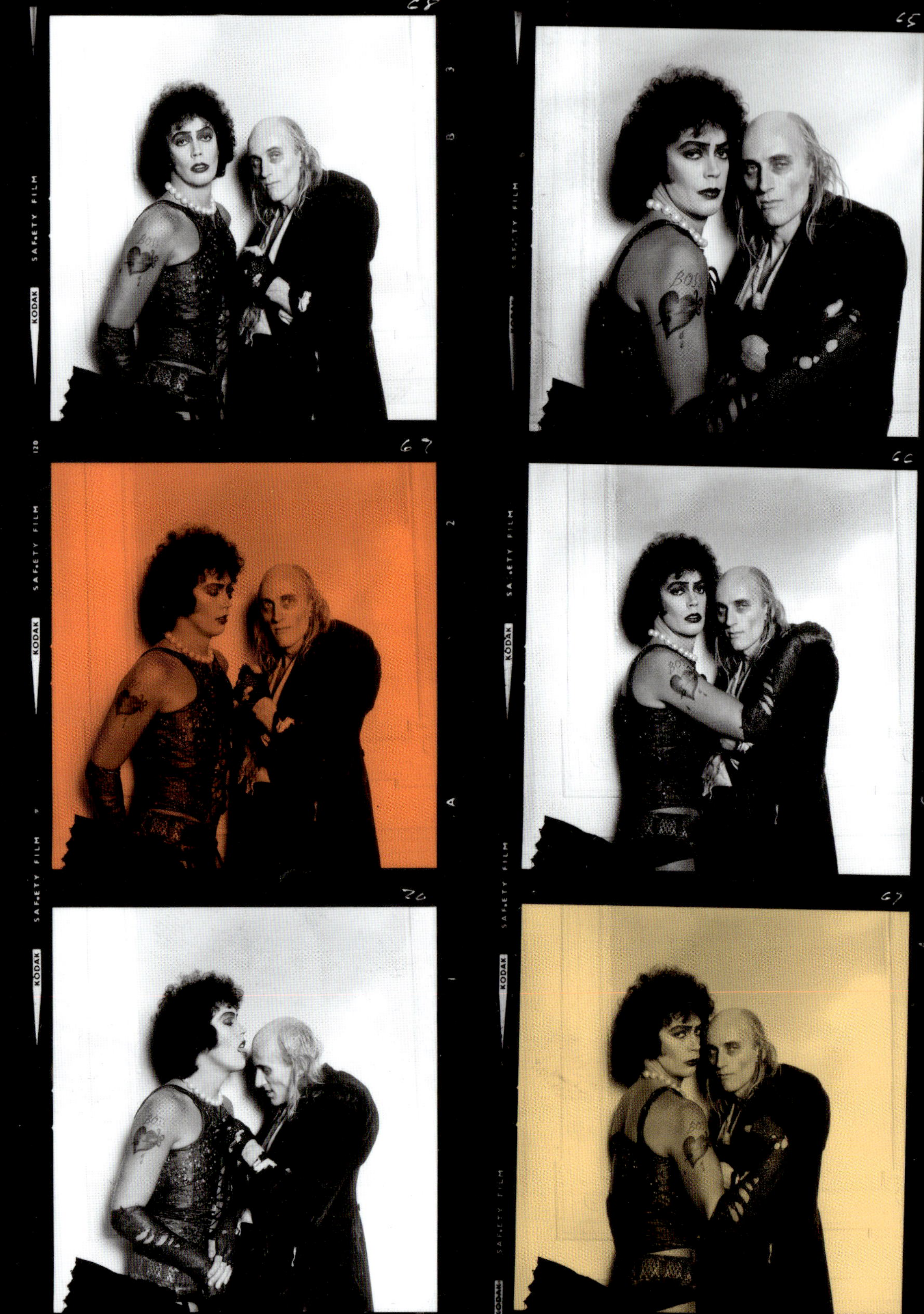

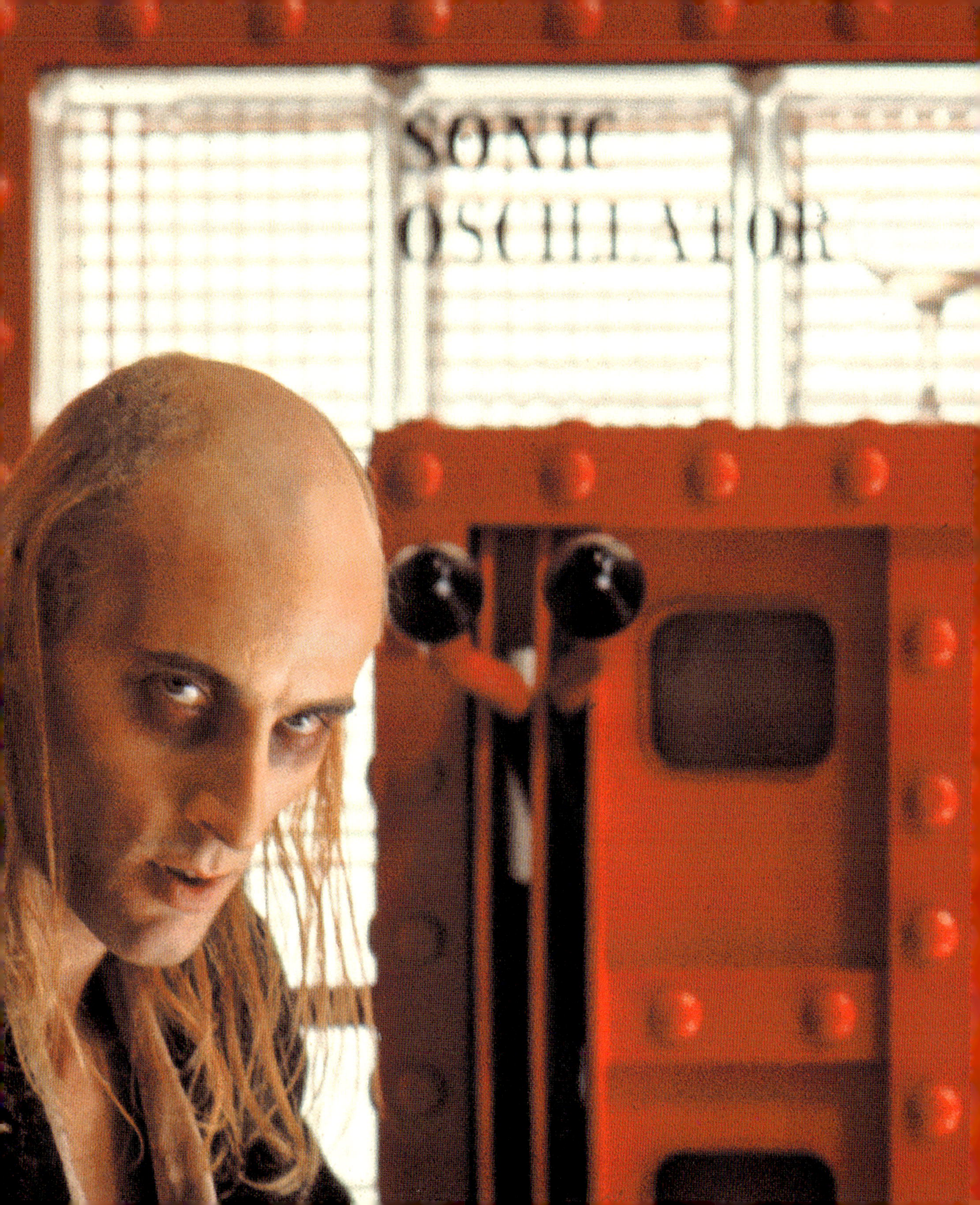
SONIC
OSCILLATOR

REEVE CARNEY, ACTOR AND MUSICIAN: "I grew up in Greenwich Village, and my elementary school happened to be just around the corner from the Waverly Theatre on 6th Avenue, which was the epicenter of the *The Rocky Horror Picture Show* midnight screening phenomenon. I remember walking by the marquee in the late eighties and being equal parts frightened and intrigued. But it wasn't until I was fourteen and living in Los Angeles that a dear friend of mine, Lindsay Felton, exposed me to the actual film for the first time. When FOX's remake version was presented to me, I began studying the film in a different way, and was mesmerized—not only by Richard O'Brien's incredibly nuanced performance but obviously by the fact that he wrote the whole dang thing. What a feat!

I found it a unique and exciting challenge to play Riff Raff, in that he is in almost every scene but in many cases not the center of attention. That is also an exciting challenge for an actor, especially on screen, because you have to keep him engaged to the fullest extent—at least that's what I felt was necessary—even in moments when you may or may not be in frame, take after take. I really enjoyed that. I remember thinking that Riff Raff would be the bass player if the ensemble were a band—that's one of the best ways I've found to describe his function within the piece as a whole. Even in moments when he intentionally remains out of focus, if you were to remove him, his absence would undoubtedly be felt, and his presence would certainly be missed.

I've loved each and every role and character I have had the opportunity to play, and I have loved the experiences for very specific reasons. But to this day, *Rocky Horror* stands as the most fun I've had on set. So much freedom exists within a character like that, combined with the sense of freedom you feel in those incredible costumes and hair and makeup design."

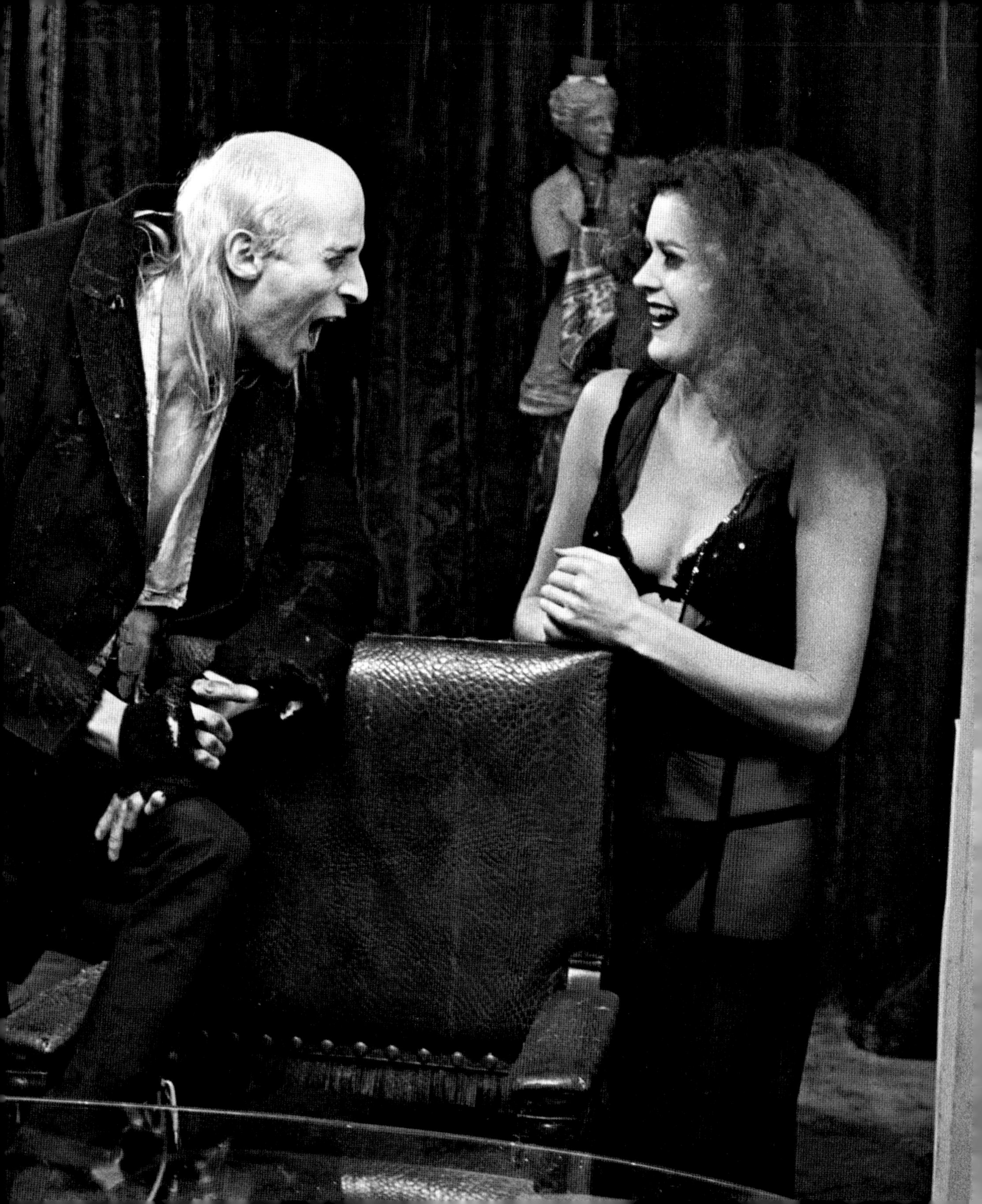

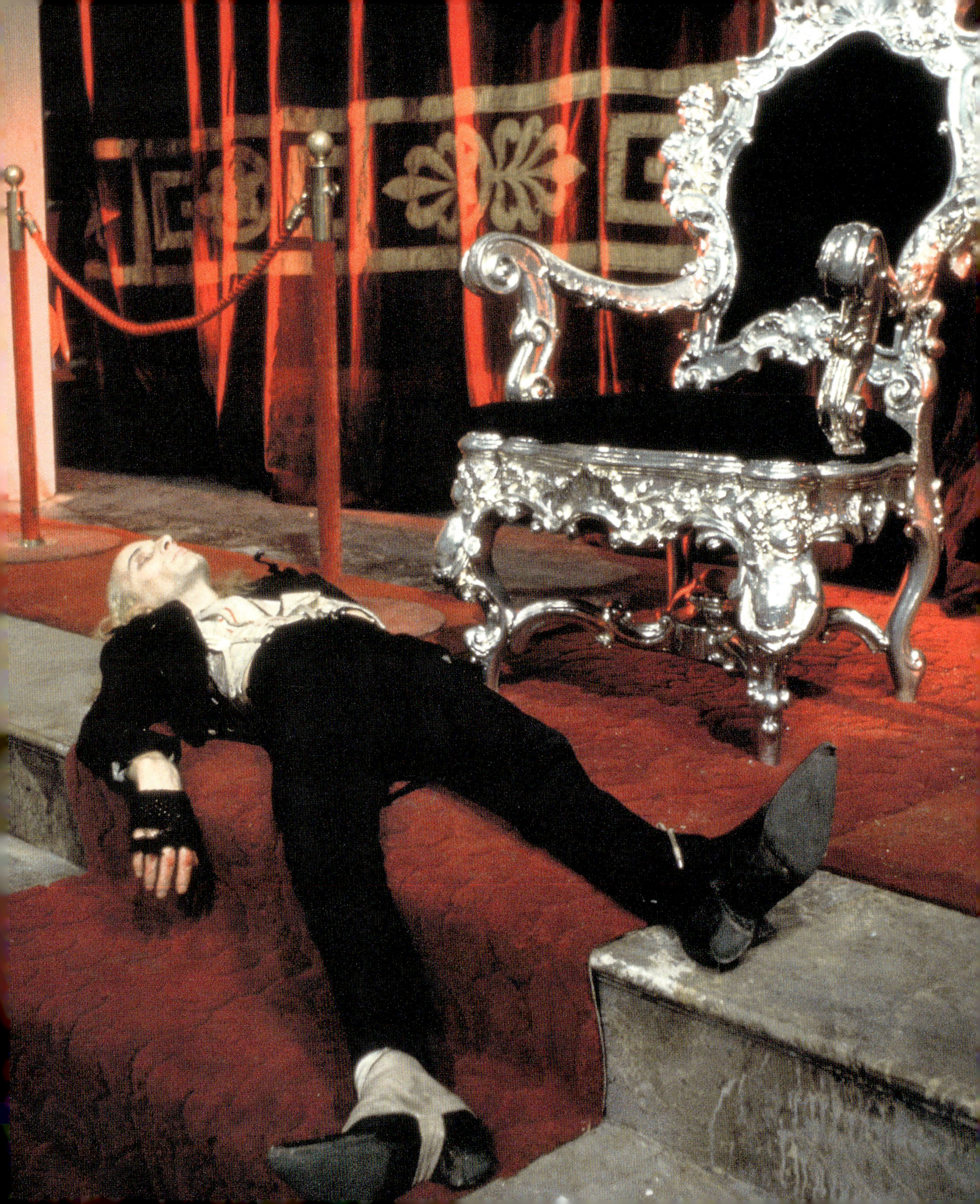

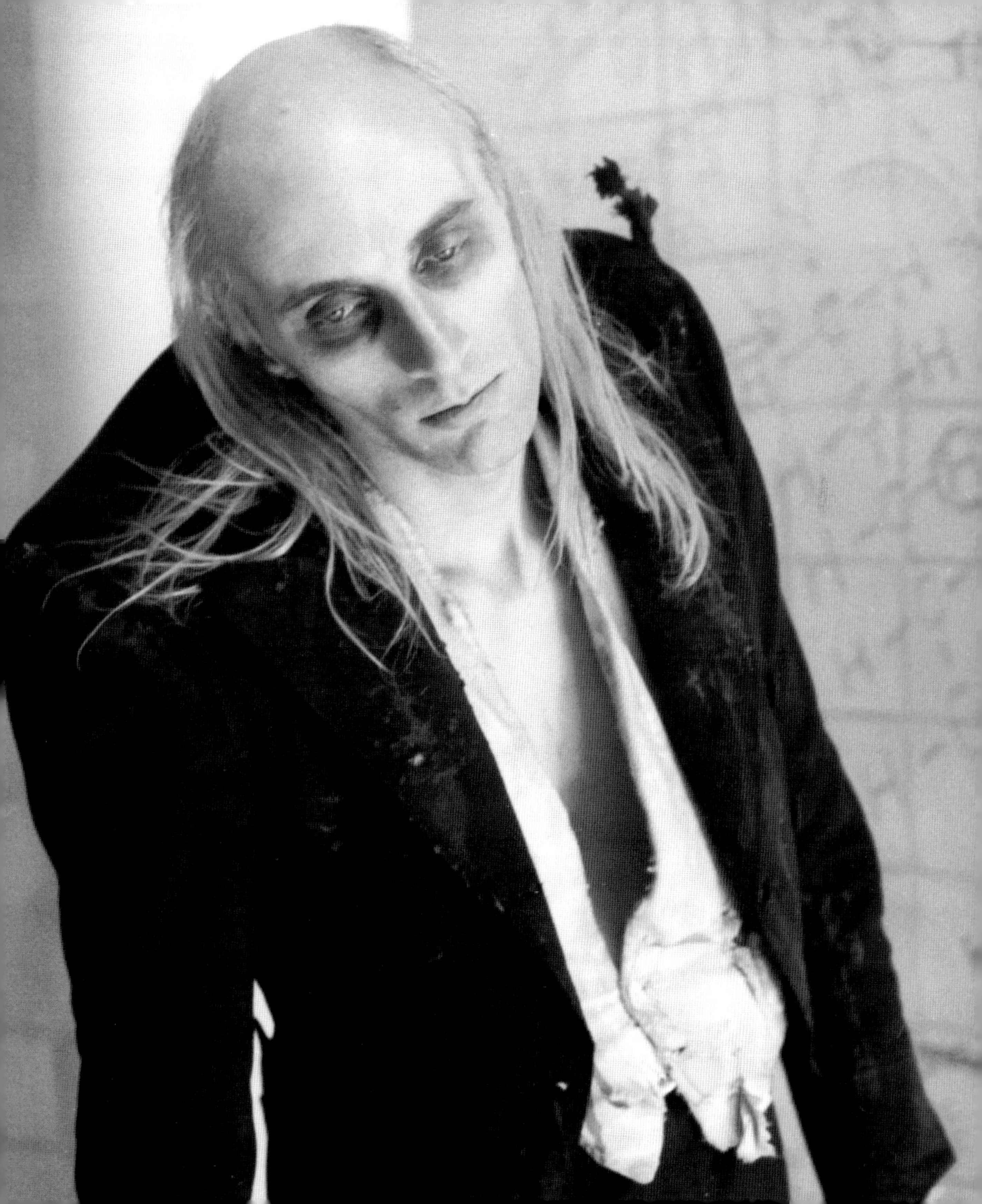

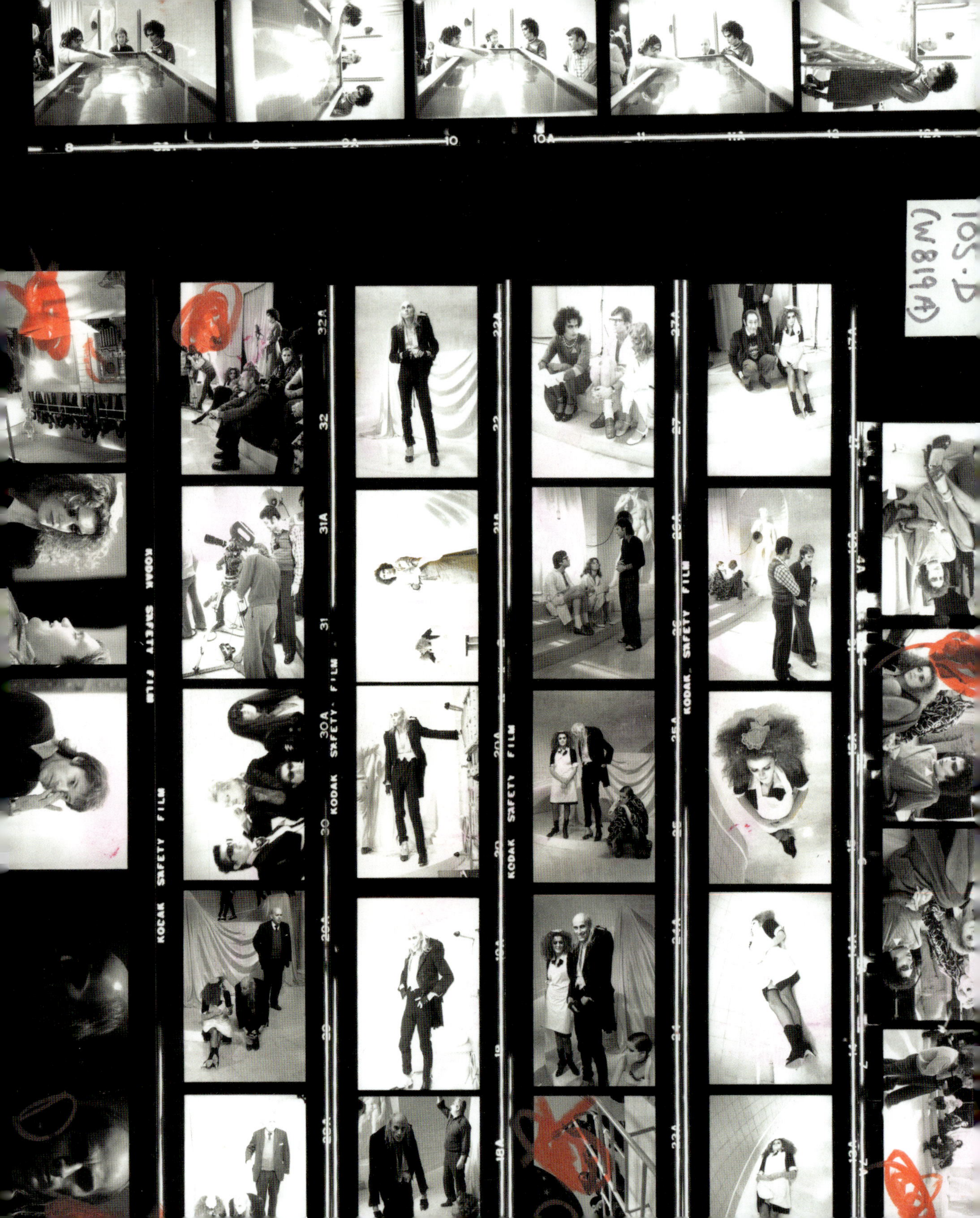

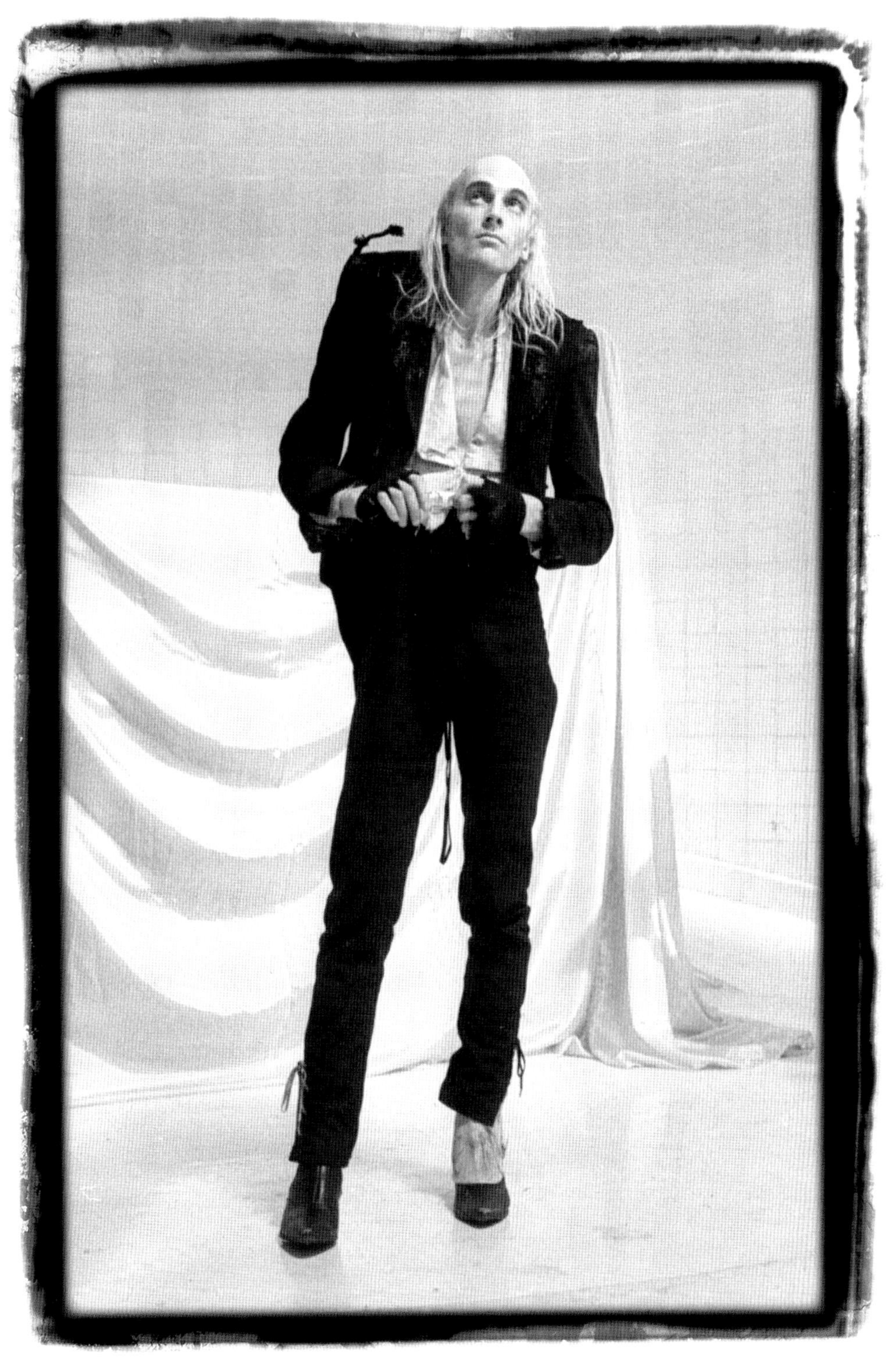

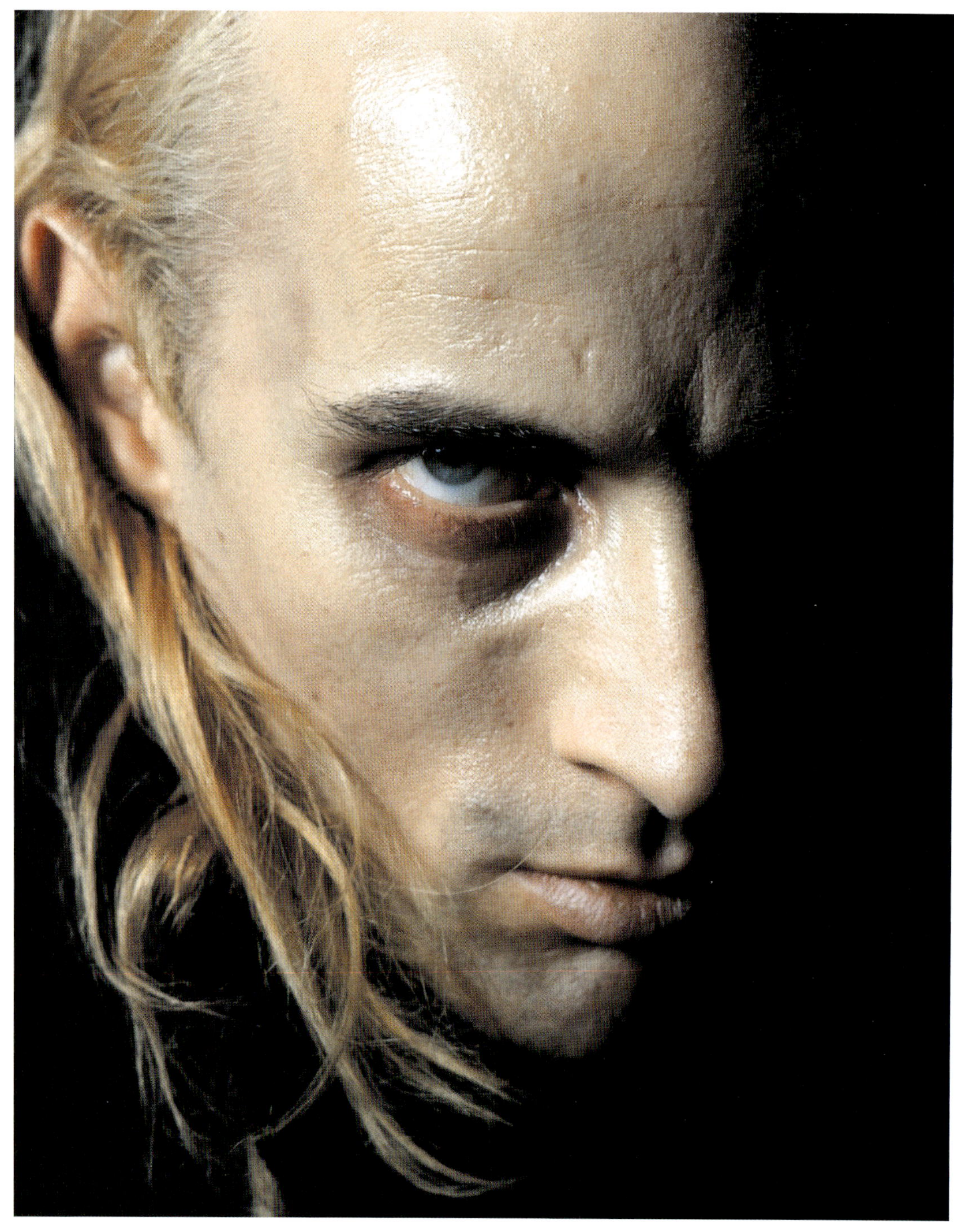

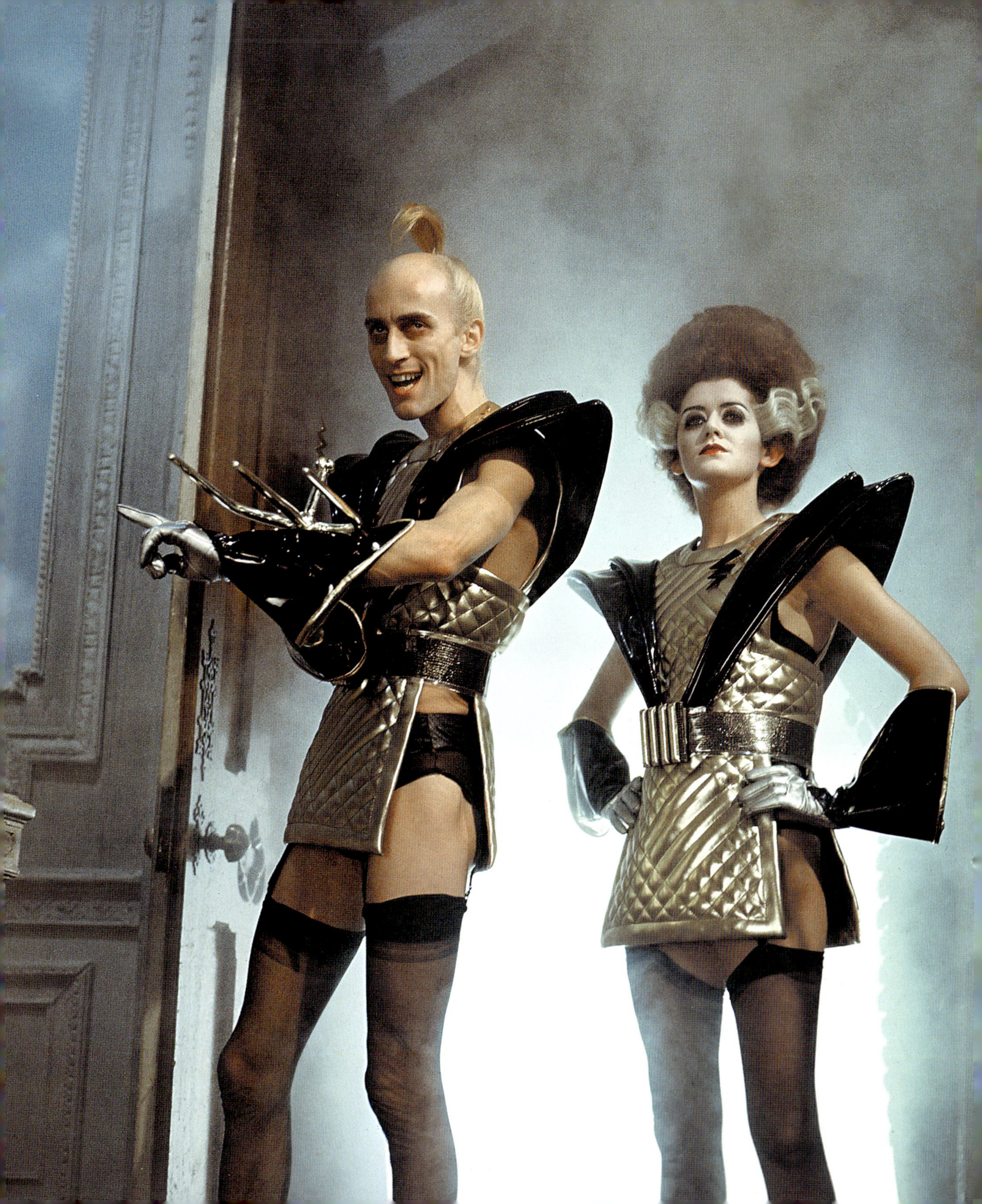

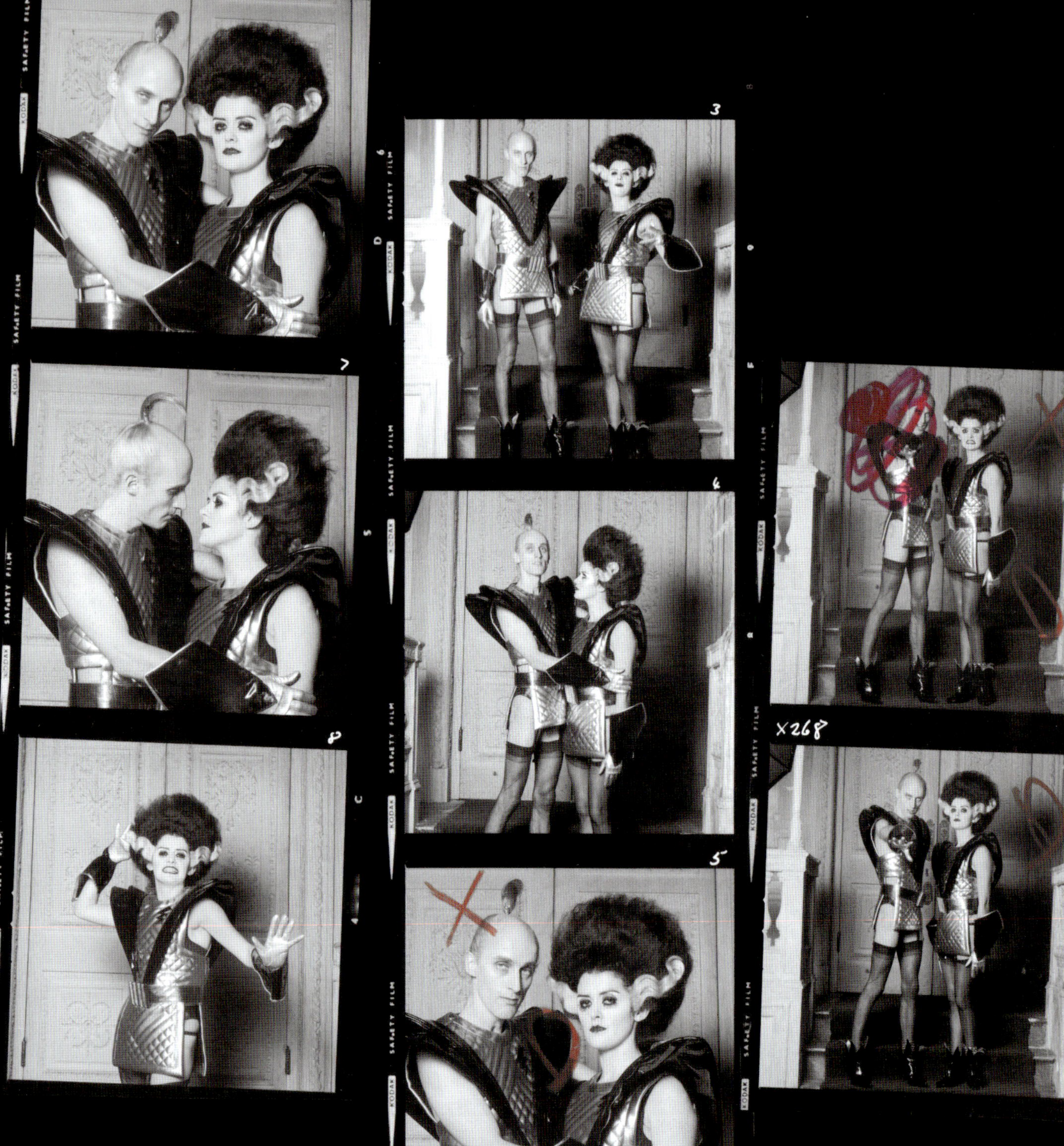

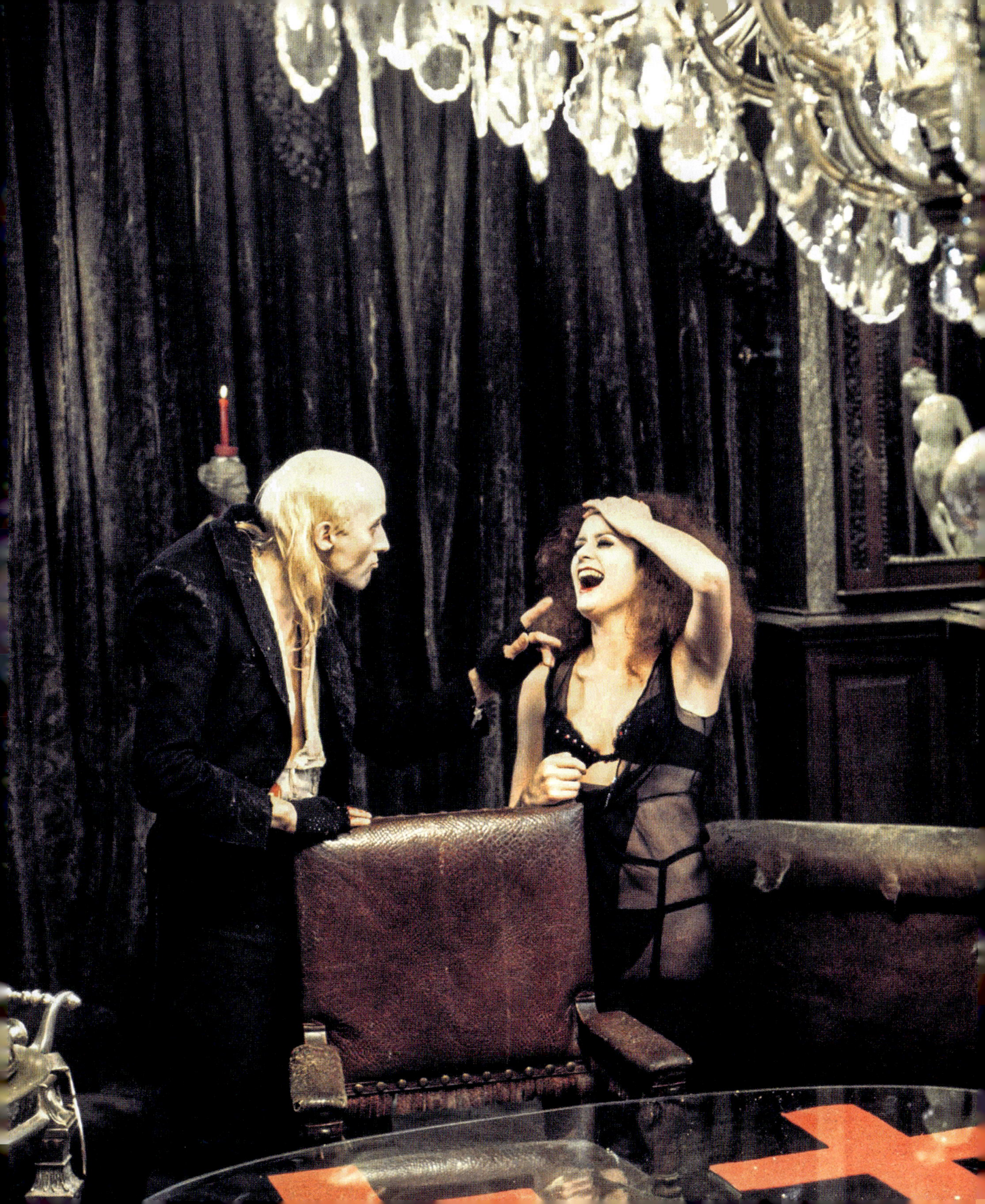

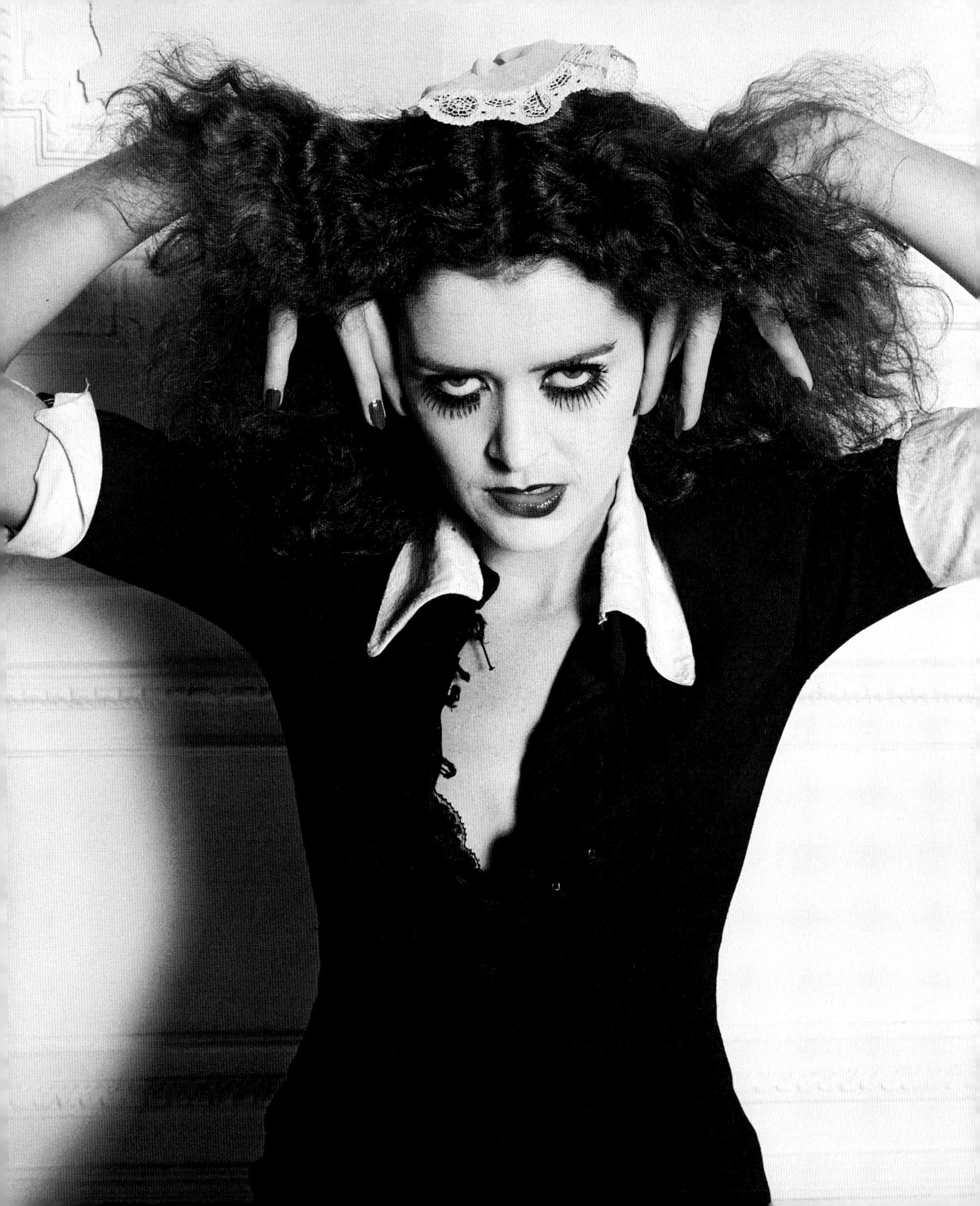

I GROW WEARY OF THIS WORLD: MAGENTA

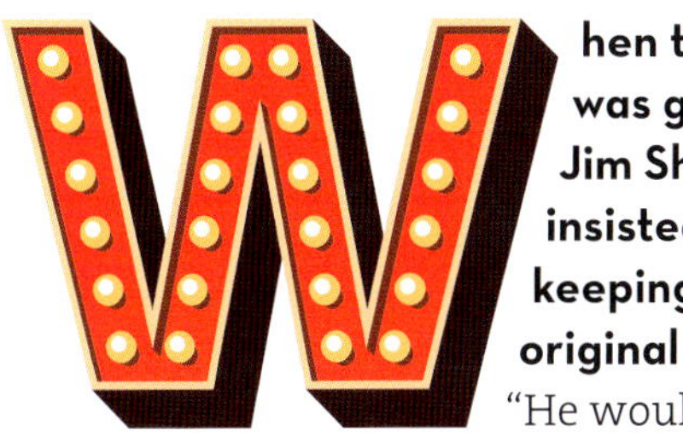

When the film was green-lit, Jim Sharman insisted on keeping the original cast. "He would only have us—and we were no-names," Patricia Quinn said in an exclusive interview in 2024.

Some concessions were made.

For the movie, for instance, famed makeup artist Pierre La Roche was brought in to do makeup that the actors had done themselves during the stage production. "I thought, *Oh my god, he's Bowie's makeup artist! He'll make me beautiful, give me cheekbones and whatnot*," Quinn recalled. "But he came in, took one look at me, and gave me a pure white face and two rows of eyelashes on both the top and bottom. I had to act in those every day. And then the red lips. Instead of making me a beauty, he got rid of my face and emphasized my eyes and mouth. He also made Tim Curry gorgeous, which Tim hated. Can you believe that?"

Quinn collected black-and-white snapshots from the continuity photographer. "I used to go up to his room every day to look at the photographs to get an idea of how the film was progressing," she said. "Then this guy called Mick Rock arrived. I assumed he was a friend of Richard's. And as this geezer started to take our pictures, he became a vital part of things. What was amazing to me about him was that he would line us up for pictures and get Nell and me to do poses, arrange us. And he sort of created relationships. It was like he was

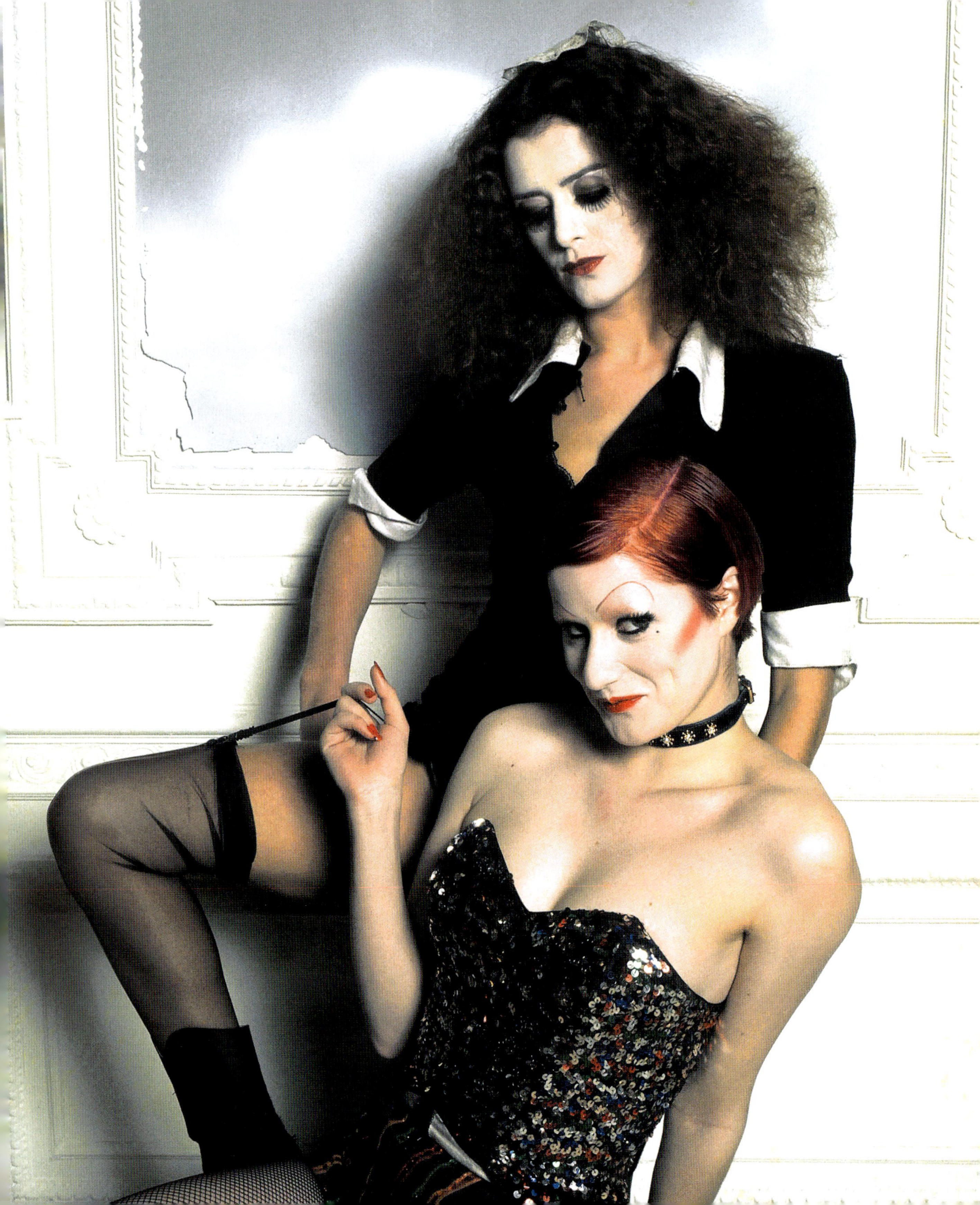

directing me—like a film director. He helped create Magenta. He brought out something. He saw the character. He was so important to the movie. To me, he was my other Jim Sharman."

As Mick said, "Pat Quinn as Frank's other little helper (and ultimately Riff Raff's soul sister) is the perfect spectral counterpoint to Nell's little dancer, and allowed me to produce some sinfully lesbian close photo setups of them both, with and without Tim's Frank. There seemed to be a genuine rapport between the two of them. In her transformation into the space-age bride of Frankenstein at the movie's end, she pairs convincingly with Richard to end Frank's reign of unbridled sexual selfishness."

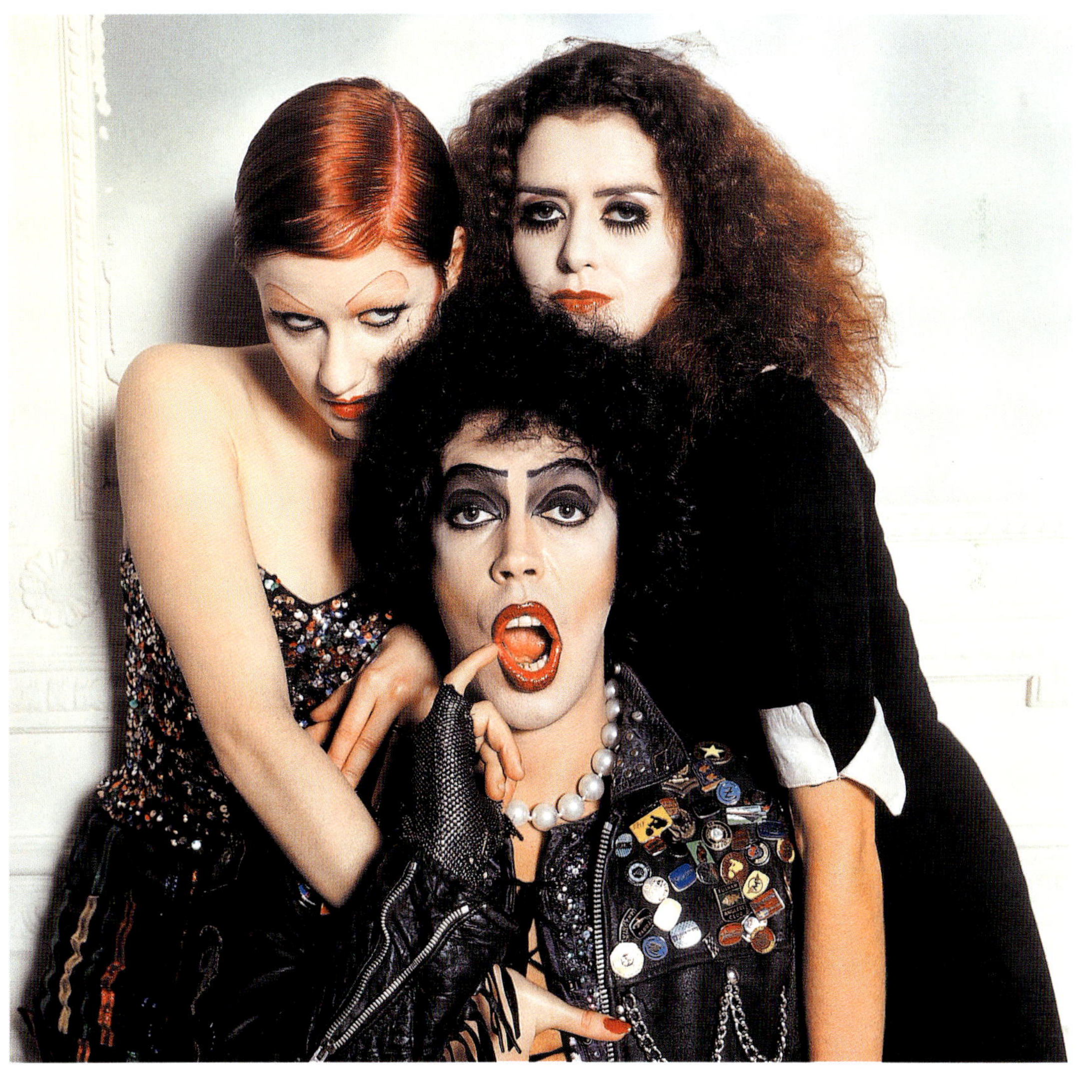

NORMAN REEDUS, ACTOR, *THE WALKING DEAD*, PHOTOGRAPHER, DIRECTOR, AND ARTIST: "I had a babysitter named Joe. He had a big red mohawk, and I idolized him. He snuck me into a midnight showing of *Rocky Horror* when I was around ten or eleven—that's how I was introduced to it. And I fell in love with the actress playing Magenta. I knew Frank-N-Furter was hot, but Magenta really threw me."

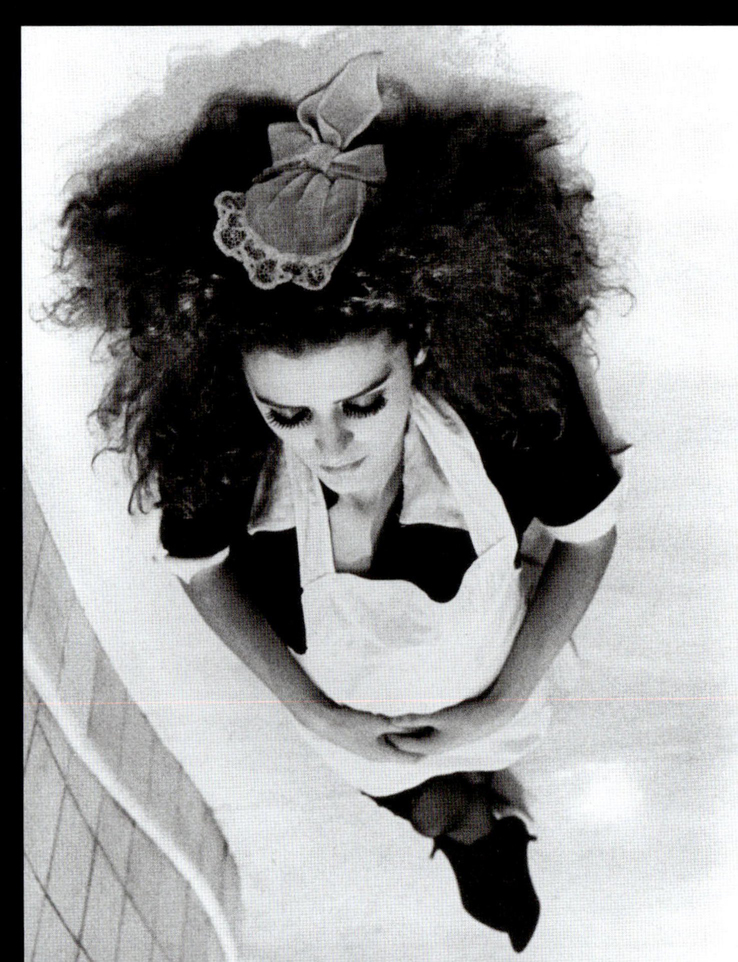

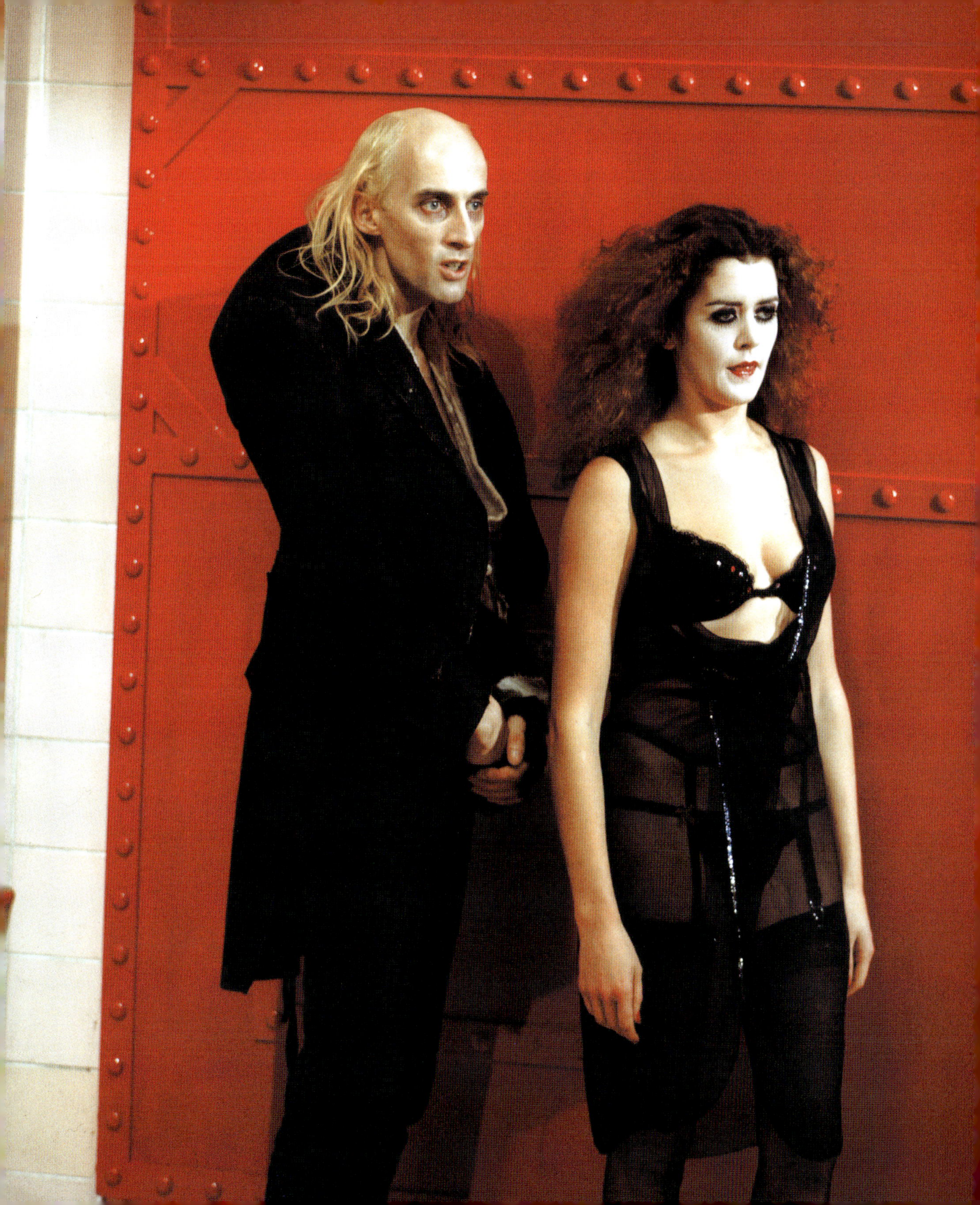

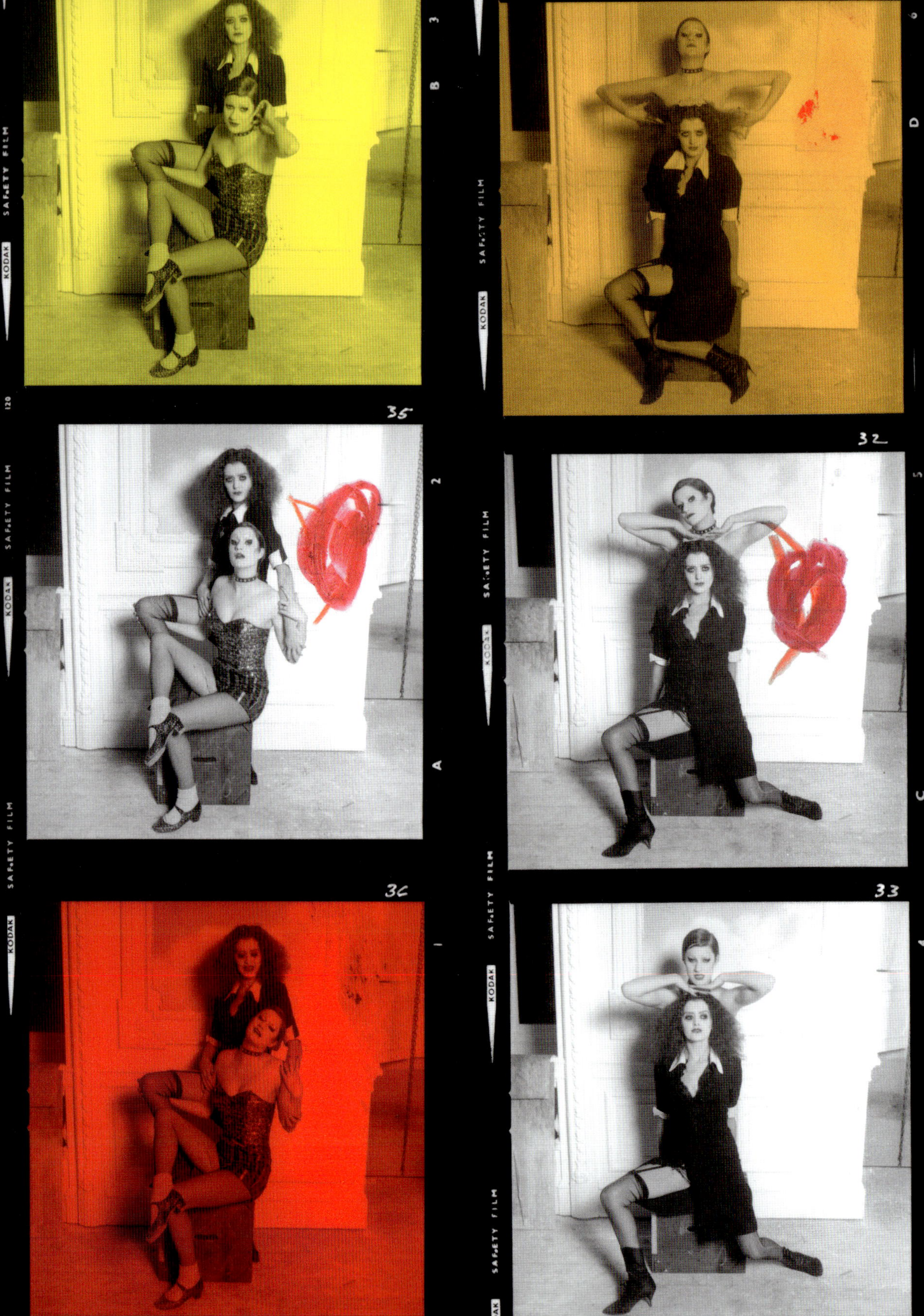

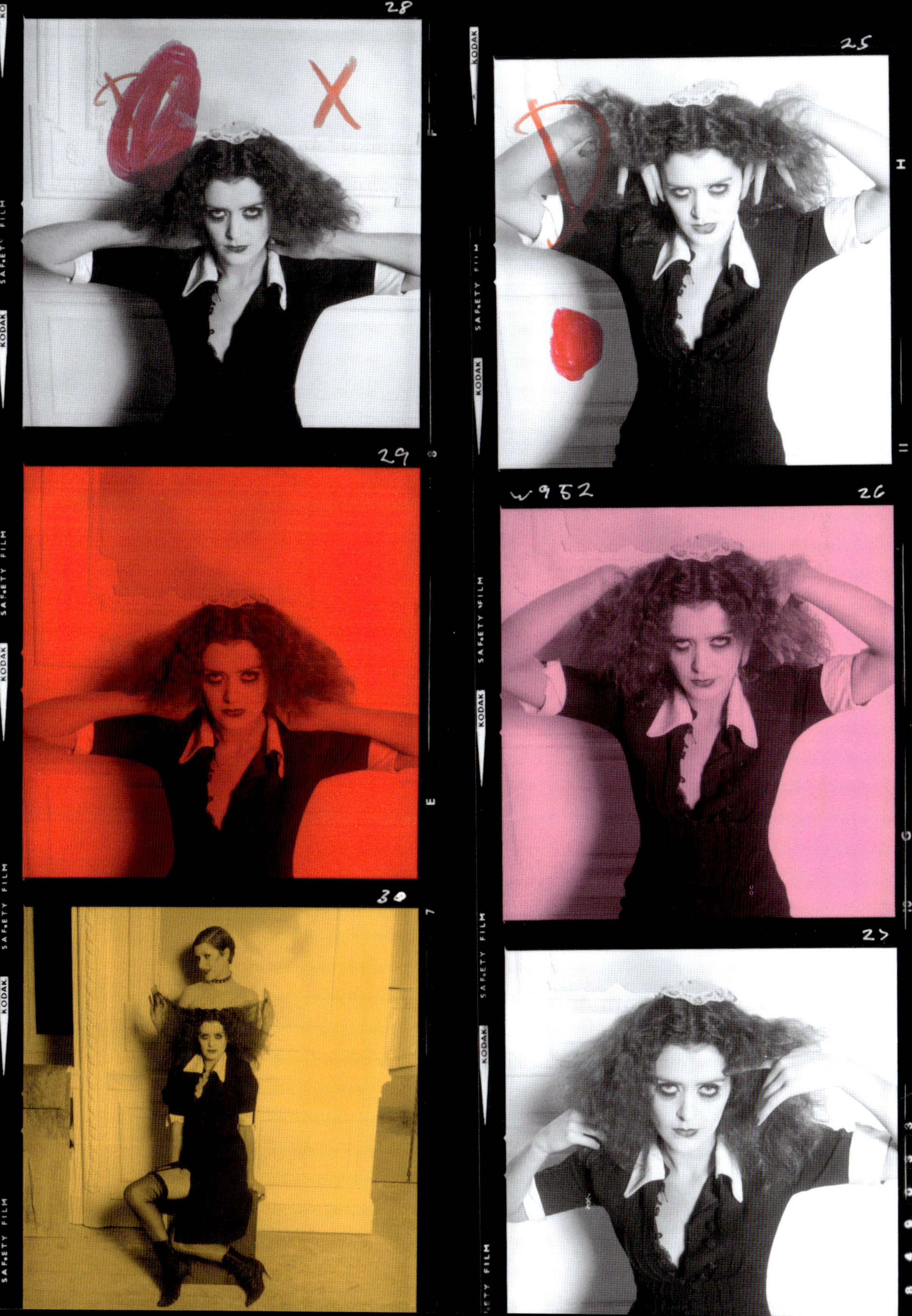

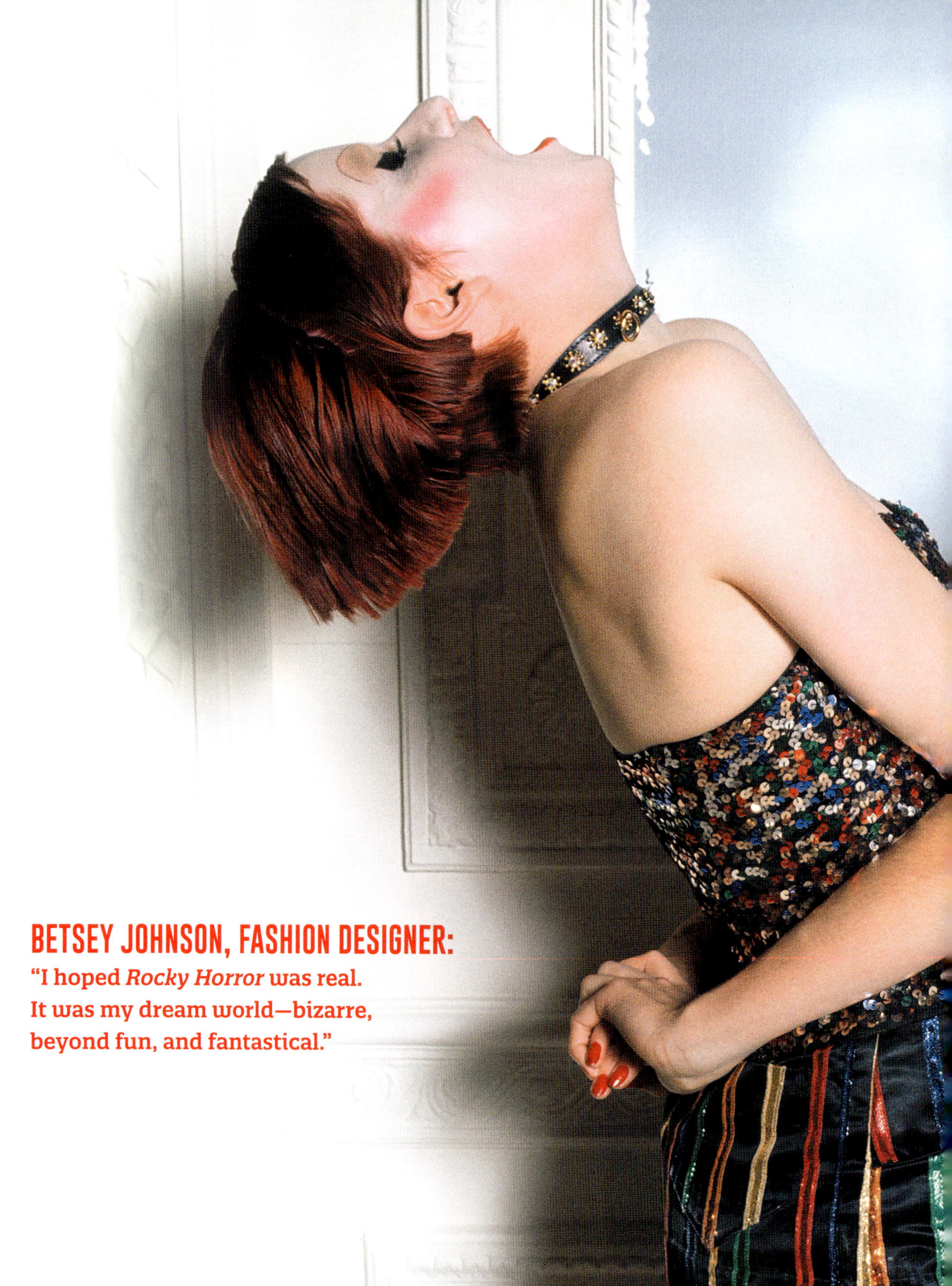

BETSEY JOHNSON, FASHION DESIGNER:

"I hoped *Rocky Horror* was real. It was my dream world—bizarre, beyond fun, and fantastical."

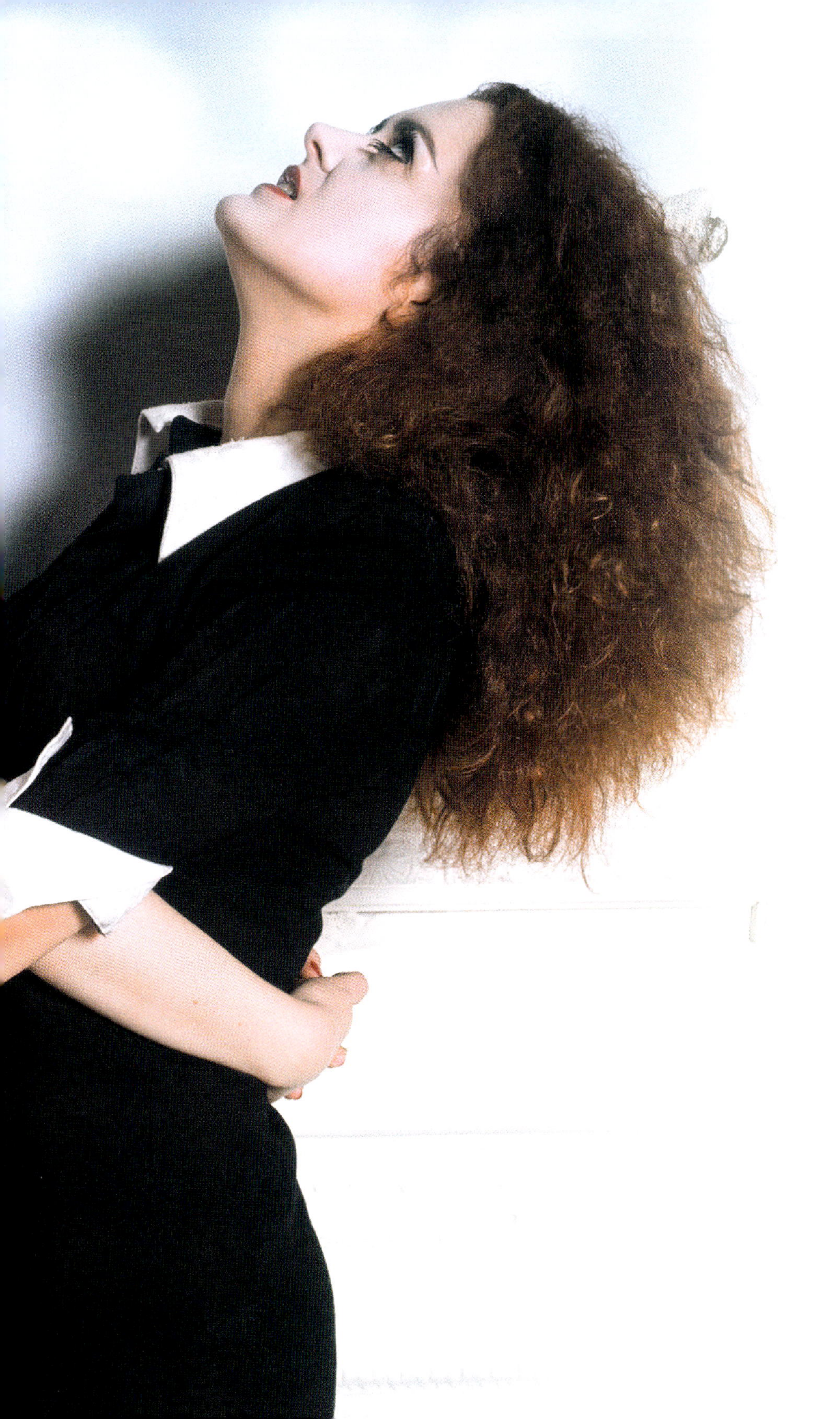

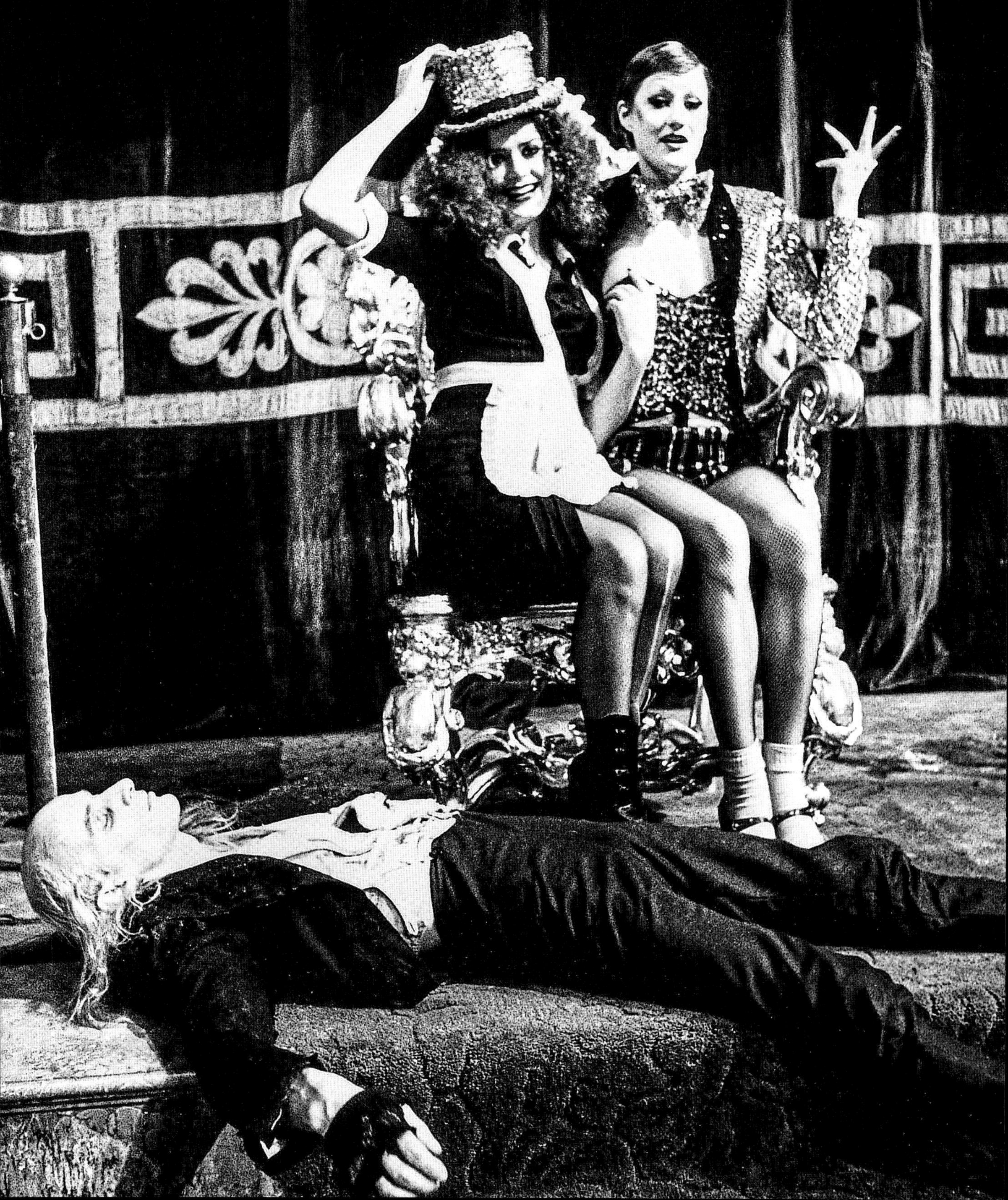

"On the last day of shooting, Jim Sharman said, 'Have you ever seen Man Ray's image of the lips? We thought we could have your mouth sing 'Science Fiction.'' I said, 'Who's singing it?' I figured they'd got Shirley Bassey or something. Eventually Richard said, 'I am.' And I thought, *You bastard. His voice coming out of my mouth?* By then I was in the West End doing a big play so I said no. But then they offered two hundred quid. It was depressing—there was a strike. I was the only person working, with a tiny crew. No special effects. They blacked out my face and tried to film just my mouth. But your face moves when you sing, so my mouth kept going out of frame. They took a lamp out of a clamp and put my head into the clamp. And it worked. That was the 'special effect.' It was amazing what came out of having no money."

—PATRICIA QUINN

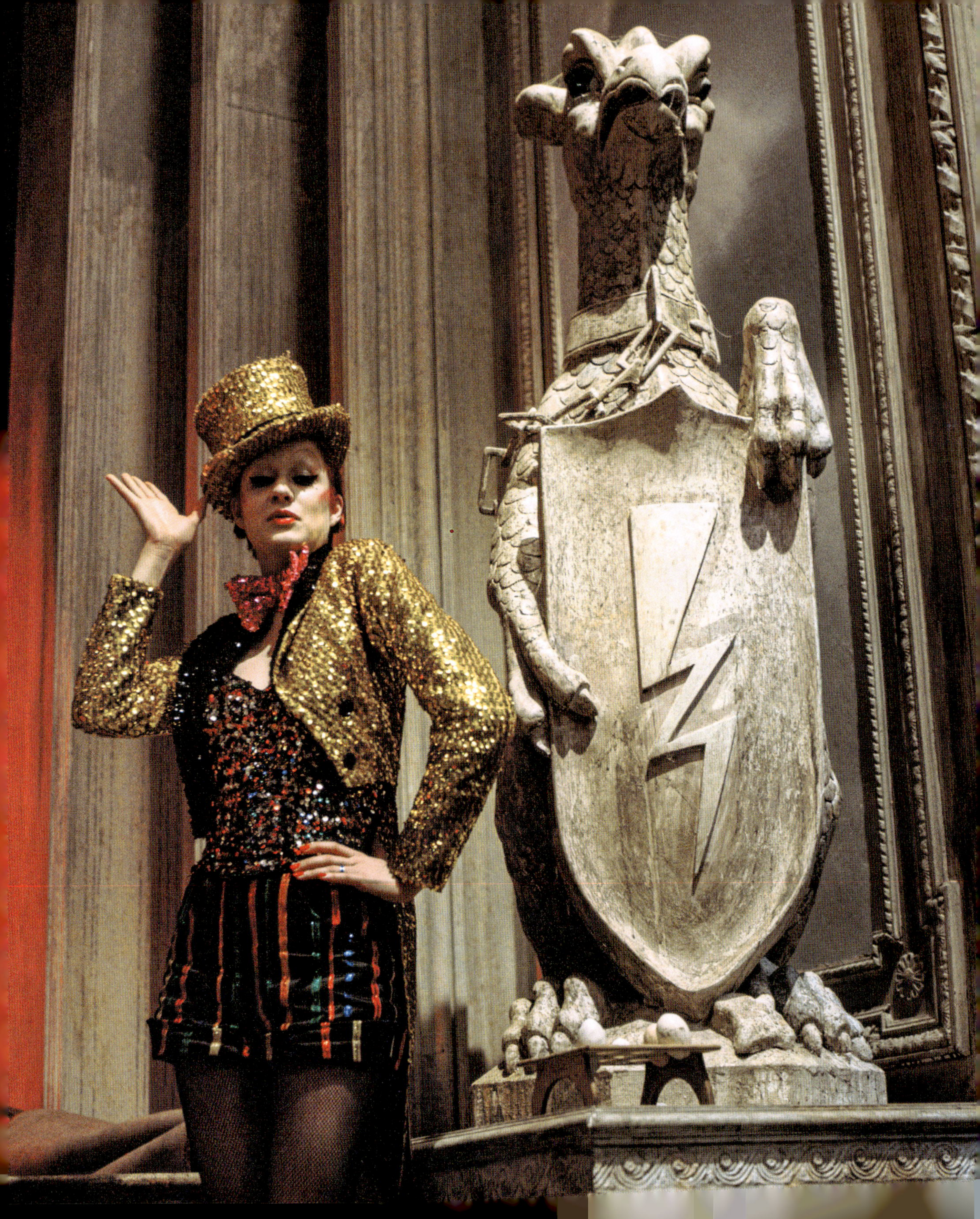

IT WAS GREAT WHEN IT ALL BEGAN: COLUMBIA

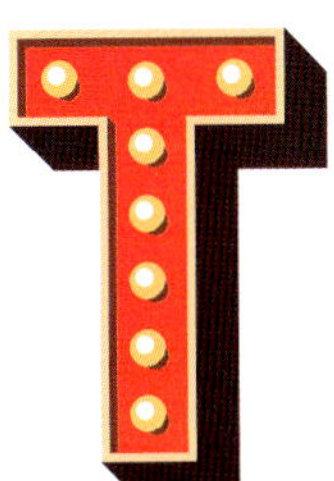

he fact is," Nell Campbell said in an exclusive interview in 2024, "Jim Sharman's imaginative casting was an absolute key detail among the many ingredients that made *Rocky Horror* endure. Jim was casting a rock musical, and you would think the first thing he would look for would be rock 'n' roll voices. But that wasn't what he was looking for. He wanted interesting characters to play the roles. I was twenty when he cast me, busking in the street and working as a waitress. Neither Pat Quinn nor I had strong singing voices. It was most unusual."

According to Campbell, the production owed its success to extraordinary teamwork and, even beyond his casting decisions, Sharman was the special sauce that brought out the flavor of the piece. "Without taking away anything from the brilliance of what Richard O'Brien wrote, you'd never have heard of *Rocky Horror*—or it probably wouldn't even exist—without Jim Sharman, Brian Thomson, Sue Blane, Richard Hartley. Because O'Brien arrived with a few pages of script. I don't think any other director would have taken on a project with such a skeletal script and a handful of songs. Jim Sharman decided to direct the musical based purely on the song 'Science Fiction/Double Feature.' He was taken by that one song; *yes, I'll do it. Anything that good, yes, I can work with this.* And he could. O'Brien could have taken his project to any other person and the result would have been totally different or might never have been made at all. Jim was the

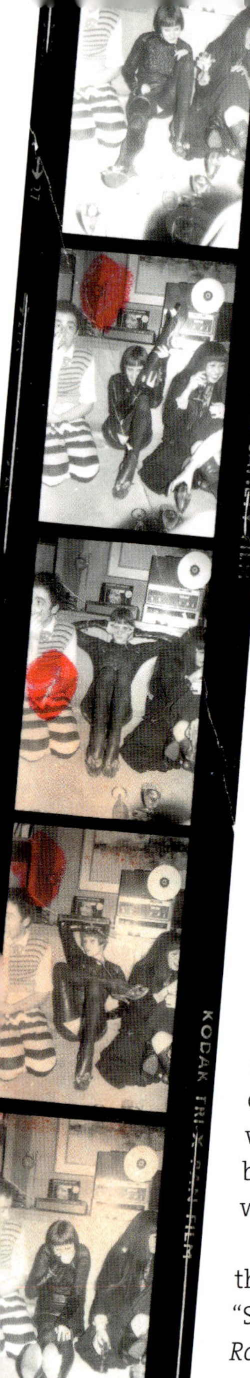

perfect person to feed Richard; Richard in turn would respond with fabulous songs, and come up with great things for the content of the play. And let's not take for granted that Jim had the imagination to invite Mick Rock to come to the set. Credit Jim again for doing something outside the box."

Campbell says the stage production's runaway success in the UK made it hard not to think everyone would love the film. But the disappointment was short-lived because she was invited to a convention in New York to celebrate the first anniversary of the film, attending along with Patricia Quinn, Sue Blane, Brian Thomson, Richard Hartley, Jonathan Adams, and others. "That was the first time we saw the phenomenon—there were costume competitions, and we saw everyone dressed up as the characters. By the way, this convention was organized by a sixteen-year-old boy. But we only found that out when we got there."

"Little Nell's energy is essential to the charm of the tale," Mick asserted. "She apparently hadn't acted before *Rocky Horror*, although she was certainly a performer. She had been discovered tap-dancing for change, in the time-honored role of a street entertainer, outside a cinema in London's West End. She had a consistently cheerful persona and came on like an old-school Broadway hoofer (think Ruby Keeler), and I would often come across her at the most fashionable and edgy parties of that period. Dancing was her thing, and she seemed to take every opportunity to set her toes a-twinkling. I have some delightfully cute pics of her dancing with Richard at Lou Adler's after-party. She had an upbeat sense of humor and a lack of inhibition that endeared her to her peers, and dressed suitably wild like the fashion icon of the scene that she undeniably was. She was a natural for the still camera and projected innocence and playful anarchy in abundance, as the photos herein attest."

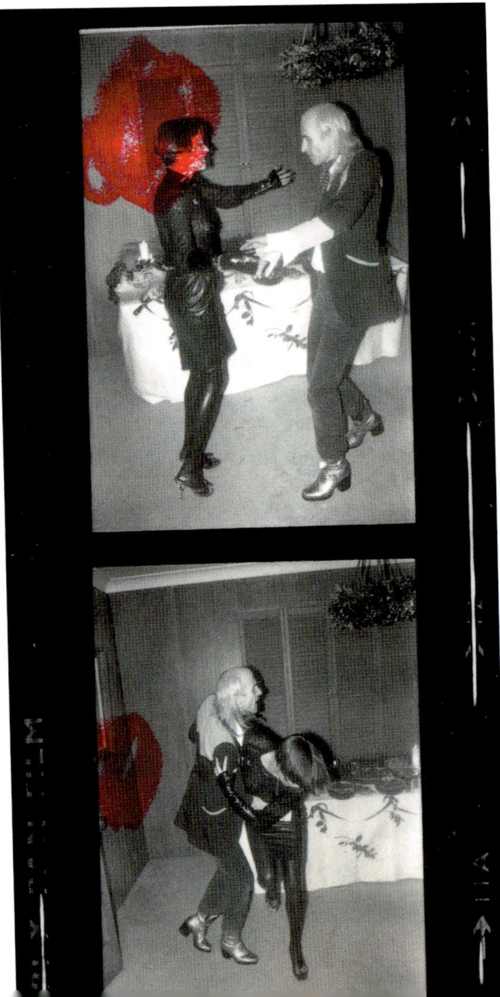

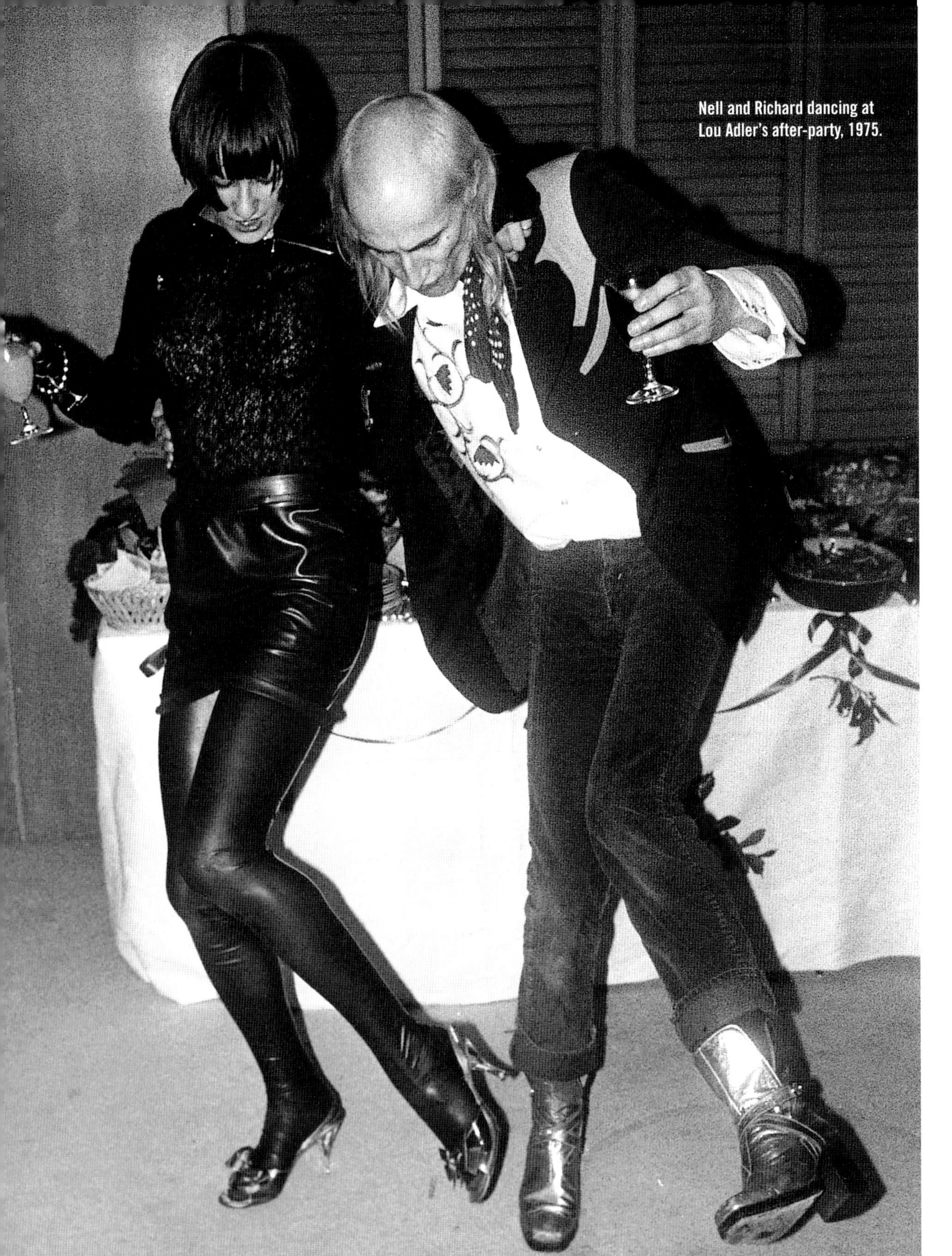

Nell and Richard dancing at Lou Adler's after-party, 1975.

SHEPARD FAIREY, ARTIST, ACTIVIST, AND FOUNDER OF OBEY CLOTHING:

"I had seen rock musicals like The Who's *Tommy* on HBO as a kid, but they did not resonate for me, and I didn't particularly love the music. *Rocky Horror* was something I'd been intrigued by just from seeing the iconography on T-shirts and posters while I was in high school. But I did not see the film until I was a sophomore at the Rhode Island School of Design, because it did not play anywhere in Charleston, South Carolina, where I grew up.

My first viewing of the film was at a midnight screening in New Jersey. I'd been warned that there would be a very campy and over-the-top crowd in attendance, but I was not prepared for the joyful and clearly therapeutic nature of the crowd participation. The vibe was punk and glam rock meets musical theater misfit, and that was precisely the kind of people I had been finding as my tribe from middle school up until that moment. The way the sensibility of the film seemed to draw the art school and creative weirdo crowd out of the woodwork was very inspiring.

By the time I got into punk rock, it had—in America, at least—entered its hardcore phase, which was ruled by angry young men and boys. Unfortunately, there was not a lot of space for women or, as far as I could tell, members of the queer community. *Rocky Horror*, on the other hand, celebrated queer culture and, in my opinion, feminism. Being an artist and hanging around people at visual and performing art schools, I understood that the queer community and women were a major force within that world, and I was happy to see a celebration of that in *Rocky Horror*. Space for weirdos and people who are at a disadvantage in the patriarchal hierarchy is something that is important to me, and I was happy to see aspects of that punk rock spirit in *Rocky Horror*—but with even more open-mindedness."

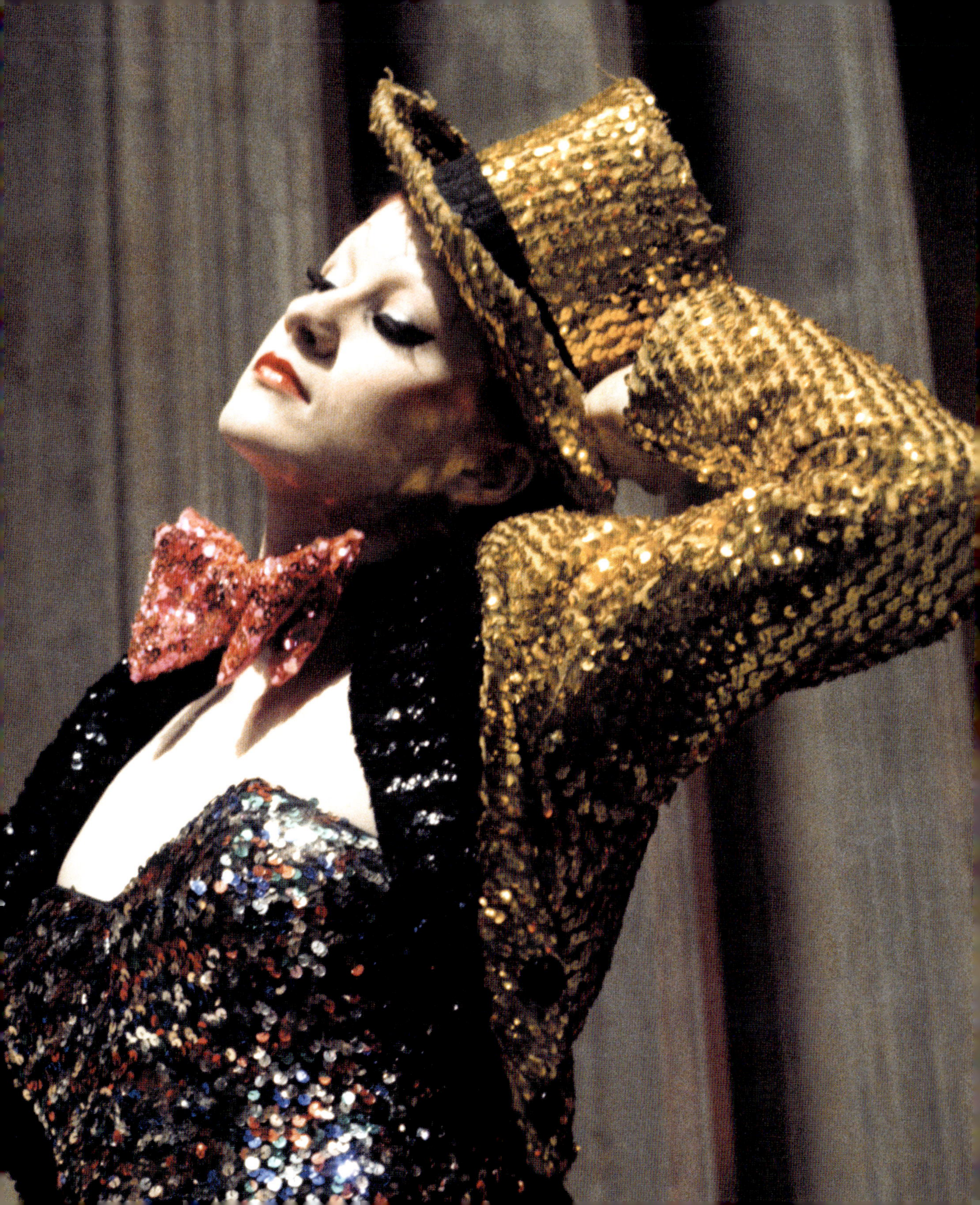

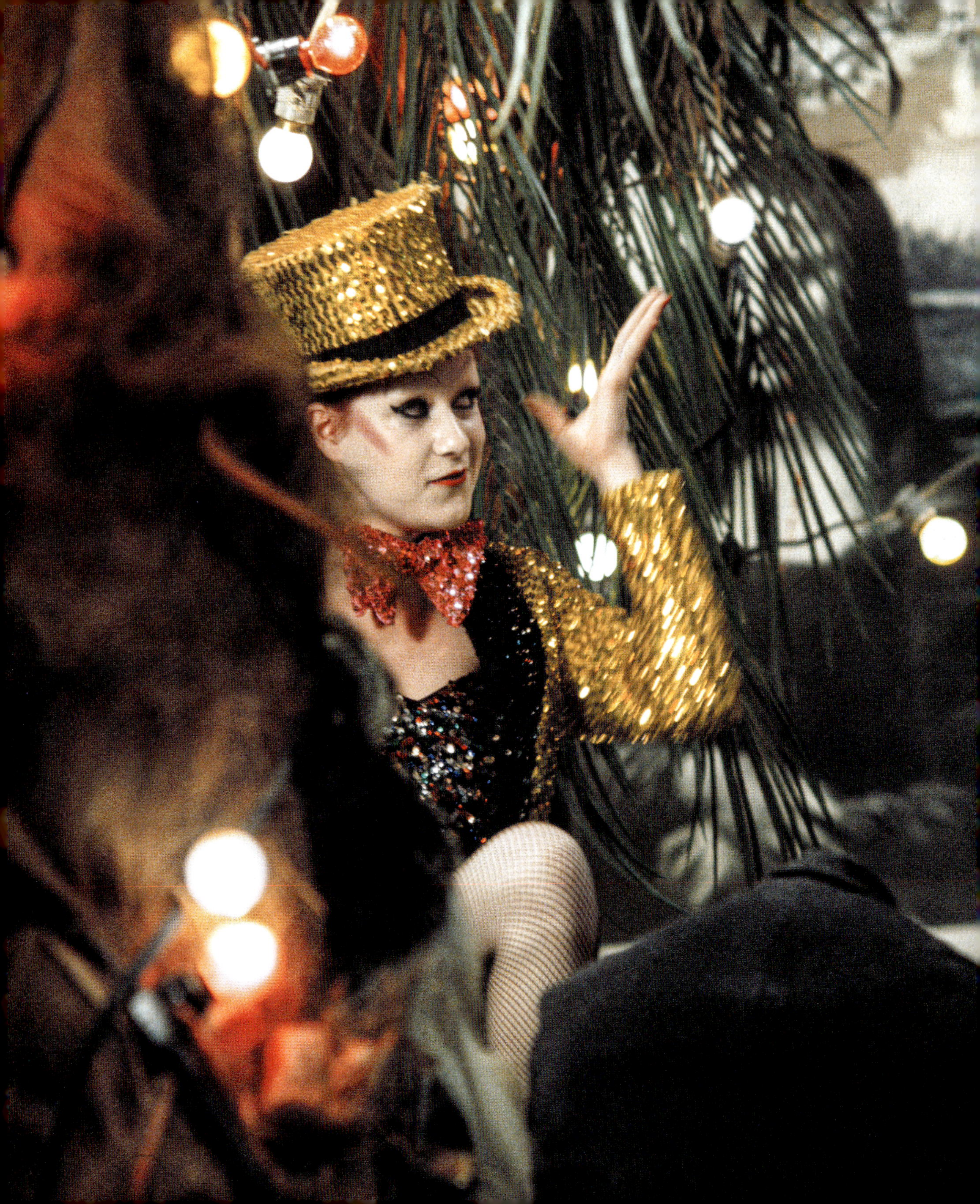

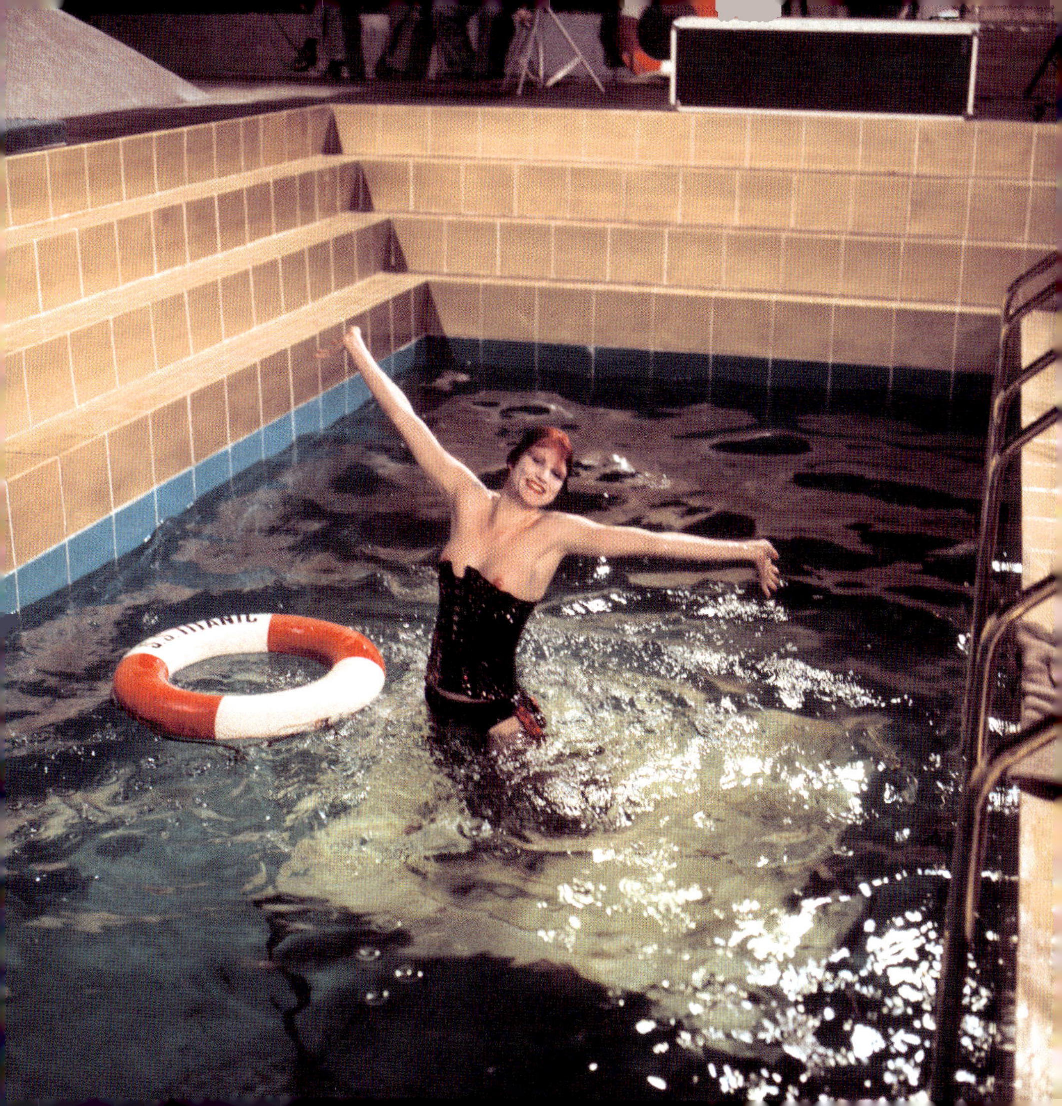

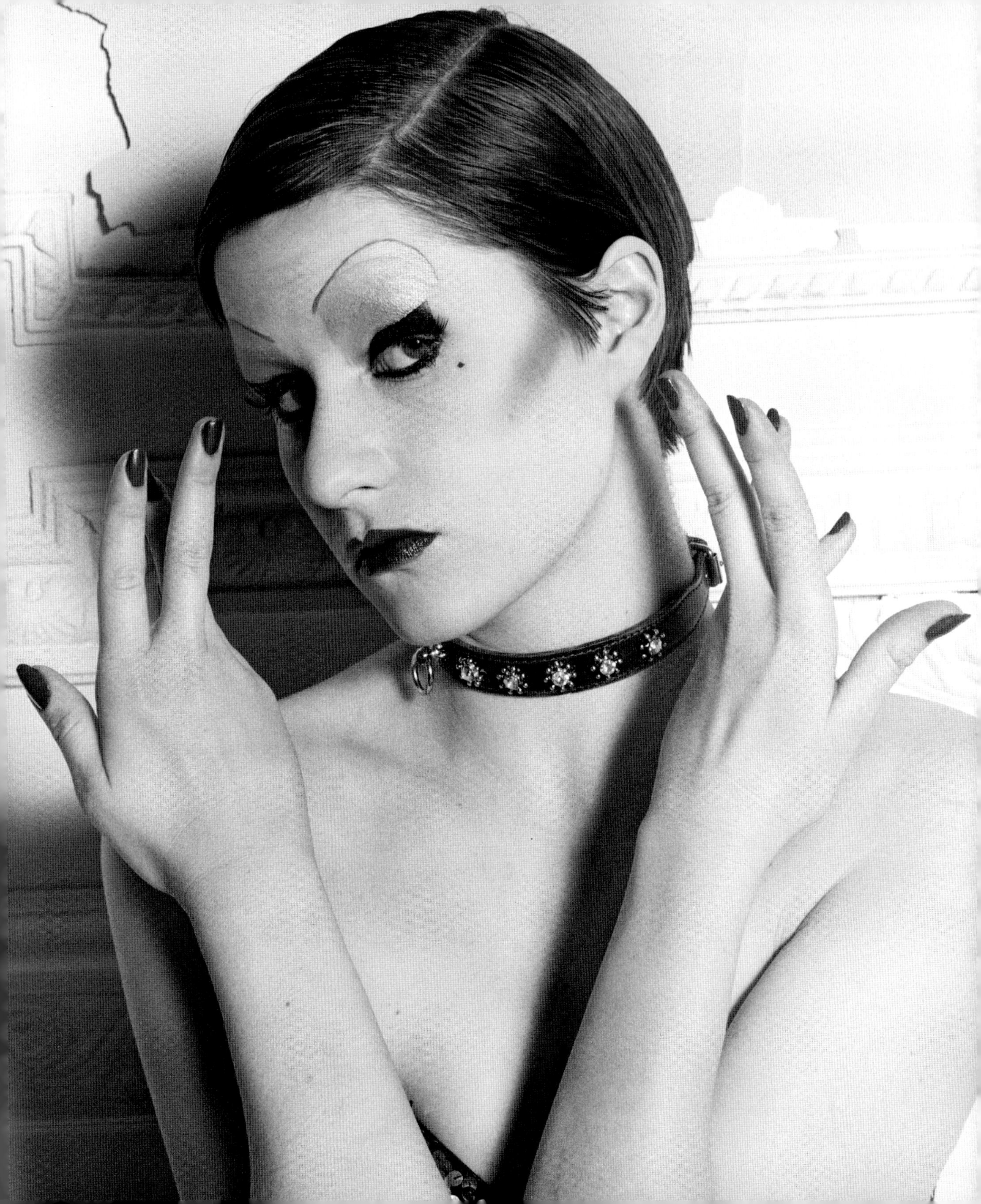

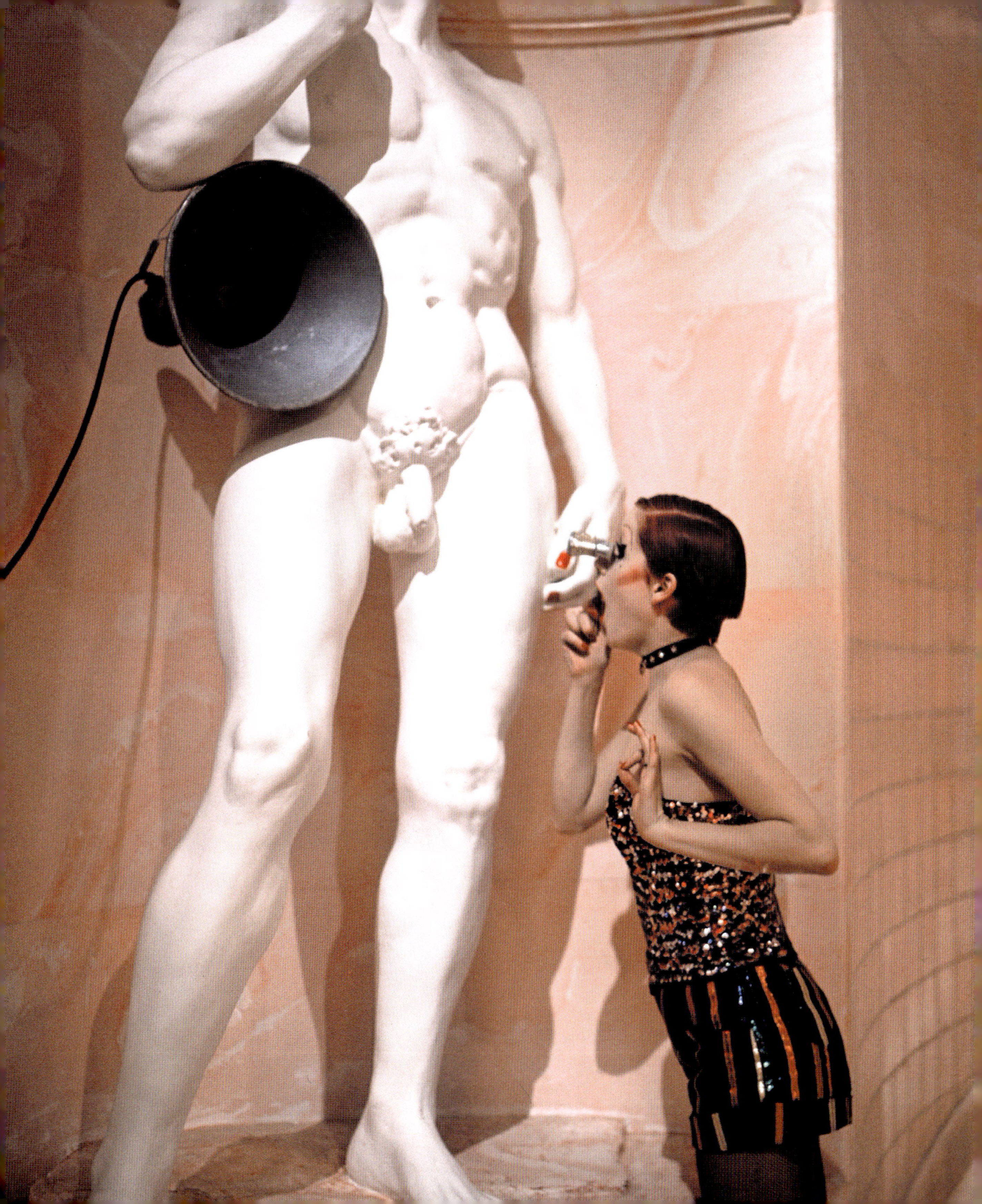

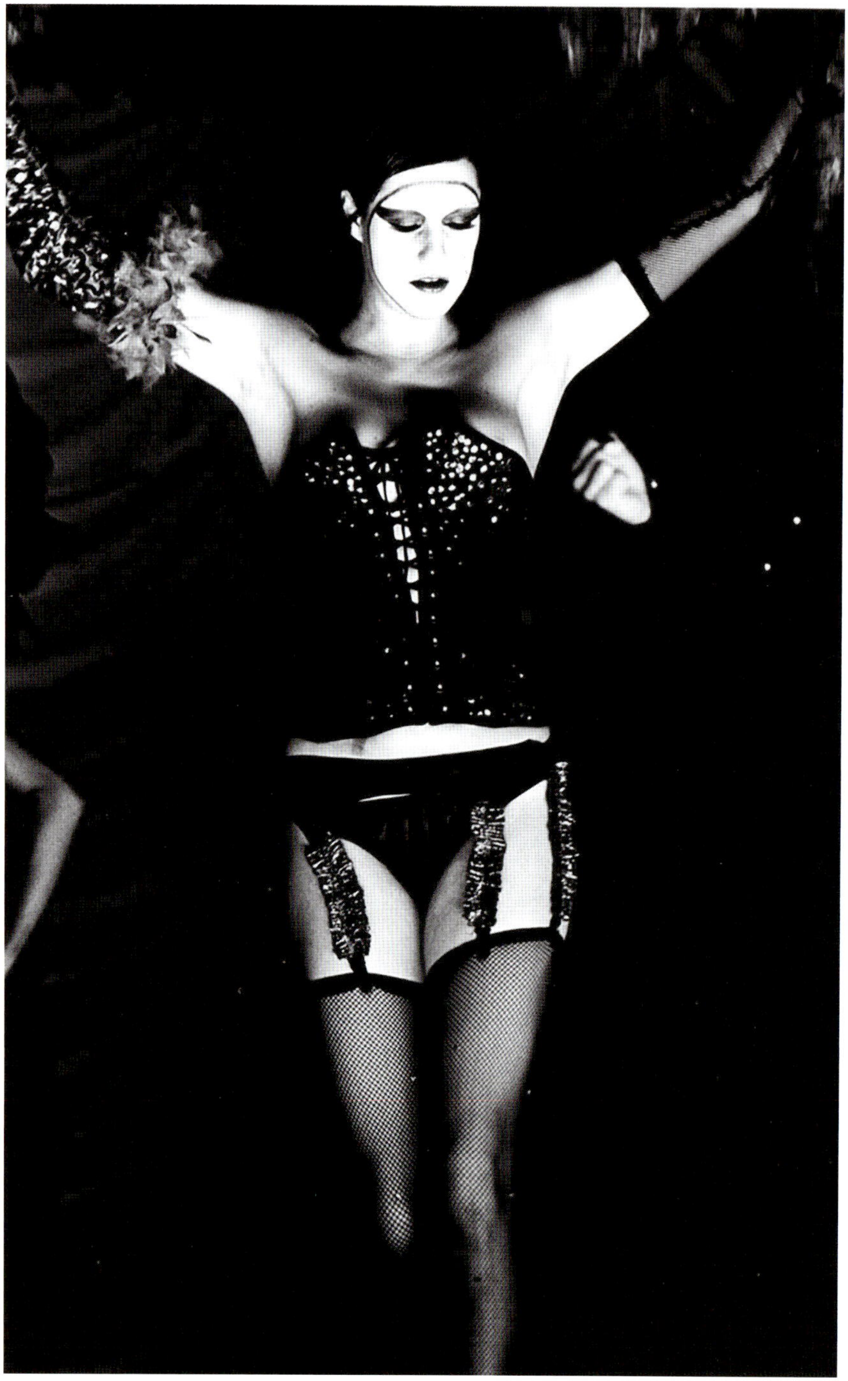

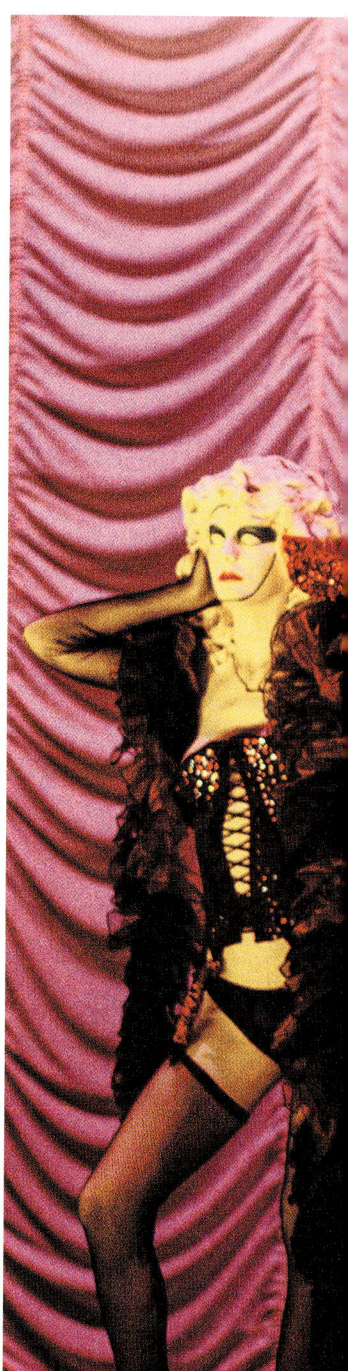

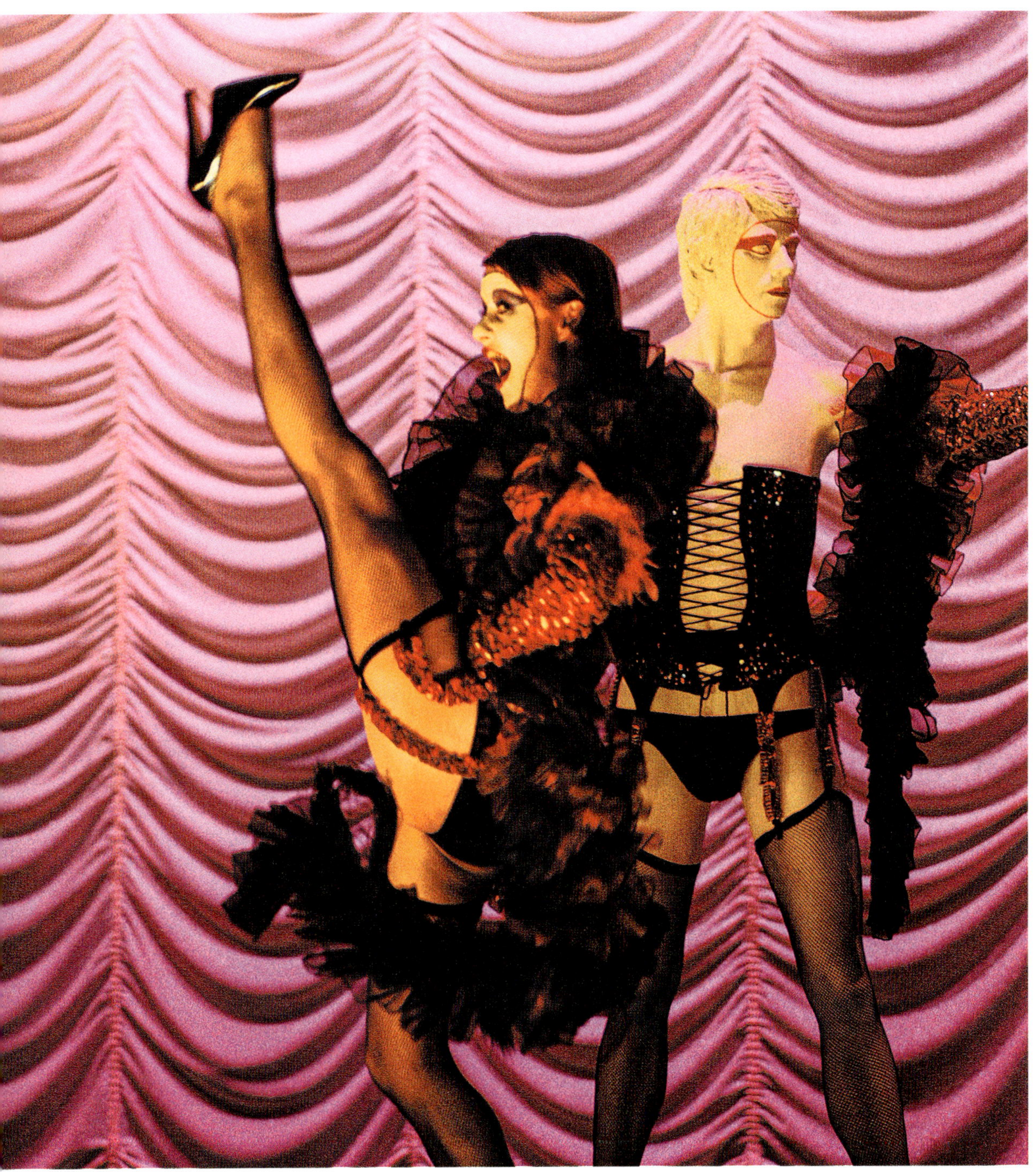

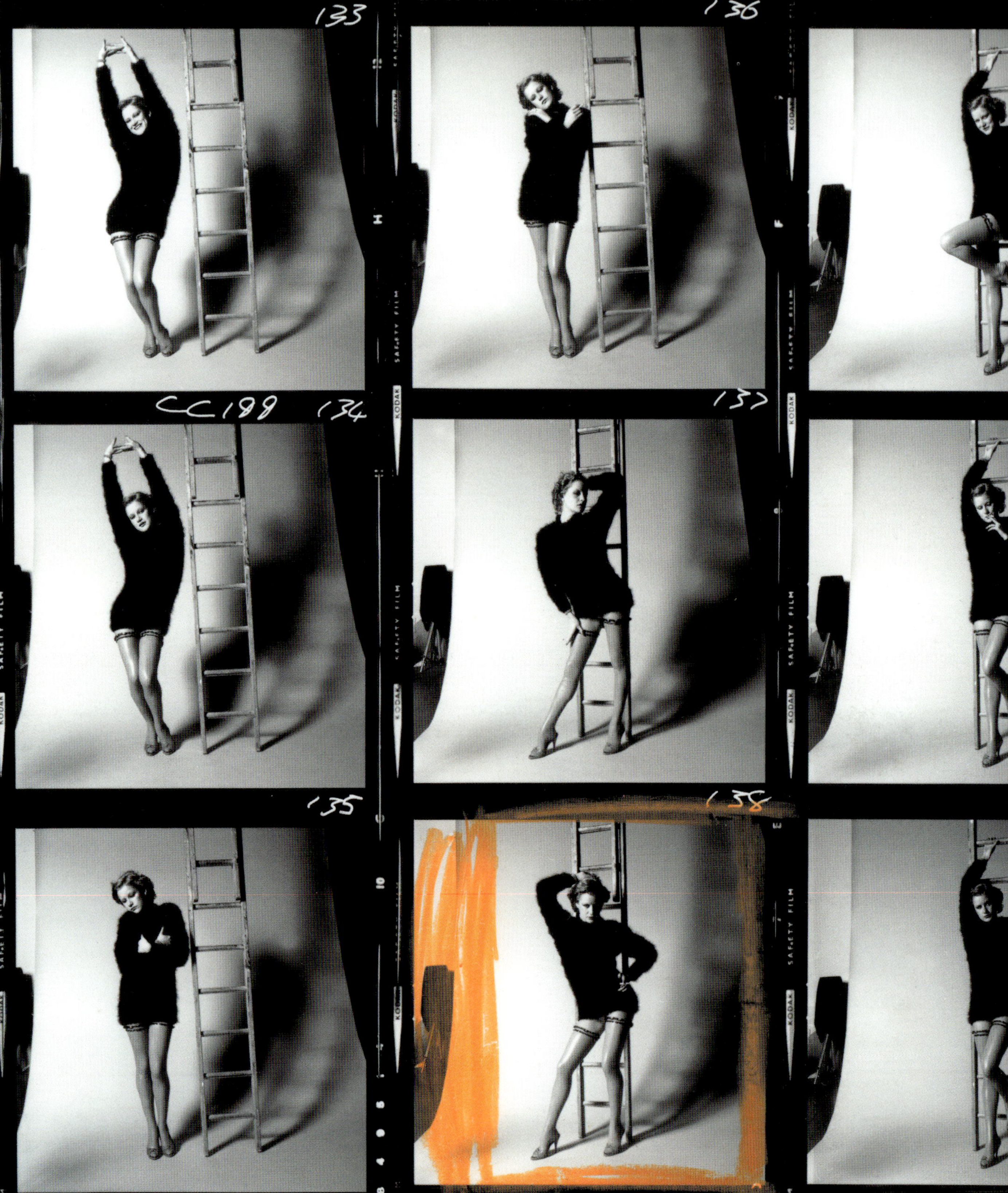
133
136
CC188
134
137
135
138
KODAK
SAFETY FILM

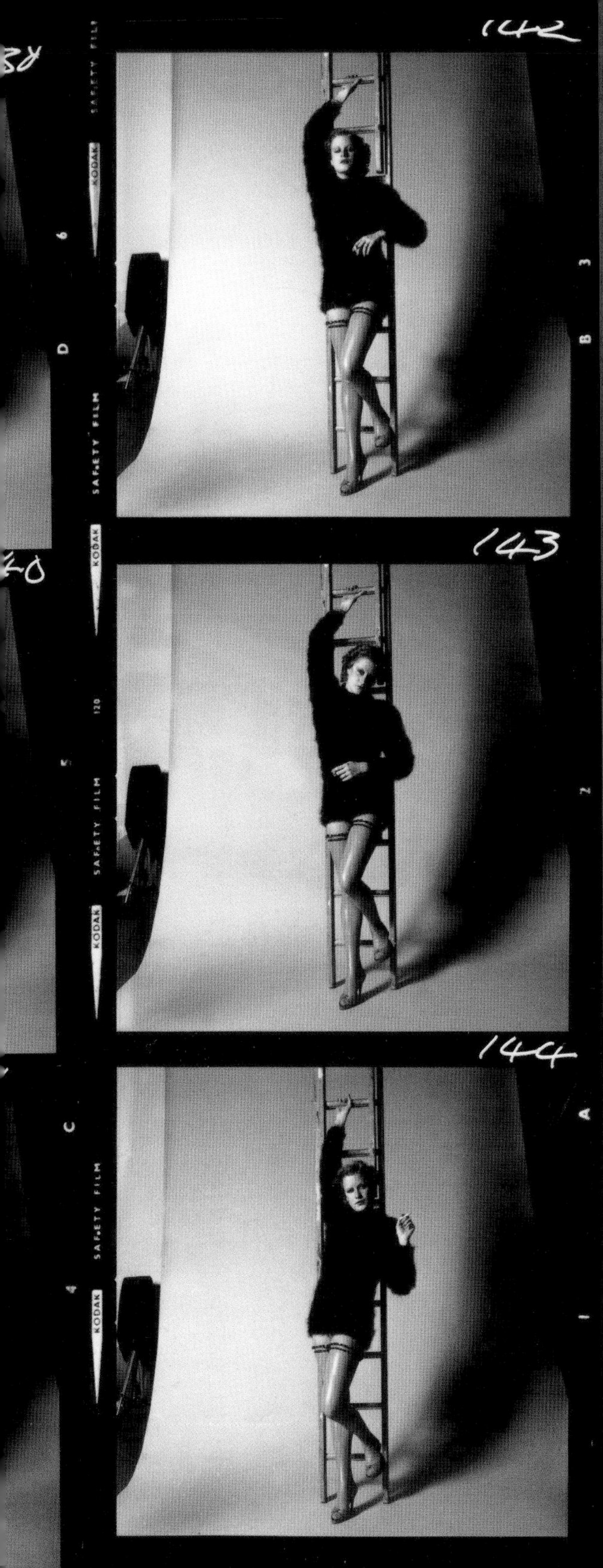

"In 1975 Little Nell and I collaborated on a shoot where she sported some early Vivienne Westwood creations: purple rubber hose, T-shirt with salacious and subversive slogans and zippers that open to allow her nipples to peek out, tight leather skirt, black mohair sweater. With her fuchsia hair color, she was an early punk princess and our photos are some of my favorite fashion statements of the period."

—MICK ROCK

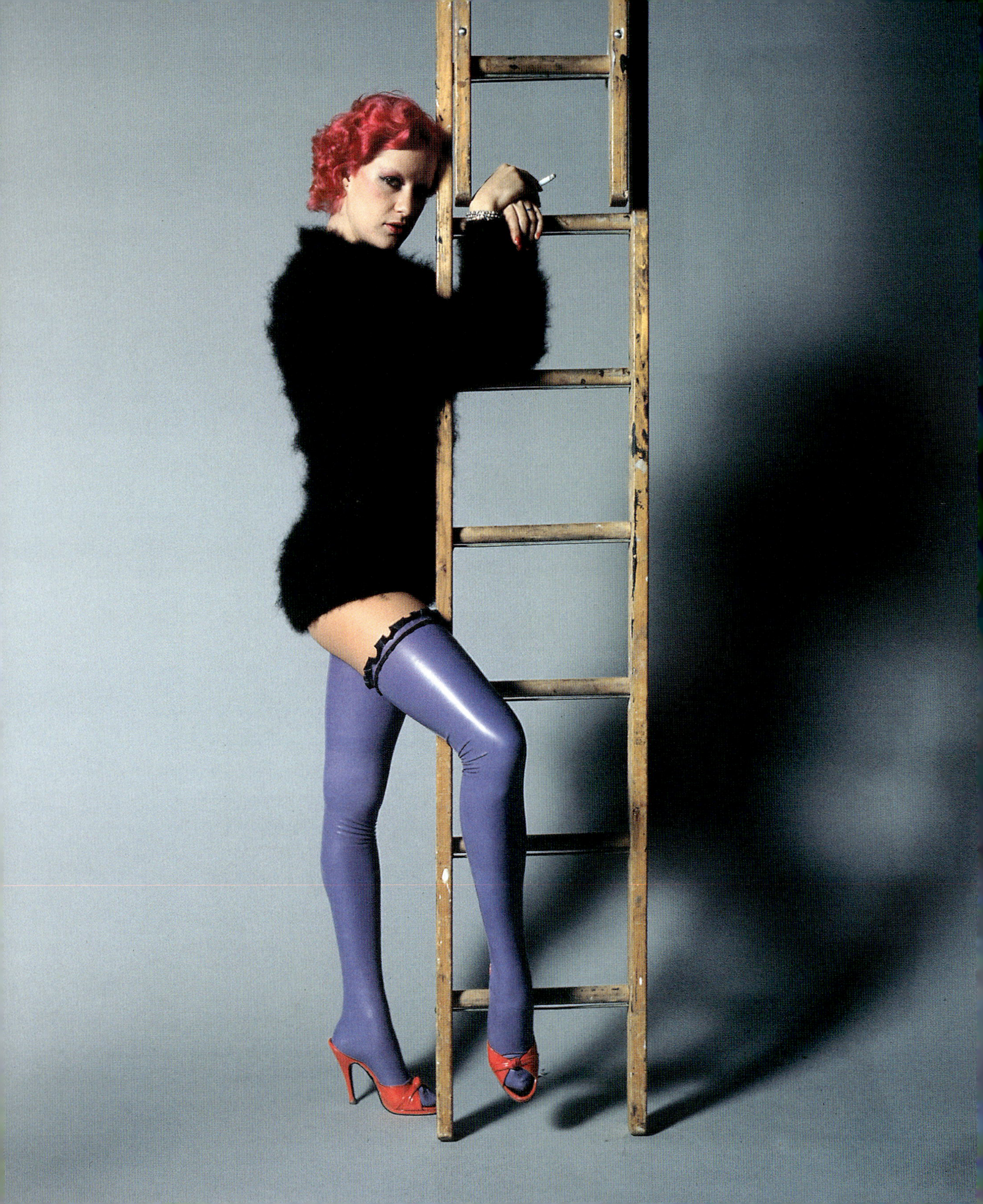

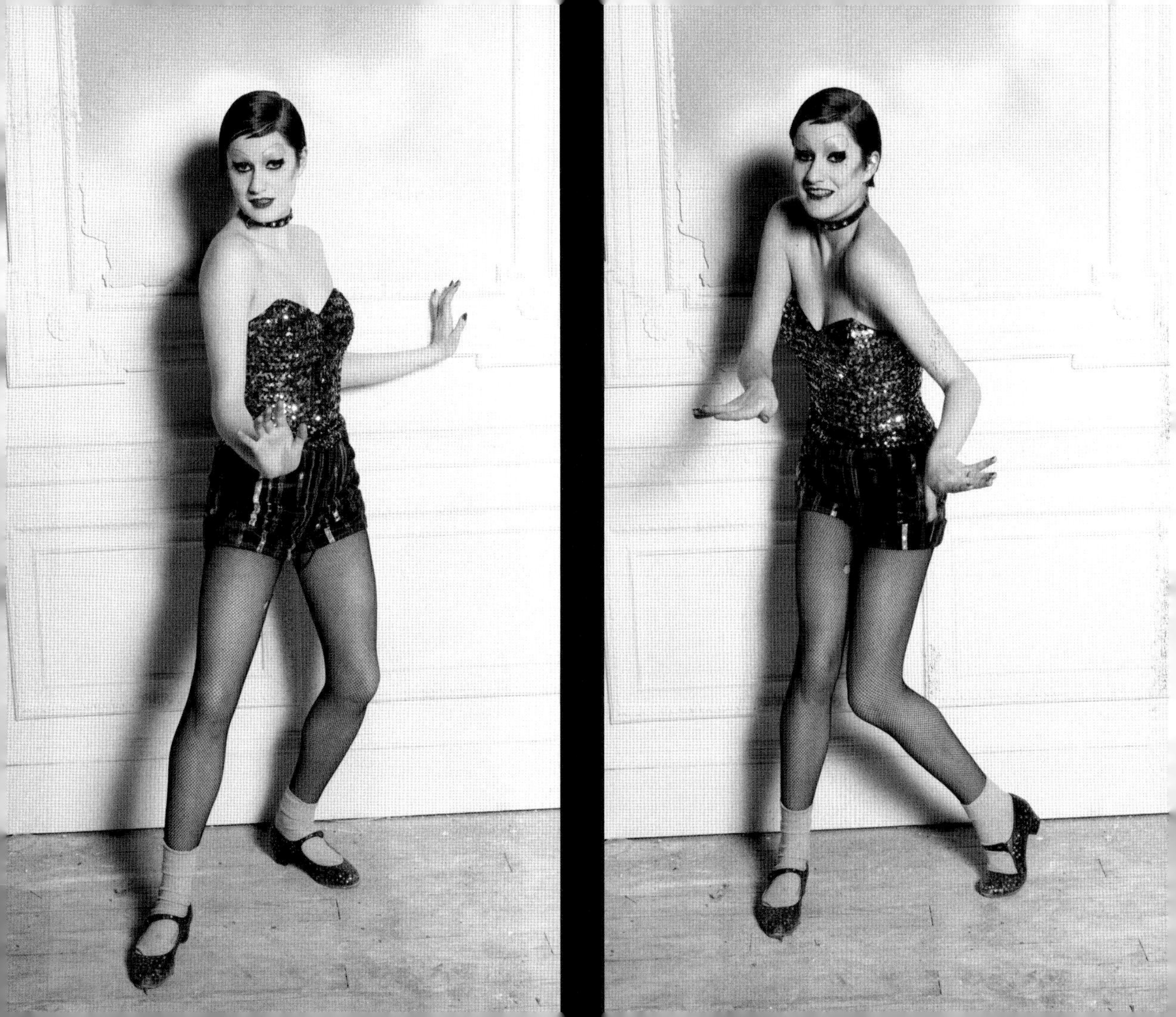

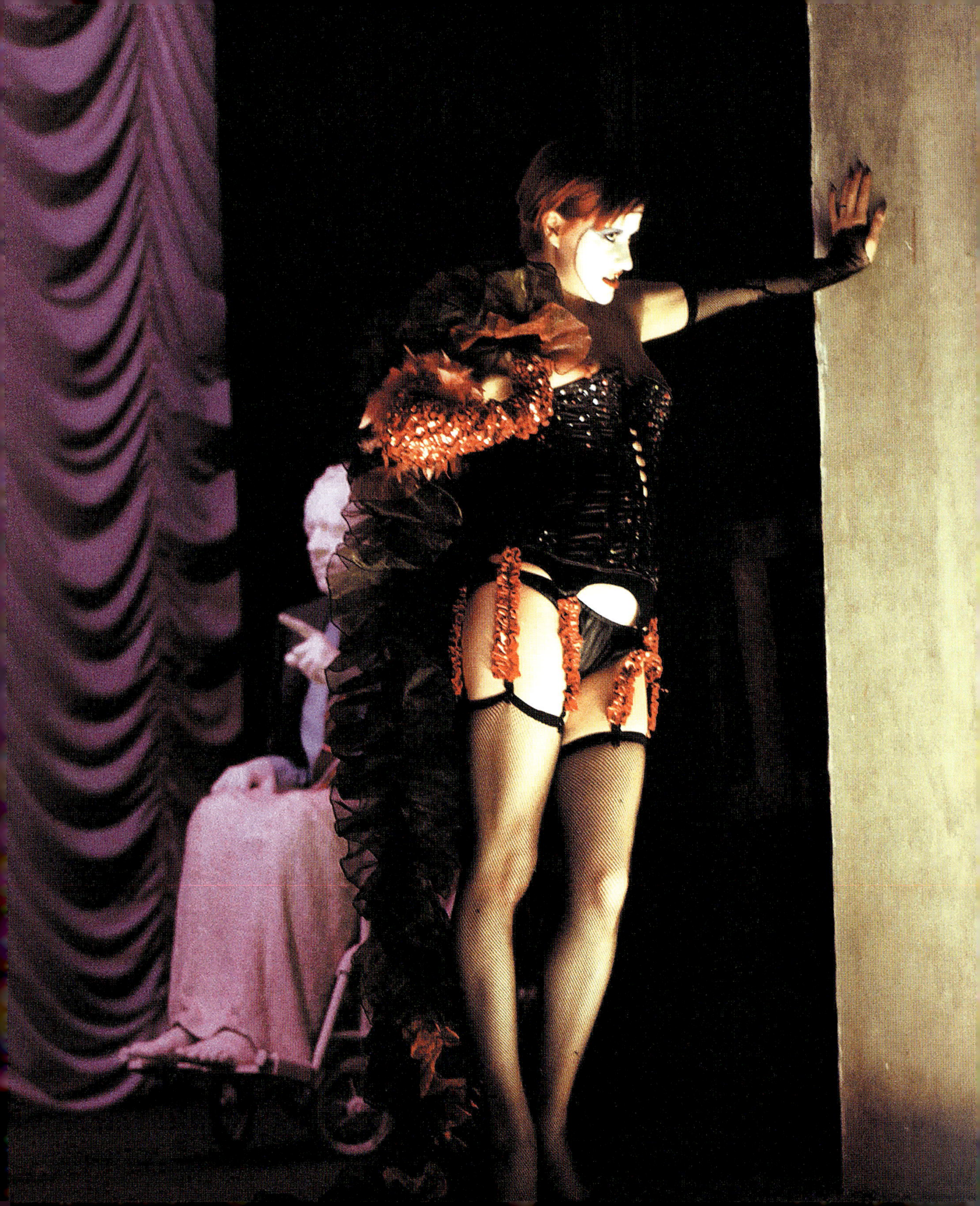

JOAN JETT, MUSICIAN: "When you're a teenager, you're changing from being that little kid into an early adult, and all these various energies awaken in you. You start to look at the world and connect with new things—ideas, fashion, music. You're figuring out who you are. I was right in that phase of life when I saw *Rocky Horror*. I'd heard about this new, weird movie, where people would go to the theater and dress as the characters. I remember being a teenager and going with my friends; there's a picture somewhere of me and my friends, with makeup on, feather boas, and stuff like that. I enjoyed the story, but I'm not so sure the story particularly mattered as much as the characters, the music, and what it all looked like. It all fit together in a cohesive sort of experience. It made me realize there was more than one way to present yourself in life. And beyond that, the music was so great, which was really important too. I was such a fan of the movie that playing Columbia—later, on Broadway—was a very cool experience; I was so familiar with the film that it was very natural. I had shaved my head for the millennium on New Year's Eve, and it ended up really working as Columbia."

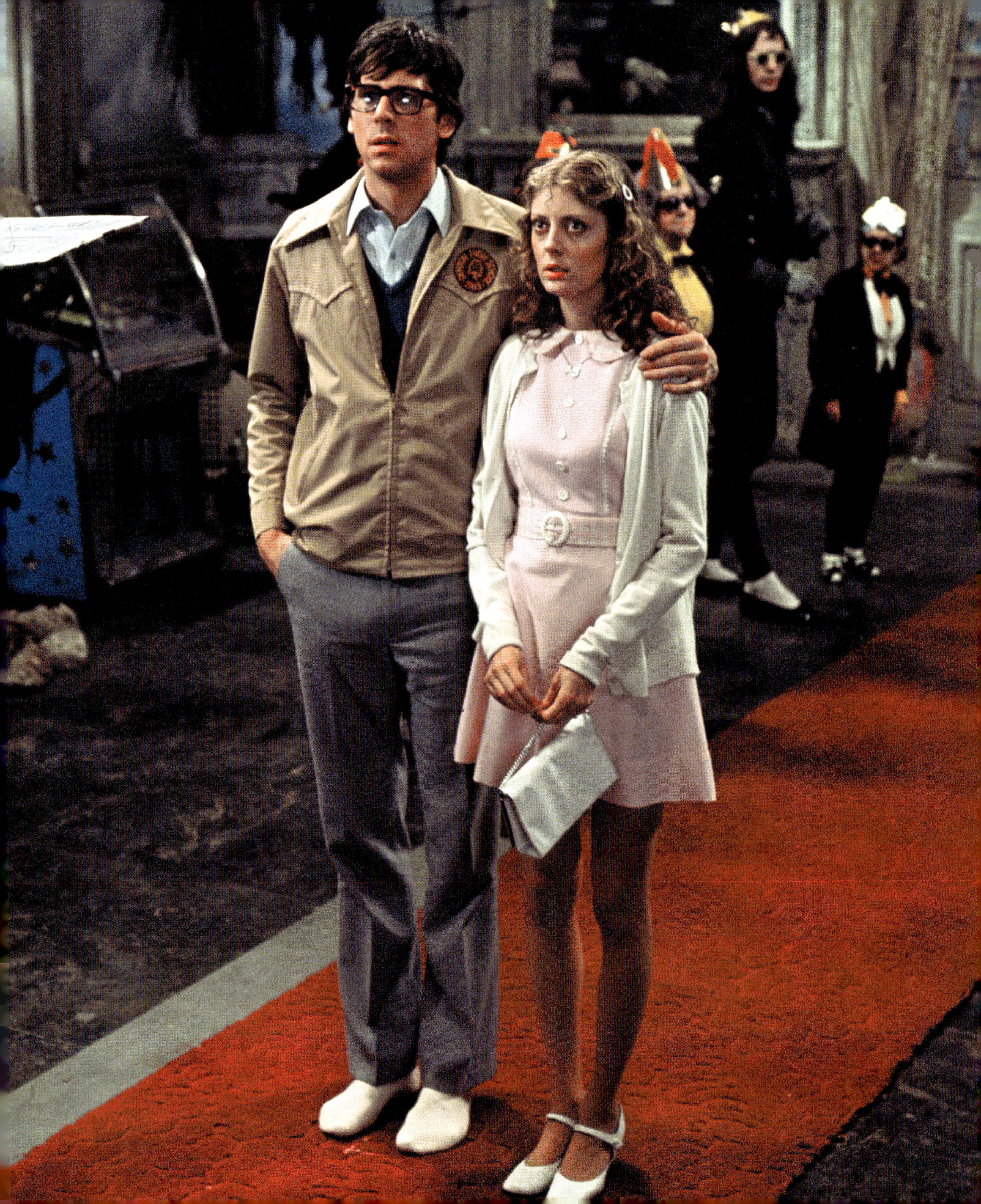

THERE'S A FIRE IN MY HEART AND YOU FAN IT: BRAD AND JANET

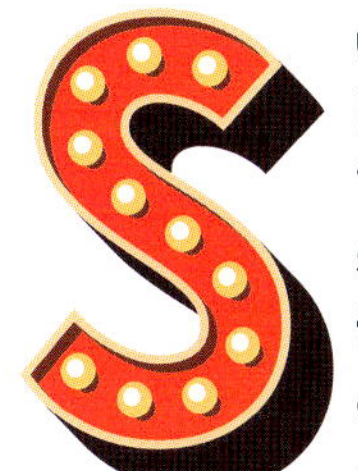

usan Sarandon and Barry Bostwick," said Mick, "were at the start of their significant careers when they boldly agreed to accept the roles of Janet and Brad. They were the perfect embodiment of young American innocents who have lost their way."

Aside from narrator Charles Gray, Sarandon was the only member of the cast who had been in a film before. That was of little consolation as she came down with pneumonia from the cold, damp conditions at Bray Studios and the partially derelict Oakley Court. "I was just trying to get through the English winter in underwear," she told *The Guardian*.

"Barry and I were the only ones that hadn't been involved with the stage show," Sarandon told *EW*. "I had become friends with Tim because I had girlfriends who were in the L.A. stage production. At one point I just ran in to give him a kiss and say hi and then they said, 'Why don't you read for this?' I didn't even know they were casting the movie. So I read and they were like, 'Oh my God!' But I said, 'Yeah, but I can't sing.' I was really embarrassed. So I thought at some point if I did this that they'd have to give me alcohol, drugs, or something to get me through it, which of course they didn't."

As Jim Sharman wrote in his memoir *Blood & Tinsel*, "How does a small-town girl greet an illustrious transvestite scientist? Does she shake hands or curtsy? It's played to perfection by the flirtatiously shrewd Susan Sarandon. More than Rocky or any

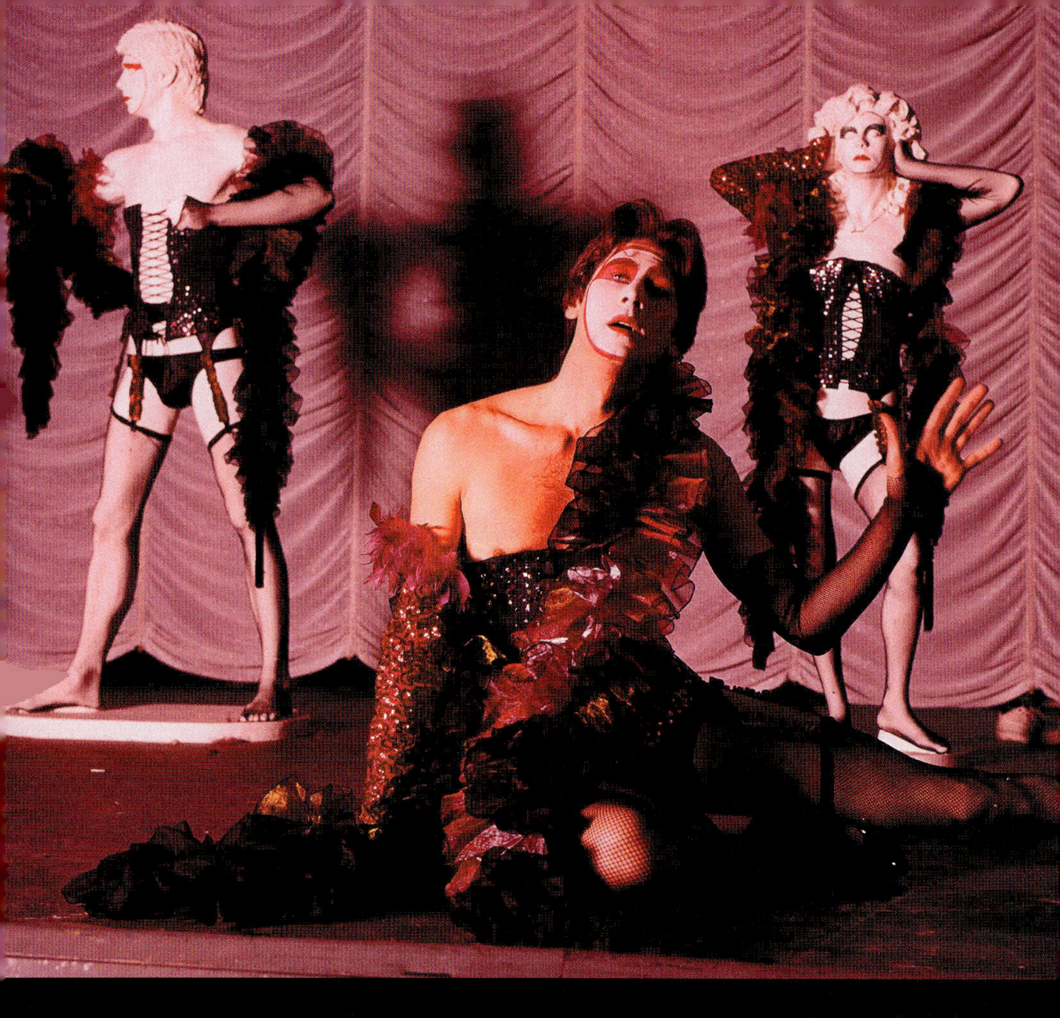

other character, it's Janet Weiss that develops through her exposure to Frank and the haunted house."

Barry Bostwick had already been nominated for a Tony as the original Danny Zuko, the lead role in *Grease*, the big-production Broadway musical that would also be filmed a few years later. Even so, *Rocky Horror* "was in my wheelhouse," he said in an exclusive interview. As Brad Majors, he enjoyed being "an exaggerated character but playing it for real." And besides, Bostwick says, he has "always been attracted to the weird, wonderful, and different."

Shuttling between London and Bray Studios, seeing England in 1974 was eye-opening for Bostwick. "It was a life-changing experience spending those six or seven weeks in the middle of the emergence of punk and the drastic changes in mores and attitudes toward the LGBTQ community. It felt like we were inventing something special, riding the times of change that were everywhere we looked."

When the film initially bombed, Bostwick said he barely noticed: "When it was finally released, I was living in New York, busy with my musical career on the stage, and it flew right over my self-concerned head."

He says it wasn't until 1981 that he realized the extent to which the movie had become a cultural phenomenon: "The cast of the Tiffany Theater in Los Angeles asked me to join them at a screening and they gifted me a gold record—and I returned the gesture by framing a pair of my tighty-whities and presenting it to the theater company. They have passed down through many hands since then."

"My only real communication with Susan and Barry came during the sexy dance sequences," said Mick, "and they both wore their scanties well and seemed to revel in that part of their roles. Certainly, they had great bodies and, divested of their initial tourist attire, they took eagerly to the liberated sexuality that Frank so forcefully inducted them into. And sex, of course, is at the core of this movie. At the time it was written, gay lib and women's lib formed the dual prongs of the culture's cutting edge and both are colorfully projected here in a spirit of pure entertainment. If Richard was proselytizing it was in a seductive and revolutionary way, and as *Rocky Horror* continues to seduce new generations of fans, also in a totally timeless way."

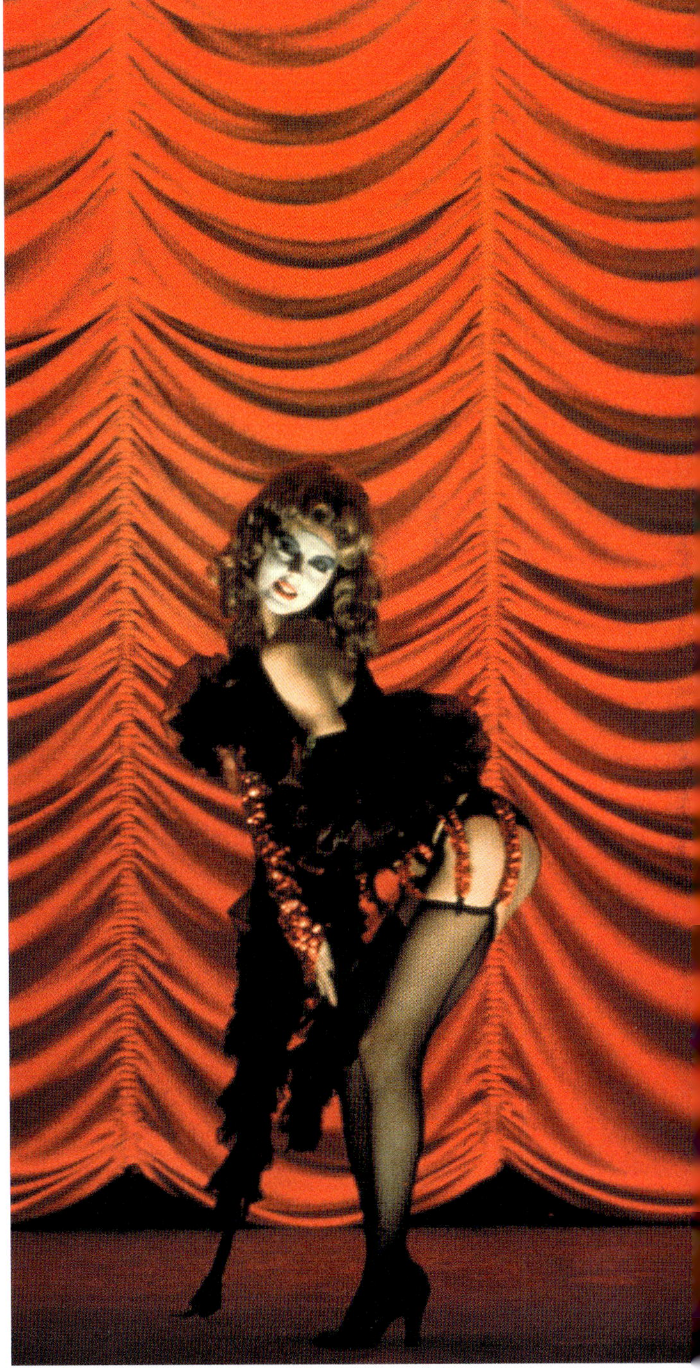

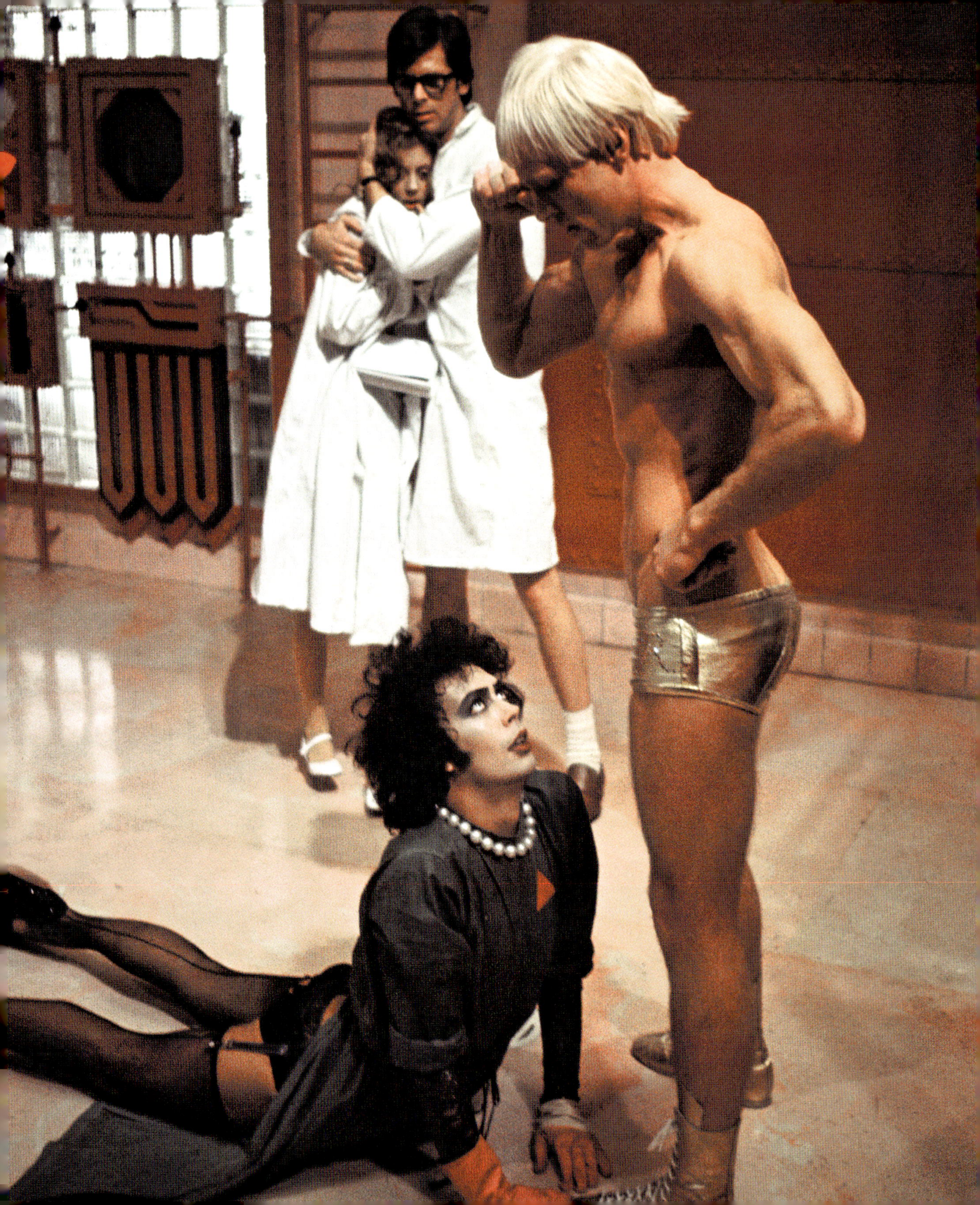

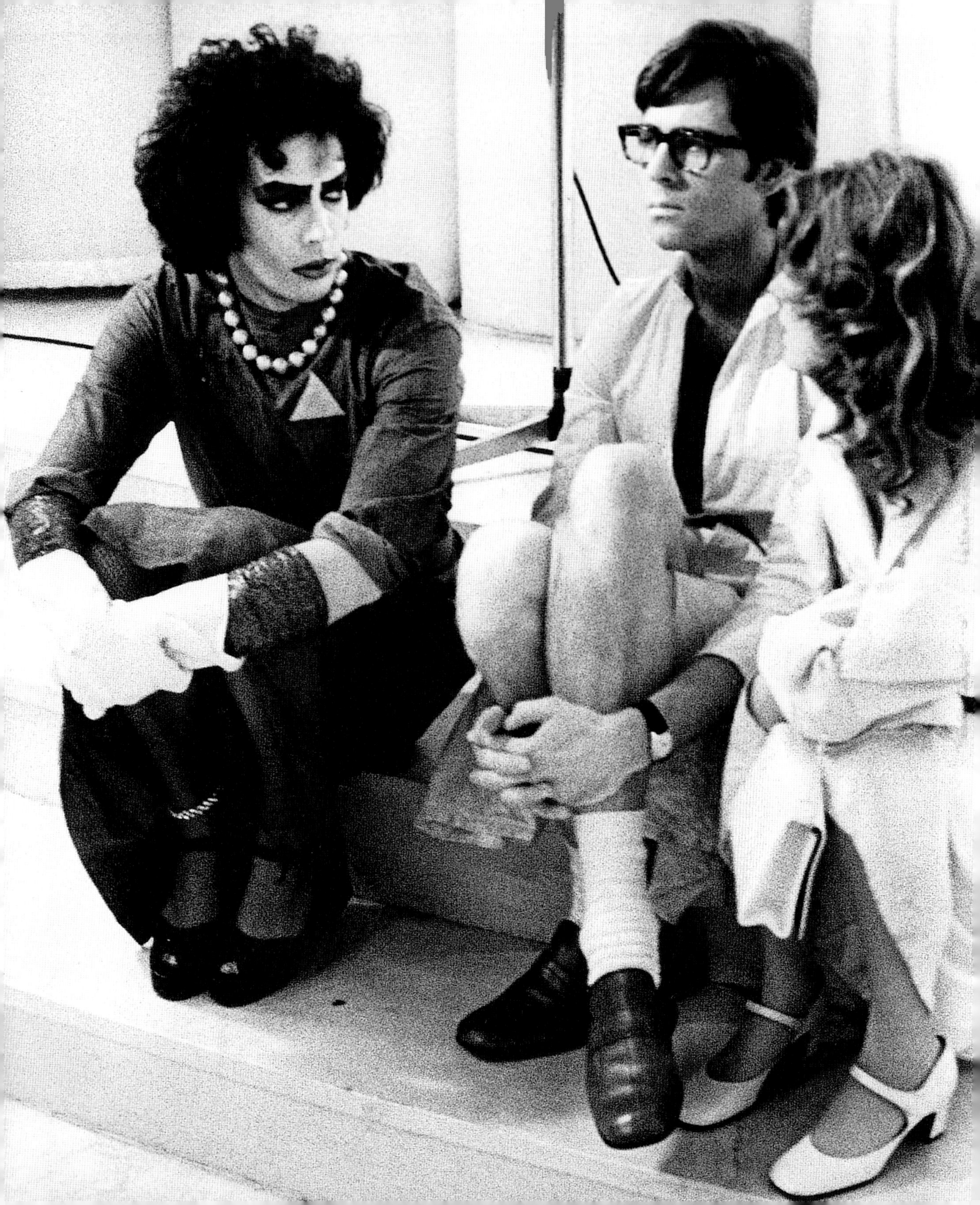

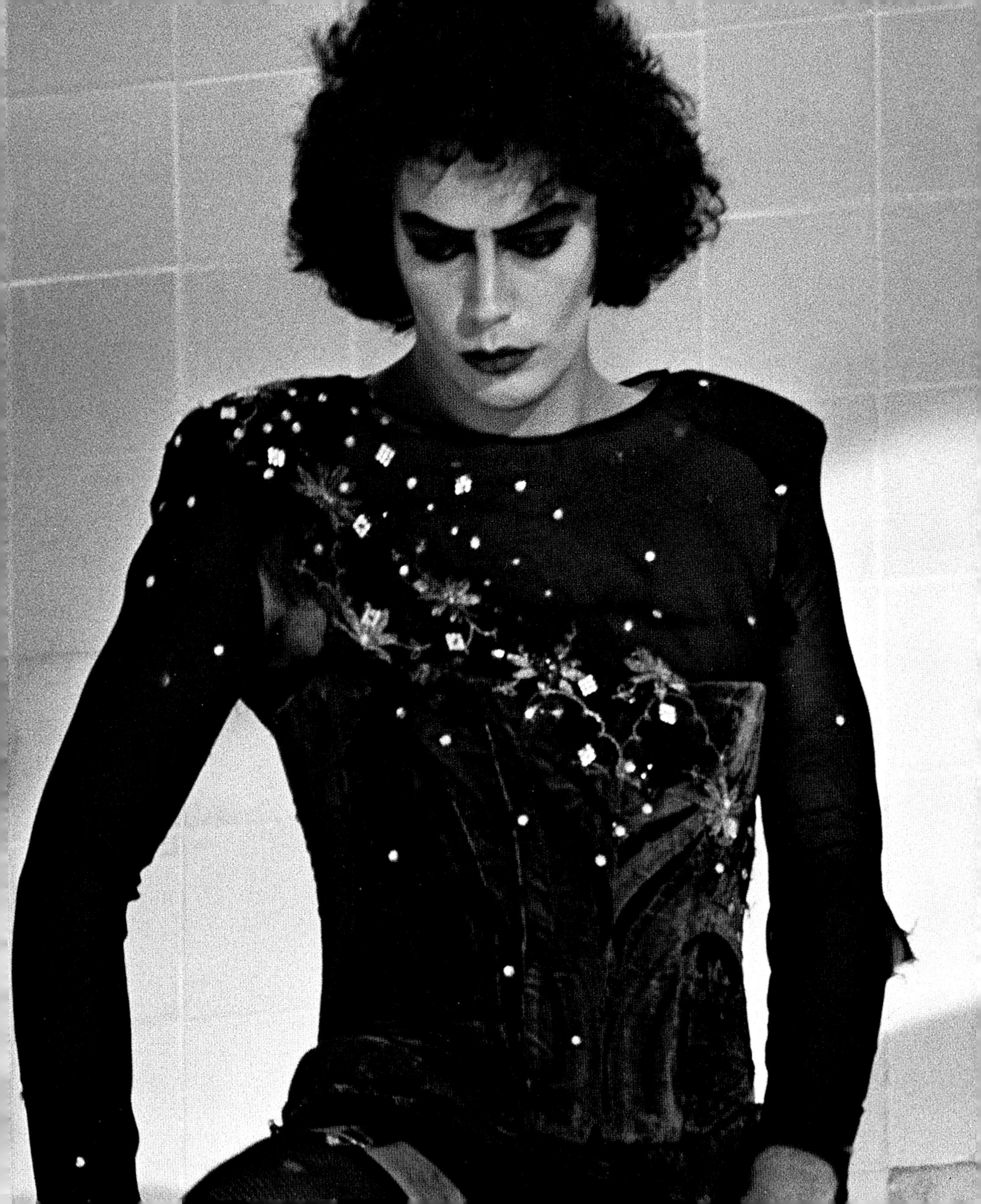

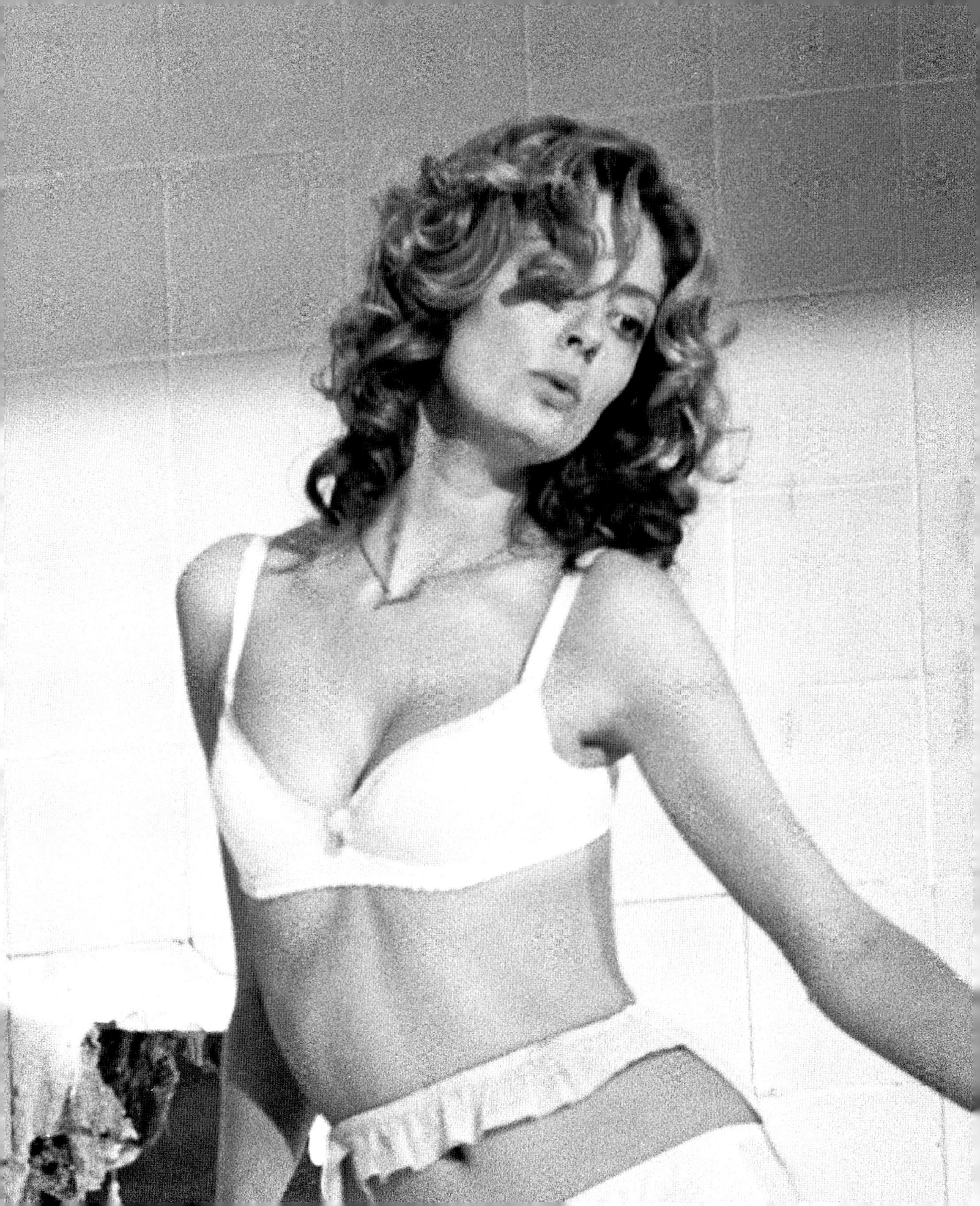

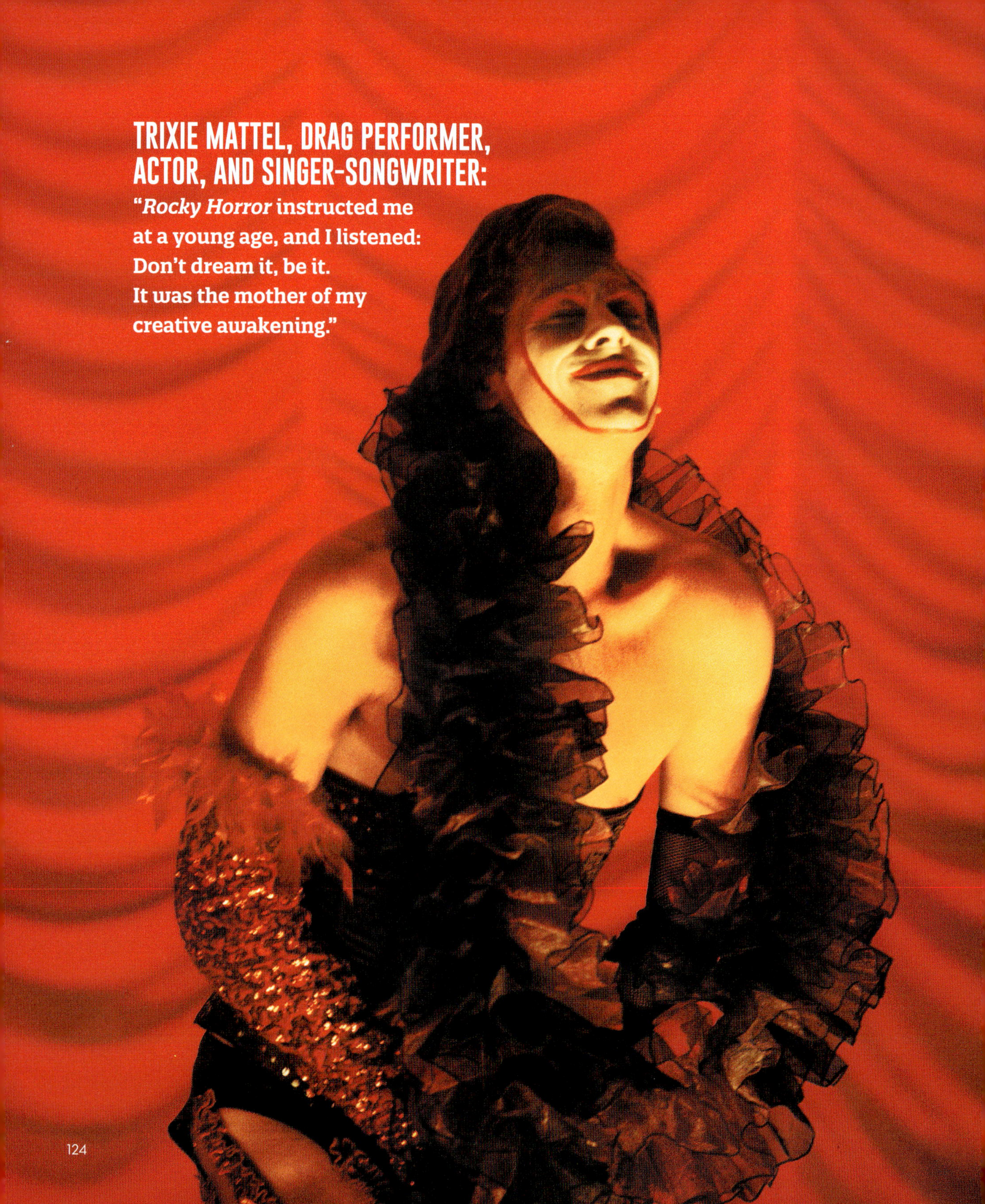

TRIXIE MATTEL, DRAG PERFORMER, ACTOR, AND SINGER-SONGWRITER:

"*Rocky Horror* instructed me at a young age, and I listened: Don't dream it, be it. It was the mother of my creative awakening."

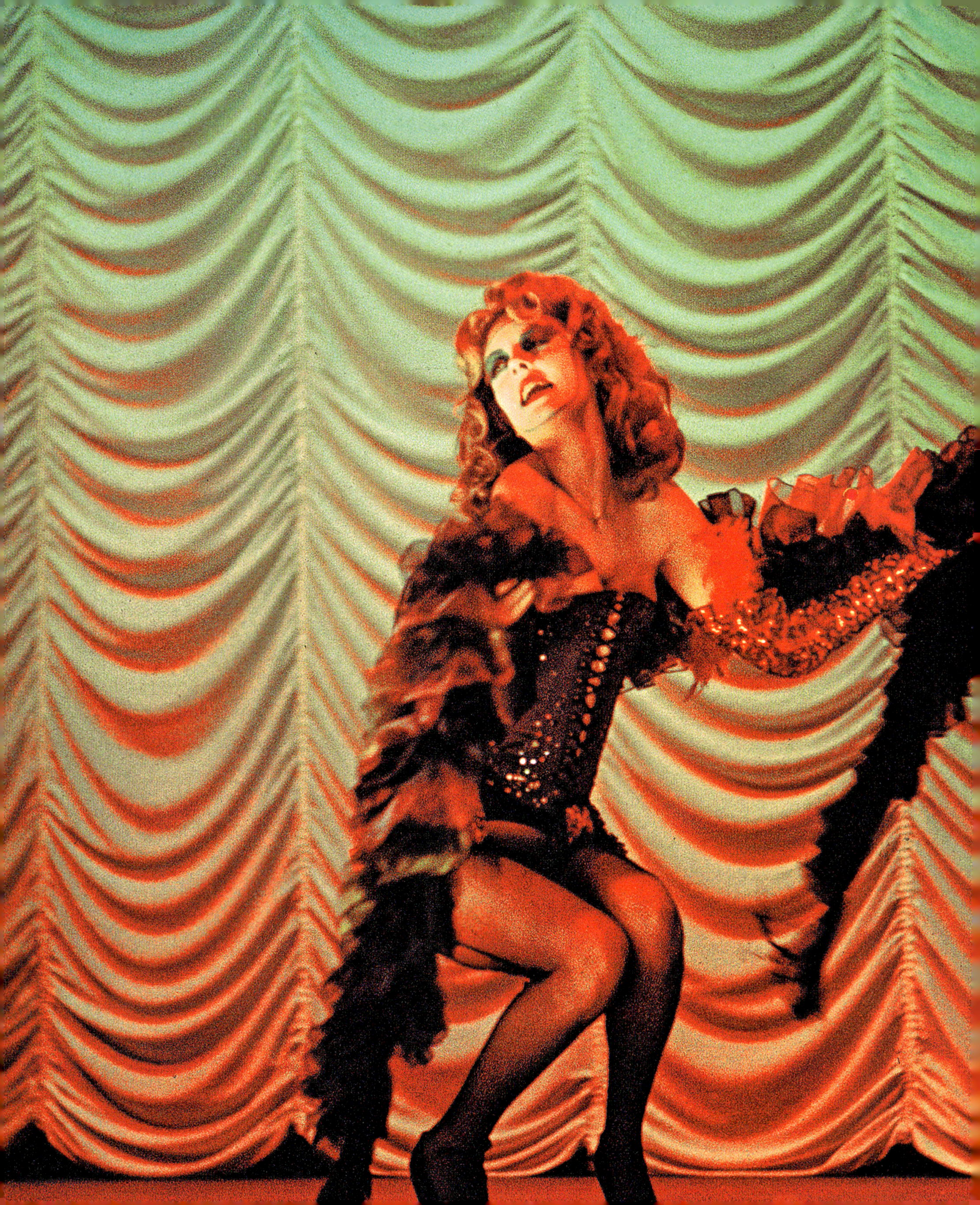

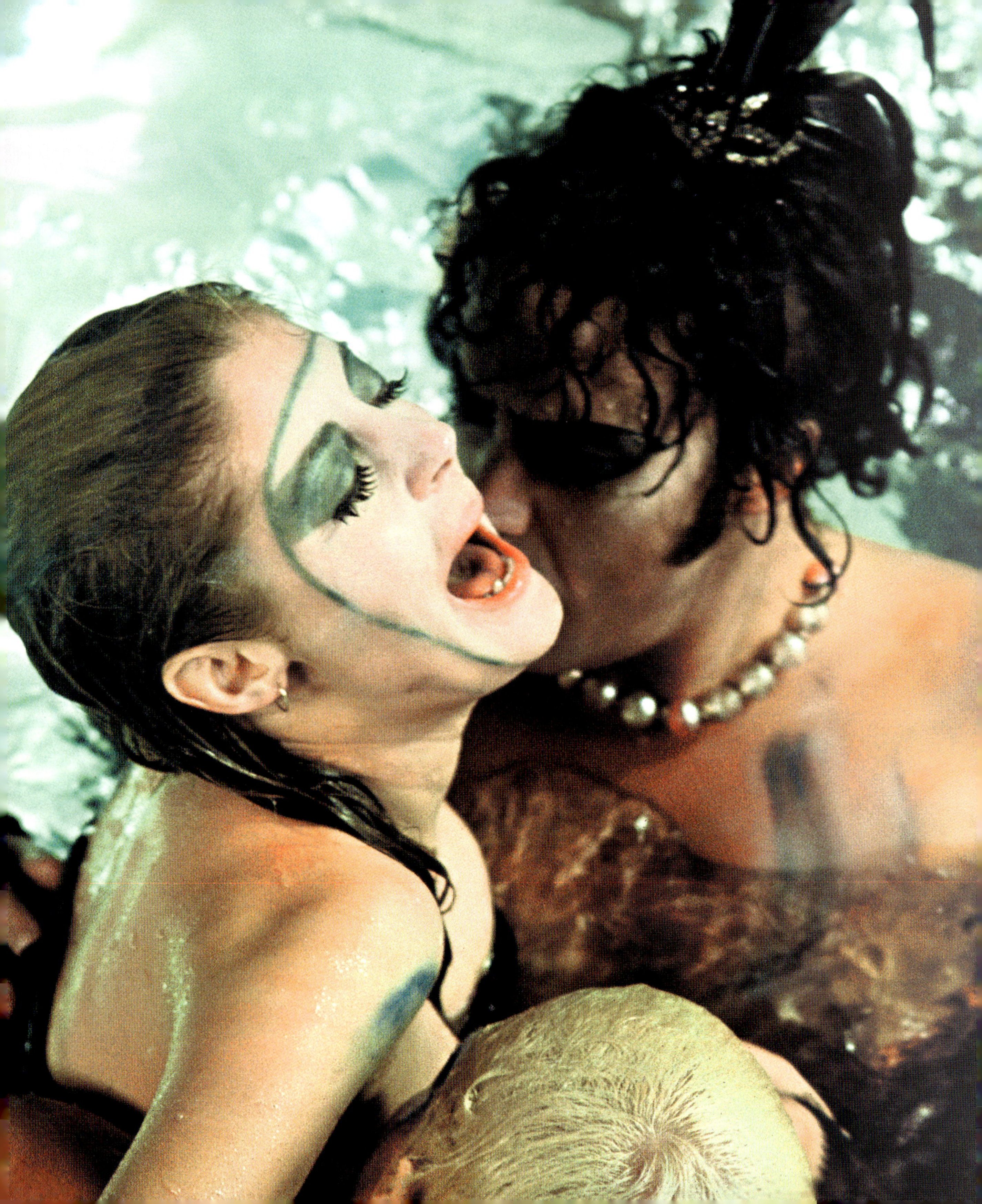

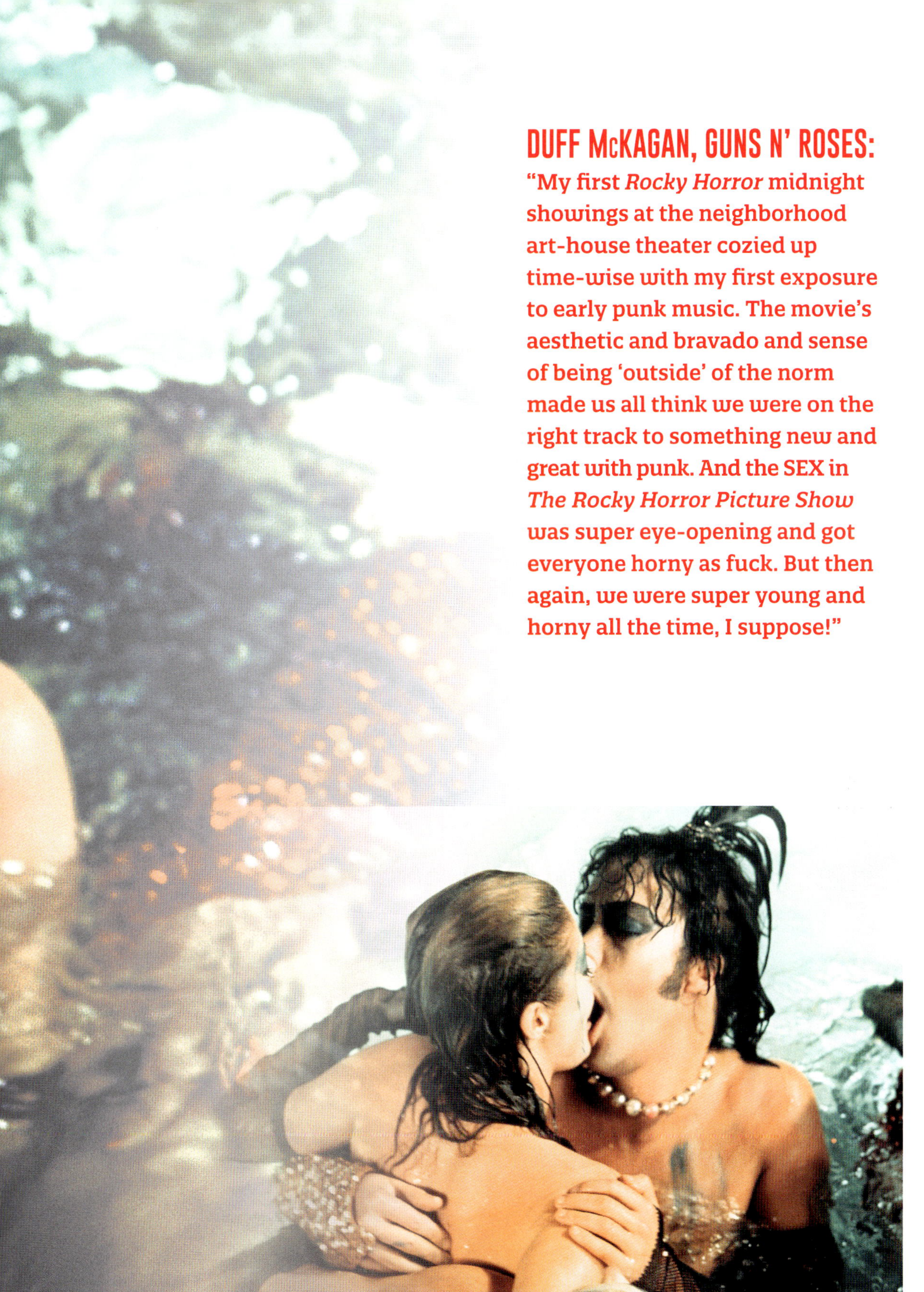

DUFF McKAGAN, GUNS N' ROSES:

"My first *Rocky Horror* midnight showings at the neighborhood art-house theater cozied up time-wise with my first exposure to early punk music. The movie's aesthetic and bravado and sense of being 'outside' of the norm made us all think we were on the right track to something new and great with punk. And the SEX in *The Rocky Horror Picture Show* was super eye-opening and got everyone horny as fuck. But then again, we were super young and horny all the time, I suppose!"

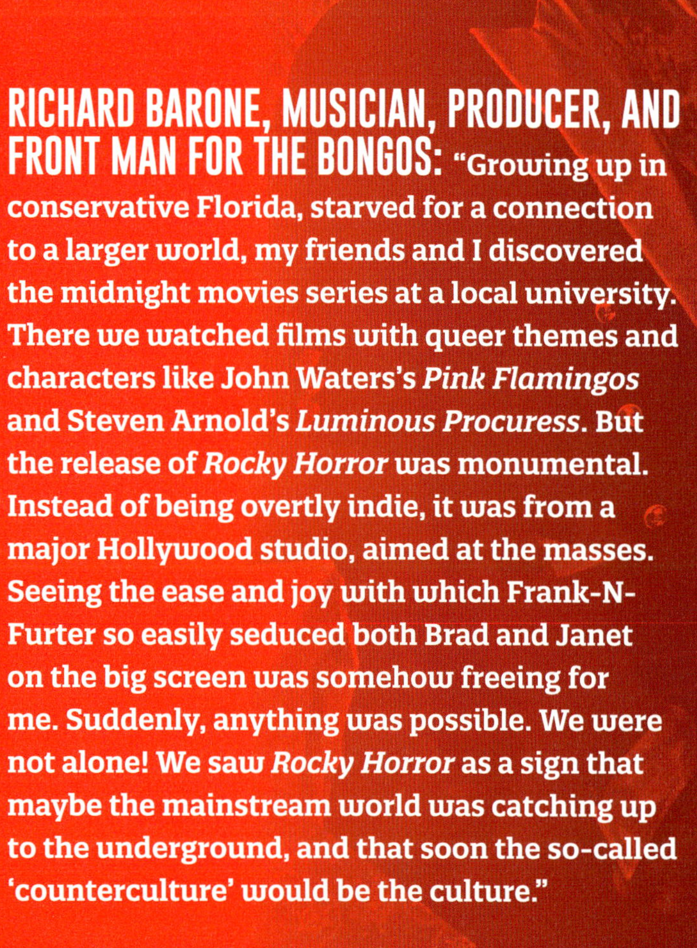

RICHARD BARONE, MUSICIAN, PRODUCER, AND FRONT MAN FOR THE BONGOS: "Growing up in conservative Florida, starved for a connection to a larger world, my friends and I discovered the midnight movies series at a local university. There we watched films with queer themes and characters like John Waters's *Pink Flamingos* and Steven Arnold's *Luminous Procuress*. But the release of *Rocky Horror* was monumental. Instead of being overtly indie, it was from a major Hollywood studio, aimed at the masses. Seeing the ease and joy with which Frank-N-Furter so easily seduced both Brad and Janet on the big screen was somehow freeing for me. Suddenly, anything was possible. We were not alone! We saw *Rocky Horror* as a sign that maybe the mainstream world was catching up to the underground, and that soon the so-called 'counterculture' would be the culture."

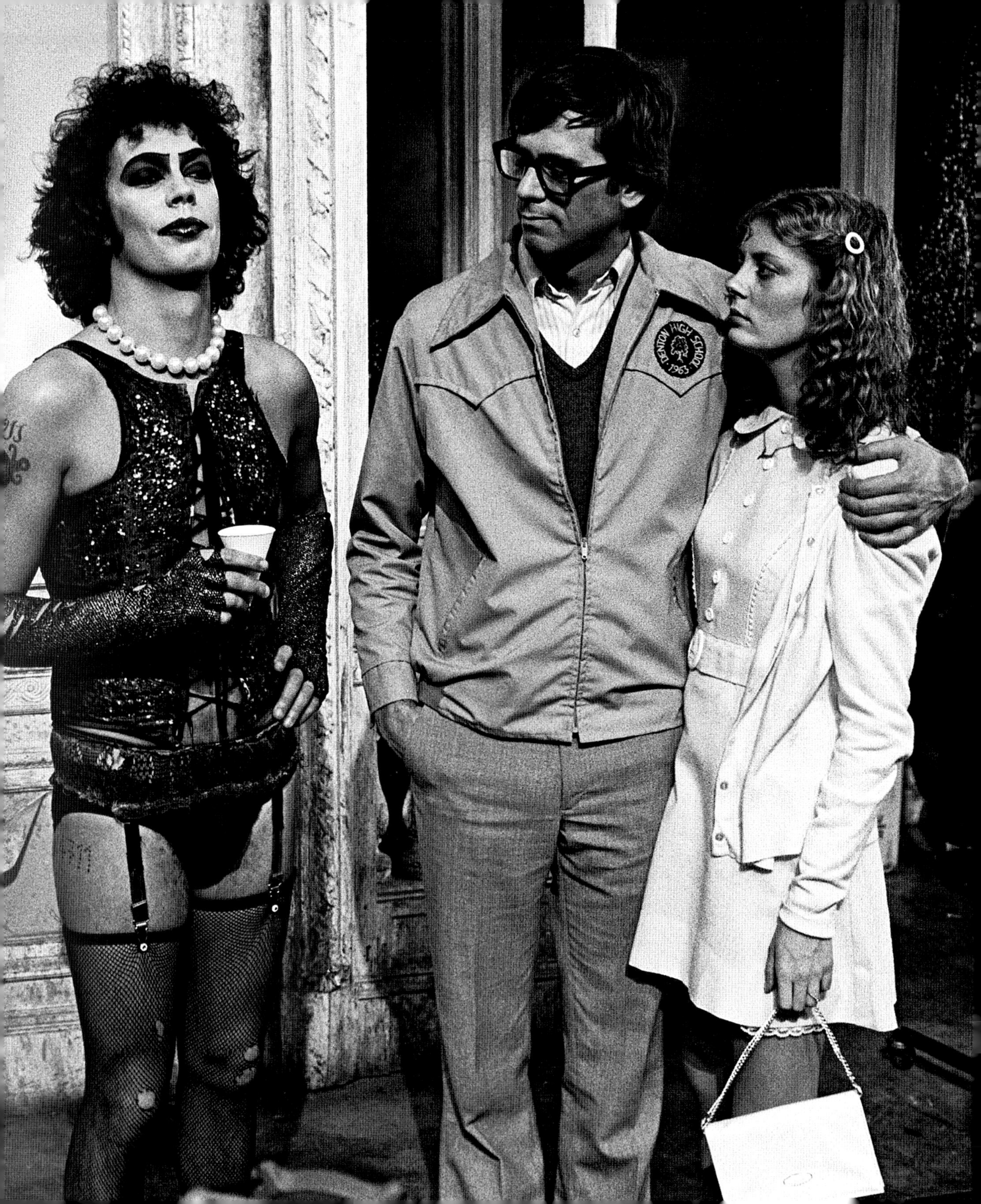
DENTON HIGH SCHOOL
1963

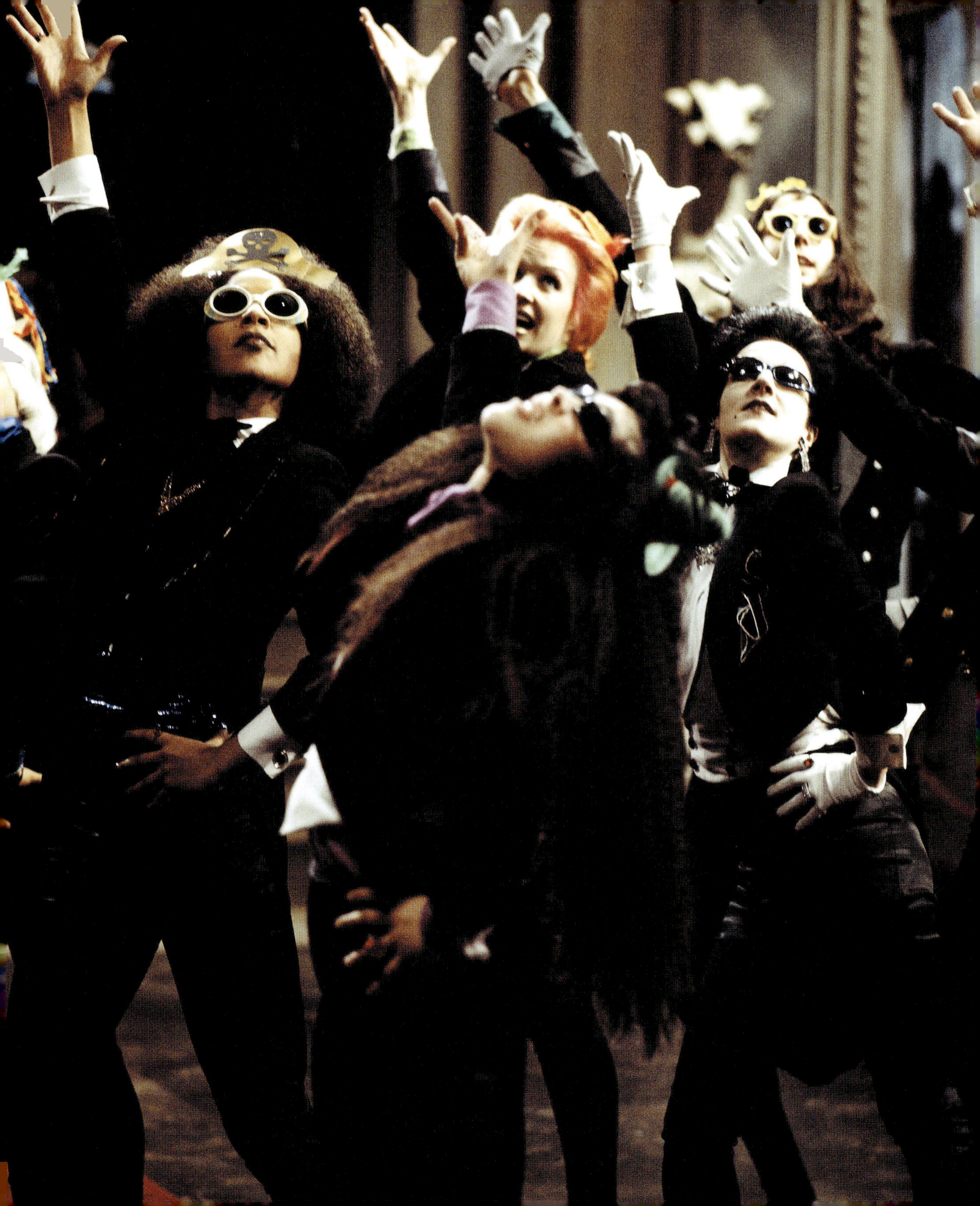

IT'S JUST A JUMP TO THE LEFT: "TIME WARP"

As Nell Campbell recalls, during rehearsals in the weeks before *Rocky Horror* was to debut, "Jim Sharman said to Richard O'Brien: 'Can you write a song for the three servants? They need a dance.' Richard went home, wrote a song, dropped it off at Richard Hartley's, they fine-tuned the chorus, and then arrived at ten a.m. rehearsals the next day with the 'Time Warp.'"

The hastily written but instantly iconic "Time Warp" became the *Rocky Horror* song that reached the furthest into the broader pop culture consciousness. As the musician and *Rocky Horror* fan Peaches says, "It's beyond rock. It's punk, but also campy. And it became a huge hit, a dance, while subverting the idea of nostalgia itself—calling itself the 'Time Warp'—and it's probably still played at weddings and whatever other heteronormative events."

Karen O of the Yeah Yeah Yeahs agrees. "It's a Halloween dance party classic. It's hooky, fun, teaches you a new dance—you'd have to try really hard not to like it."

In some ways, "Time Warp" may have functioned as a sort of Trojan horse to get the film's subversive message to go mainstream. As Peaches further explains, "The best thing about *The Rocky Horror Picture Show* is: the music is fantastic. That's what leads it. It is such a feat that the music is so great because otherwise it would have been shifted to the side as some weird, queer musical. But instead, it became huge."

As for the bold look of the "Time Warp"

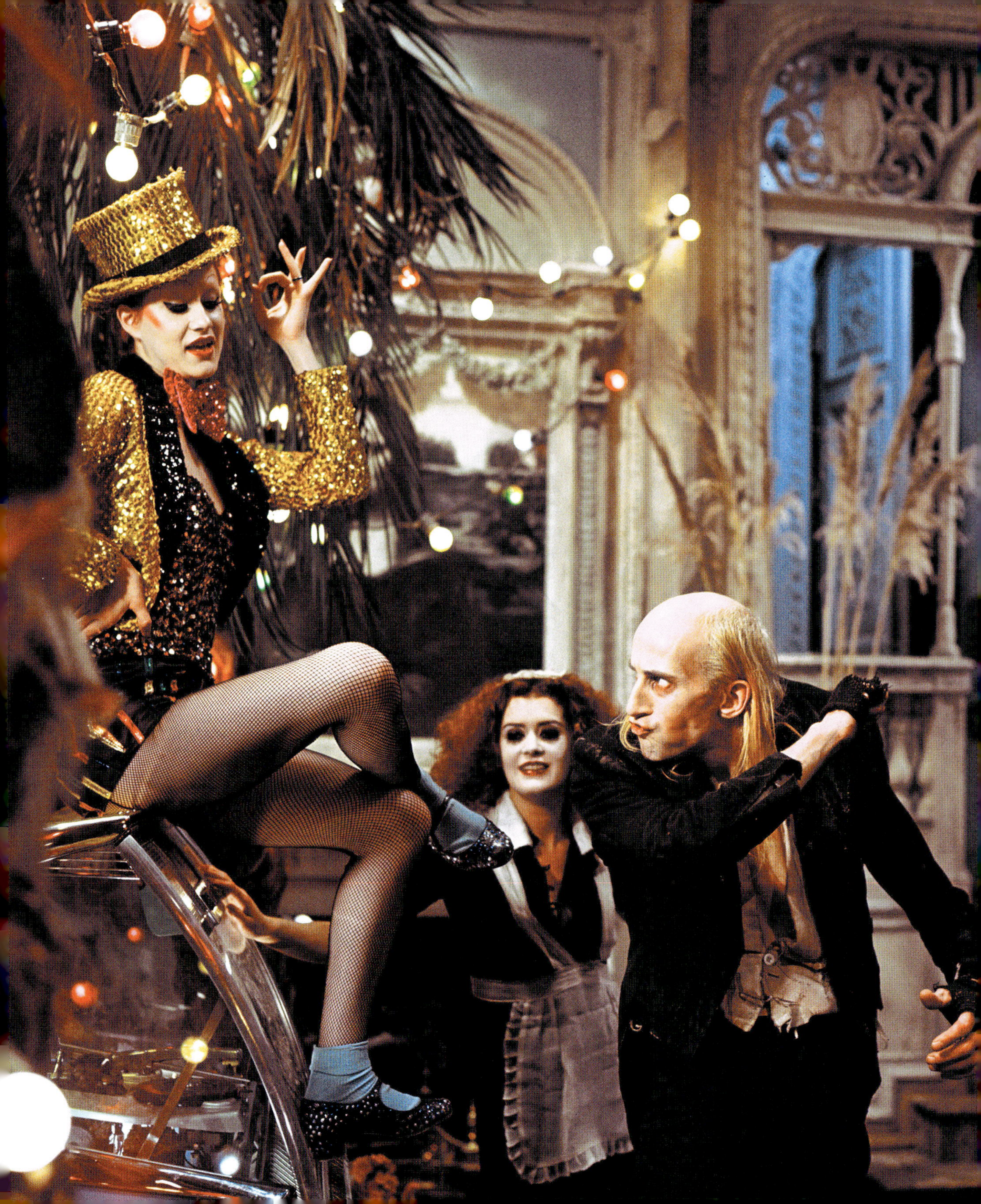

scene, costume designer Sue Blane says an original vision for the movie to switch from black and white to color led her to make the dance routine particularly visually striking. "The Transylvanians have all these fluorescent bits on them because I thought once we get into color I really want people to know immediately that we're in color, not for them to realize slowly as they're watching the 'Time Warp.' So that was more heightened, and so were all the other colors, Janet's pink, Brad's blue, than if we hadn't planned on that changeover."

KAREN O, THE YEAH YEAH YEAHS:

"It's a Halloween dance party classic. It's hooky, fun, teaches you a new dance—you'd have to try really hard not to like it."

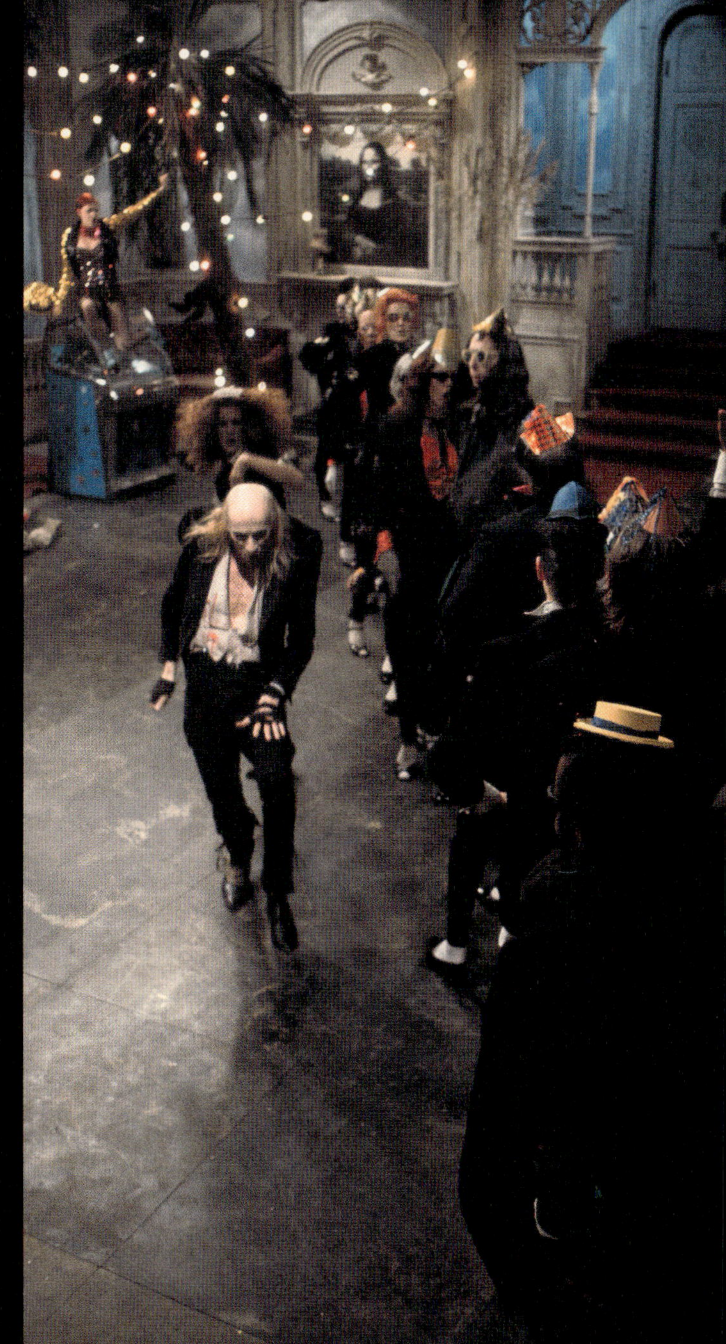

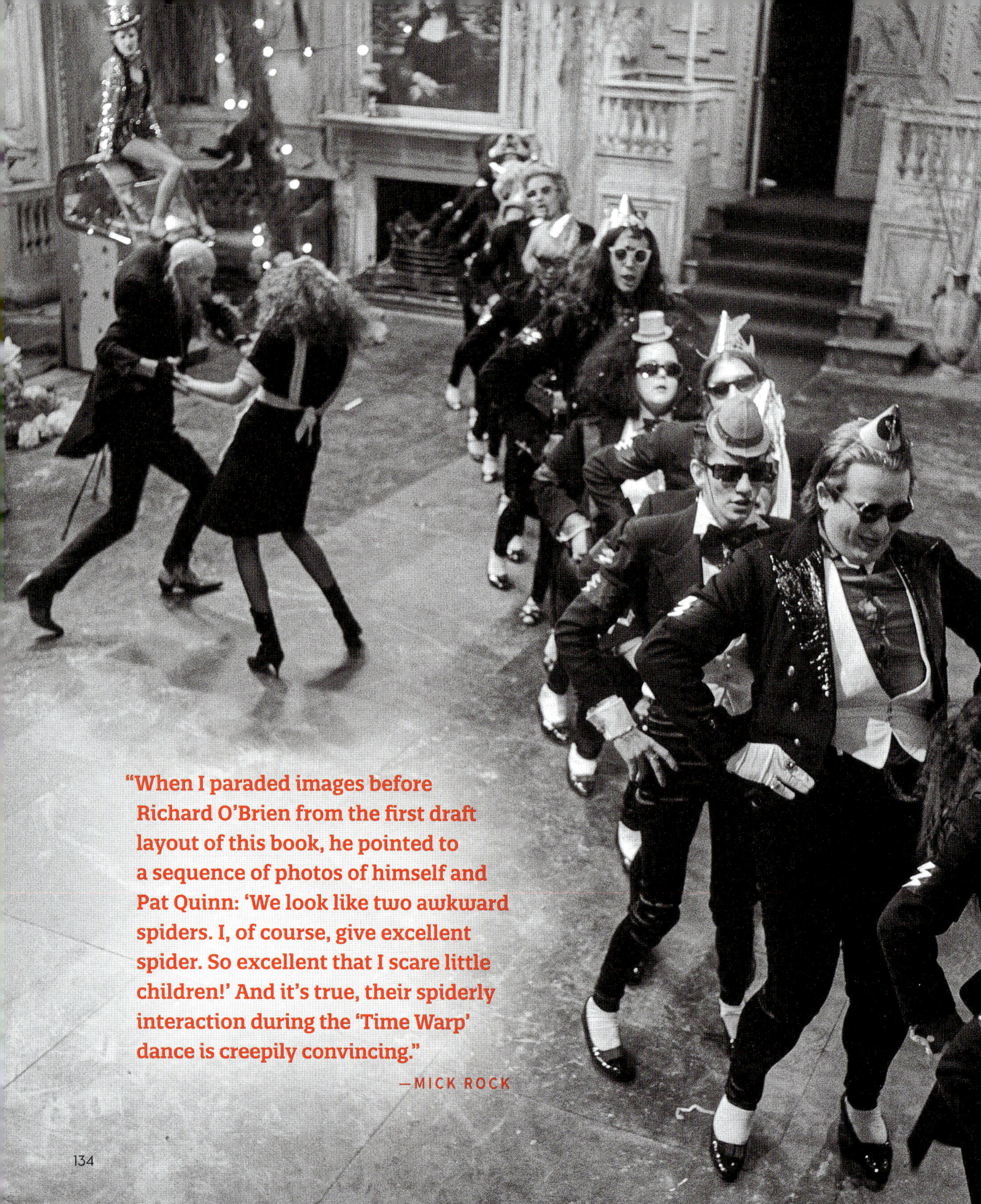

"When I paraded images before Richard O'Brien from the first draft layout of this book, he pointed to a sequence of photos of himself and Pat Quinn: 'We look like two awkward spiders. I, of course, give excellent spider. So excellent that I scare little children!' And it's true, their spiderly interaction during the 'Time Warp' dance is creepily convincing."

—MICK ROCK

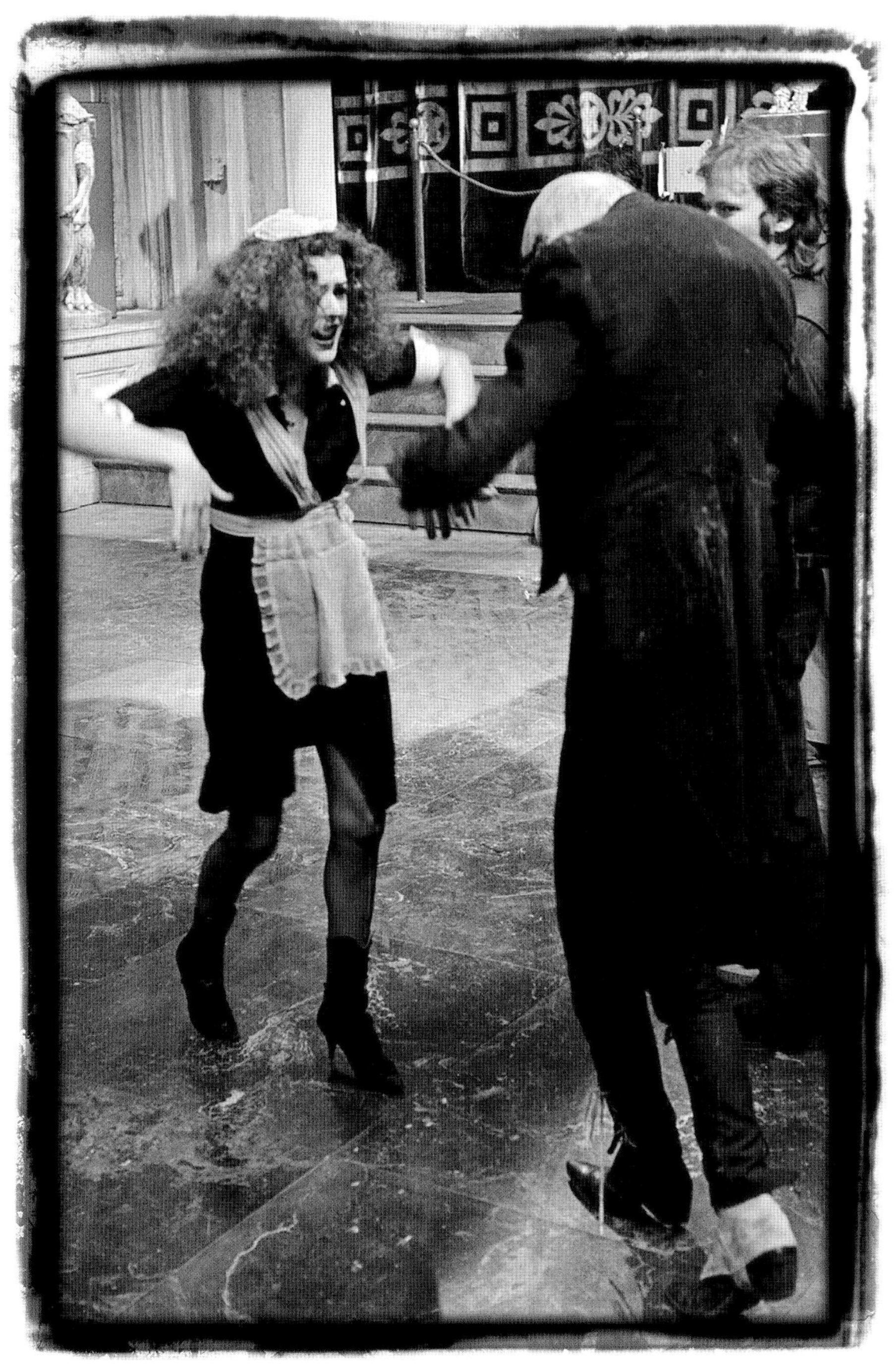

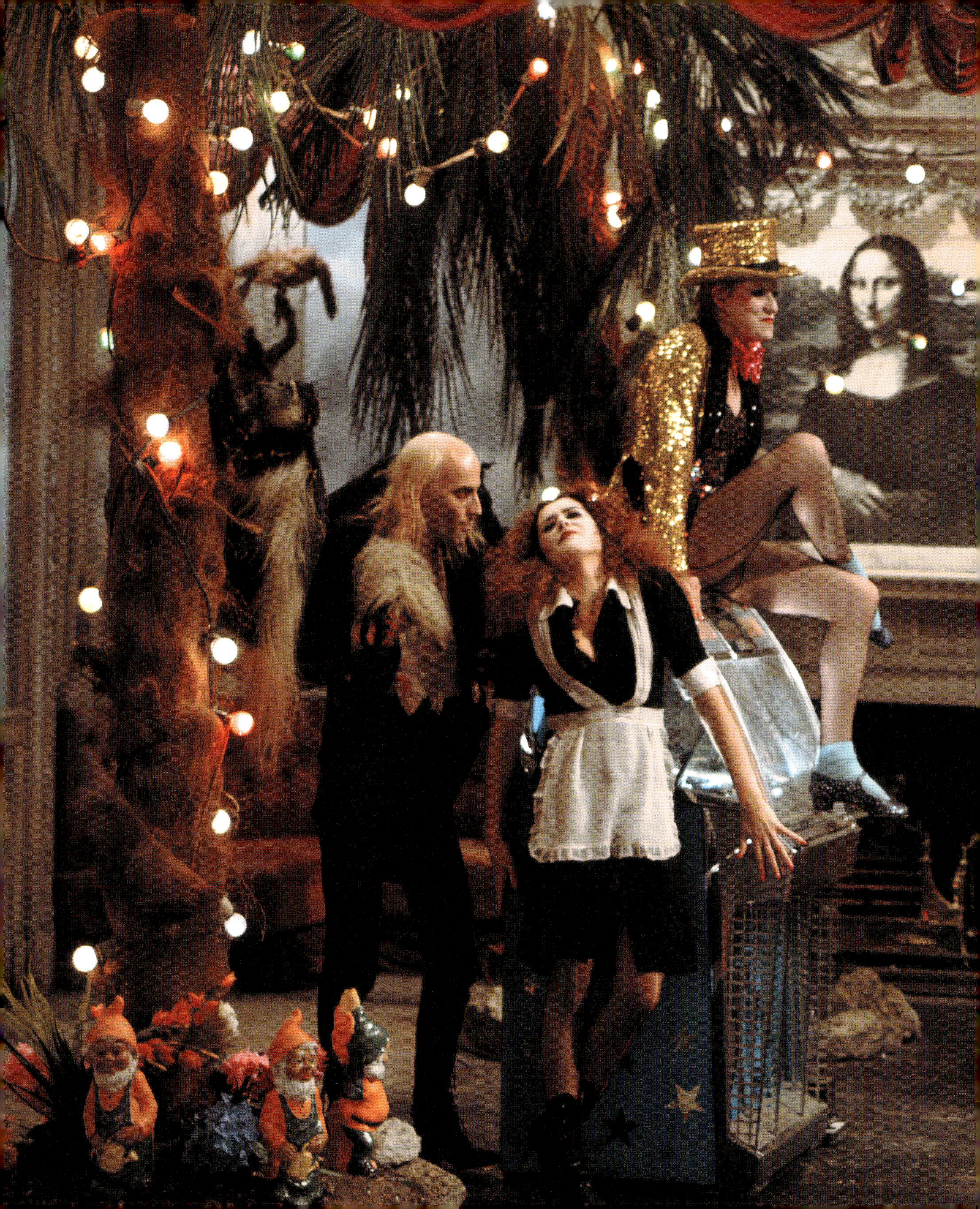

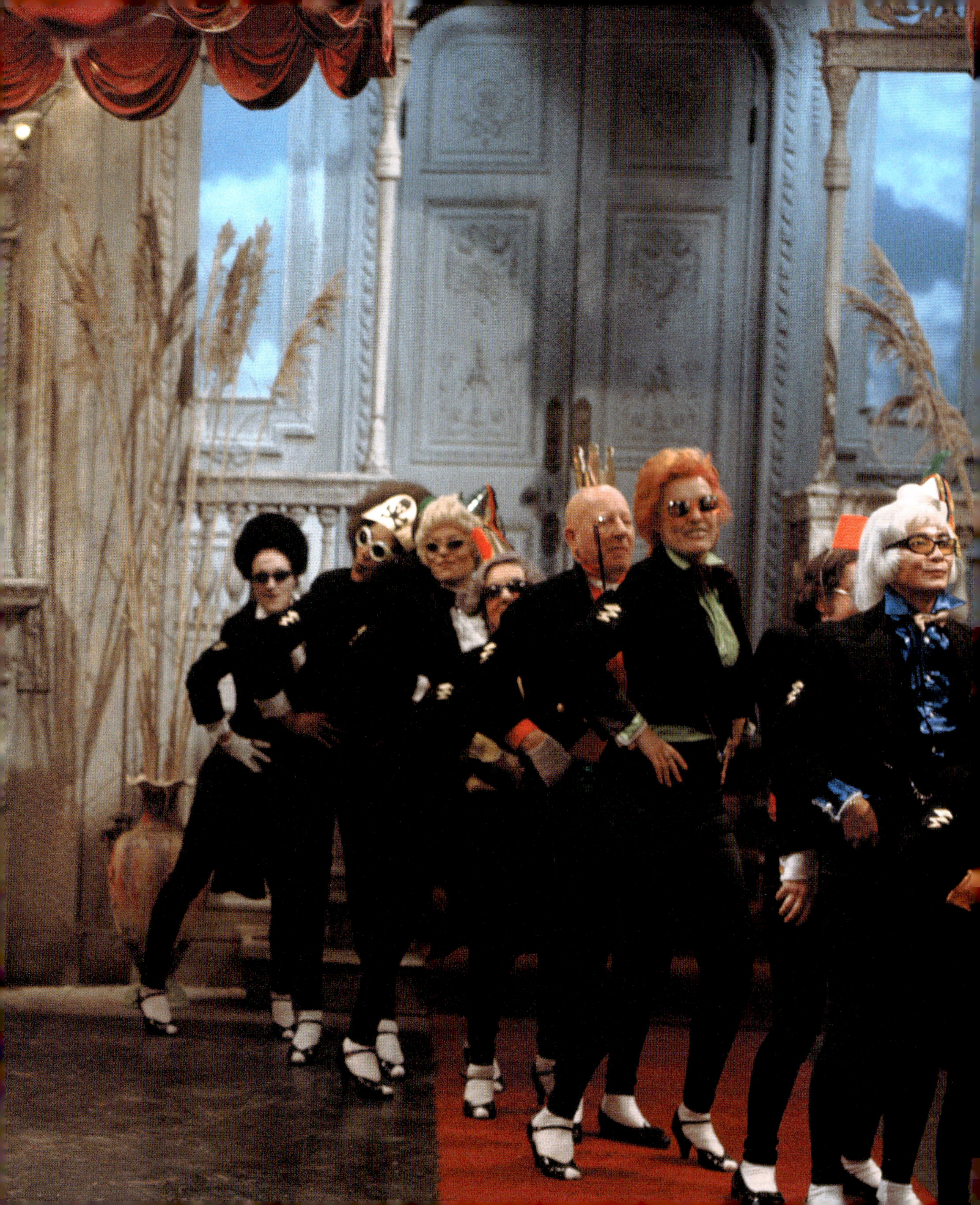

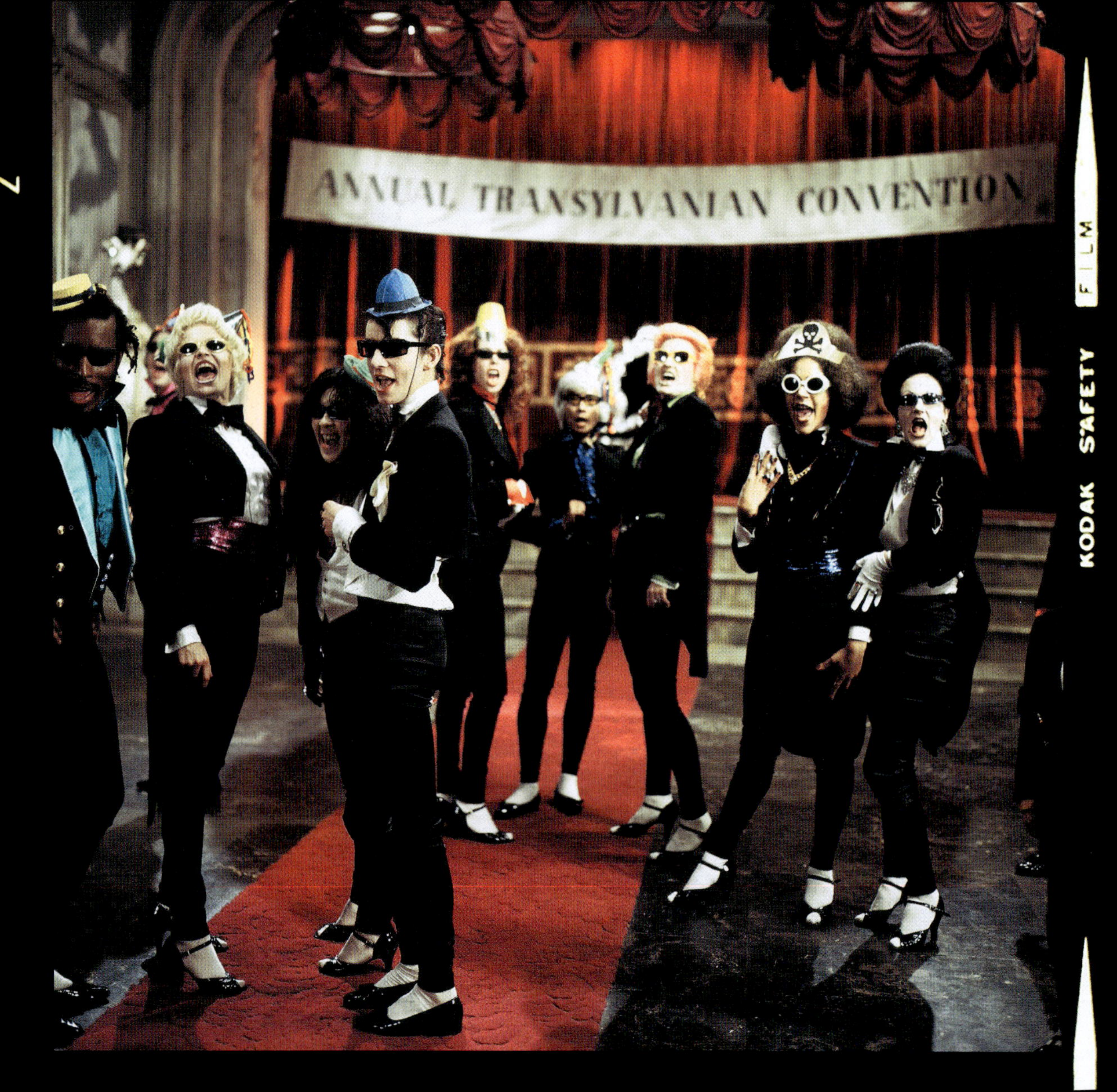

ANNUAL TRANSYLVANIAN CONVENTION
KODAK SAFETY FILM

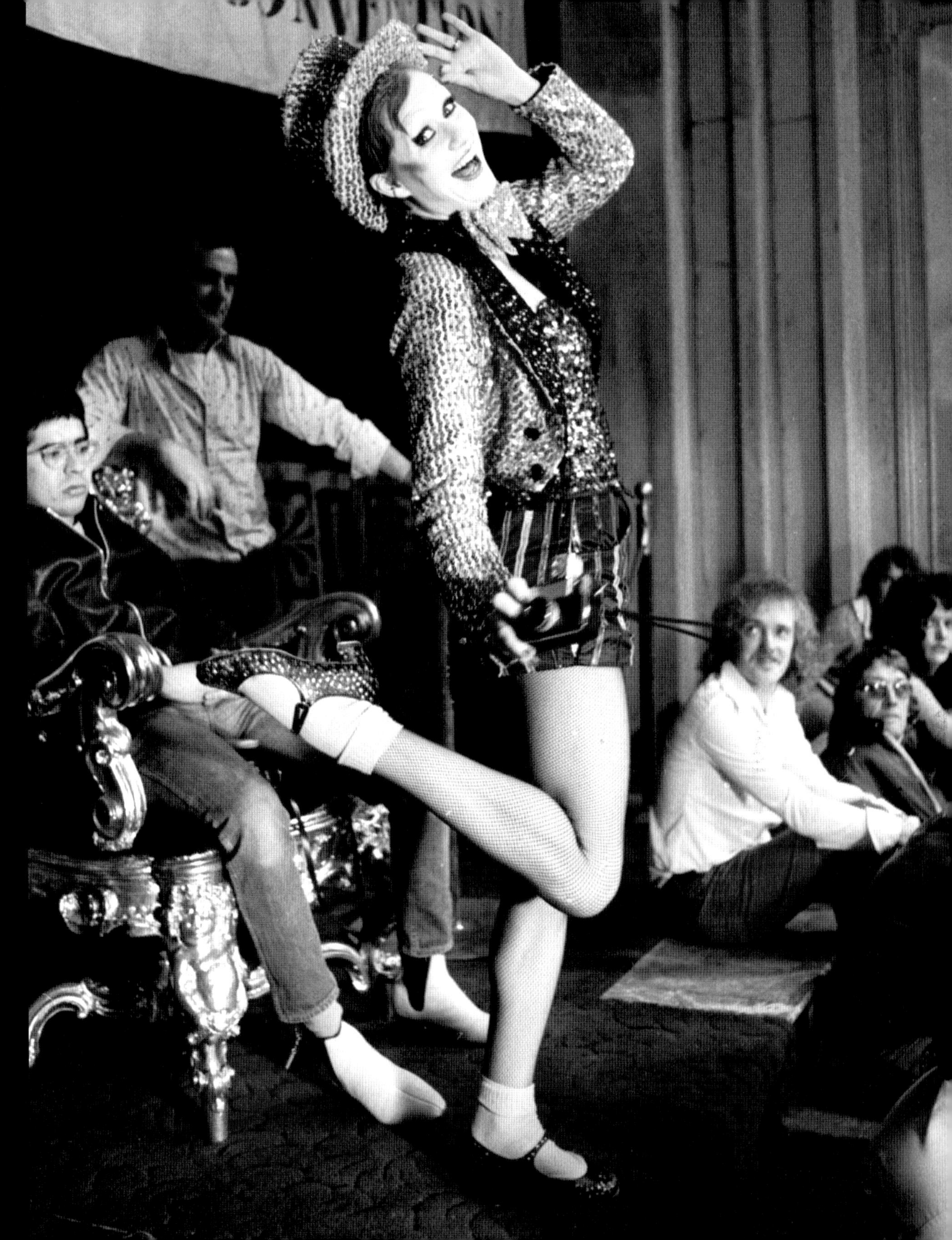

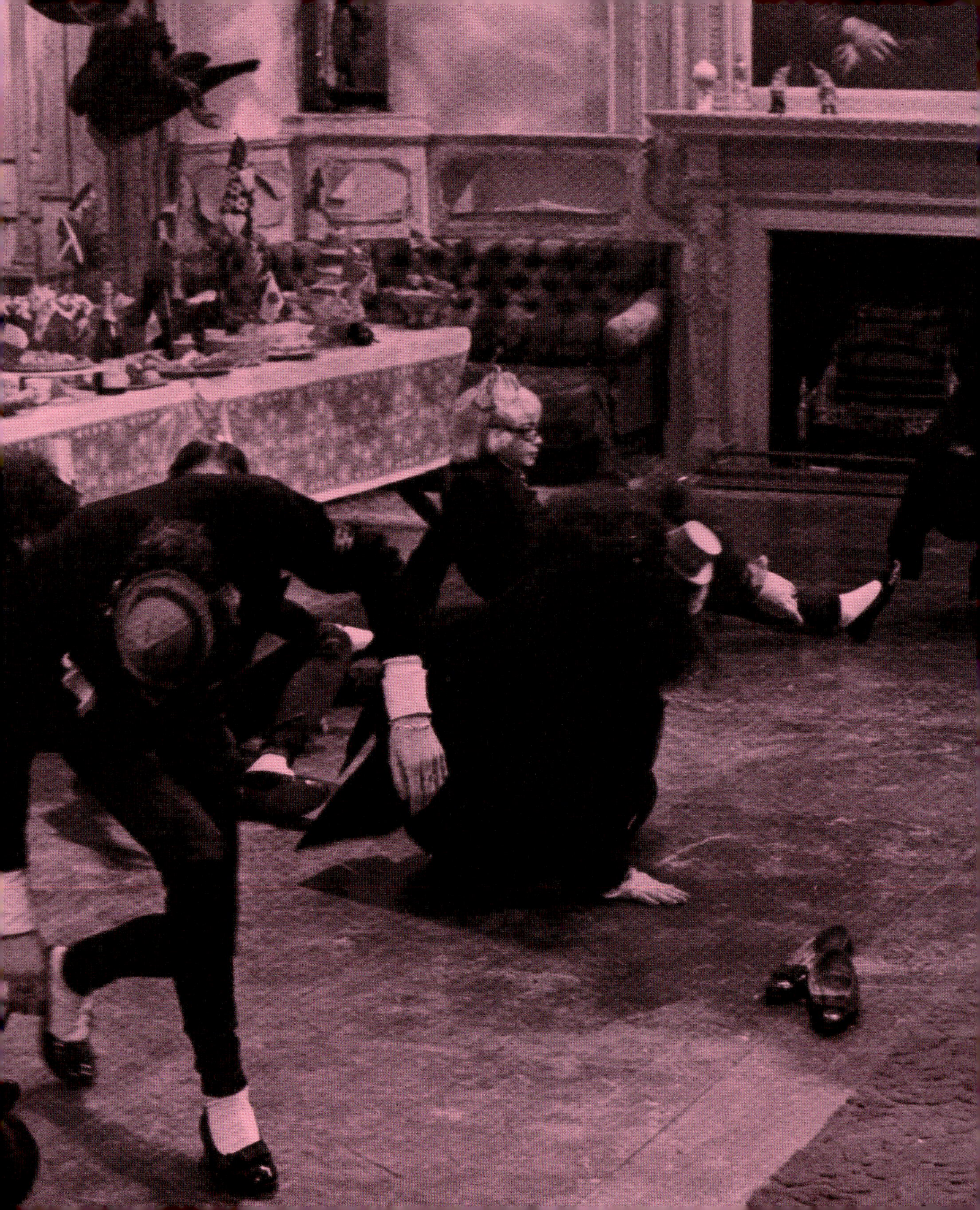

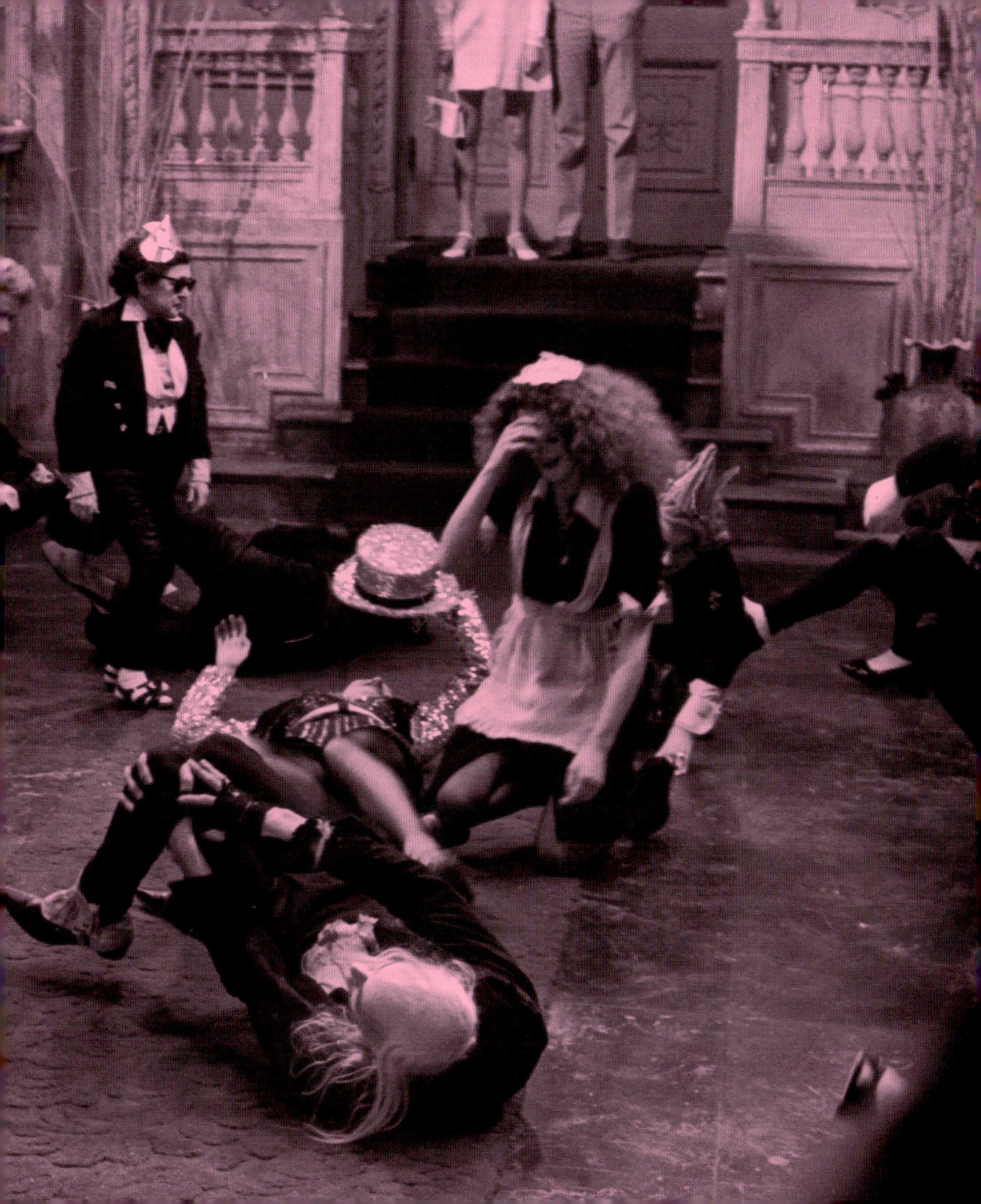

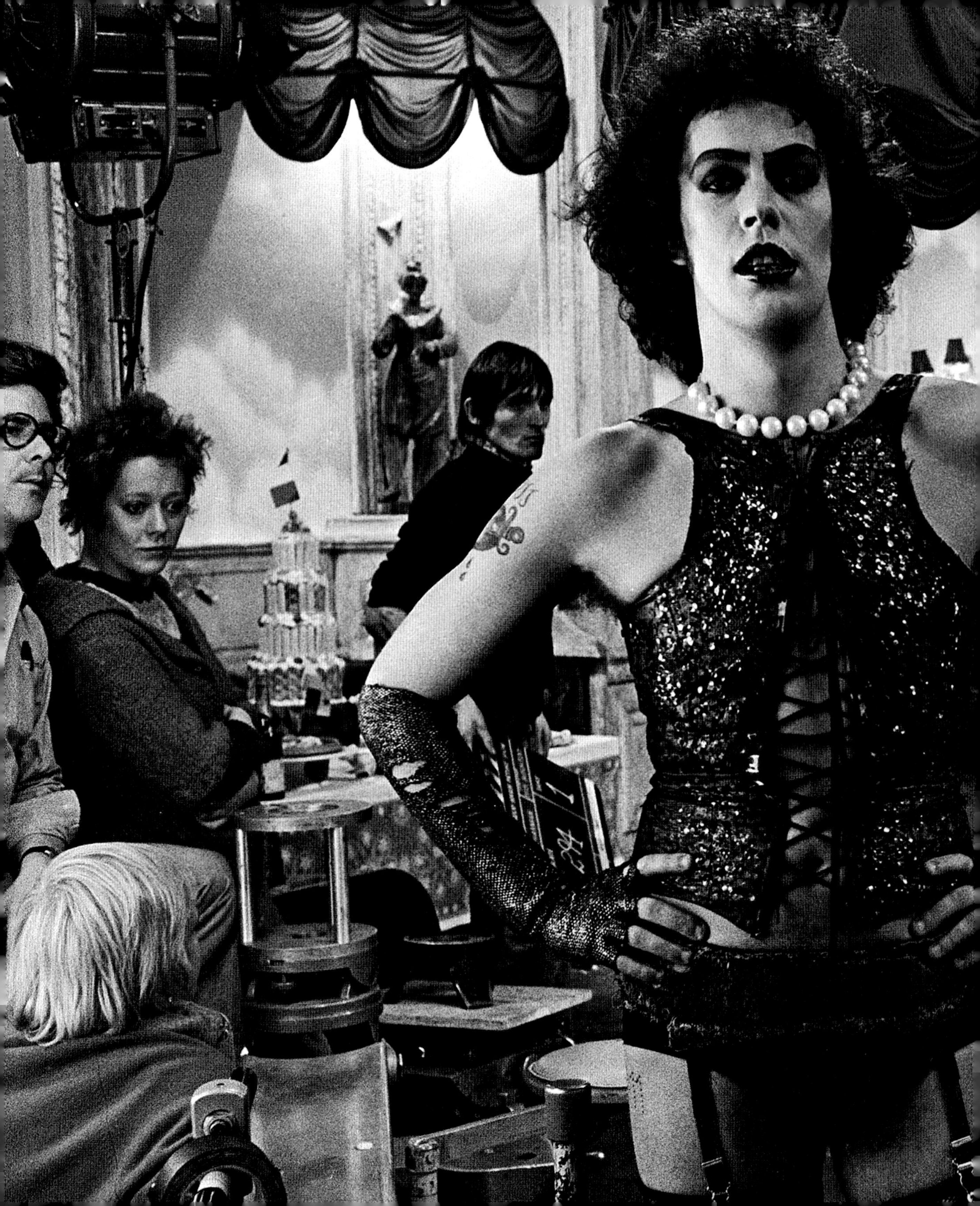

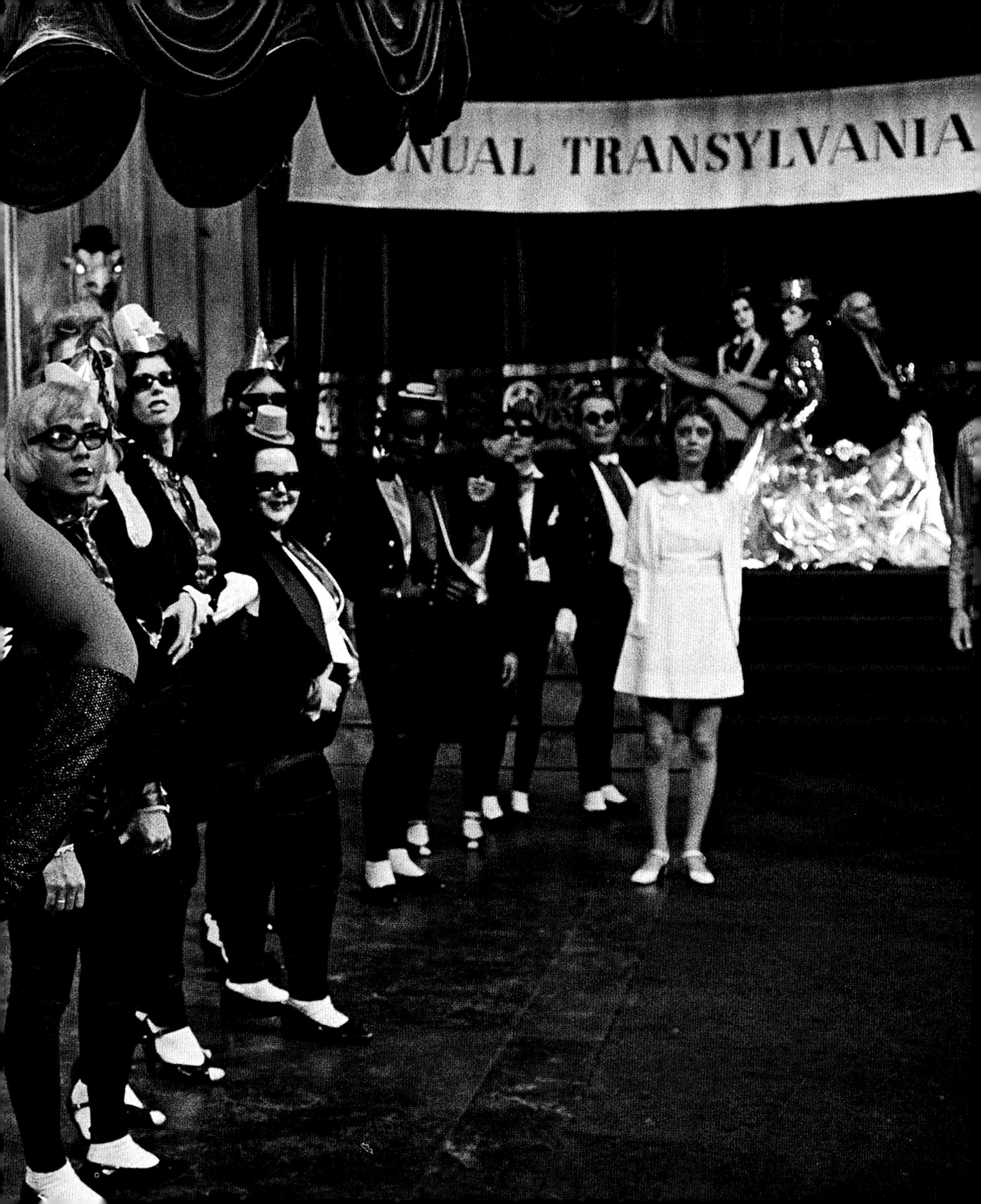

TRANSYLVANIA

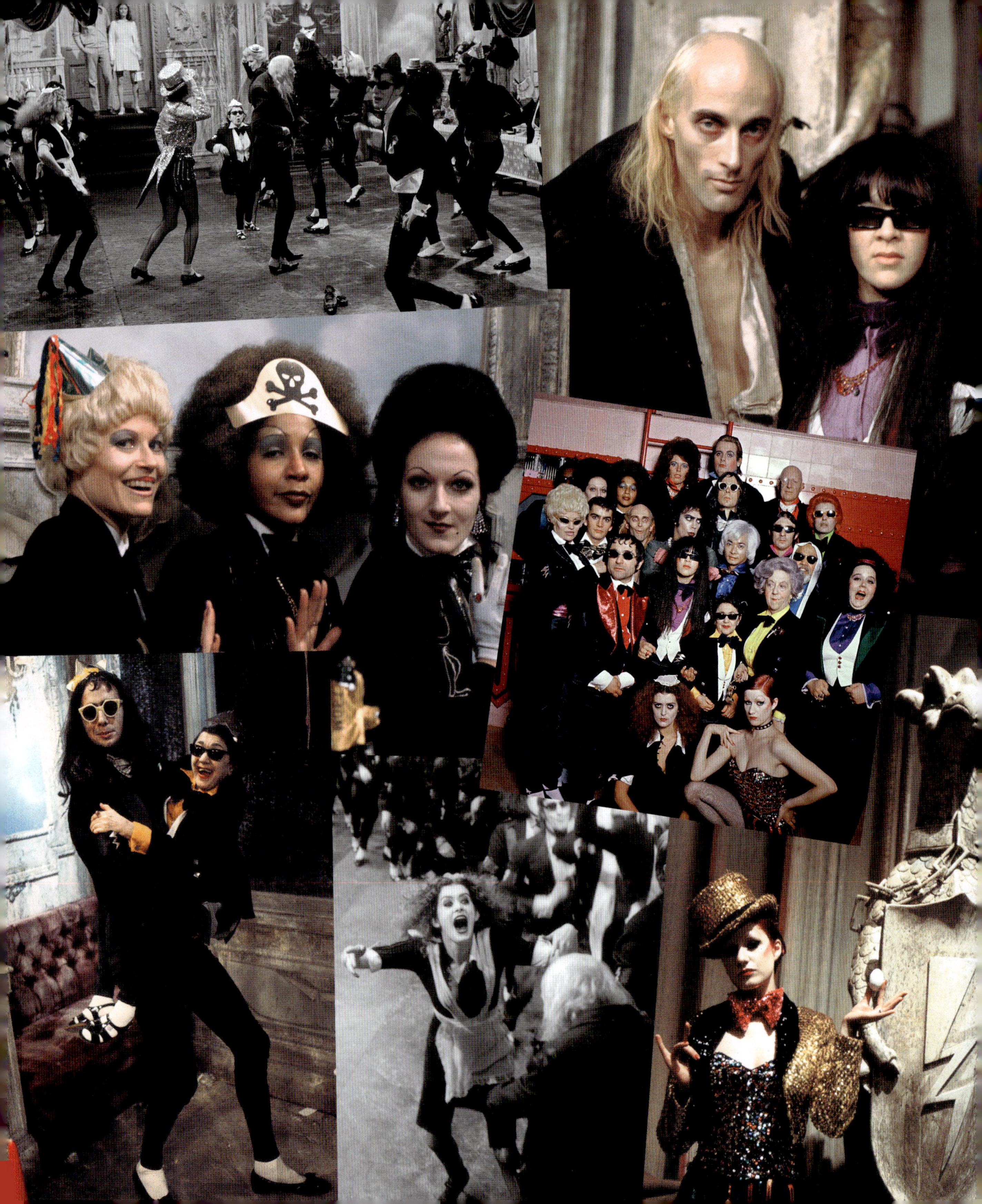

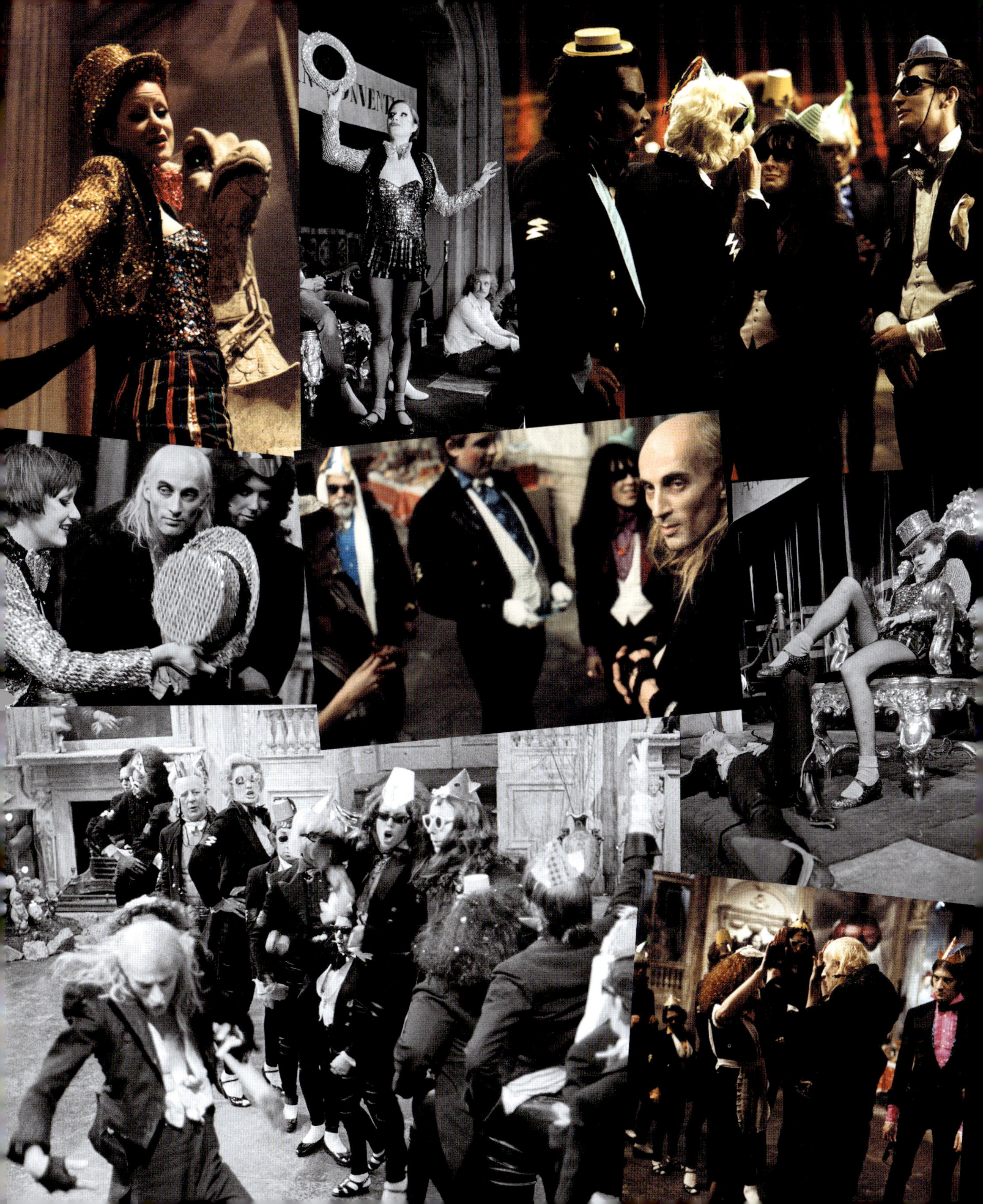

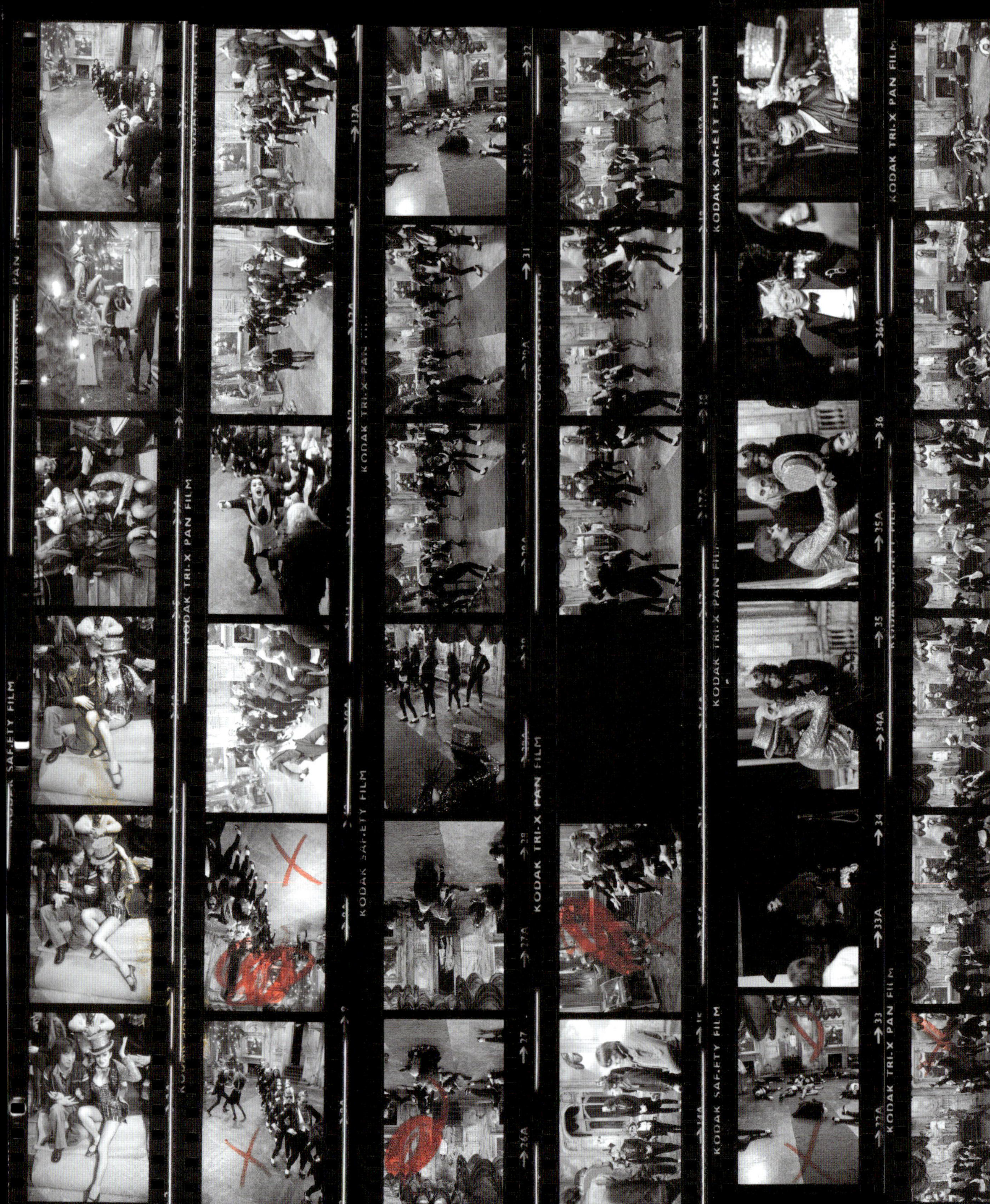

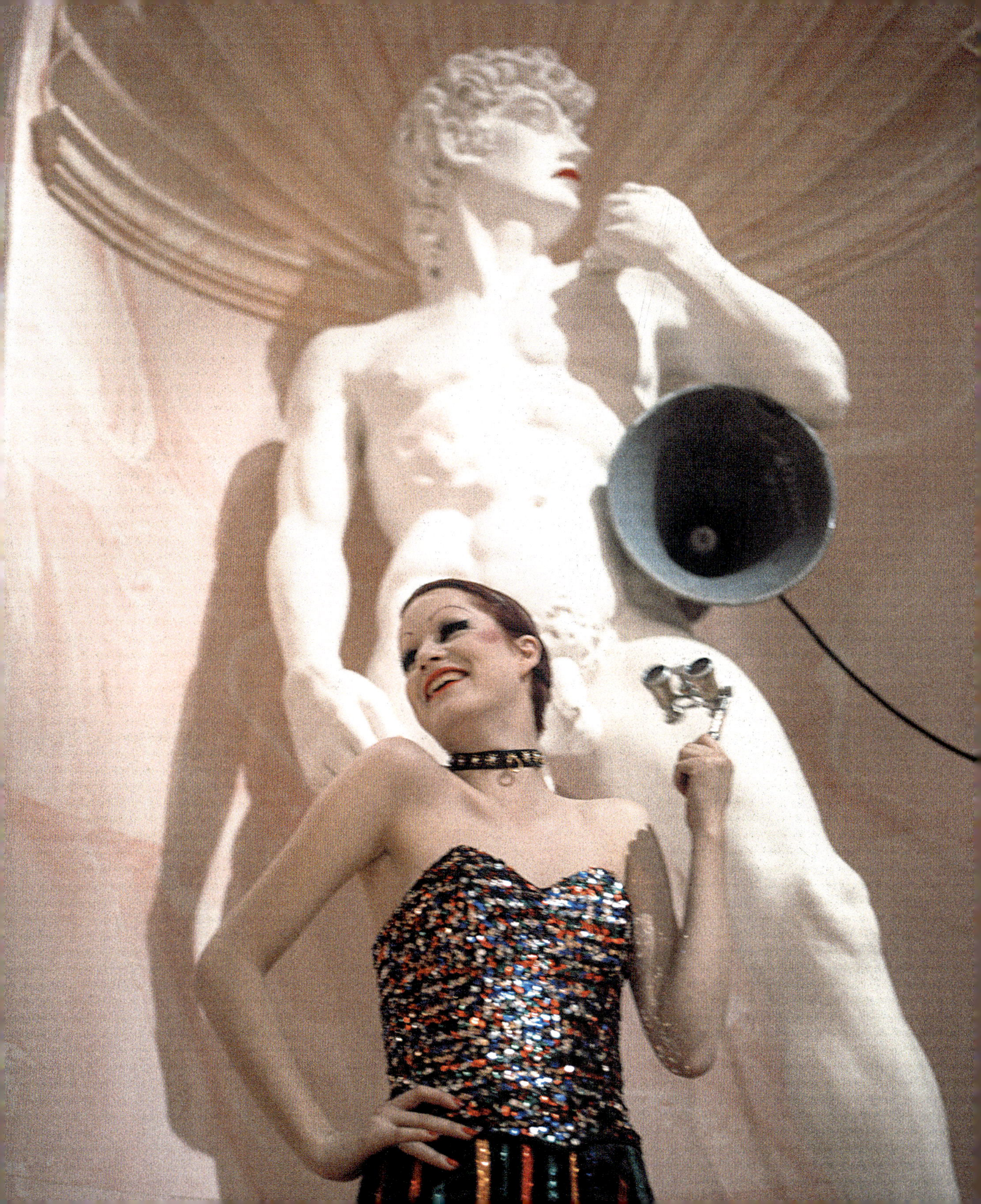

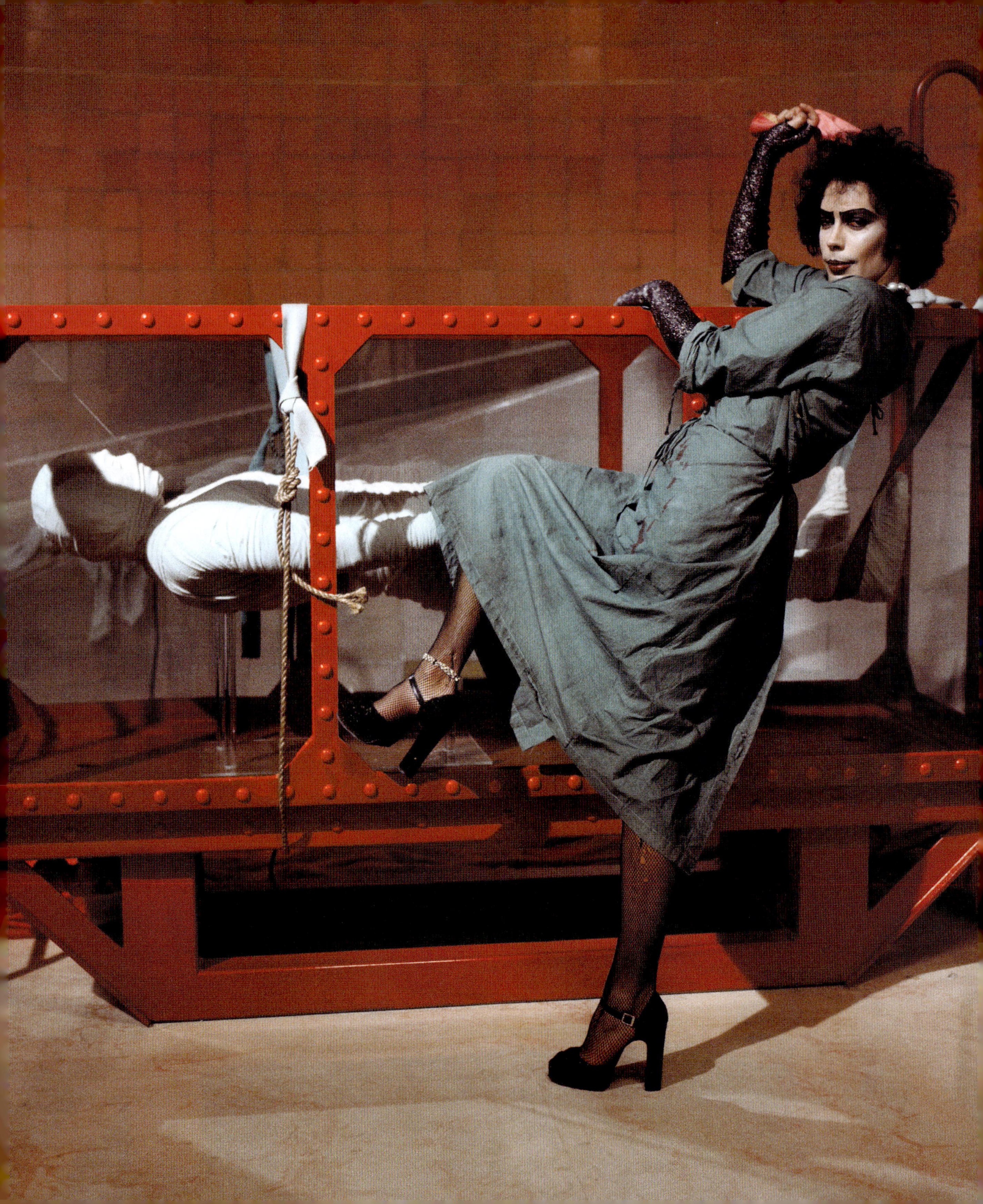

DIANNE BRILL, FASHION DESIGNER, MODEL, QUEEN OF THE NIGHT, AND ICONIC IT GIRL:

"I remember my confusion as a preteen, feeling a bit uncomfortable in my movie theater seat as I wasn't sure what I was seeing. Quickly I knew it was a place/music/style where I would fit in and maybe even be welcomed. Friendly, sexy, and inclusive, the *Rocky Horror* movement gave a lot of us sitting in our suburb bedrooms around the world a place to feel understood."

BILLY CORGAN, THE SMASHING PUMPKINS:

"Mick's photography made beautiful work of the lost people, the set asides, and those who'd never have been models or on the covers of magazines; except when presented as freaks and nothing more. Creating a tender equanimity where that has been none, and a new kind of power, by unleashing what has previously been hidden away and secreted."

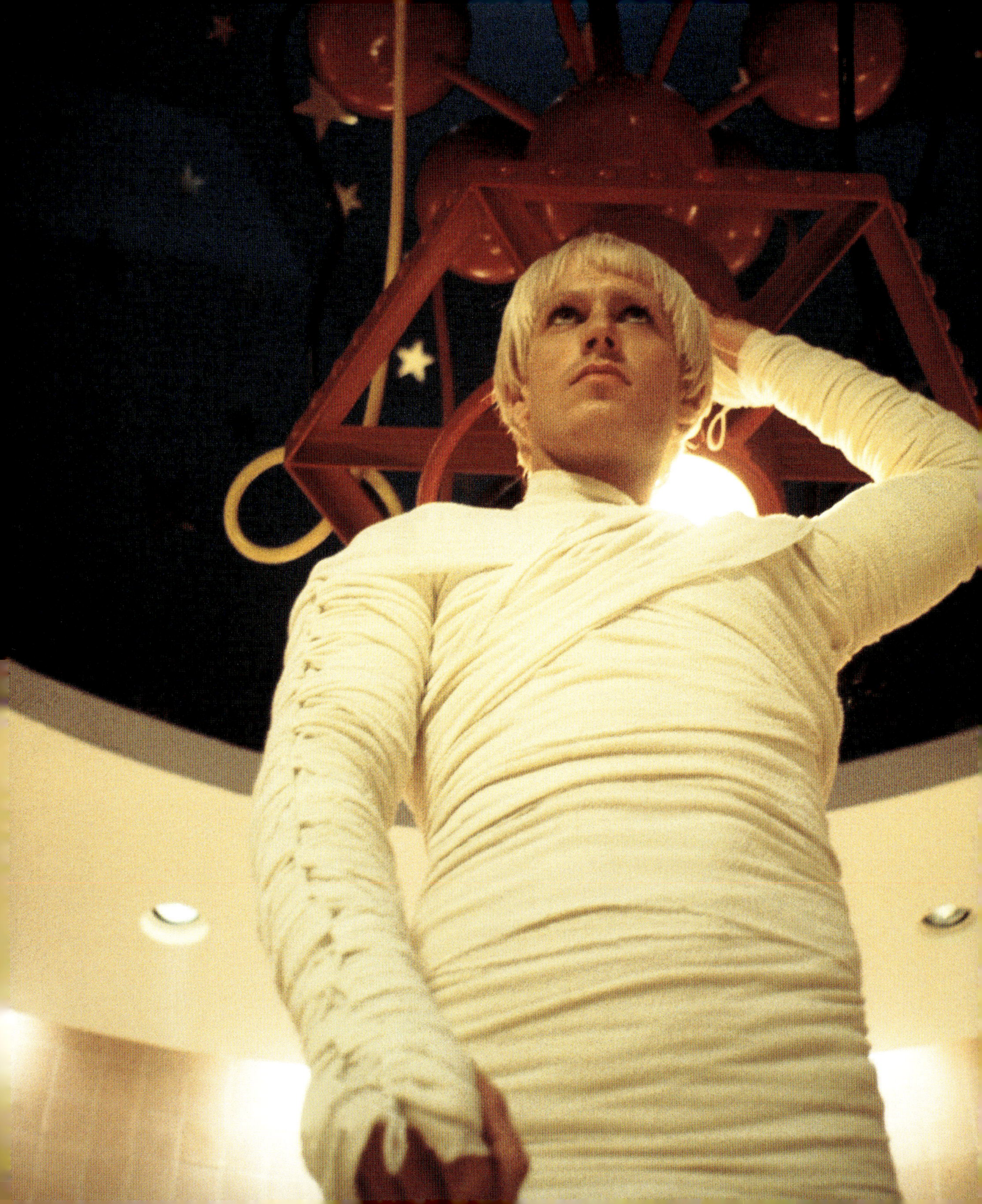

I CAN MAKE YOU A MAN: ROCKY

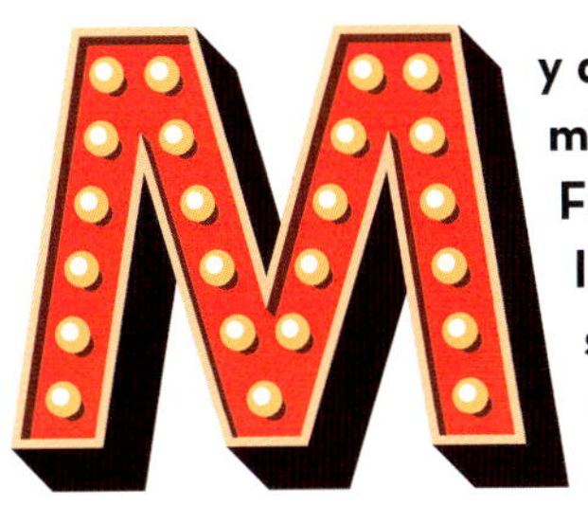

"My audition was miming Bryan Ferry's song 'The In Crowd' and subsequently I landed the challenge of playing Rocky," Peter Hinwood recalled in an exclusive interview in 2024. "As for the underground spirit of the moment, I was engulfed in it anyway, flower power, LSD—Chelsea was buzzing at that time."

Hinwood had loved *Rocky Horror* on stage—"the original live show was completely wonderful"—but he was surprised to be offered a role in the film adaptation. "I wasn't an actor. My face had been seen in the odd fashion shoot and occasionally, I had to strip off for swimwear. But the idea [of having me] play Rocky in the film seemed ridiculous. Having the right look doesn't necessarily mean you have self-confidence. But Richard O'Brien and Jim Sharman picked me up in a car every morning, and Jim patiently guided me through it. It was a new experience, but rather than feeling excitement, it was just a challenge—I didn't want to let everyone down. When shooting was completed, I had no idea how satisfactory my performance had been. As soon as it was over, I was ready to escape from that world. When the movie was released, I had moved on, even avoided viewing it."

After his role in the movie, Hinwood quit acting, preferring to lead a life out of the public eye. That changed—to an extent—decades later when he first appeared at a *Rocky Horror* convention. "I was amazed by

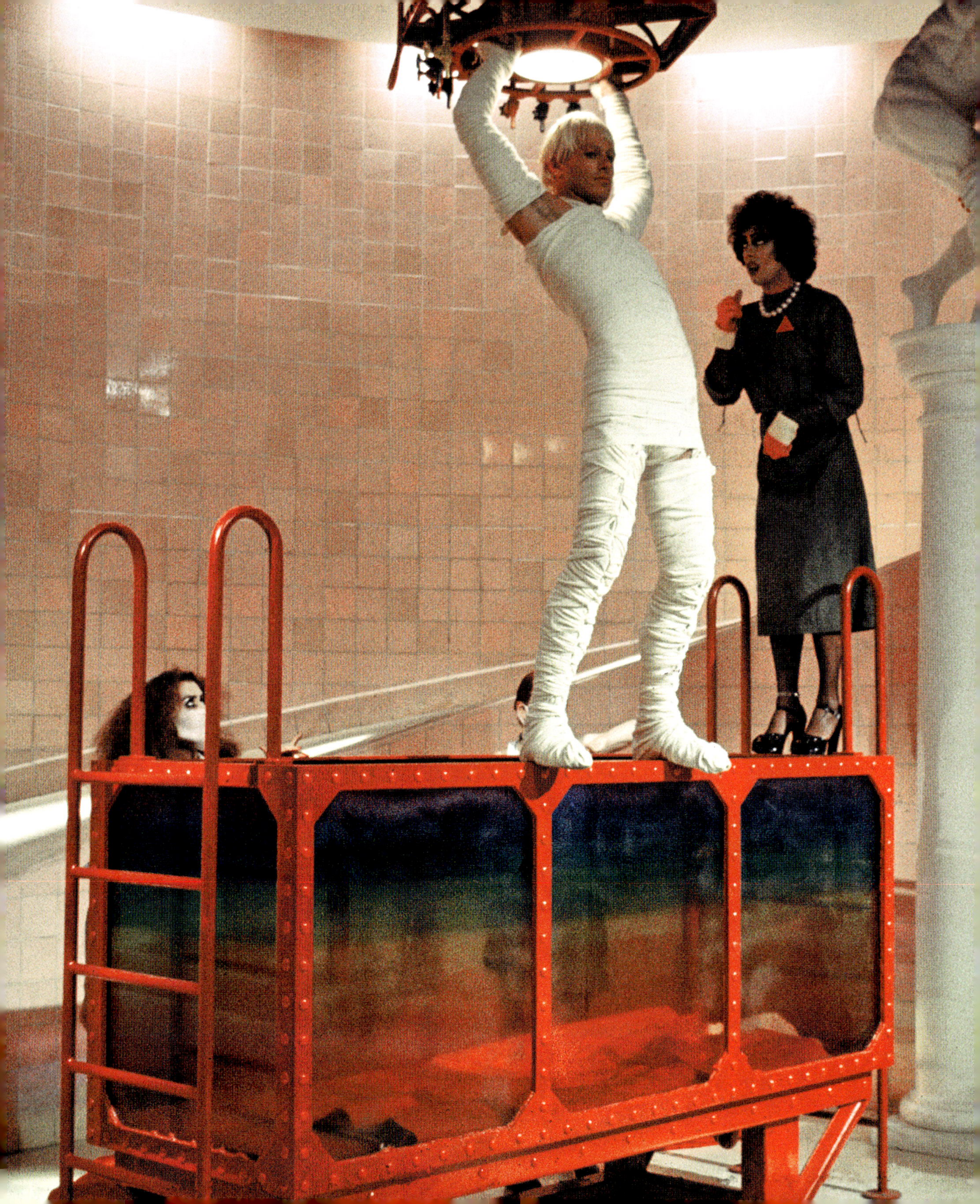

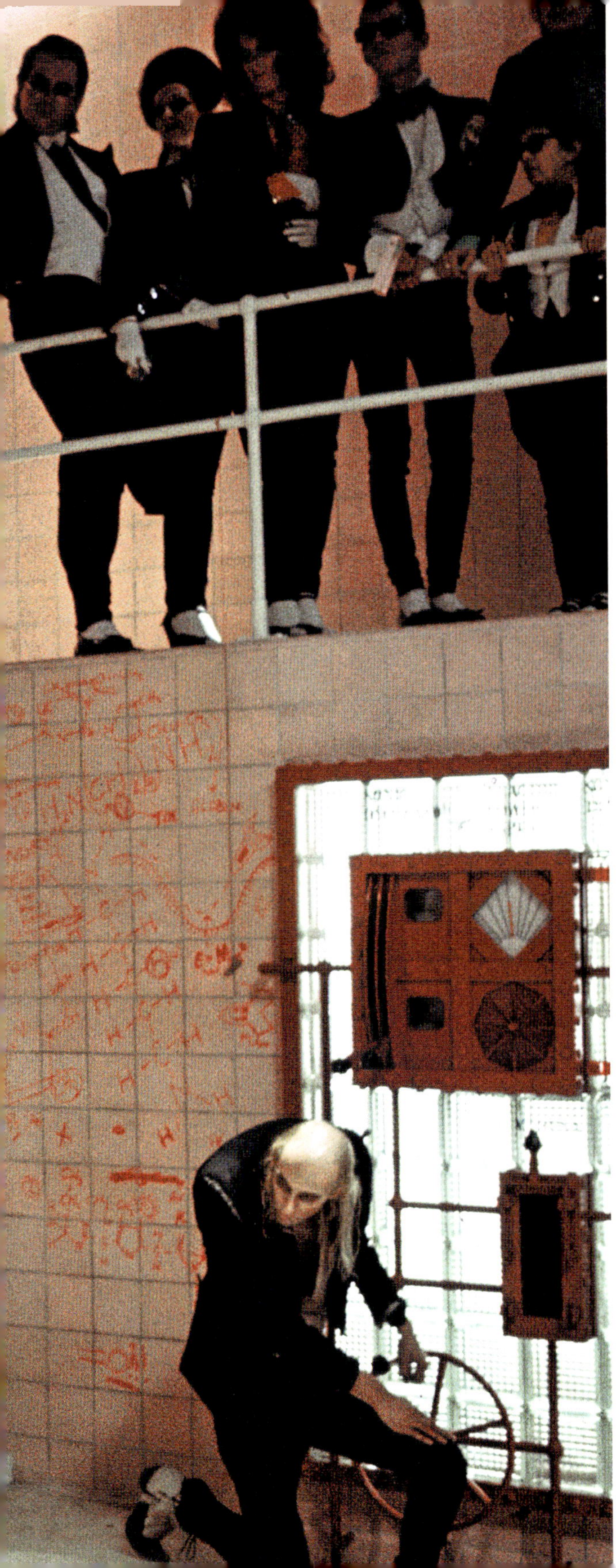

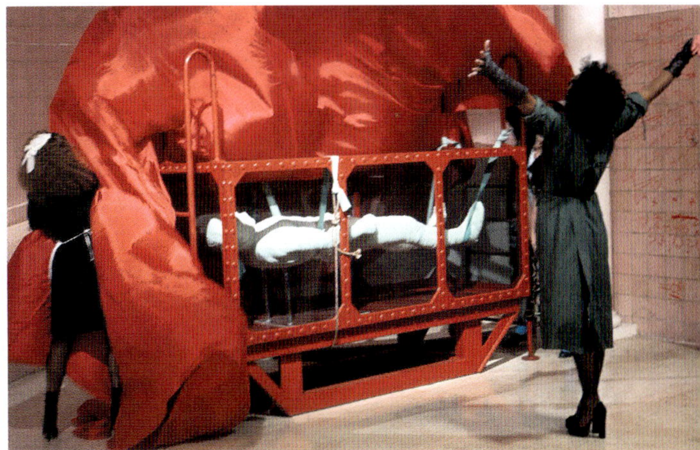

the attention it generated, with queues of fans wanting autographs and selfies, and the whole experience left me feeling that I had contributed to something important. I realized I had to embrace this moment from my past."

Mick Rock knew Hinwood before *Rocky Horror*. "Amanda Lear, a deep-throated and socially decorative blonde persona who was best known at the time for appearing on the second Roxy Music album cover with a black panther and for her sexual liaisons with top rockers such as Brian Jones and David Bowie, first introduced us. Peter was, of course, stunningly handsome and had been at one time a successful model before starting a successful antiques business. He had never been in front of a movie camera in his life and was quite tentative and inhibited in his movements. This inexperience and his lack of necessity to deliver a single line of dialogue, combined with his physical beauty, turned out to be a stroke of casting genius for his role as Frank's love monster creation."

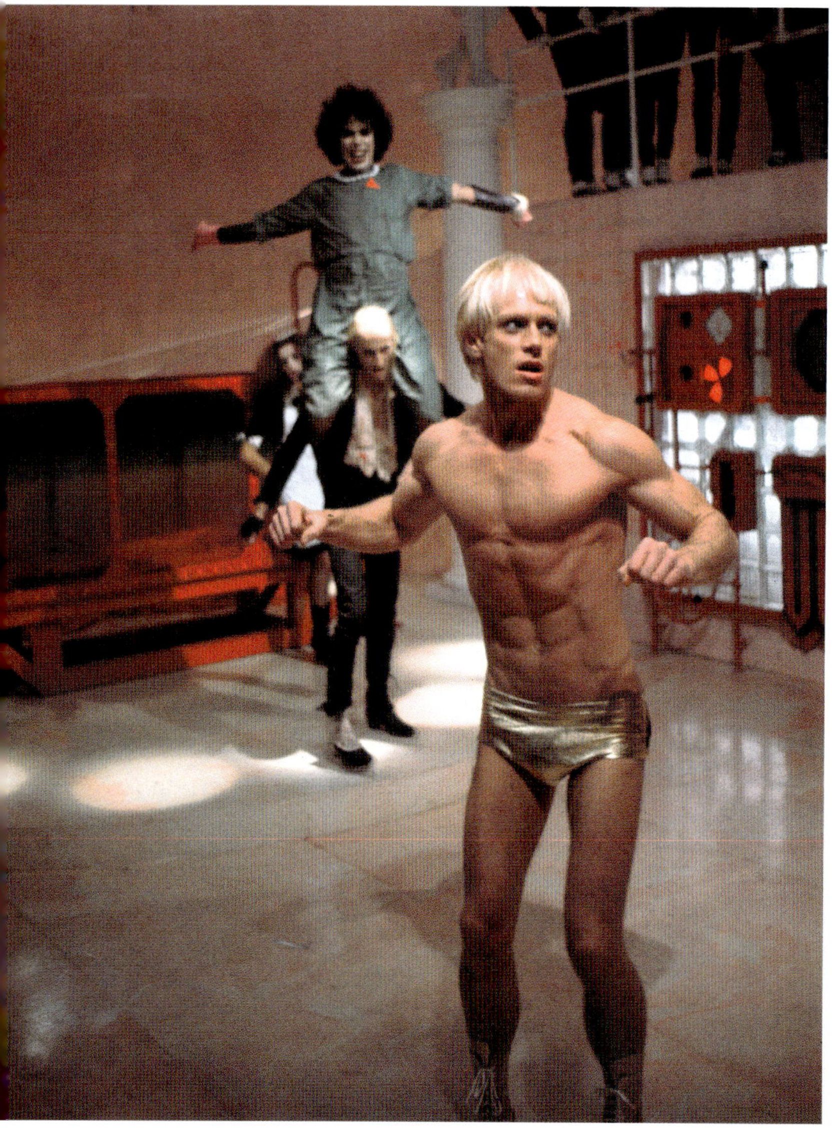

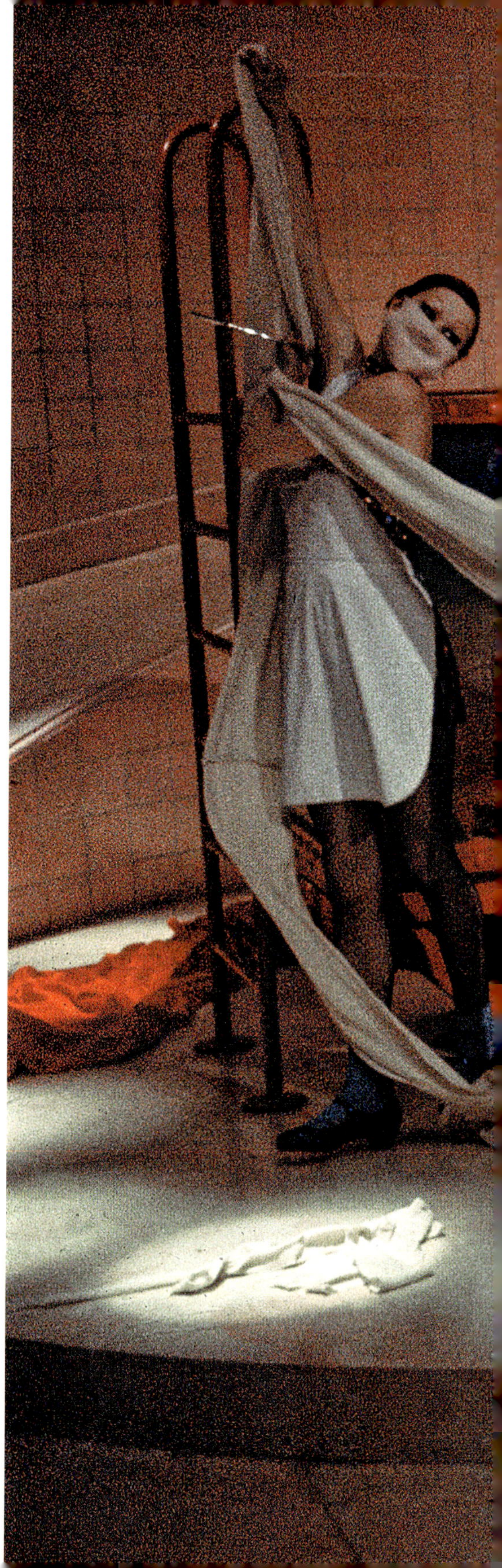

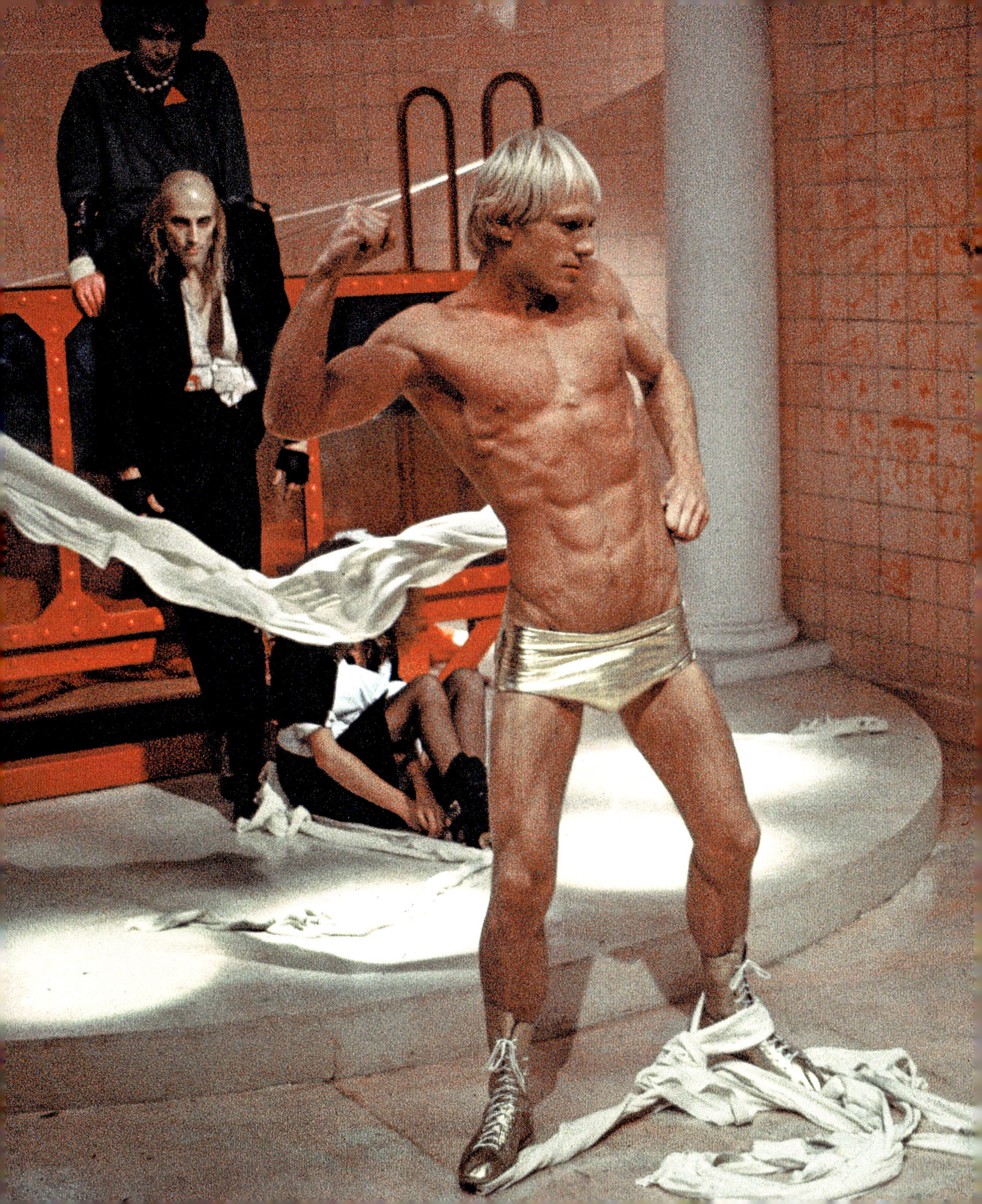

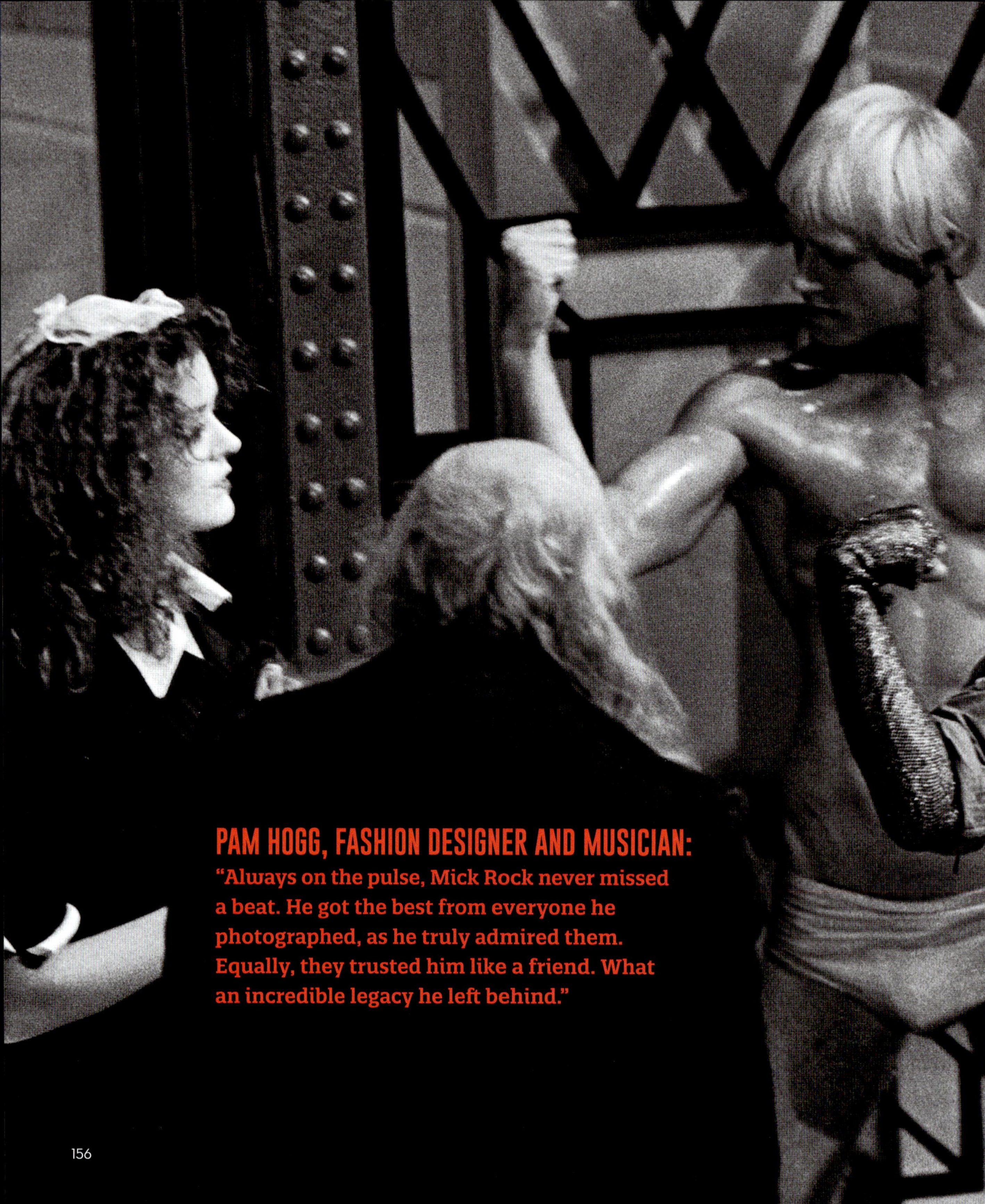

PAM HOGG, FASHION DESIGNER AND MUSICIAN:

"Always on the pulse, Mick Rock never missed a beat. He got the best from everyone he photographed, as he truly admired them. Equally, they trusted him like a friend. What an incredible legacy he left behind."

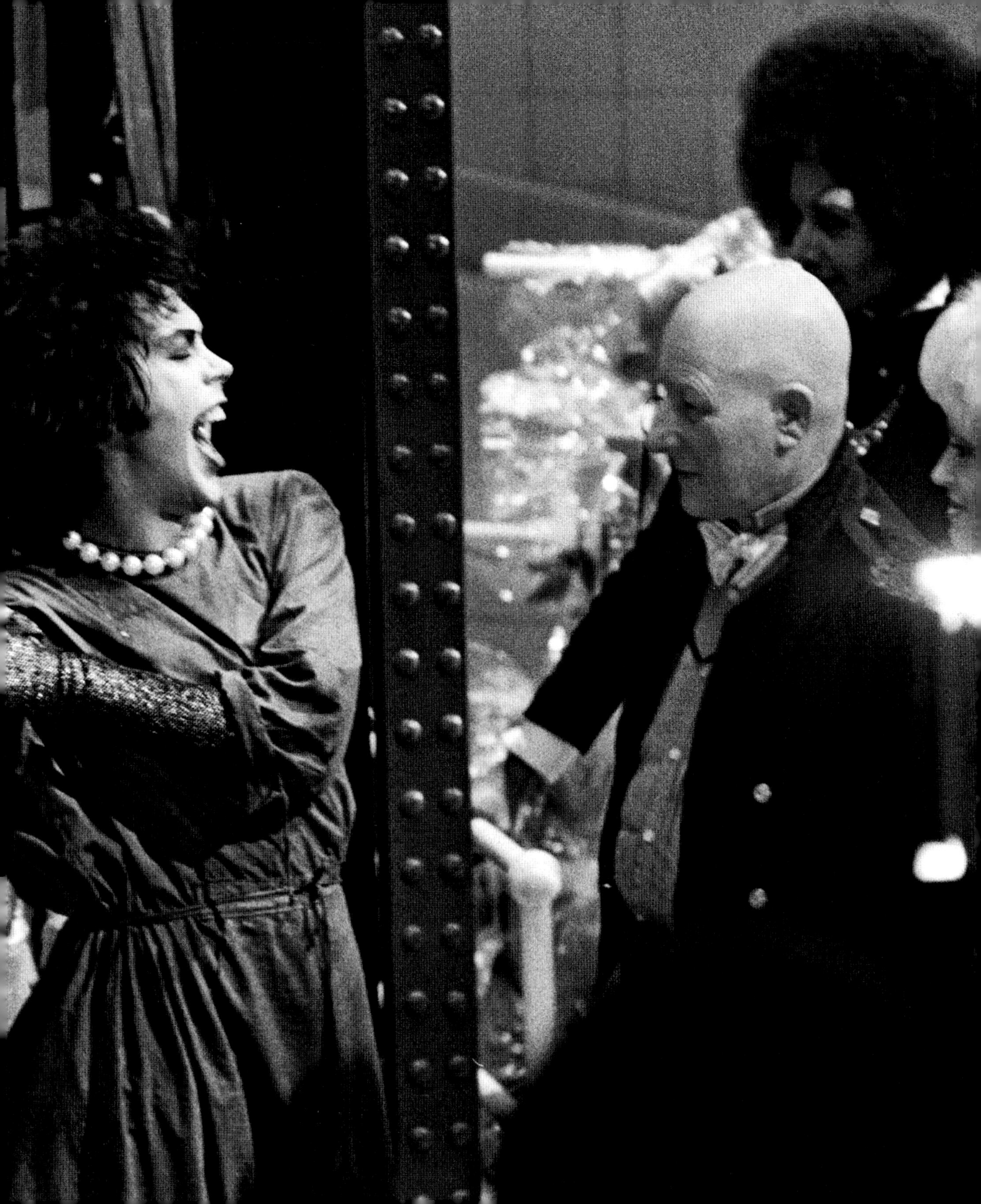

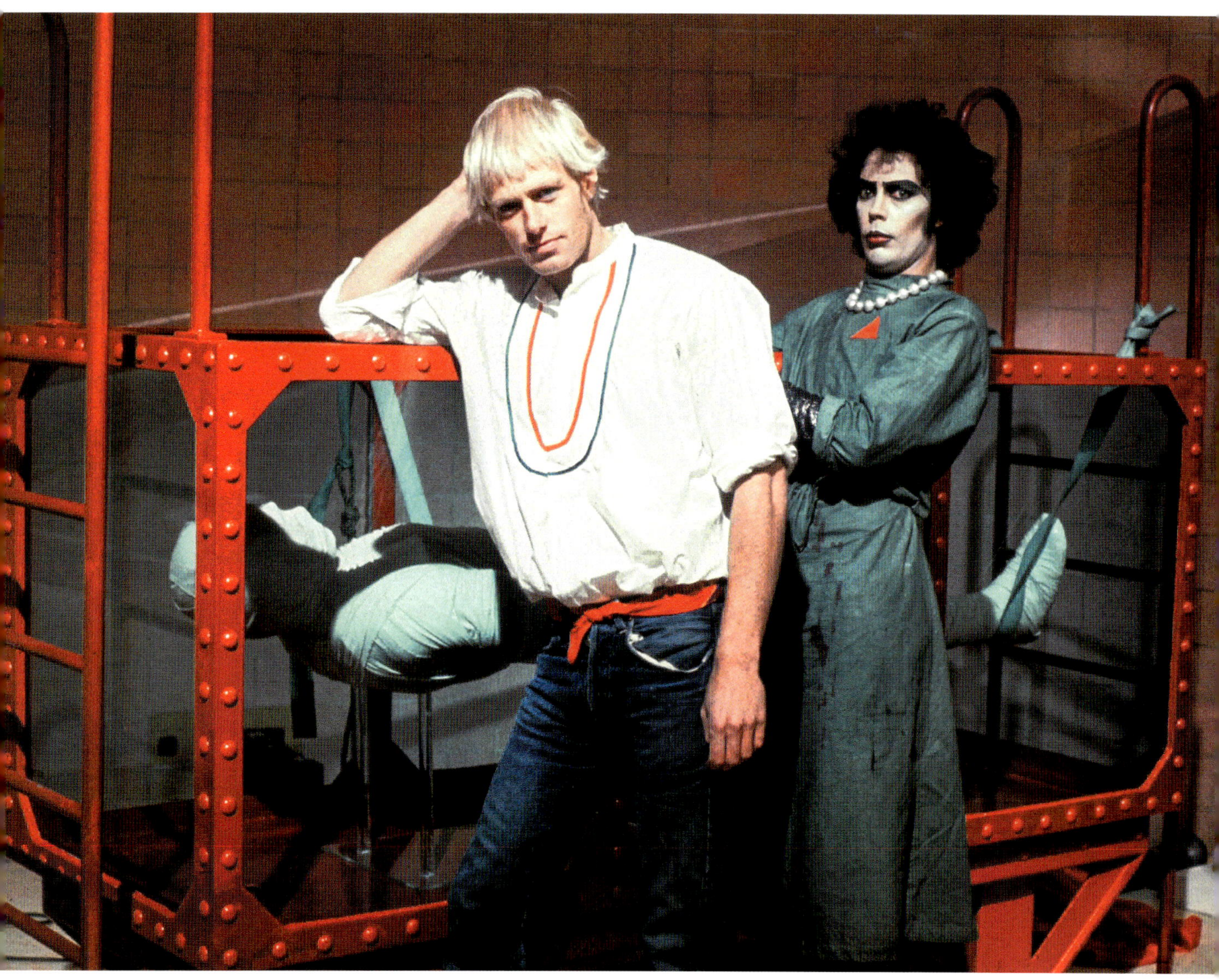

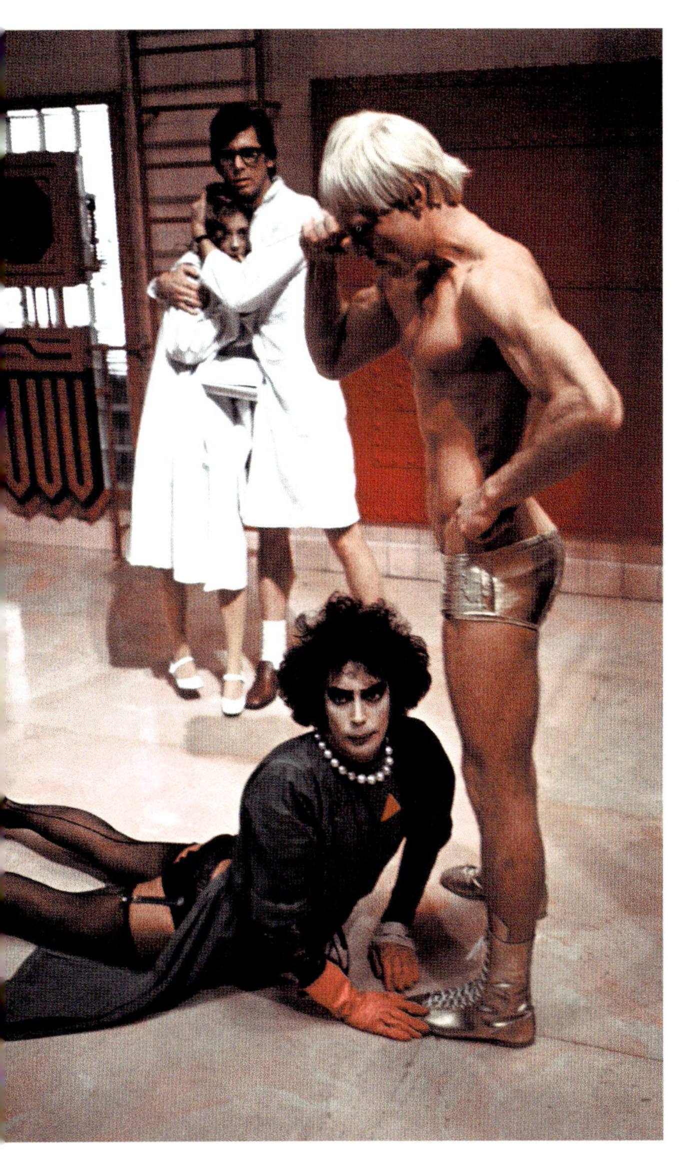

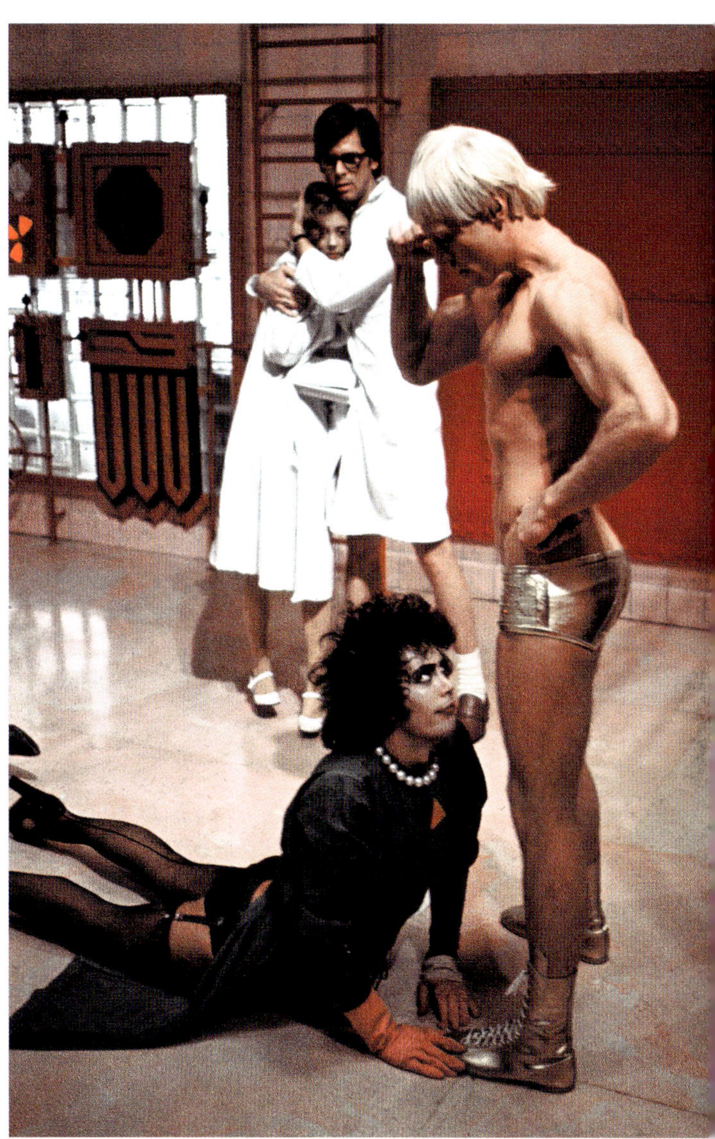

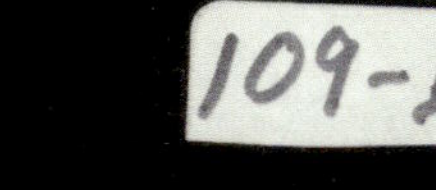
109-D

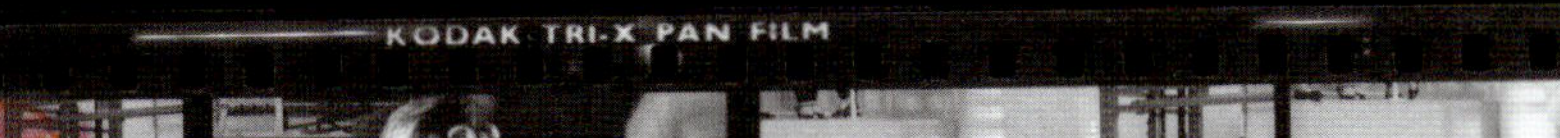

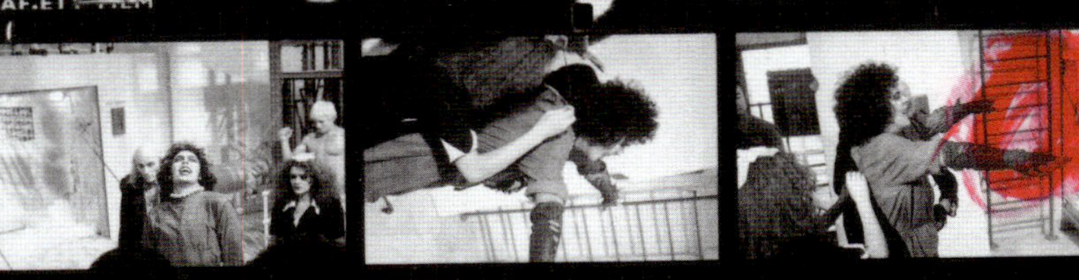

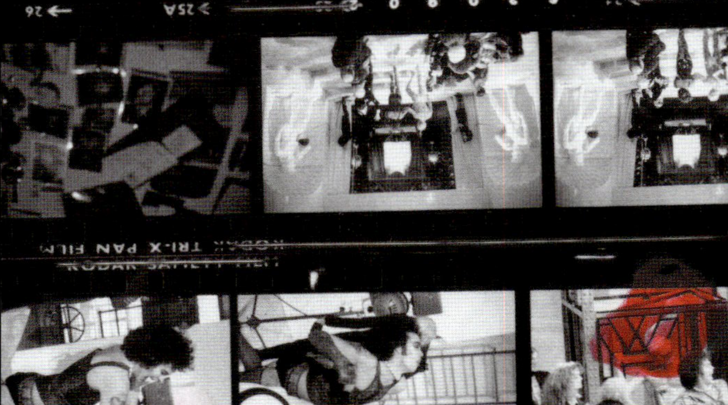

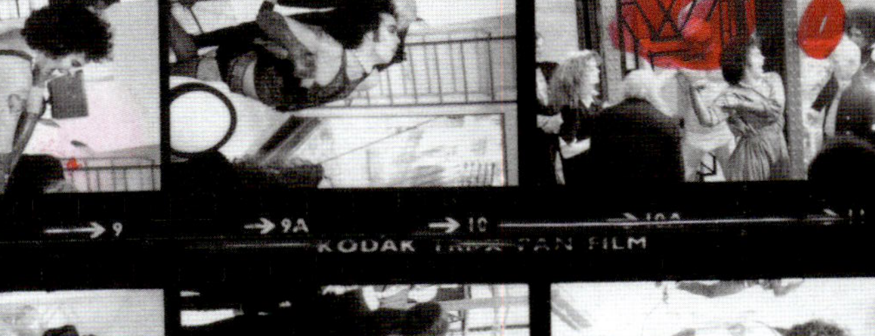

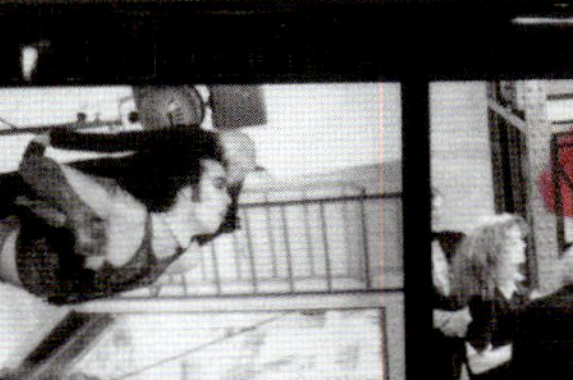

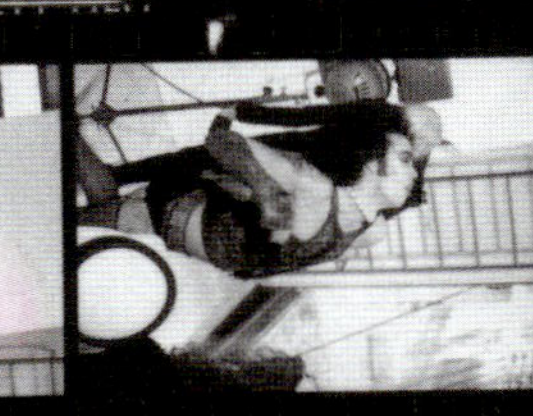

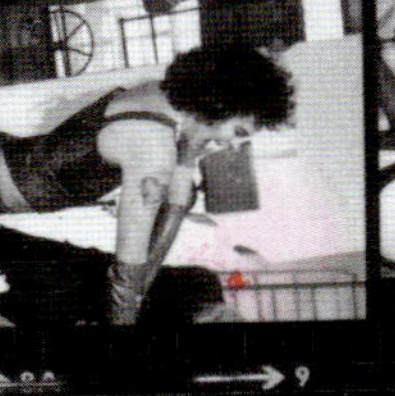

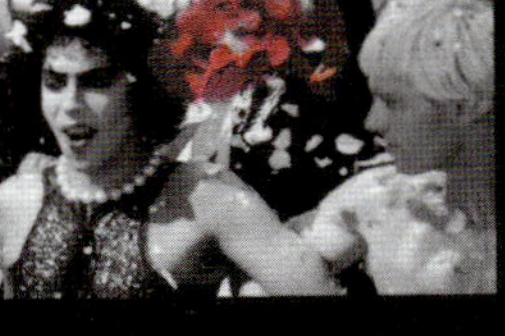

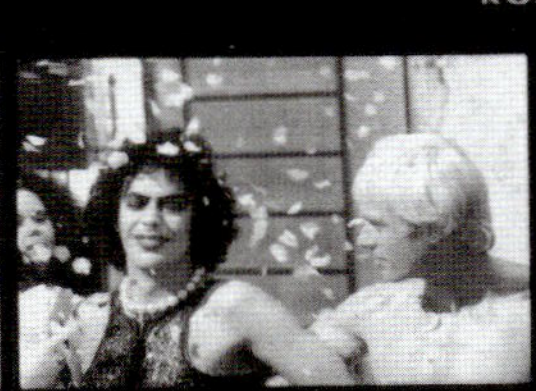

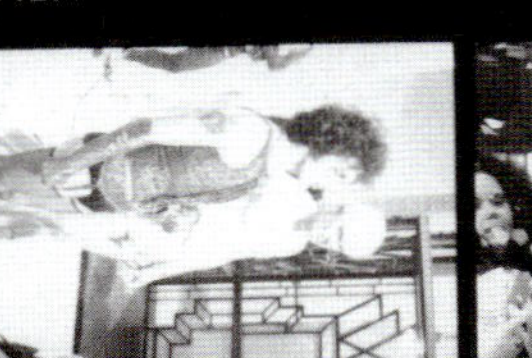

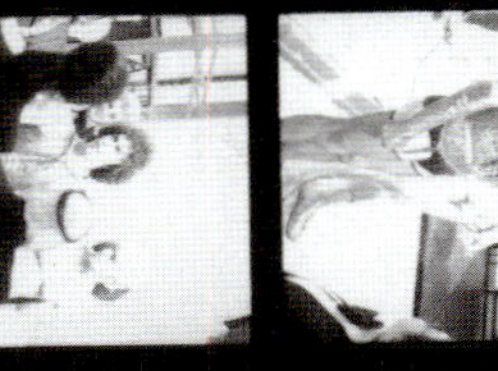

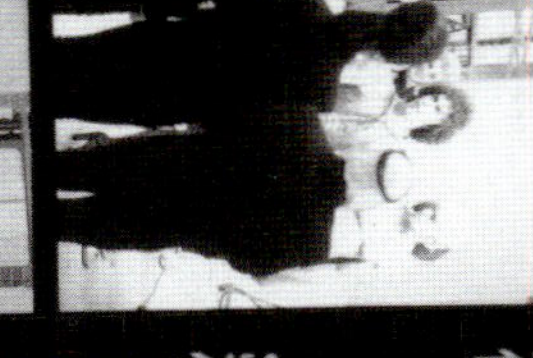

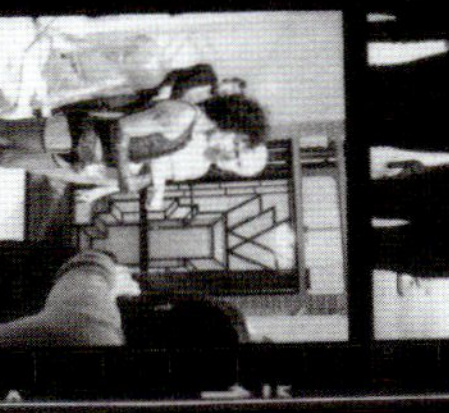

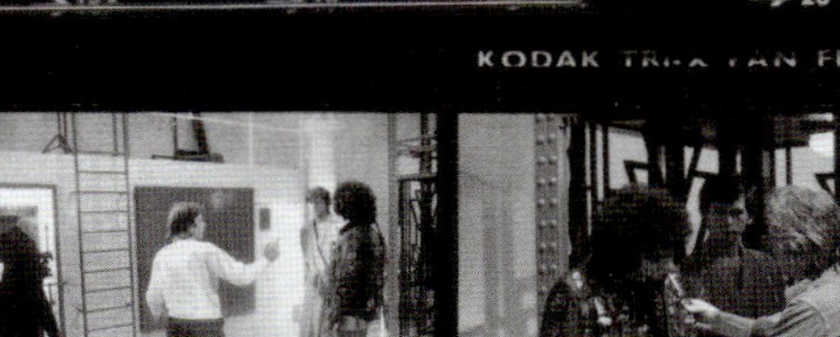

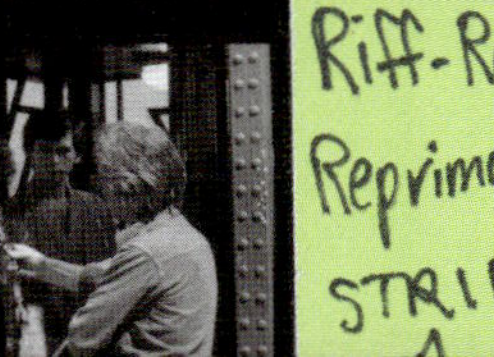
Riff-Raff
Reprimand
STRIP

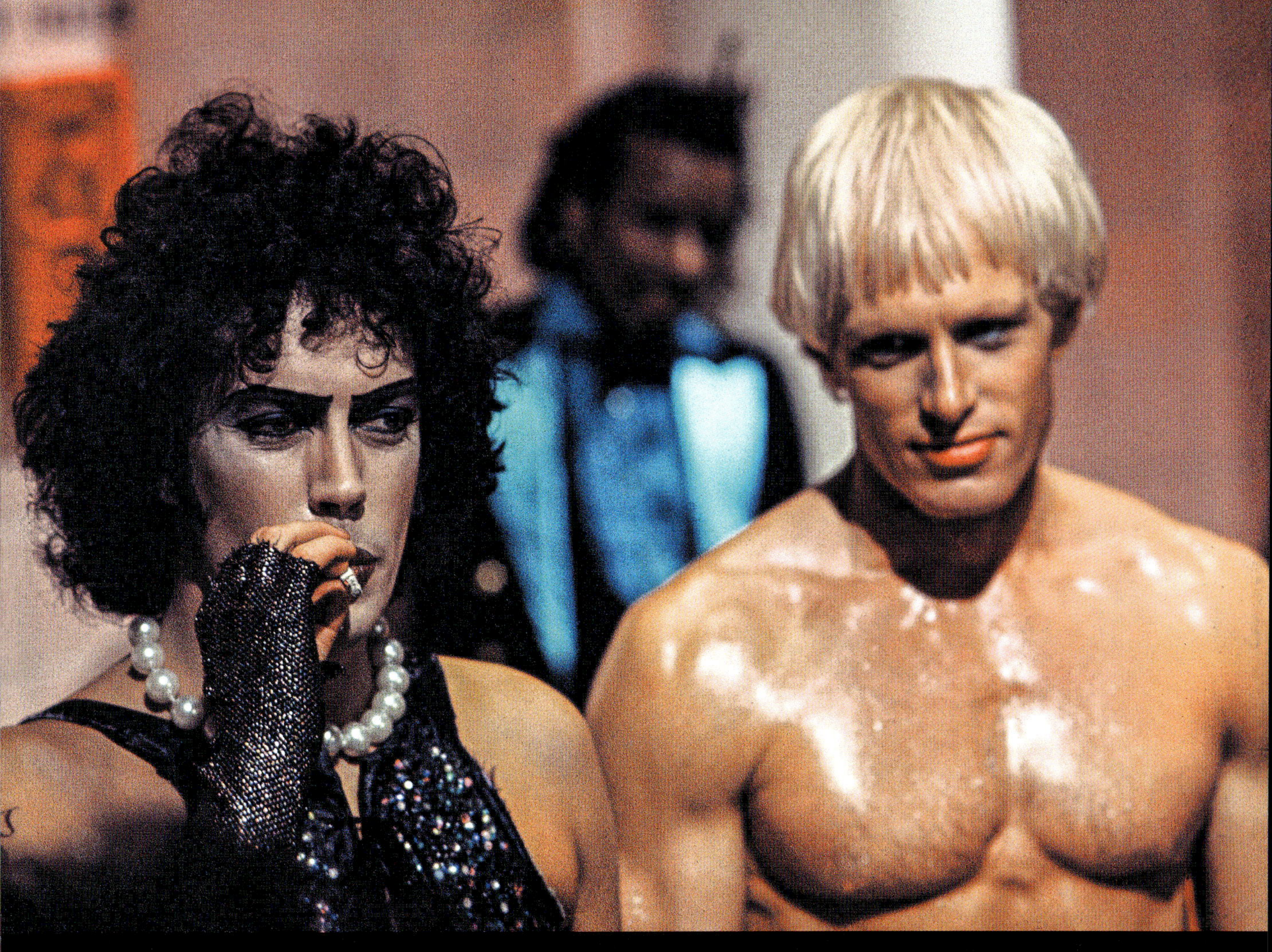

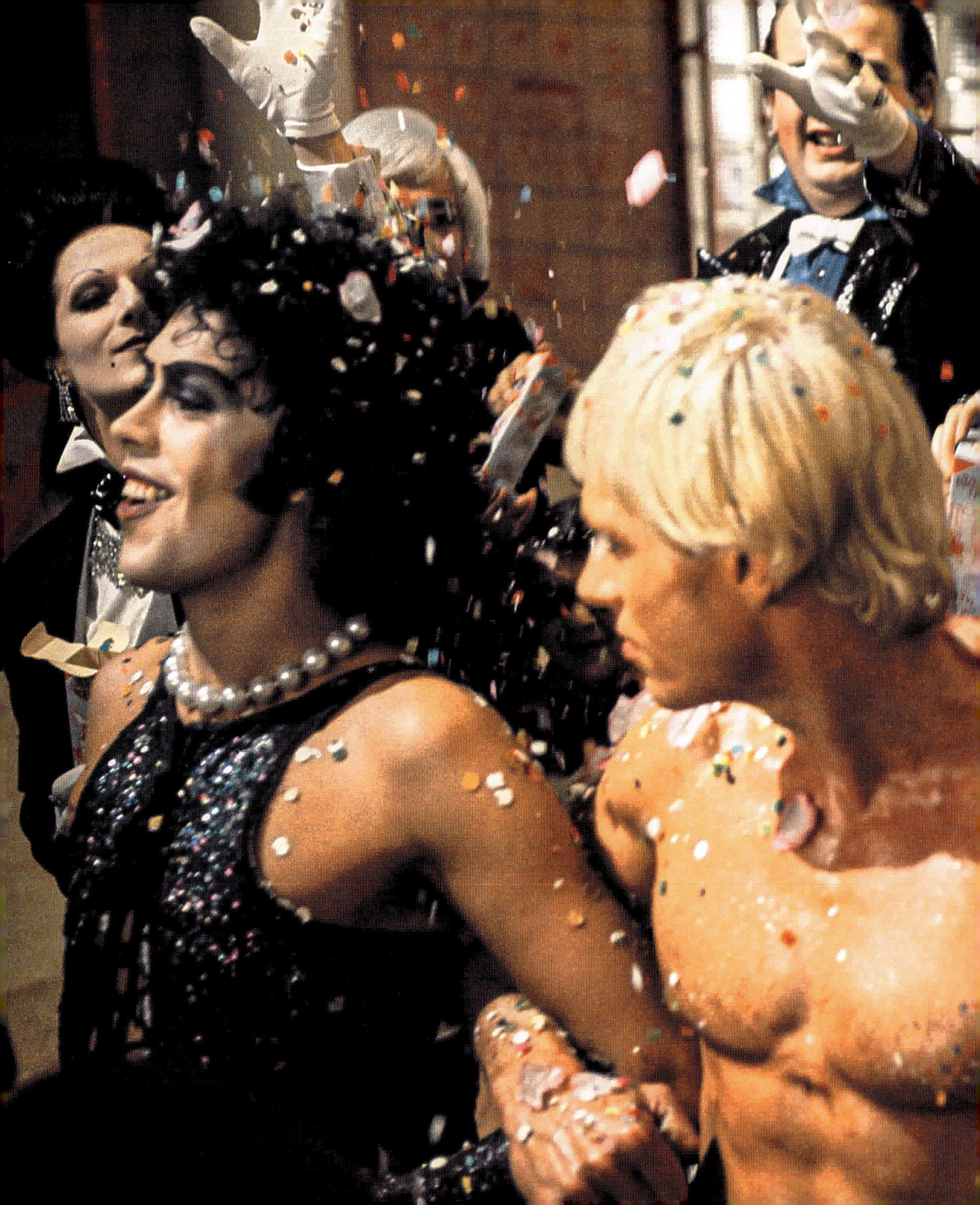

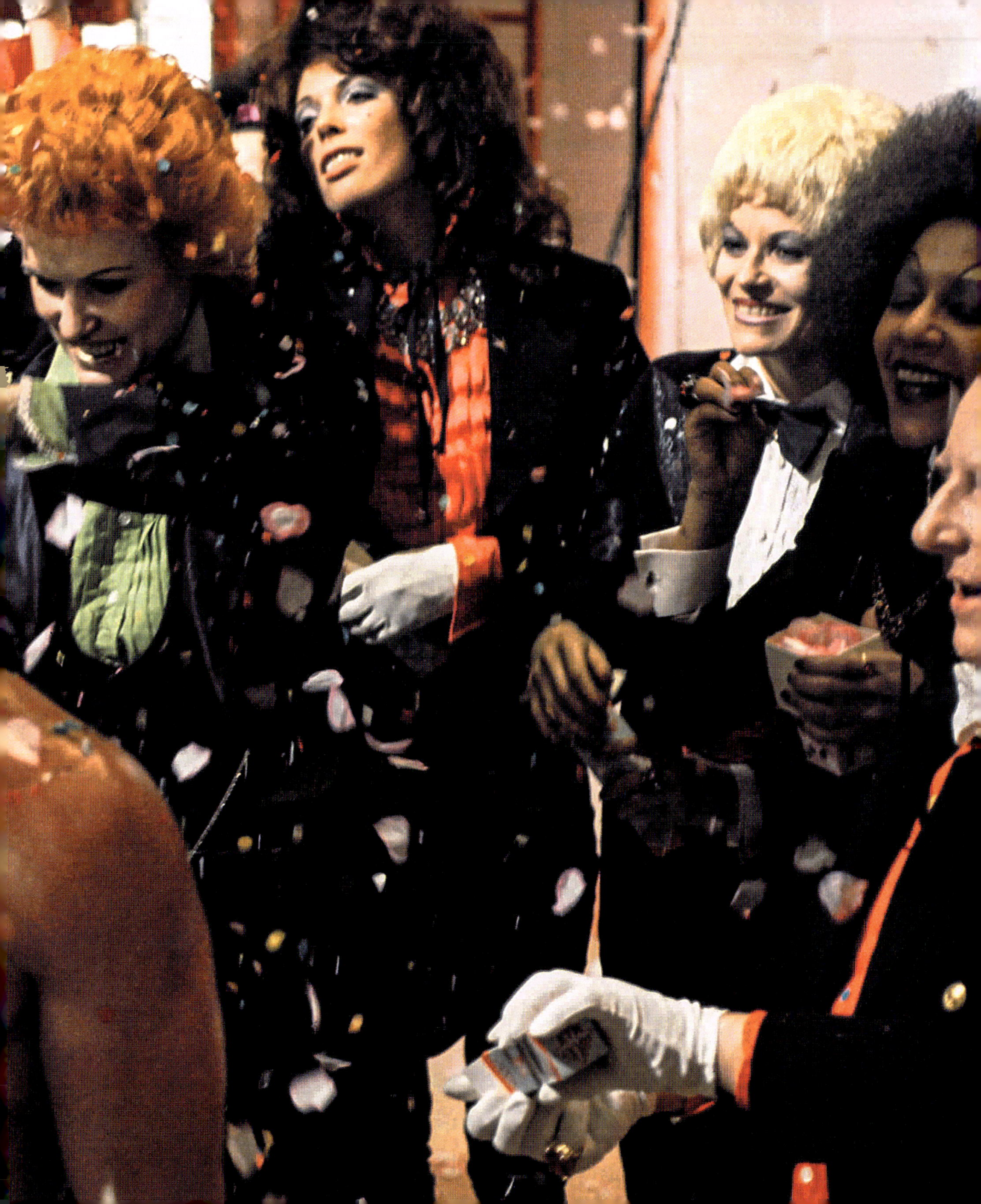

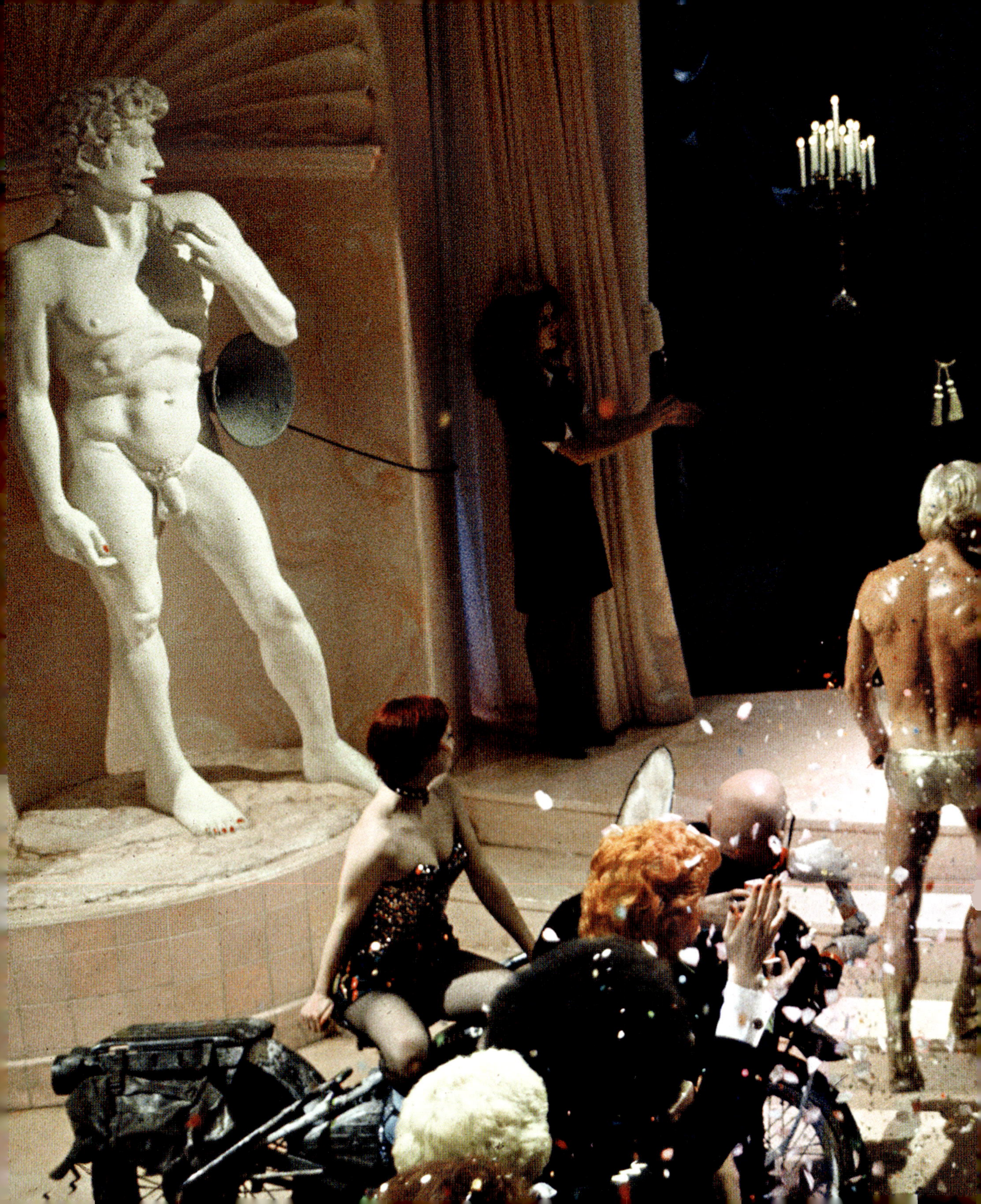

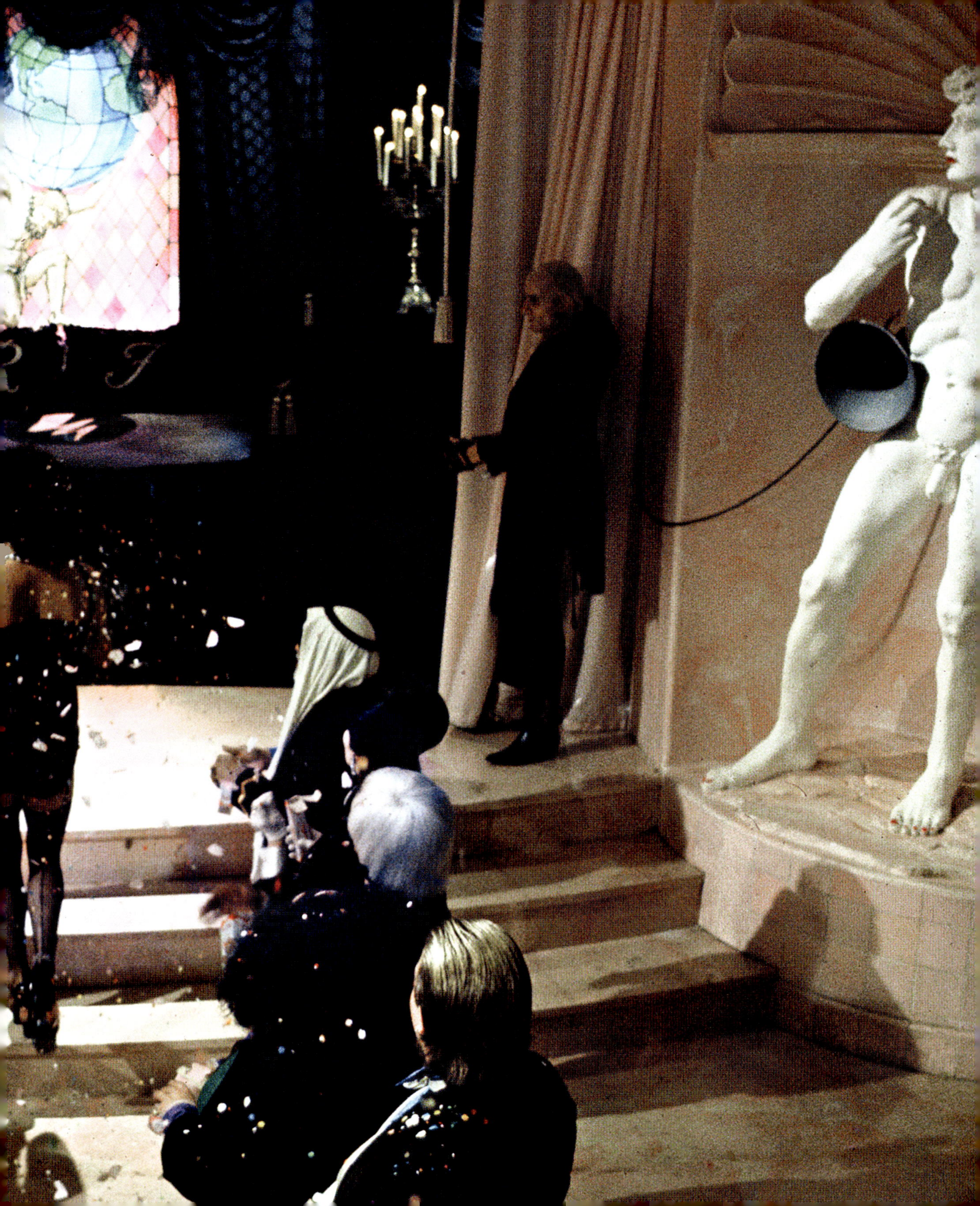

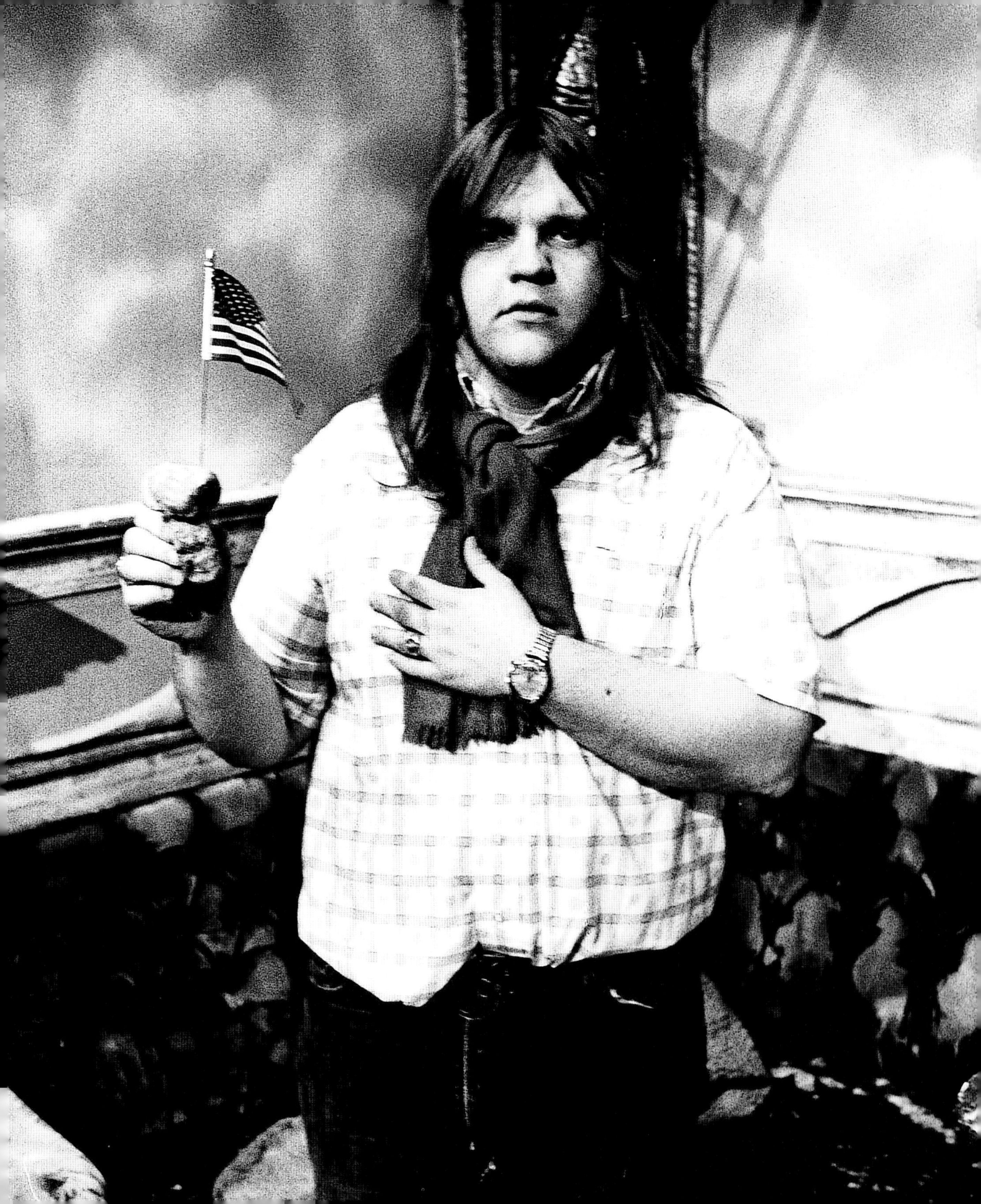

FROM THE DAY HE WAS BORN, HE WAS TROUBLE: EDDIE

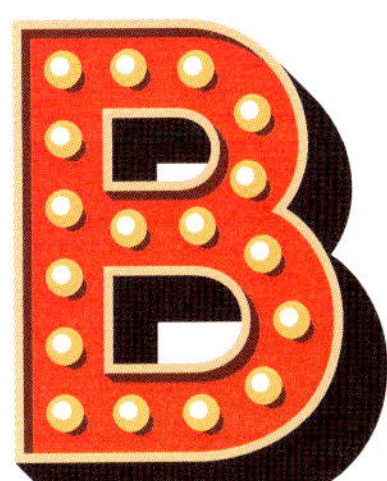

By the time Meat Loaf joined *Rocky Horror* for the LA production at the Roxy Theatre, he was known regionally for several bands, one of which, Floating Circus, had opened for The Who and Janis Joplin, among other acts.

As Meat Loaf told *EW* on the occasion of the fortieth anniversary of the movie, "When they called for *Rocky Horror*, I had no idea what it was. All I knew was they wanted me to come to L.A. in the play. I played Eddie as well as Dr. Scott."

In his memoir, *To Hell and Back*, Meat Loaf described the run-up to the show's opening. "We're finally ready to rehearse Curry's entrance, but we still haven't seen him. Doors in the back of this little theater open, and a guy with big black hair and a leather jacket comes walking down the aisle singing 'Sweet Transvestite.' As he gets closer, we see that he's got a garter belt, fishnet stockings, and enough make-up for a cosmetics counter. I'm sitting next to Graham Jarvis, the show's Narrator. I turn to him and say, 'I'm leaving!' I walk across the street against the light and get a ticket for jaywalking. Graham followed me out and I asked, 'What is this? What's going on? These people are nuts. I'm not doing a drag show.'" But he obviously reconsidered.

As for nailing the role, Meat Loaf said, "The first two weeks when we were doing the play all we did was the music, they had not given us a script. They come to me on the part of 'Hot Patootie,' and Richard

O'Brien is here at these rehearsals. He said, 'On this song, you'll never be able to get all the words in—I wrote it and I can't sing all the words.' Nobody could ever get in and just make those words fly through it. I looked at him and said 'I can sing all the words.' I just love telling people 'I can do that' and then being able to do it."

As Mick Rock recalled, "Meat Loaf, who had played Eddie in the Los Angeles production of the stage show, enjoyed his short but powerful role in the movie. He was on set for only a few days, but you can see that he enjoyed himself. He was a brief but memorable blast of rock 'n' roll that added another layer to the richness of the tale. He was very happy to mug for my camera and gave me images that stand outside his character in the film. A few years later, I met him again in Todd Rundgren's Woodstock studio while they were working on his first album *Bat Out of Hell*, which would propel him to international fame as a rock star in his own right."

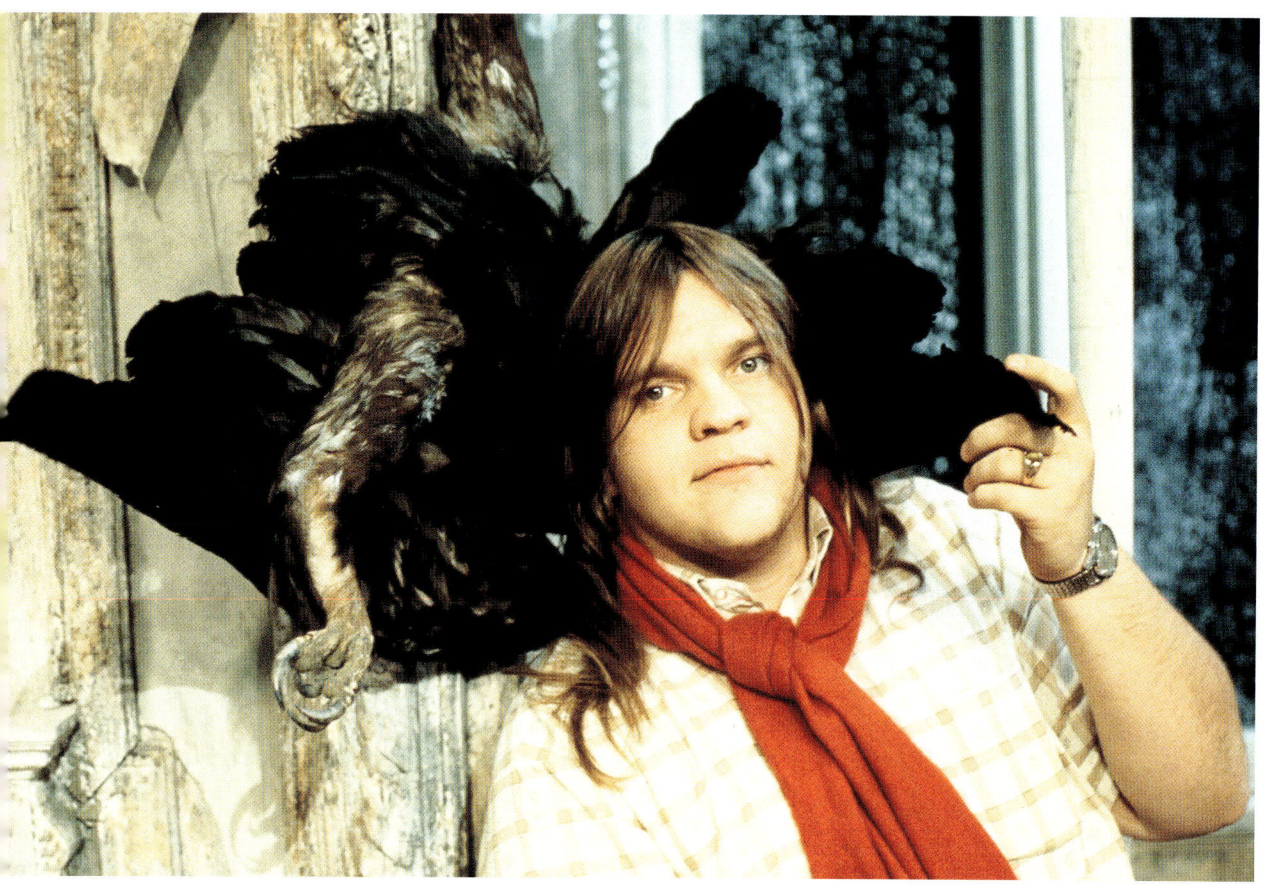

LUKE SPILLER, THE STRUTS: "Jesse Hughes, the singer of the Eagles of Death Metal, hosts a *Rocky Horror*–themed Halloween party at a club in West Hollywood. He gets a band together and does all the music for the entire show. I'd known Jesse for years and we had texted back and forth about the show, and the possibility of my singing 'Hot Patootie' with them. I love that song—it's probably my favorite from the whole musical. Ironically enough, the night of the party I was dressed as David Bowie in *Labyrinth*. I was probably six or seven tequilas in, and I was in the audience when Jesse called me up on stage and said, 'Are we doing this?' And I sang my ass off for those three minutes. I might not have the build to ever play Eddie, but I ride motorcycles, I've got the voice, and I'd love to."

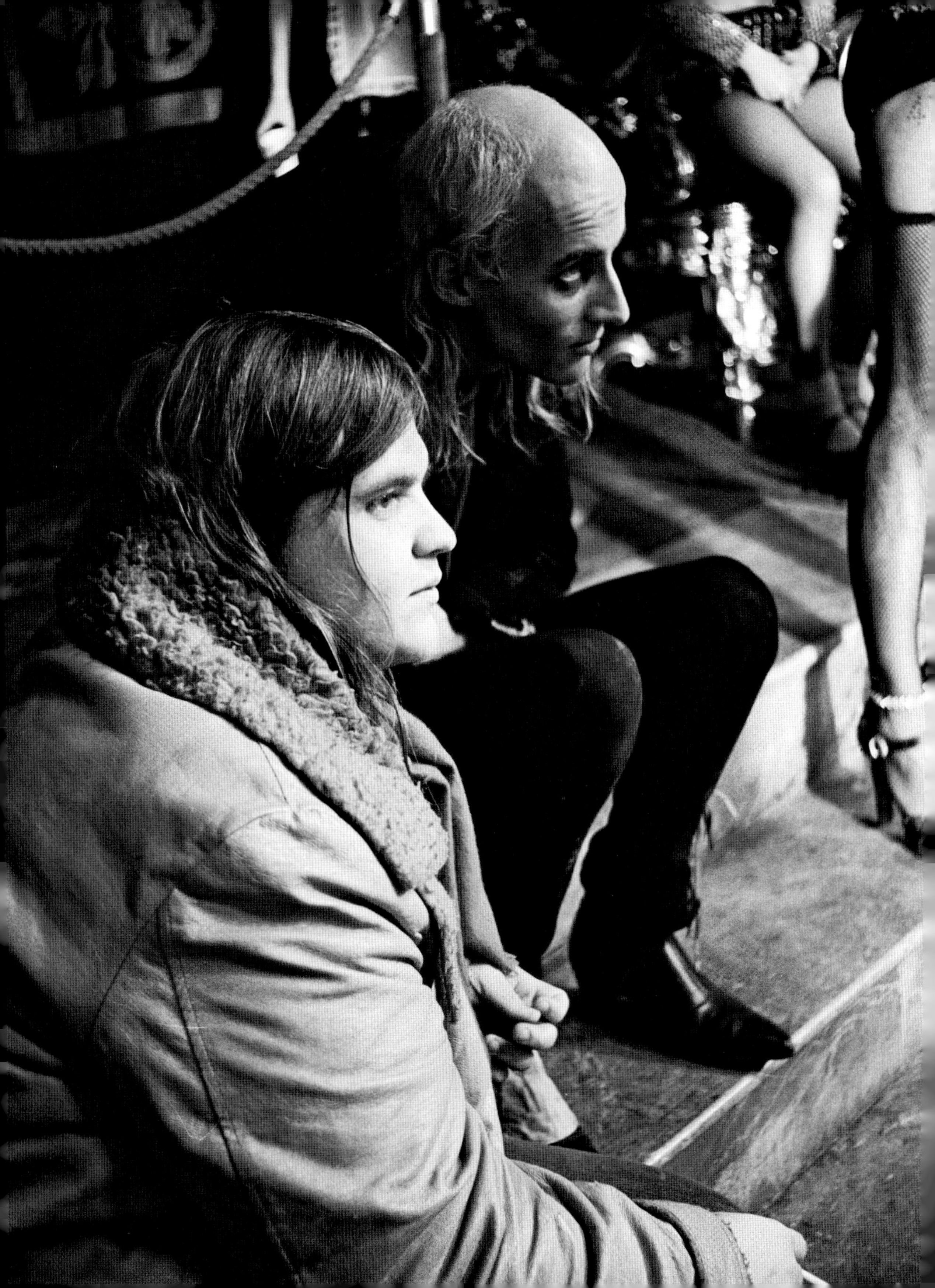

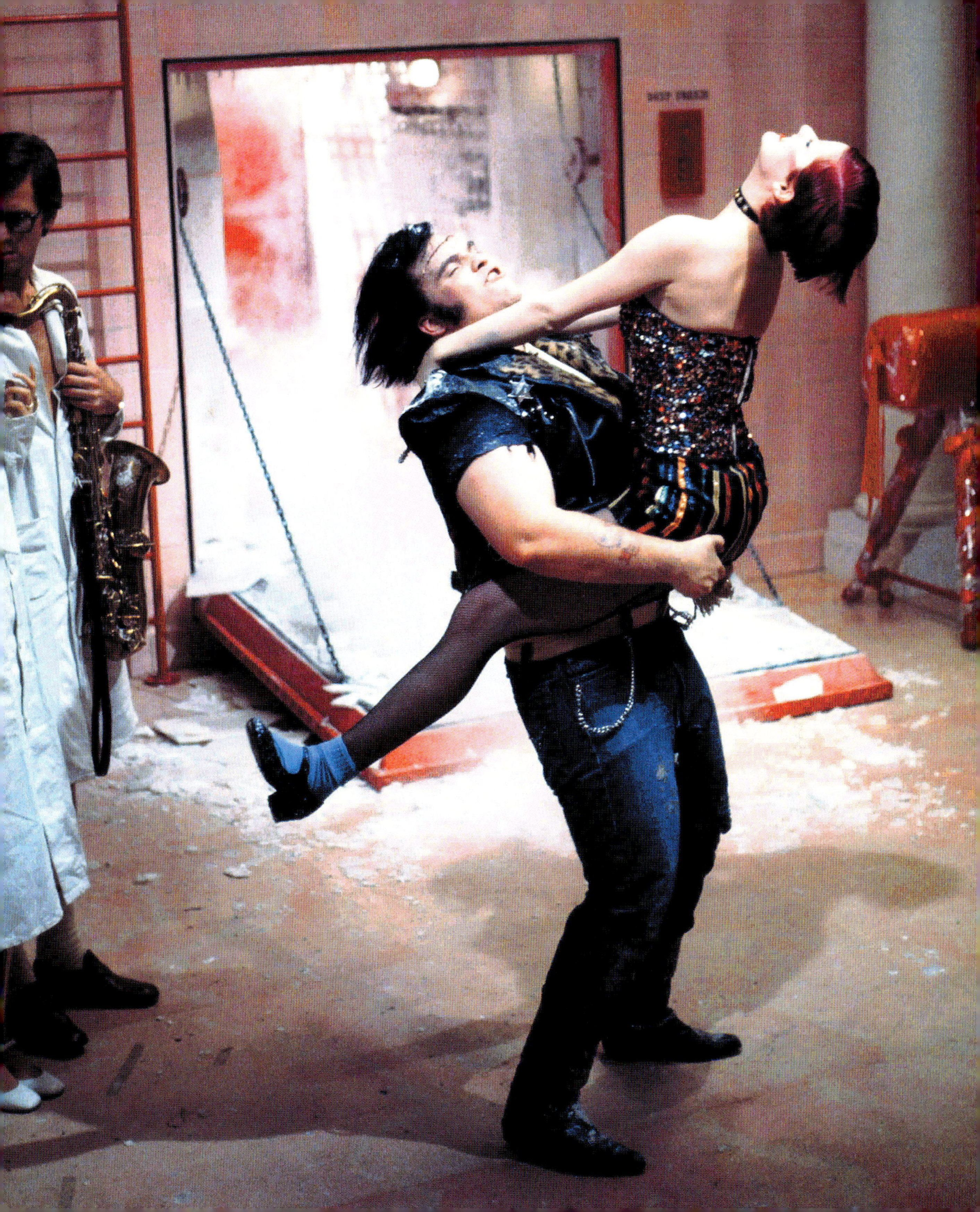

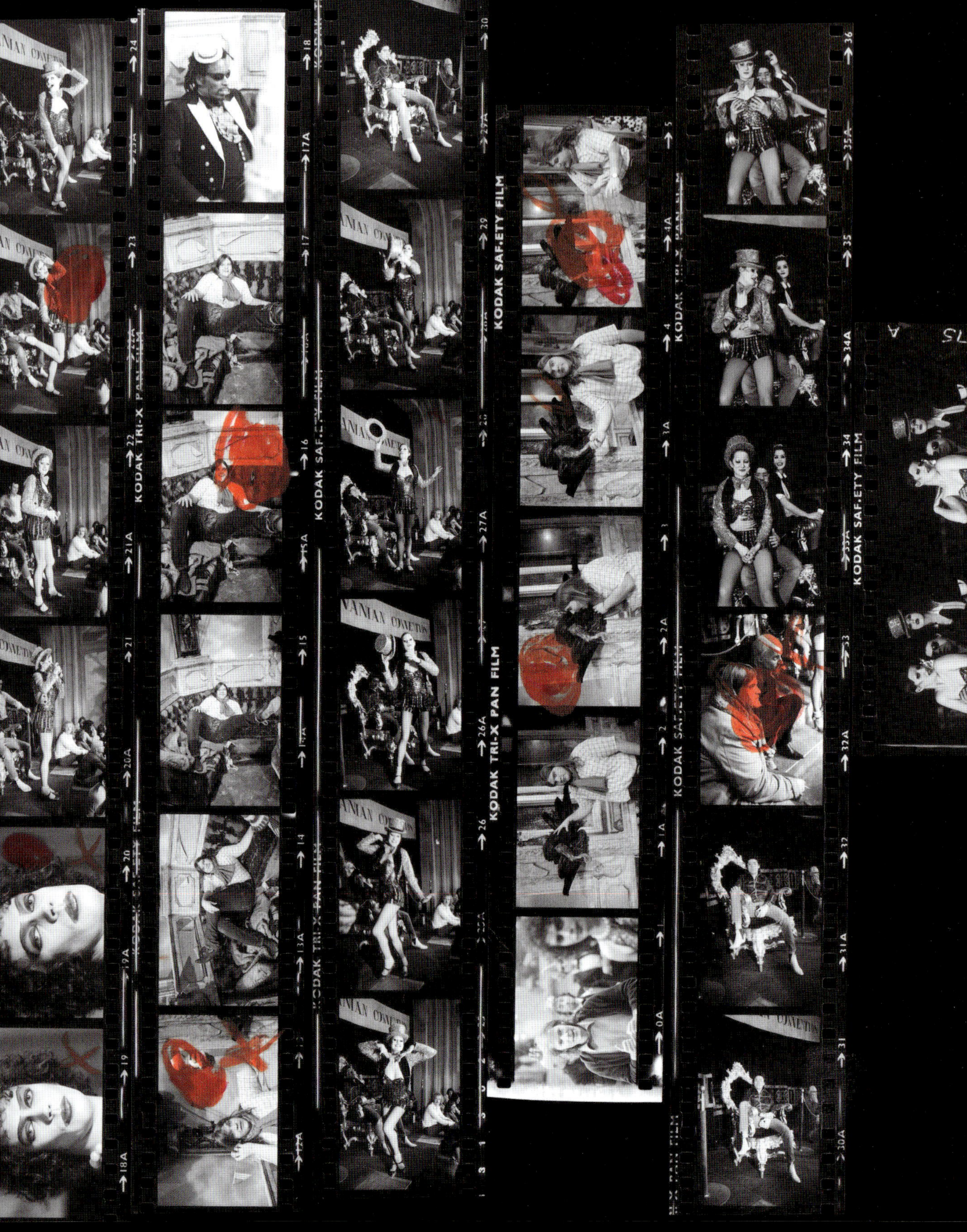

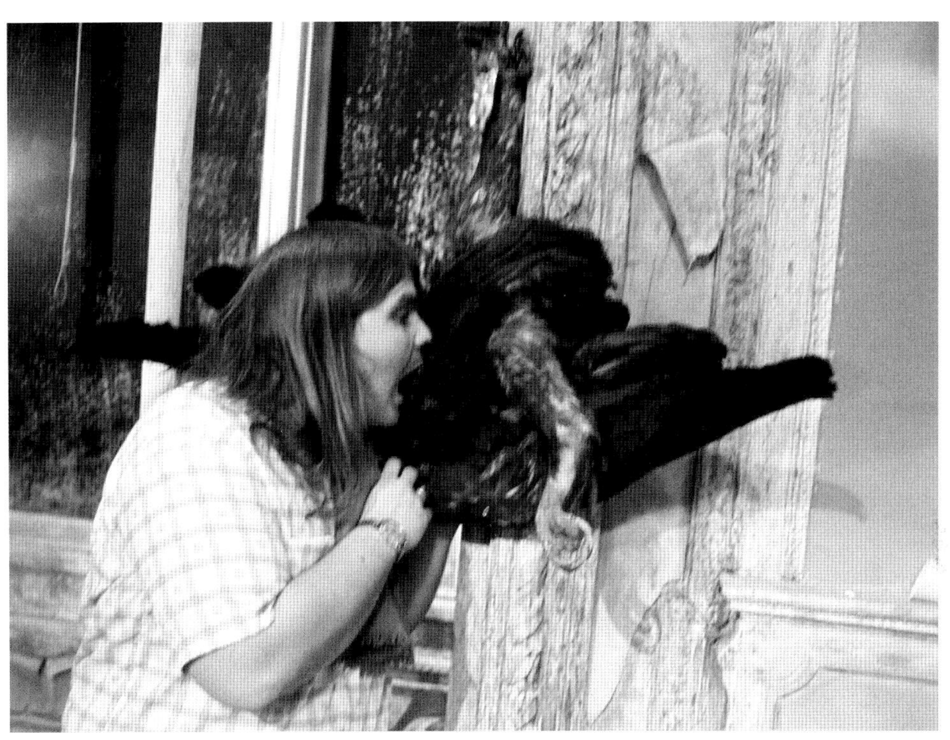
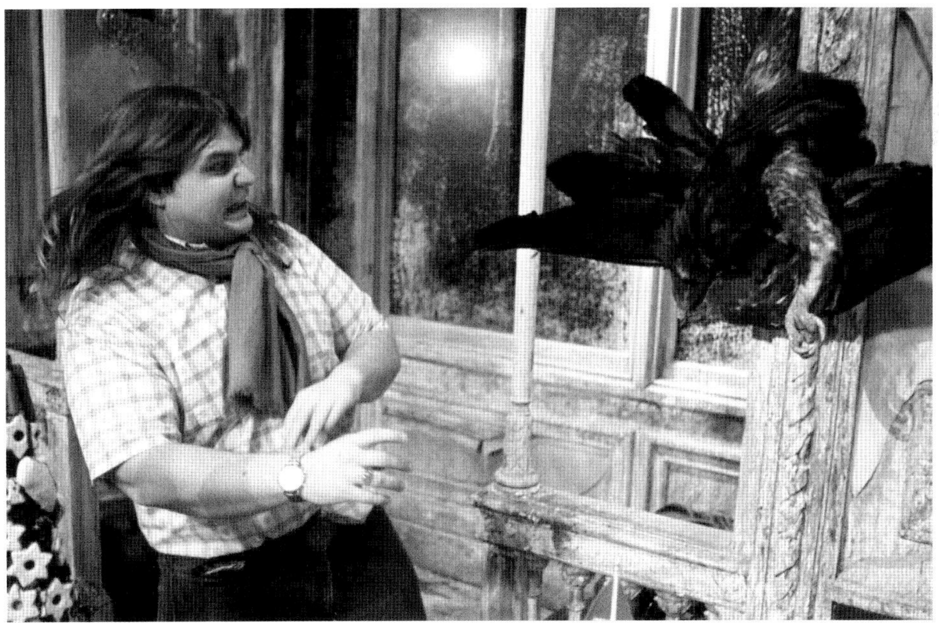

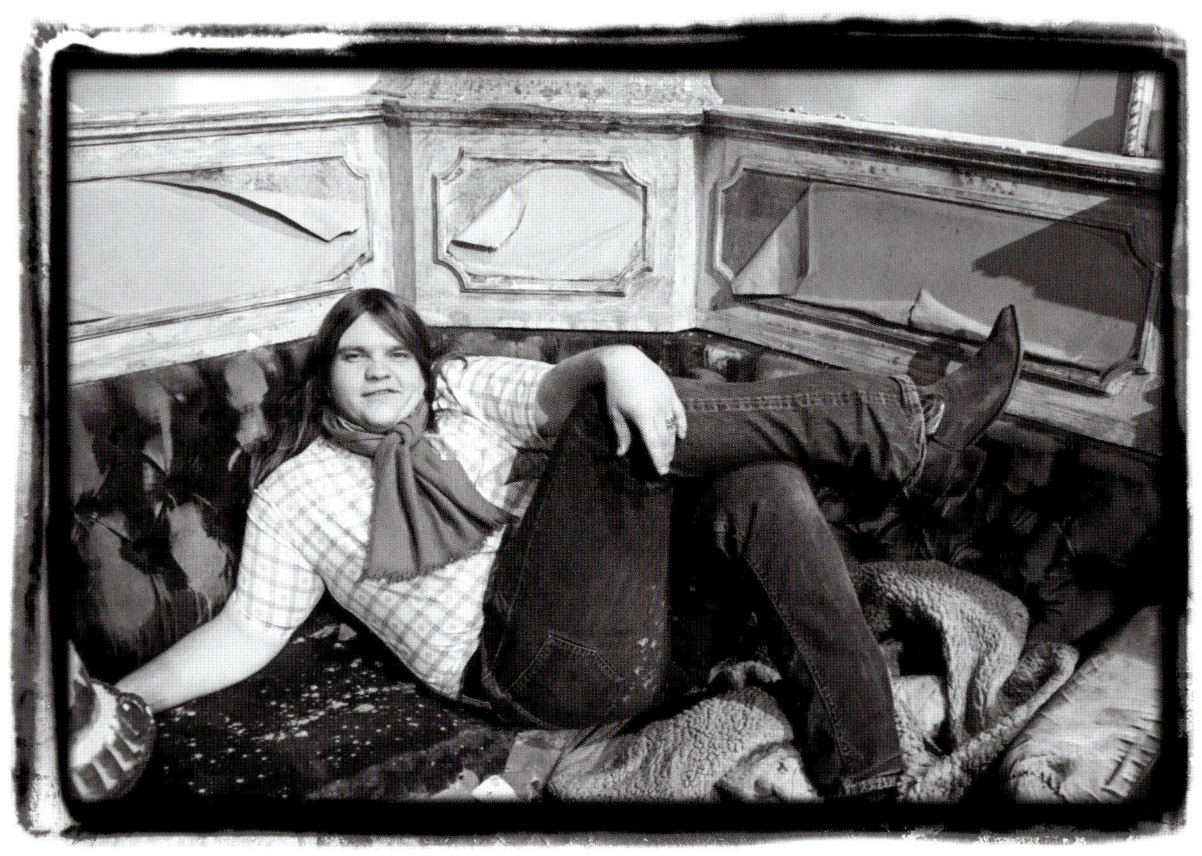

The buzz surrounding *Rocky Horror*'s run at the Roxy lured in celebrities, including the King of Rock 'n' Roll himself, who subsequently wanted to meet the cast.

"We went to meet Elvis, who had seen the show, and he said to me, 'I hear everyone that has done Eddie has only done an impersonation of me—and you didn't do that.' And I went, 'No, there's only one you.'"

—MEAT LOAF, *EW*

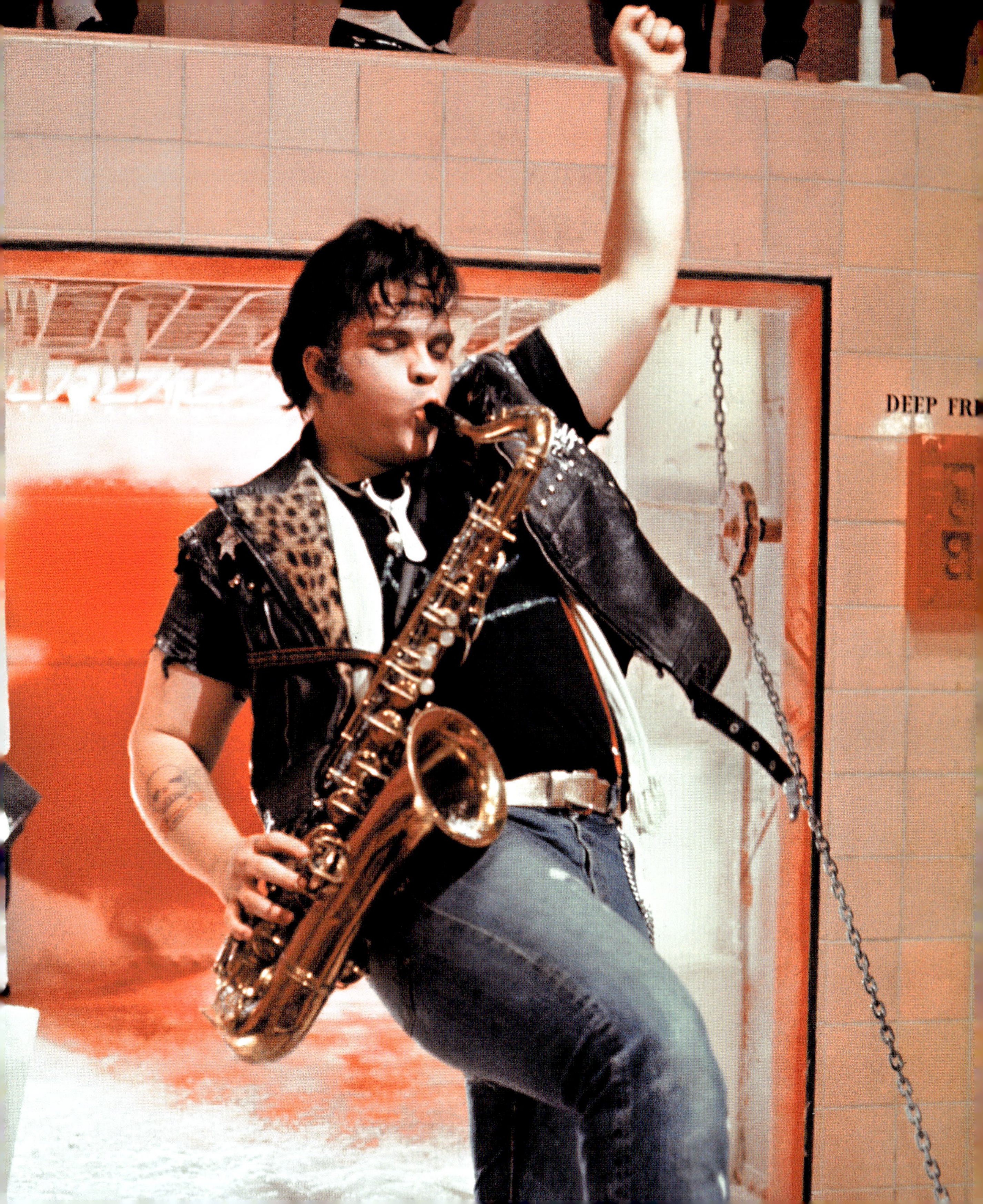
DEEP FR

A TIRELESS FORCE ON SET: JIM SHARMAN

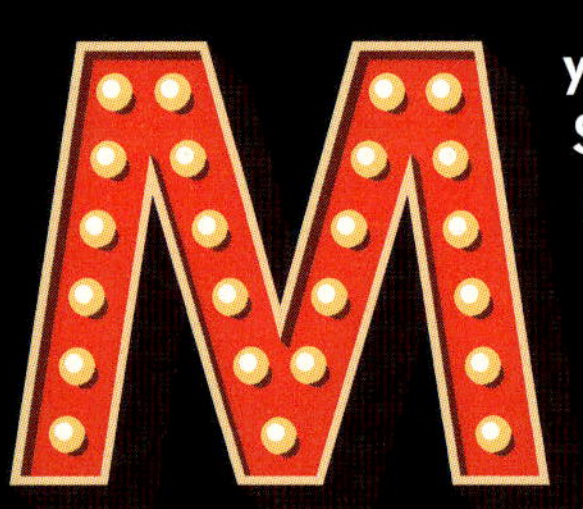

y own background," Sharman explained to the *Los Angeles Times* in 2015, "was divided between a very conventional city upbringing in a very conservative Australia—I think I did a little bit to correct that starting with *Hair*—but the rest of the time my family ran traveling sideshows."

He said his decision to go to theater school reflected his "serious side," while his involvement in *Rocky Horror* was "kind of the fairground side."

When it came time to adapt the stage production for film, Sharman told RockyHorror.com, "I always aimed to stay true to its modest origins because, from the moment when a storm broke over London on the first chord at the opening night, there was something magical about *Rocky Horror*. You don't mess with that; not without betraying what's special about it. Insisting on staying with the original cast for Frank and his trio of servants—Tim, Richard, Pat, and Nell—and to keep the original designers—Brian Thomson and Sue Blane—was part of staying true to the source. In the short term, this attitude may have appeared unrealistic, or too idealistic, but, over time, it brought its own rewards."

One thing that did change from stage to screen: the music. "There's a view that the film is just a stage show recorded, but this is far from true. The music for the film was re-arranged by Richard Hartley to suit the musical strengths of the cast. We also

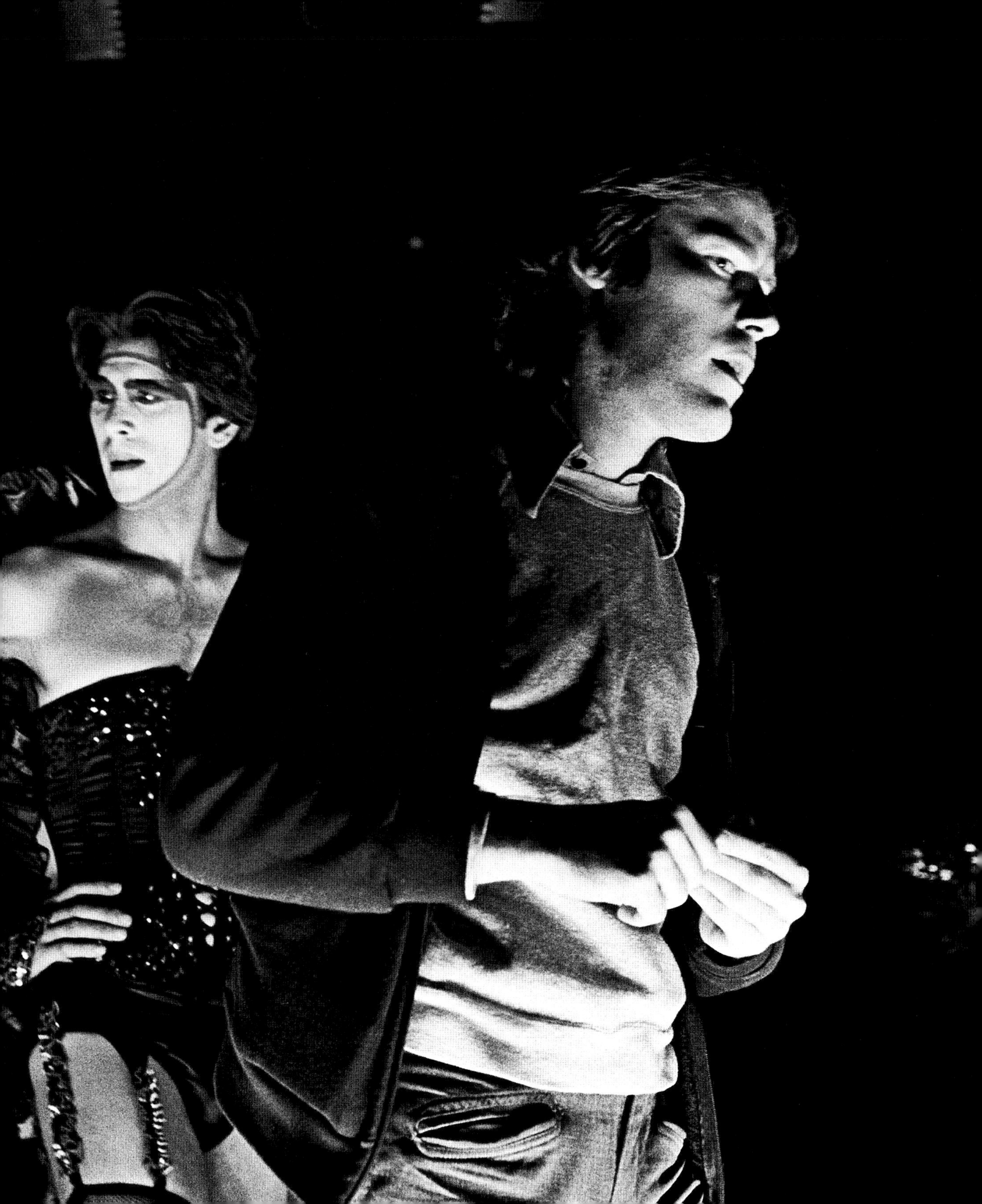

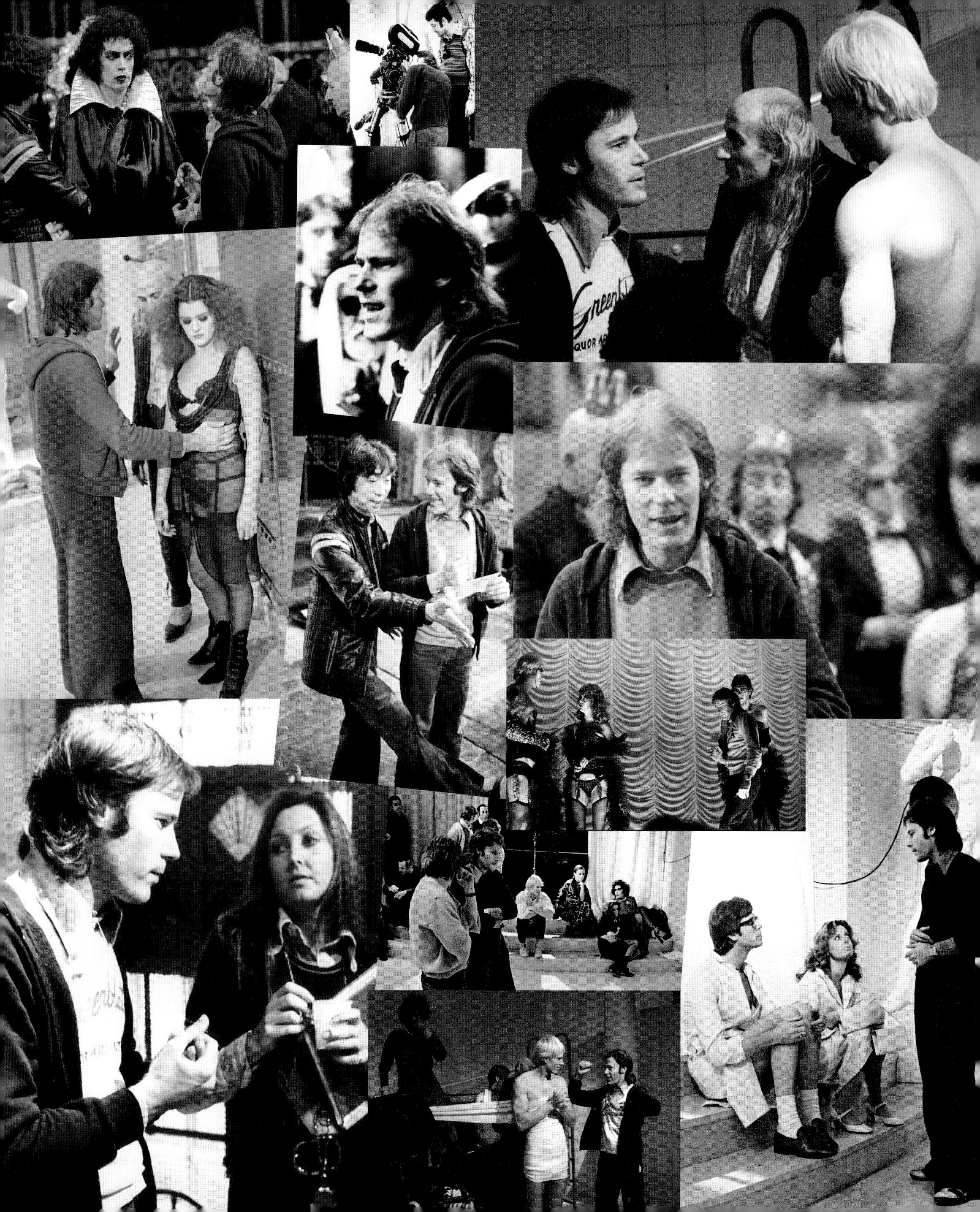

rehearsed before we recorded, so the songs were performed with a clear idea of the action involved, allowing the actors to characterize their songs. This resulted in a shift in interpretation between stage and film. For instance: 'Science Fiction' onstage is a chirpy, witty, up-tempo song—abrasive and attention-demanding. It is, after all, the opening number of a stage show. In the film, it's slow, sinuous, and seductive—it draws you in."

As for how Mick Rock ended up on set, Sharman explained in an exclusive interview in 2024, "Mick's rock star photography revealed his sharp eye for serious people kicking up their heels. When I invited Mick to take stills on *The Rocky Horror Picture Show*, I sensed that he might capture the subversive glimmer beneath the surface glitter. And he did. We both had a desire to capture lightning in a bottle, and this resulted in fond memories of our on-set encounters and a bunch of now iconic images."

"Jim Sharman was a tireless force on the set," said Mick. "You can see his concentration and energy in many of the stills. He was a very hands-on director and worked closely with all the main characters. In many ways, this was nearly as much his baby as Richard's. He had apparently nursed it from the start. He knew Richard from the original London production of *Jesus Christ Superstar*, which he directed while Richard played Judas Iscariot, and it had been a huge success. But this was more personal, closer to his real tastes. He had also co-written the shooting script with Richard. *Rocky Horror* was 'cult,' but as time has proven, much more significant culturally than *Superstar*, and I'm sure that

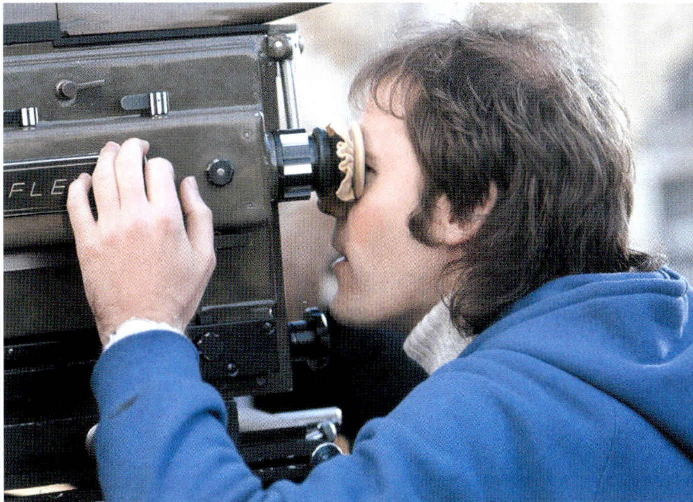

over the years it has generated much more dinero than the tepid film version of *Superstar*—which wasn't directed by Jim.

"He seemed very comfortable with me flitting in and out with no warning and no obvious timetable and encouraged everyone to cooperate when I wanted to do special setups. He had invited me to dine at the apartment he shared with his young South American boyfriend, Gustavo, and was thrilled when I gave him a *Transformer* print for his wall. He seemed an intrinsically shy man. I never saw him at any parties—even the private one at Lou Adler's apartment after the shoot was done. He was in a way an old-school workaholic and later returned to Australia. Although he directed the most significant stage show and film to come out of that whole glammy, androgynous scene, he wasn't really part of it. He could deal with it creatively, but he was probably in essence voyeuristic. He had left his mark and moved back to what he knew best: live theater."

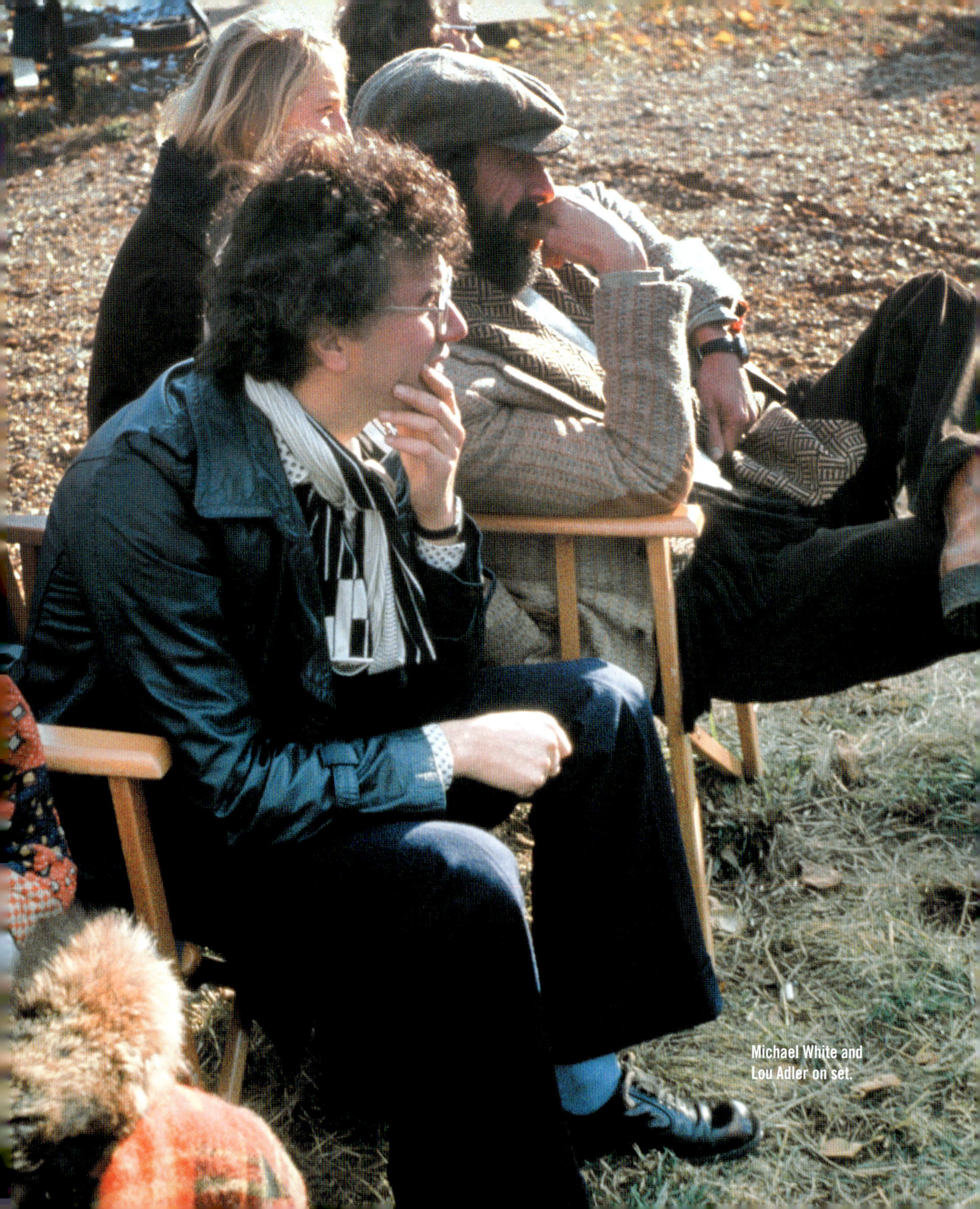

Michael White and
Lou Adler on set.

A STUDY IN CONTRASTS: LOU ADLER AND MICHAEL WHITE

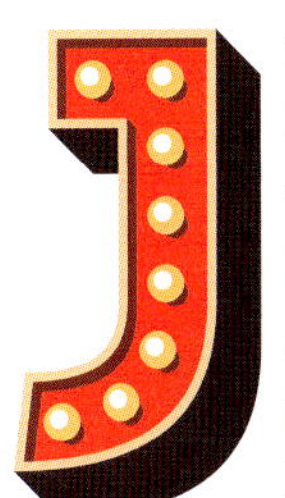

Jim Sharman's producers, Michael White and Lou Adler, were a study in contrasts," Mick said. "Michael was first a stage producer and had financed the original production, while Lou Adler was best known as a music producer for Jan and Dean, The Mamas and the Papas, and Carole King, among others. He was brought in by Michael to finance the US productions of the stage show in Los Angeles and New York. Neither Lou nor Michael was around the set that much when I showed up, although I do have a few pics of Lou from a couple of different occasions. They seemed to give Jim free rein, although I know the film was produced for a very modest sum. Jim seemed very focused and certainly brought the project in on budget."

By his own account, Adler was always on the lookout for new subcultures and the next big thing, but in *Rocky Horror*, he saw something more practical. "What I saw in the show was the way it would fit into the Roxy, which I owned in LA," Adler said in an exclusive 2024 interview. "I wasn't that familiar with Broadway theater; I wasn't thinking that far in advance. I was thinking of the Roxy."

In fact, Adler didn't necessarily foresee *Rocky Horror* as the next big thing at all—and certainly not the success it became. "I didn't always choose my projects based on whether I thought they would work. They worked *for me*. I did what felt right for me to do at the time. Eventually I saw how much it was ahead of its time, and how much it did for so many people."

The failure of the Broadway version of *Rocky Horror* half a year ahead of the cinematic release of the film didn't deter him. "Once I start on something I'm so straight ahead that something like that wouldn't make me stop, wouldn't even make me think about stopping. Broadway was the wrong venue."

Of course, the film initially flopped too. "We previewed it in Santa Barbara, which is both a college town and a retirement community. We showed it with the wrong film—you usually previewed with another film that brought you the right audience. But there was no other film like it. So when most of the audience walked out, we were dejected. I was sitting on the curb with Tim Deegan, a Fox executive, after pretty much the whole audience left. Then about fifteen college kids came up and said, 'We loved the movie.' And they talked about it in the terms that would eventually be the way people thought about *Rocky Horror*. So we knew there was an audience, but we had to find it, or it had to find us. It was a taste of what could be a potential audience."

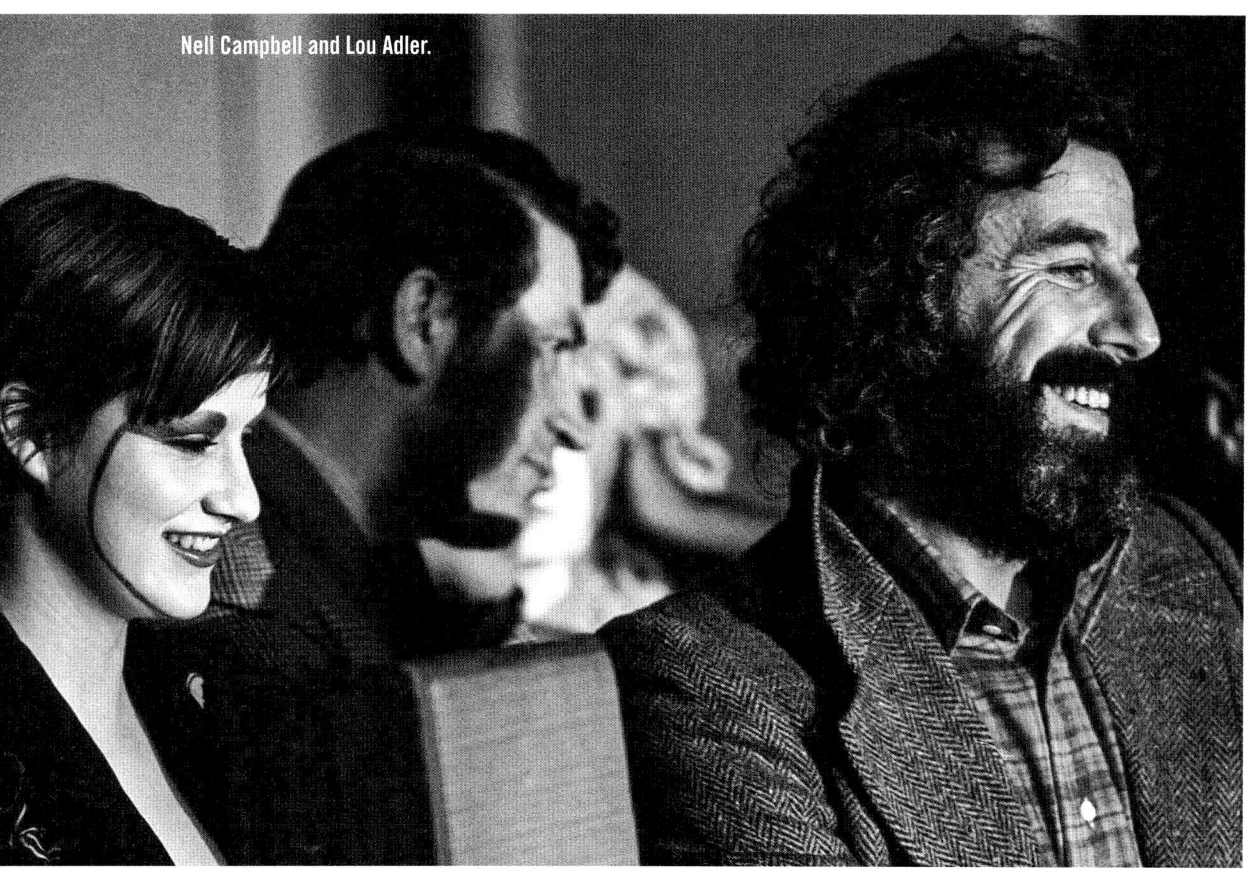

Nell Campbell and Lou Adler.

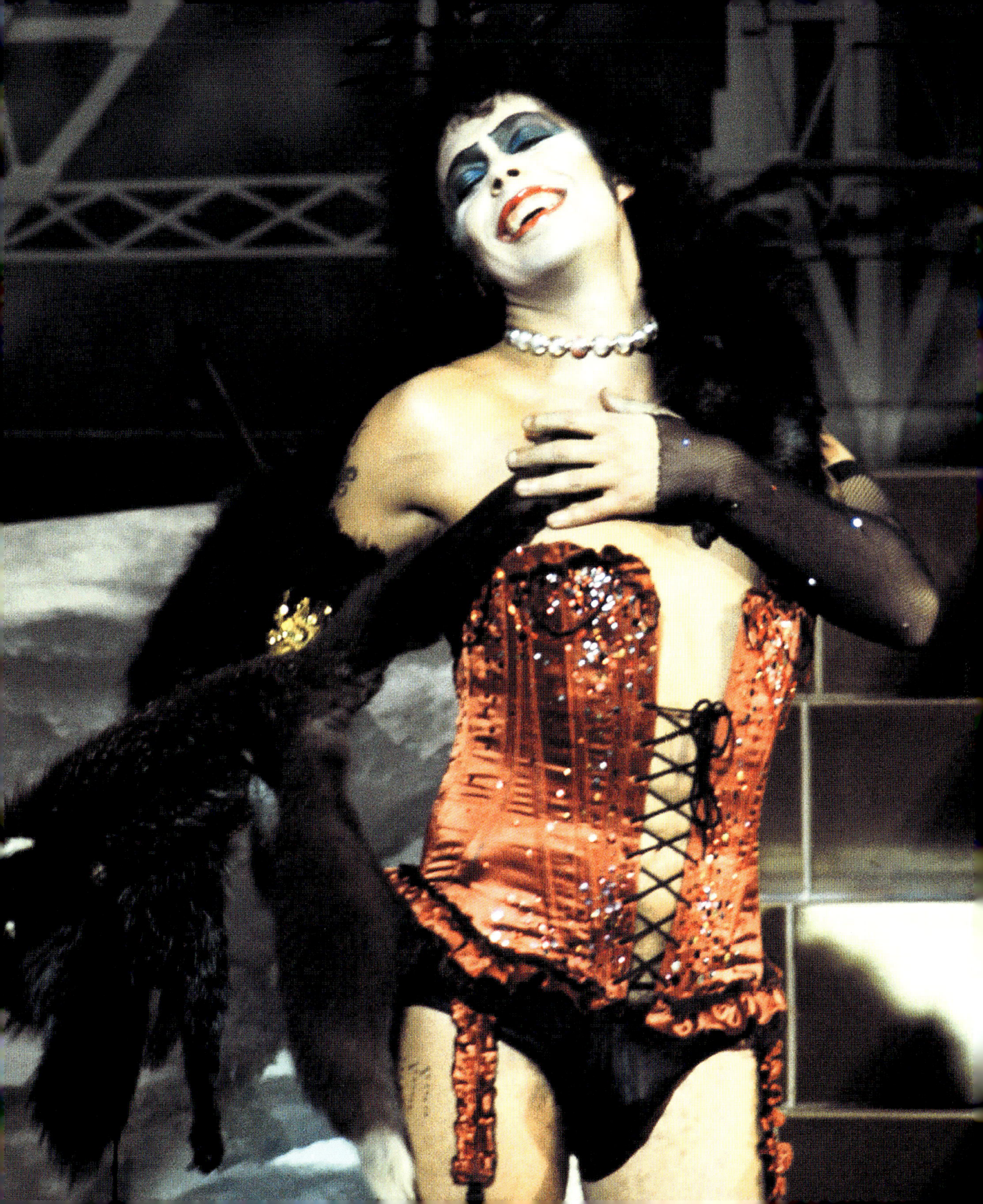

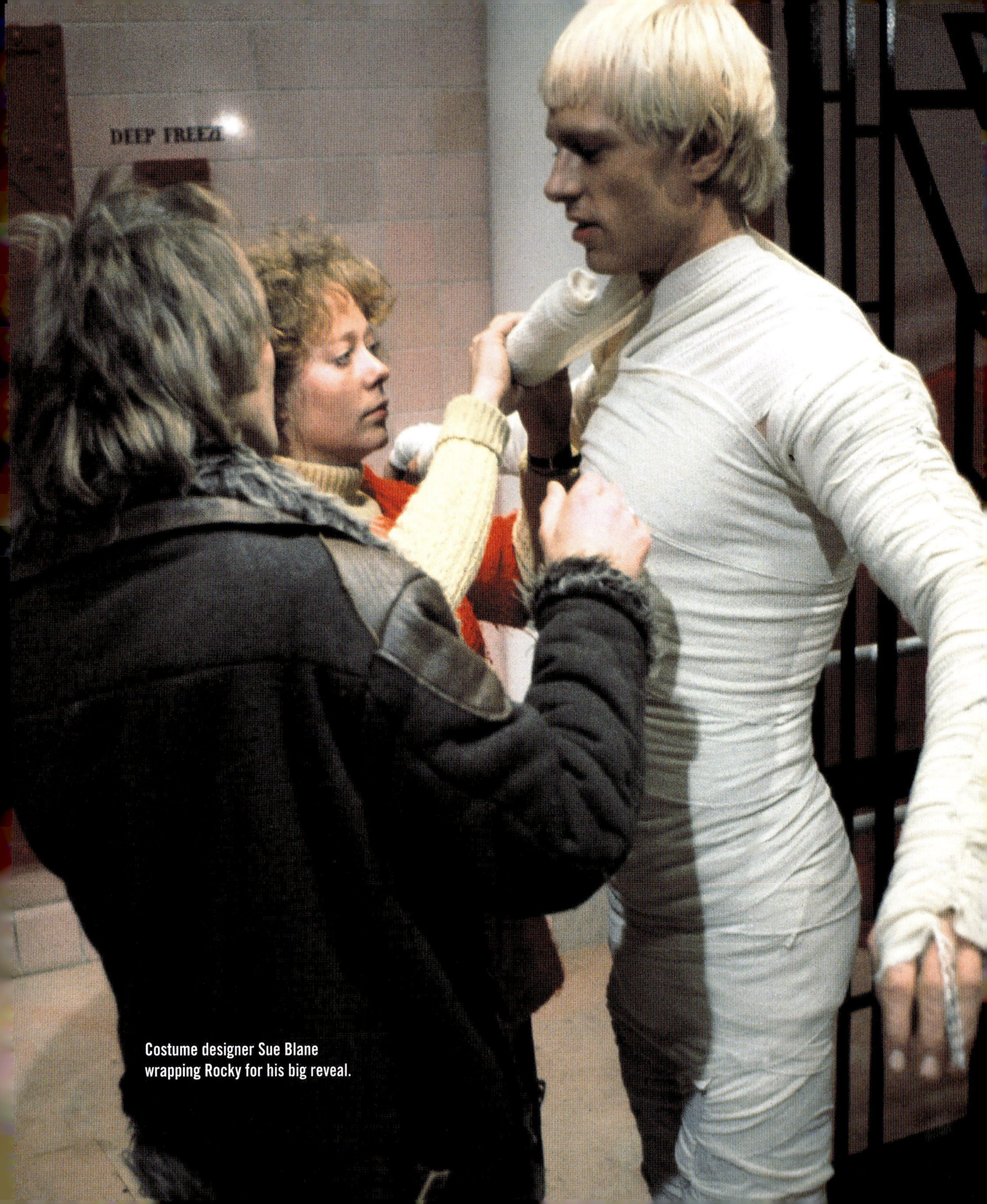

Costume designer Sue Blane wrapping Rocky for his big reveal.

FORMAL DRESS IS TO BE OPTIONAL: SUE BLANE

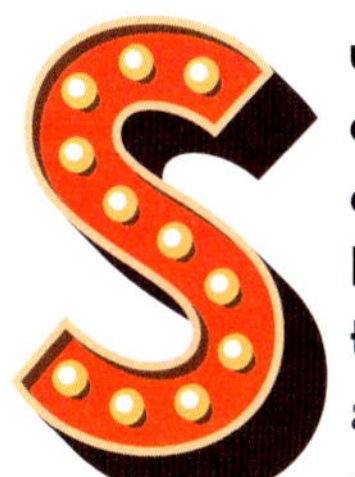

ue Blane served as the costume designer for the original stage shows in London and LA, as well as the movie. "I was skeptical about the show," she explained in an exclusive interview in 2024, "but I knew so many of the people involved. I knew Tim Curry, for instance, and the stage manager, the manager of the Theatre Upstairs, so it was like going to work with family. I'd never met Jim Sharman or Brian Thomson or for that matter Richard O'Brien, but it just seemed like a nice job. I fitted in ideally, as they couldn't find any other costume designer who was willing to take it on. They said they'd tried anybody who was any good and they'd all said no, so would I give it a go? With a compliment like that, what could I say? I arranged to meet Jim Sharman and we got on like a house on fire. And within twenty-four hours I was halfway through designing it."

Blane humbly deflects whenever she's asked about the huge impact her *Rocky Horror* designs had on the larger fashion and pop culture world. "Everyone else seemed to know more about what was fashionable and hip in London than I did," she says. "I'd moved to London only five or six months before we did *Rocky Horror*, so I was soaking up what was around me."

Blane again deflects when it comes to her work's influence on the then-nascent punk scene, but will admit, "One thing I did have an influence on was the sort of beaten-up effect of the costumes, for the initial

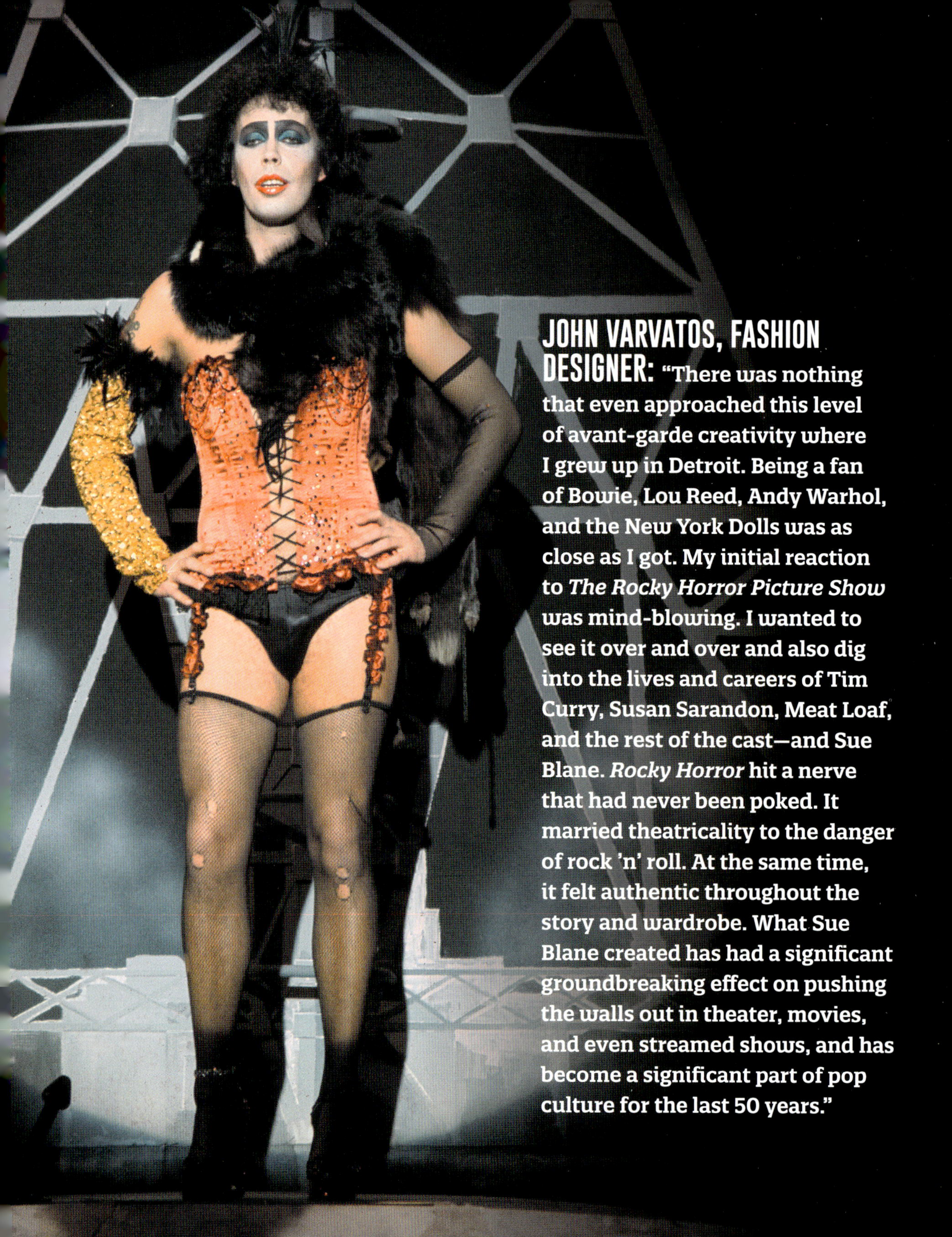

JOHN VARVATOS, FASHION DESIGNER: "There was nothing that even approached this level of avant-garde creativity where I grew up in Detroit. Being a fan of Bowie, Lou Reed, Andy Warhol, and the New York Dolls was as close as I got. My initial reaction to *The Rocky Horror Picture Show* was mind-blowing. I wanted to see it over and over and also dig into the lives and careers of Tim Curry, Susan Sarandon, Meat Loaf, and the rest of the cast—and Sue Blane. *Rocky Horror* hit a nerve that had never been poked. It married theatricality to the danger of rock 'n' roll. At the same time, it felt authentic throughout the story and wardrobe. What Sue Blane created has had a significant groundbreaking effect on pushing the walls out in theater, movies, and even streamed shows, and has become a significant part of pop culture for the last 50 years."

show particularly: the ripped fishnets, everything used, old, patched, painted, dyed. It was very theatrical in that old-fashioned sense, and I think that bit of punk—where the kids could go and see the show and basically put together a similar look relatively cheaply with secondhand clothes and bits of old stuff, and throw together different looks—was in the spirit of *Rocky Horror* and in the spirit of punk as it was then developing."

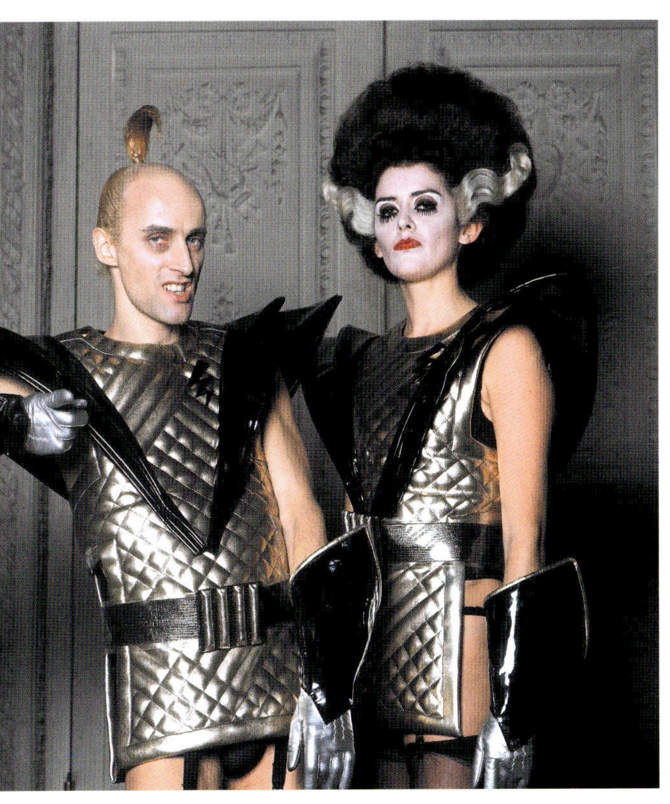

SIMON DOONAN, AUTHOR, FASHION COMMENTATOR, AND ON-AIR TALENT: **"I am part of the *Rocky Horror* generation. The fusion of camp, drag, and glam rock spoke LOUDLY to me and my pals. *Rocky Horror* connected the dots between early-seventies glam rock and late-seventies punk, bringing fishnets, corsets, and heavy makeup to suburban and small-town kids, gay and straight, opening the door to goth and so much more. It was a reaction to the stuffy conventionality of class-riddled British society, and even though there was more than a whiff of nostalgia to it, the nostalgia—like in Lou Reed's 'Walk on the Wild Side' or Andy Warhol's work—was dark and wicked and decadently glamorous. That is why it became iconic."**

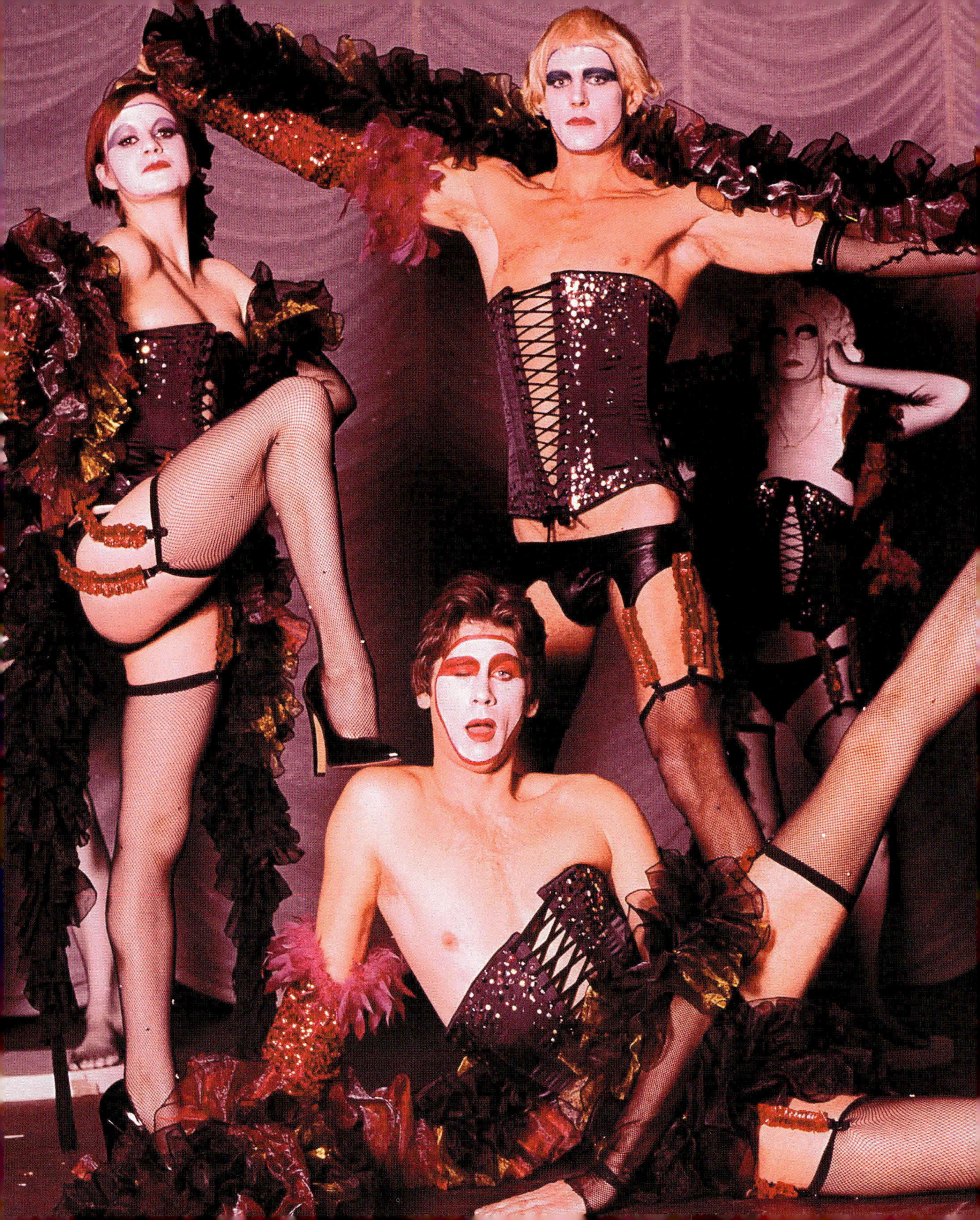

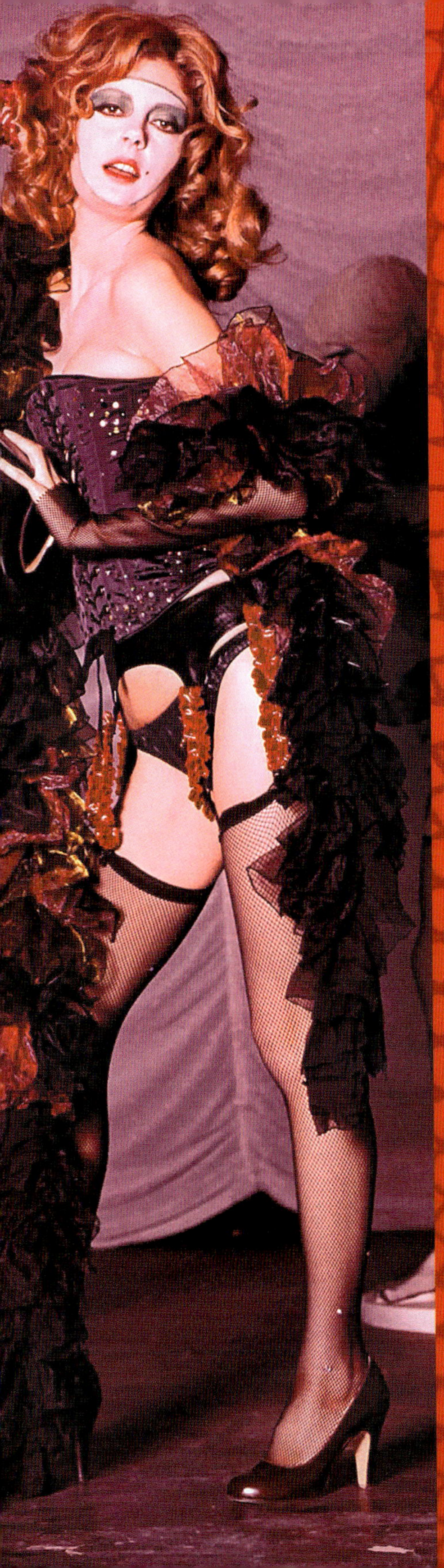

ARIANNE PHILLIPS, OSCAR, TONY, AND BAFTA-NOMINATED COSTUME DESIGNER:

"Sue Blane's costumes have absolutely informed me. There was a true DIY aspect to her work, an authenticity, world-building, and such brilliant character development that was true and honest. *Rocky Horror* was the original cosplay. A recurring theme in my work has been transformation, identity, androgyny, and self-expression, all stemming from my personal aesthetics and experiences, and *RHPS* formed the nucleus of that inspiration.

When I read the script for *Hedwig and the Angry Inch*, my first reaction was, This is my *Rocky Horror*! I was inspired and aspired to create characters that were outrageously authentic, just as Sue Blane had for *The Rocky Horror Picture Show*. I hoped and dreamed that I could strike a chord in the zeitgeist that resonated with the audience the way *The Rocky Horror Picture Show* had influenced and informed me."

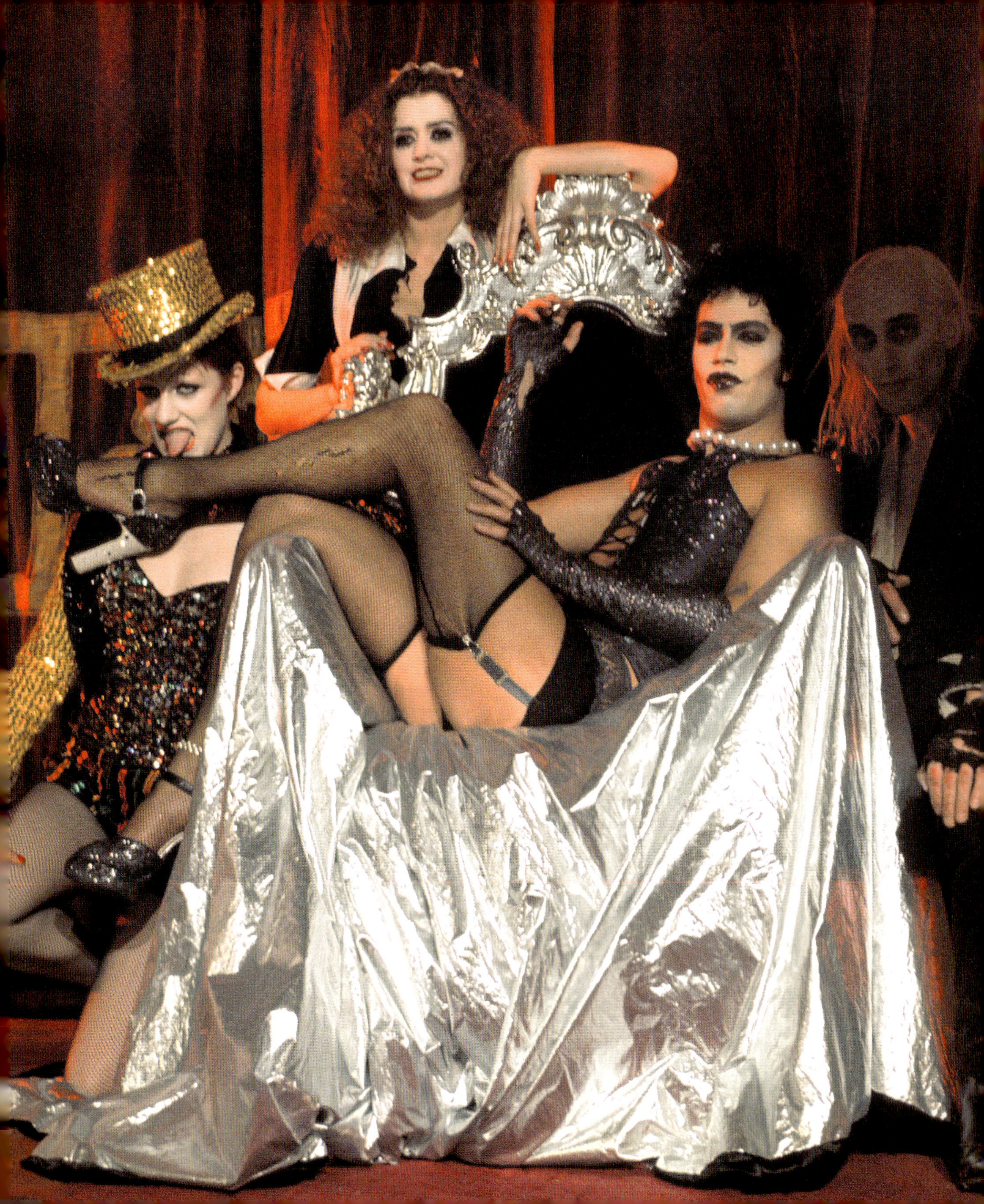

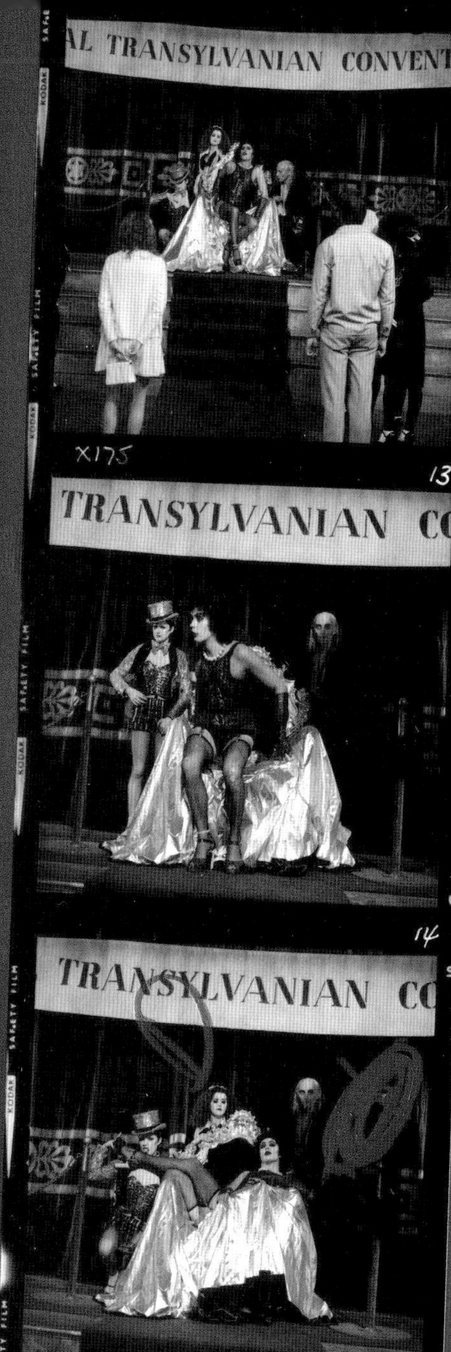

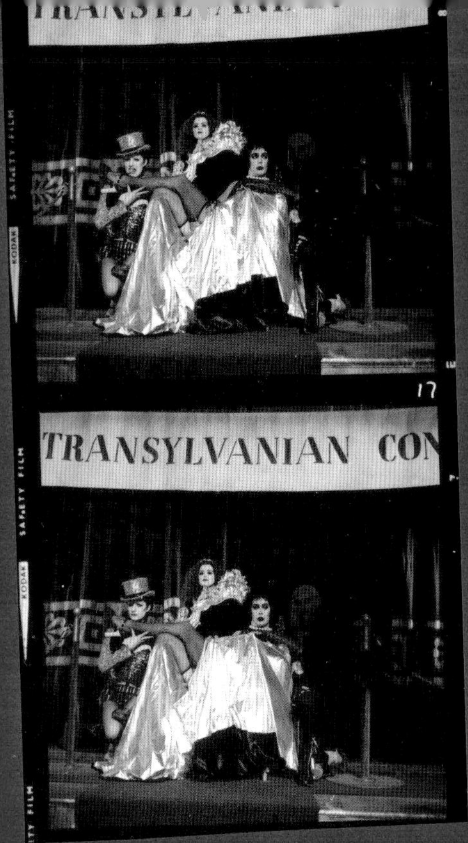

"I hadn't always realized that quite a lot of the pictures I'd looked at over the years were actually Mick's stills as opposed to stills from the film itself. I just assumed they were stills from the film. Like the iconic one of Tim, as Frank-N-Furter, on the sofa with Columbia and Magenta and Riff Raff—I had assumed that was a still from the movie. But clearly, it isn't. It was set up by Mick." —SUE BLANE

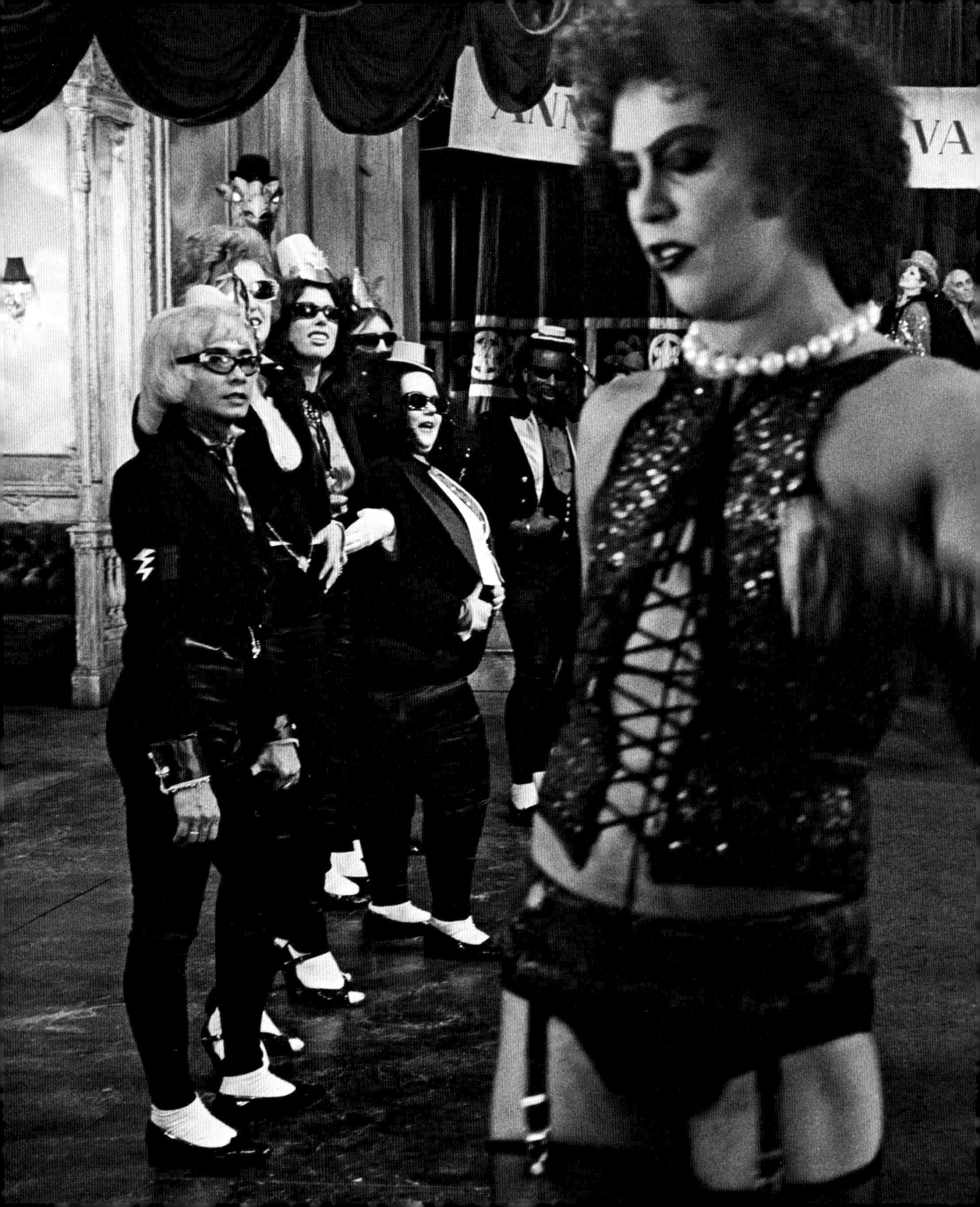

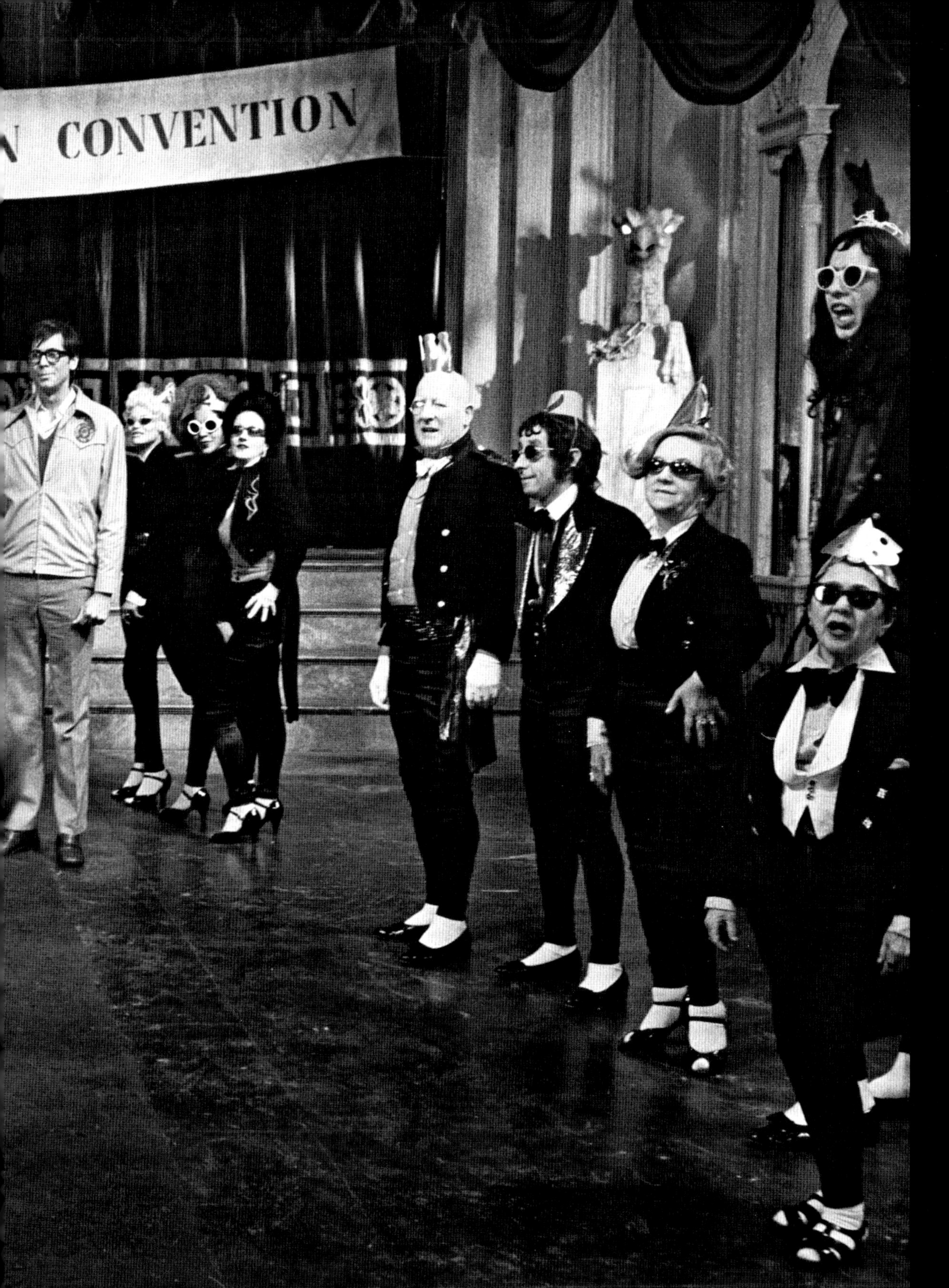
N CONVENTION

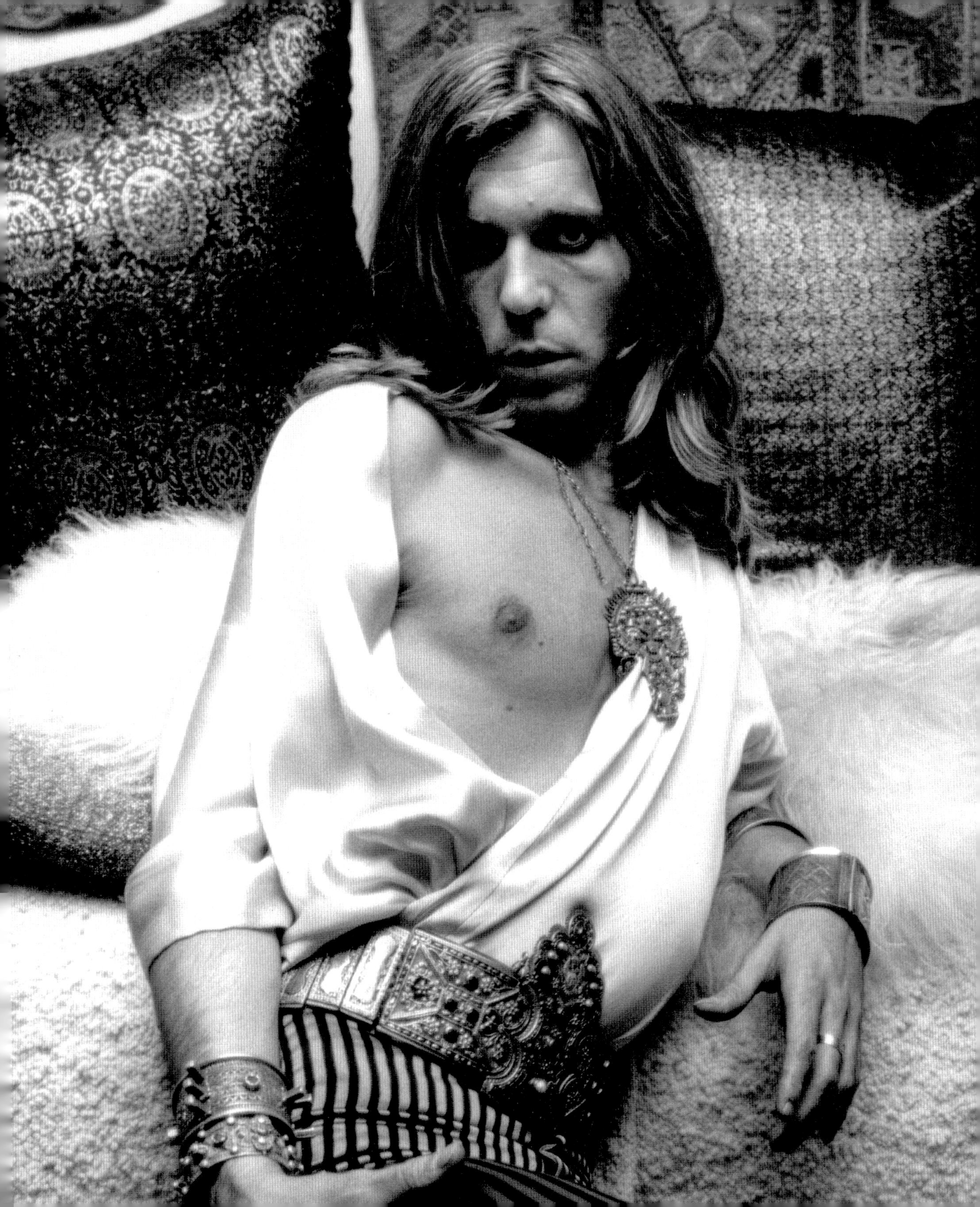

A WILD AND UNTAMED THING: PIERRE LA ROCHE

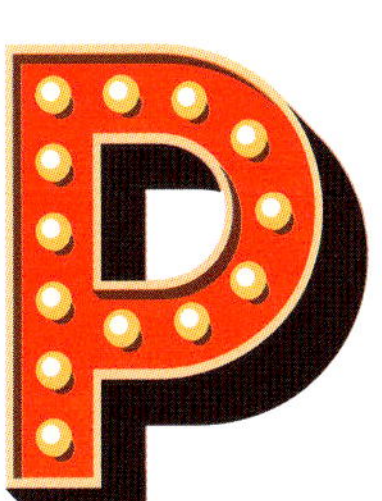

Pierre La Roche had grown up in Algiers before moving to France and then England, where he became a star makeup artist for Elizabeth Arden. When the company tried to rein in his more outré creative impulses, he quit. He started working with musicians, helping to popularize the glitter look and heavy, dark eye shadow—apparently influenced by the use of kohl that he knew from Algeria. His clients would include Mick Jagger and—most famously—David Bowie.

In the space of just two years, La Roche helped craft Bowie's Ziggy Stardust persona, including the astral sphere on his forehead; he designed the lightning bolt on Bowie's face for the cover of *Aladdin Sane*, which became one of the most recognizable images in pop history; he created Bowie and Twiggy's look for the cover of *Pin Ups*; and he did Bowie's makeup on the set of Mick Rock's iconic video shoot for "Life on Mars?"

During the stage production of *Rocky Horror*, the actors had done their own makeup, but when it came time to make the film, La Roche was brought in.

As designer and model Susie Cave wrote on Instagram of La Roche, who died in 1991, "Pierre La Roche was in my opinion the greatest, most inventive makeup artist the world had ever seen, but back then these extraordinarily talented people did not receive the same recognition as they would today. A visionary genius and the most beautiful friend."

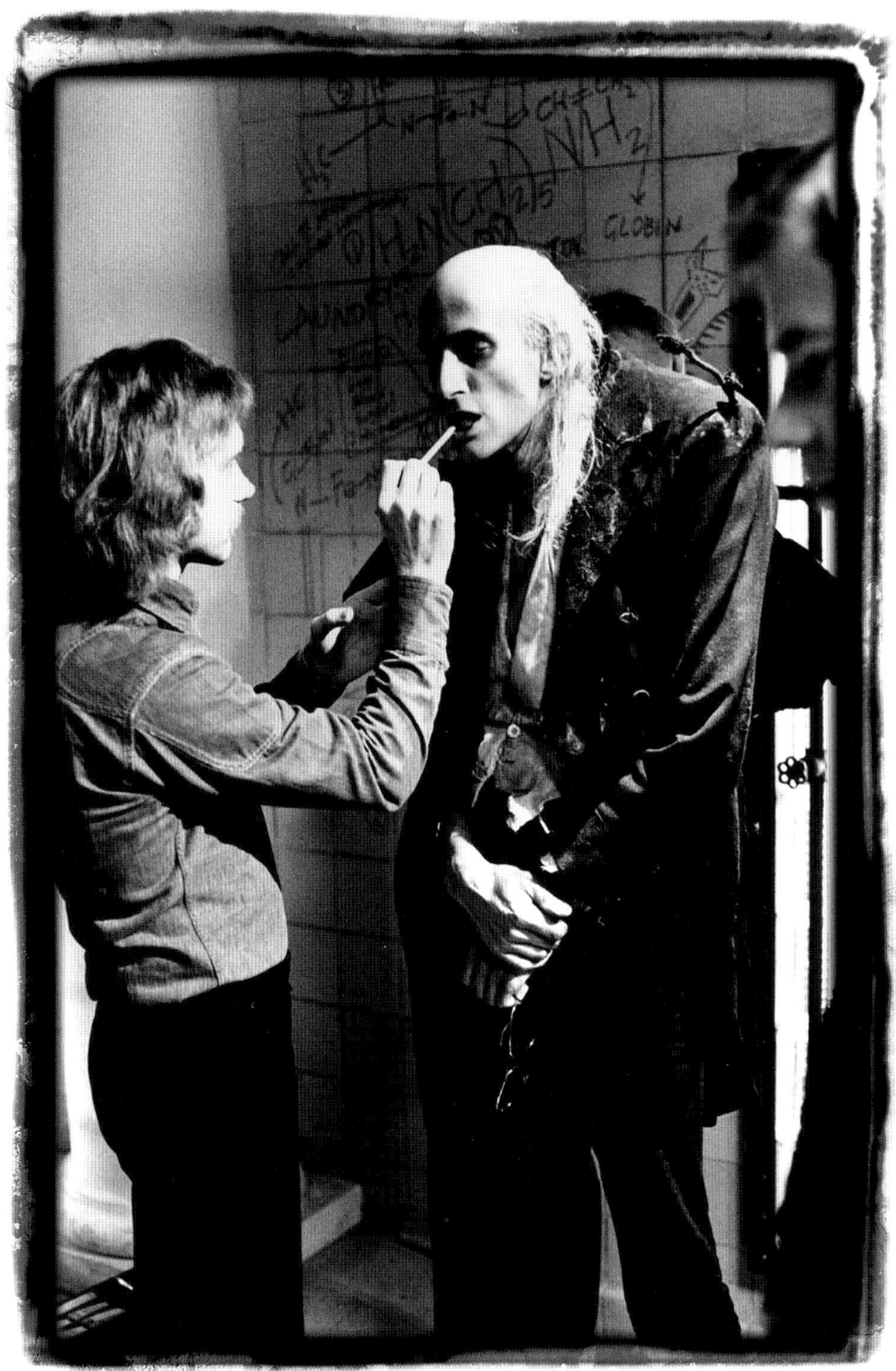
GLOBIN

ARIANNE PHILLIPS, OSCAR, TONY, AND BAFTA-NOMINATED COSTUME DESIGNER: "I first heard of *Rocky Horror* when I was 11—my older and very cool cousins, who lived in Los Angeles, saw the live show at the Roxy with their mother, my aunt, who was dating a well-known rock 'n' roll lighting designer. It wasn't until a few years later, when the film was released, that I happened to see it—by accident.

I was 14 and was with a bunch of friends who were going to see David Lynch's *Eraserhead* at a midnight showing in Berkeley, California. Without any notice, they showed *The Rocky Horror Picture Show* instead. My adolescent mind was blown. I was already a theater kid, and I loved rock 'n' roll musicals like *Hair*, *Godspell*, and *Jesus Christ Superstar*, but *The Rocky Horror Picture Show* was beyond anything I had ever seen. Watching this film when I myself was just a kid, figuring out who I was, the message of *don't dream it be it* resonated on a very deep level. *The Rocky Horror Picture Show* for me was punk and irreverent, and empowered self-expression through makeup, hair, dressing up, sexual ambiguity, being different, being free with sexuality, and belonging to a tribe of similarly like-minded people. After that midnight screening, I was never the same."

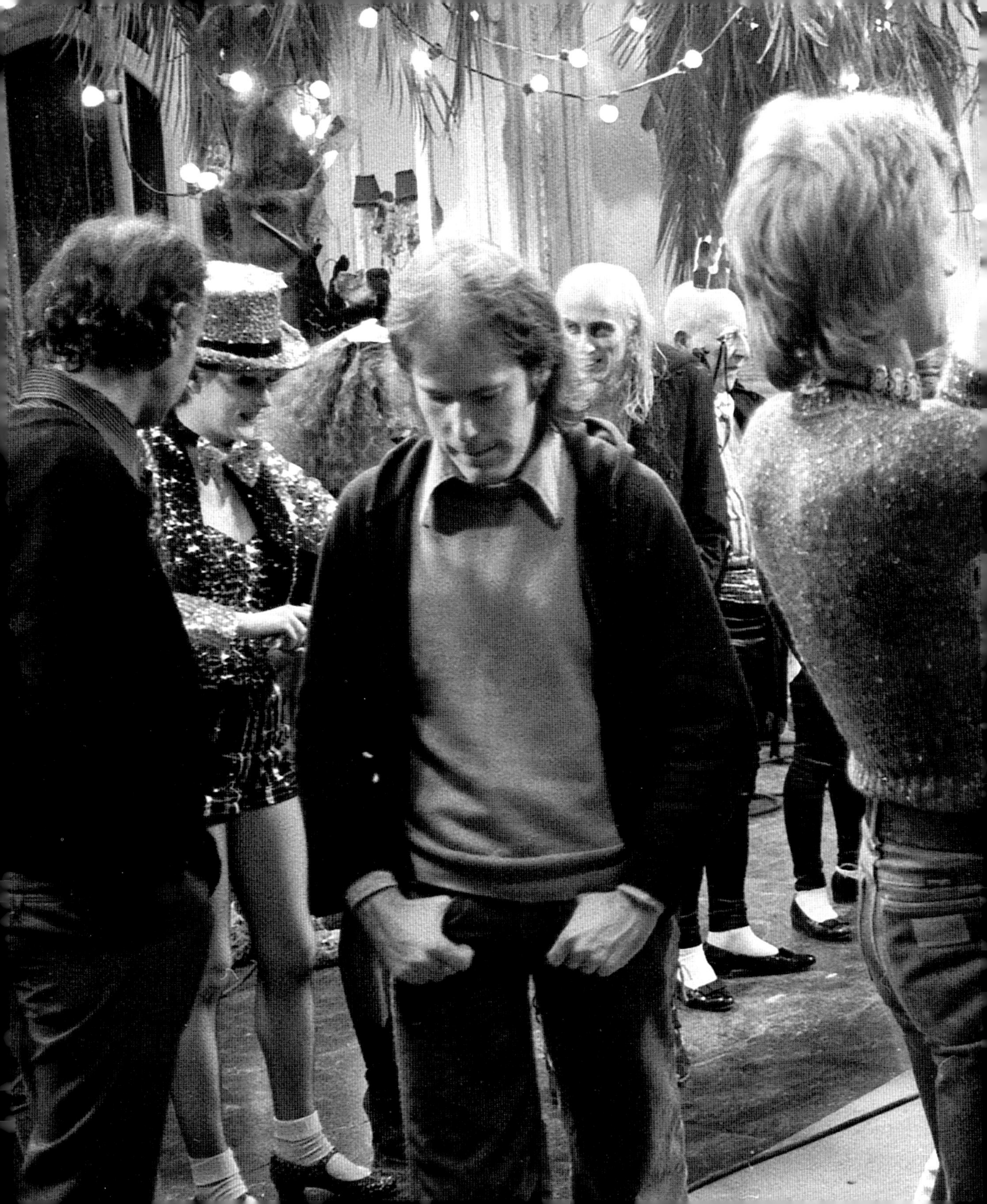

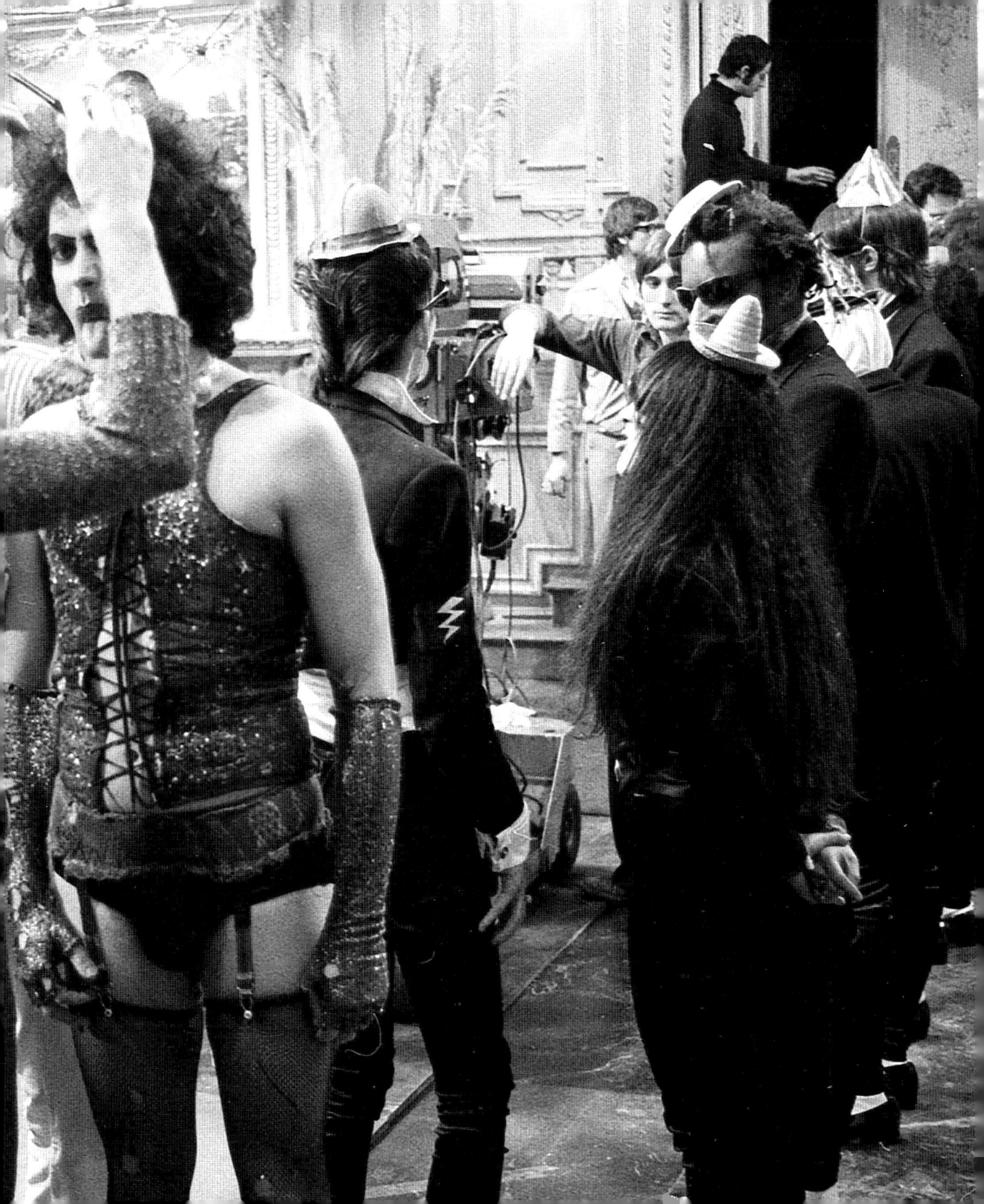

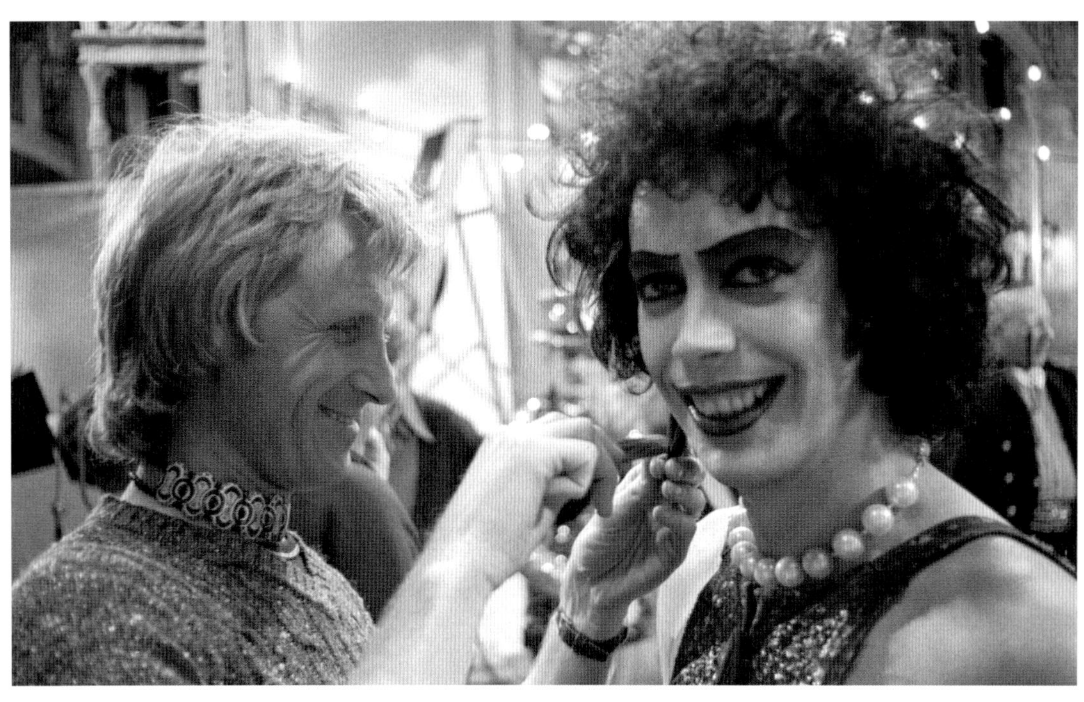

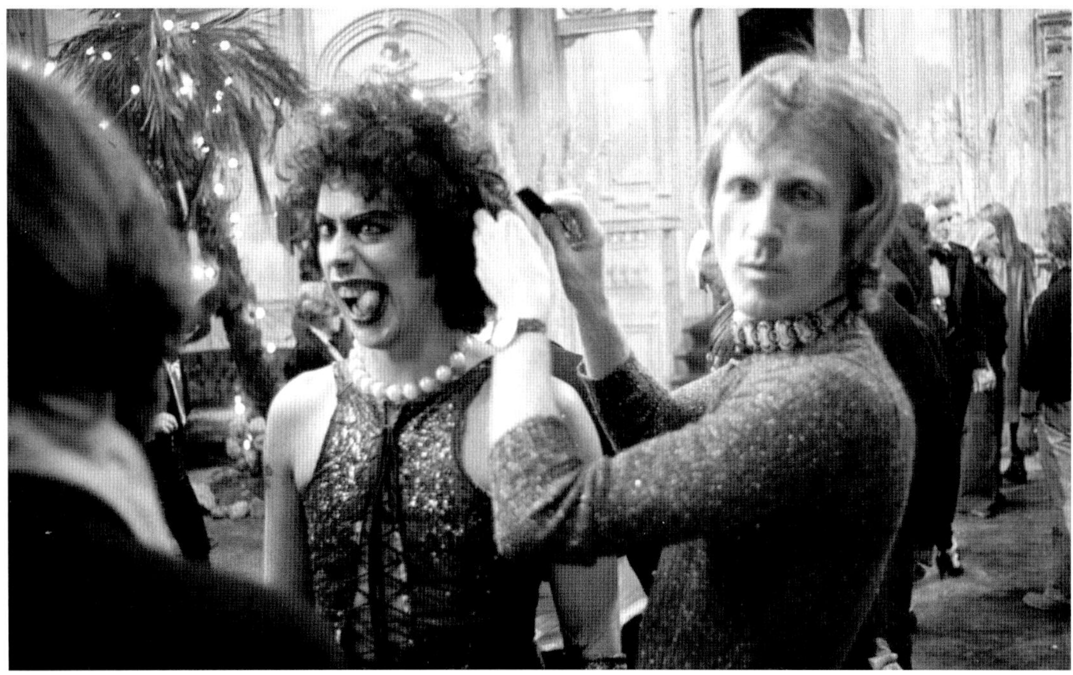

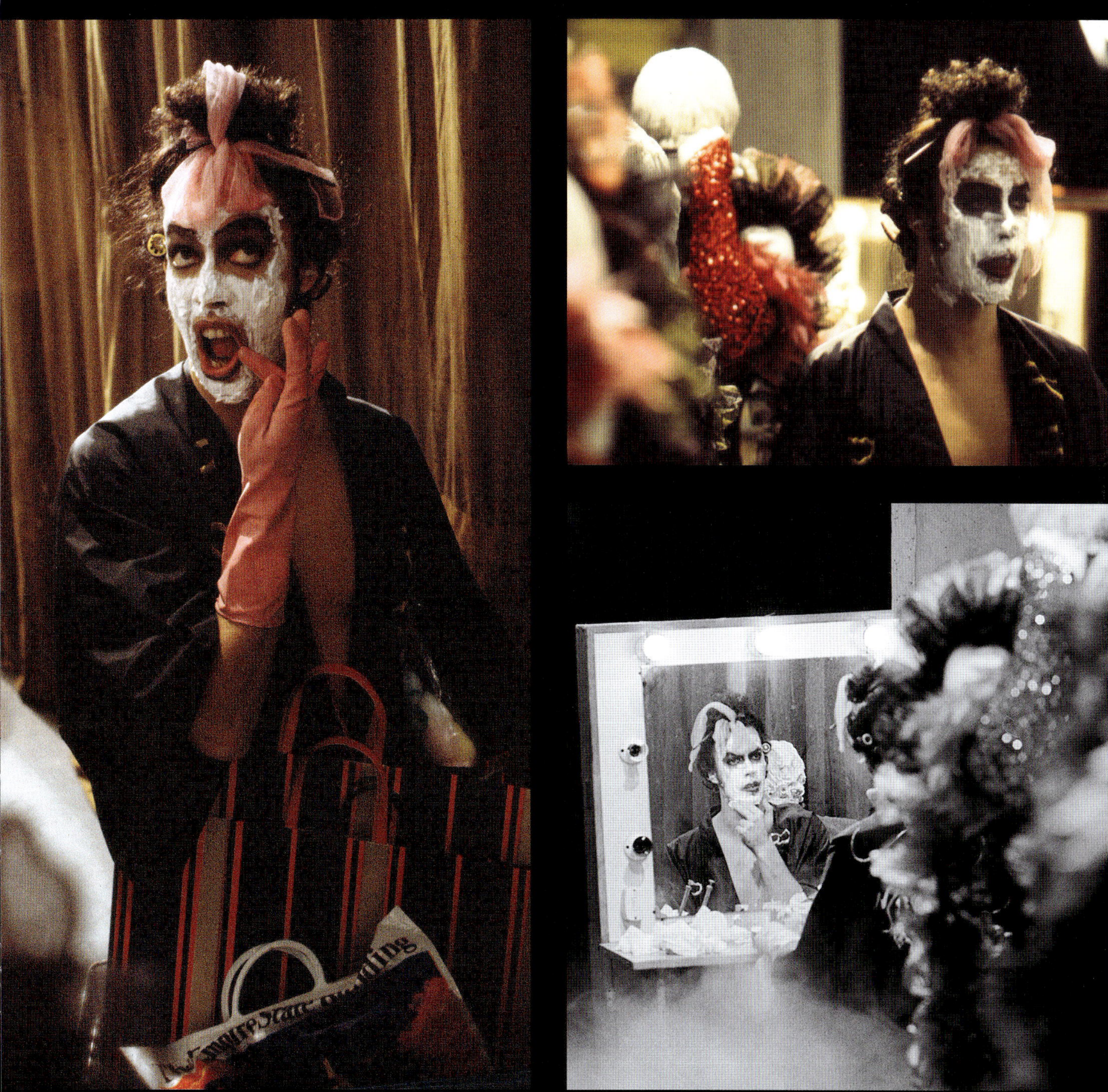

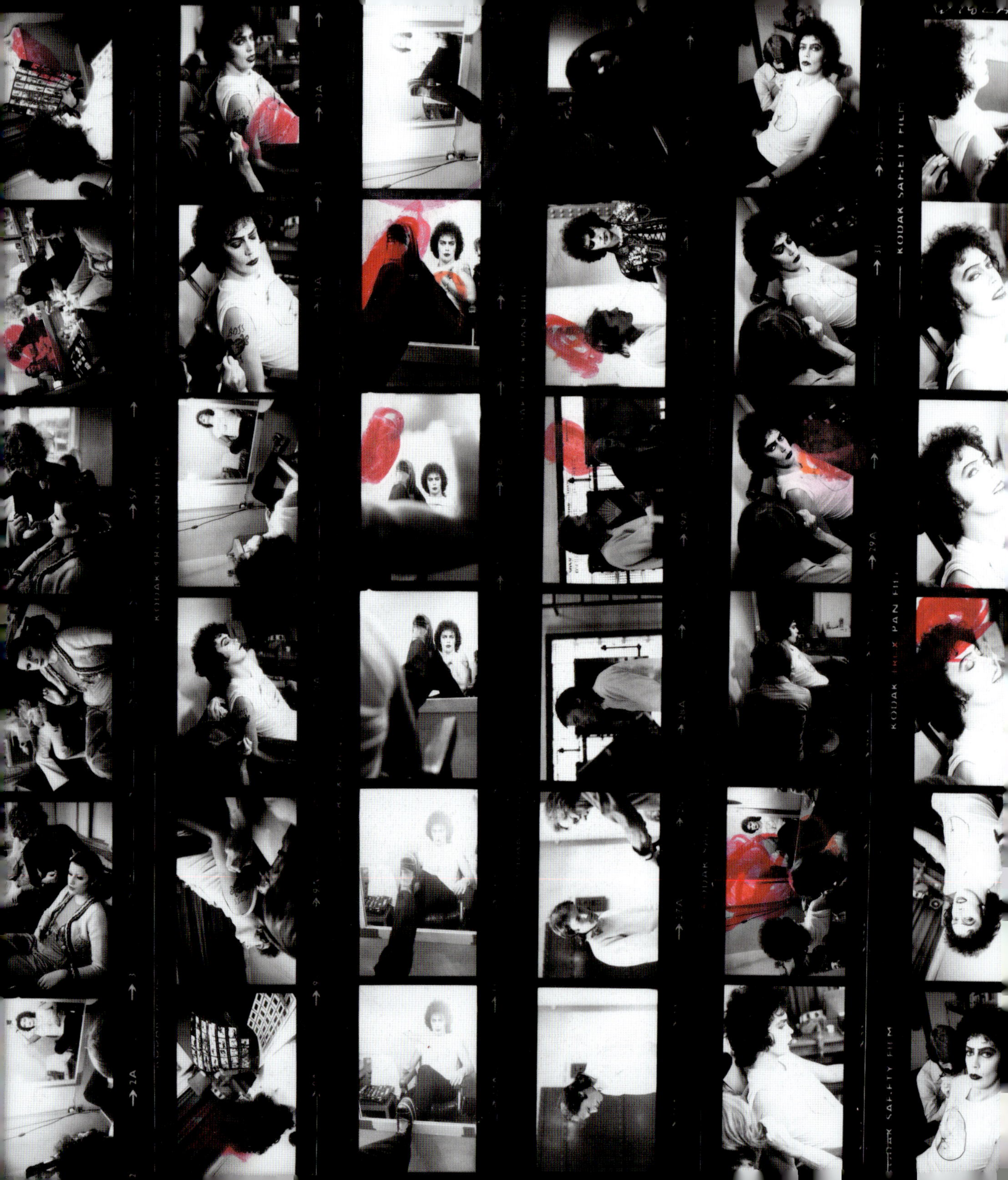

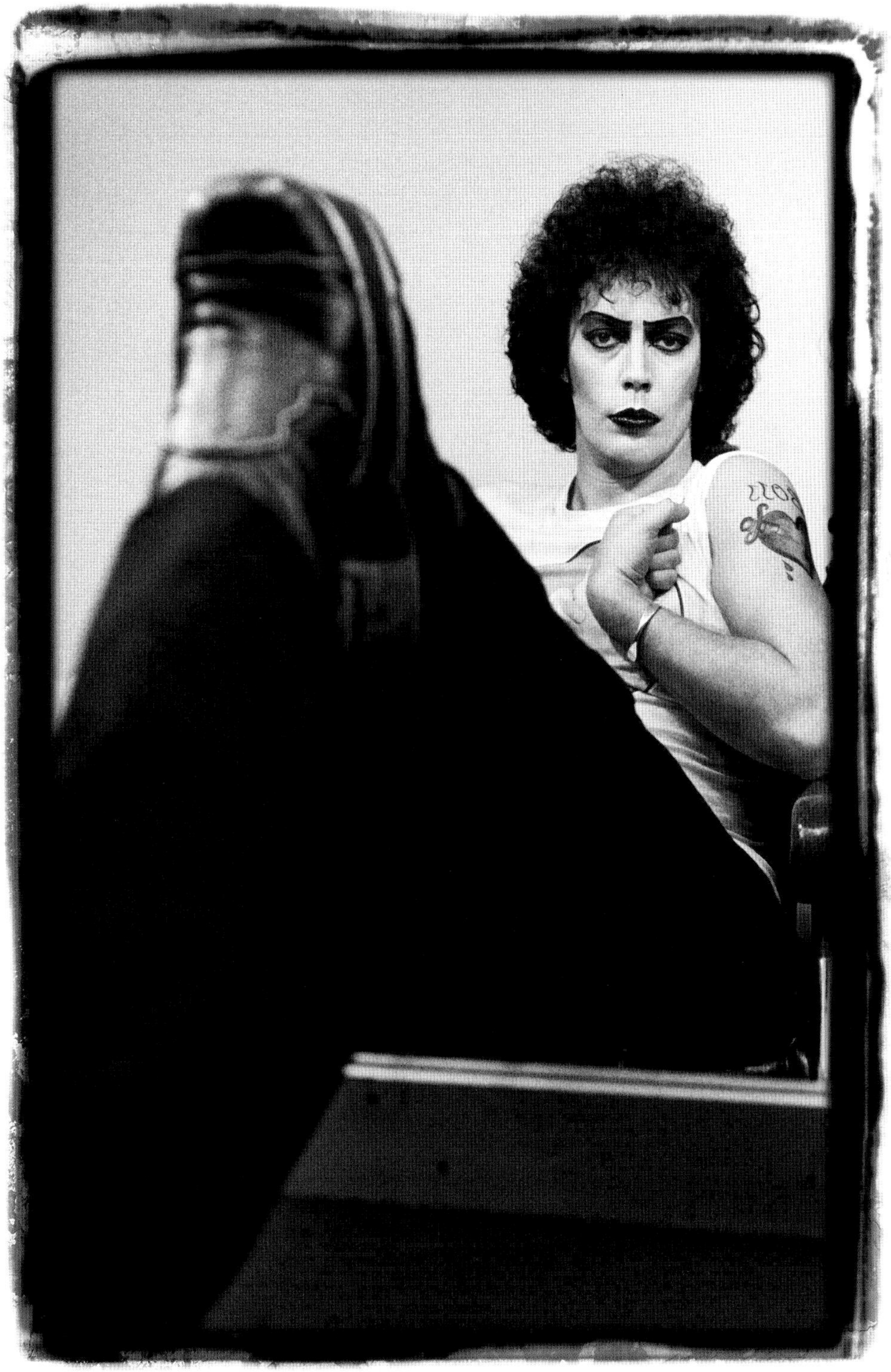

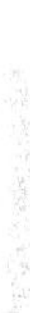

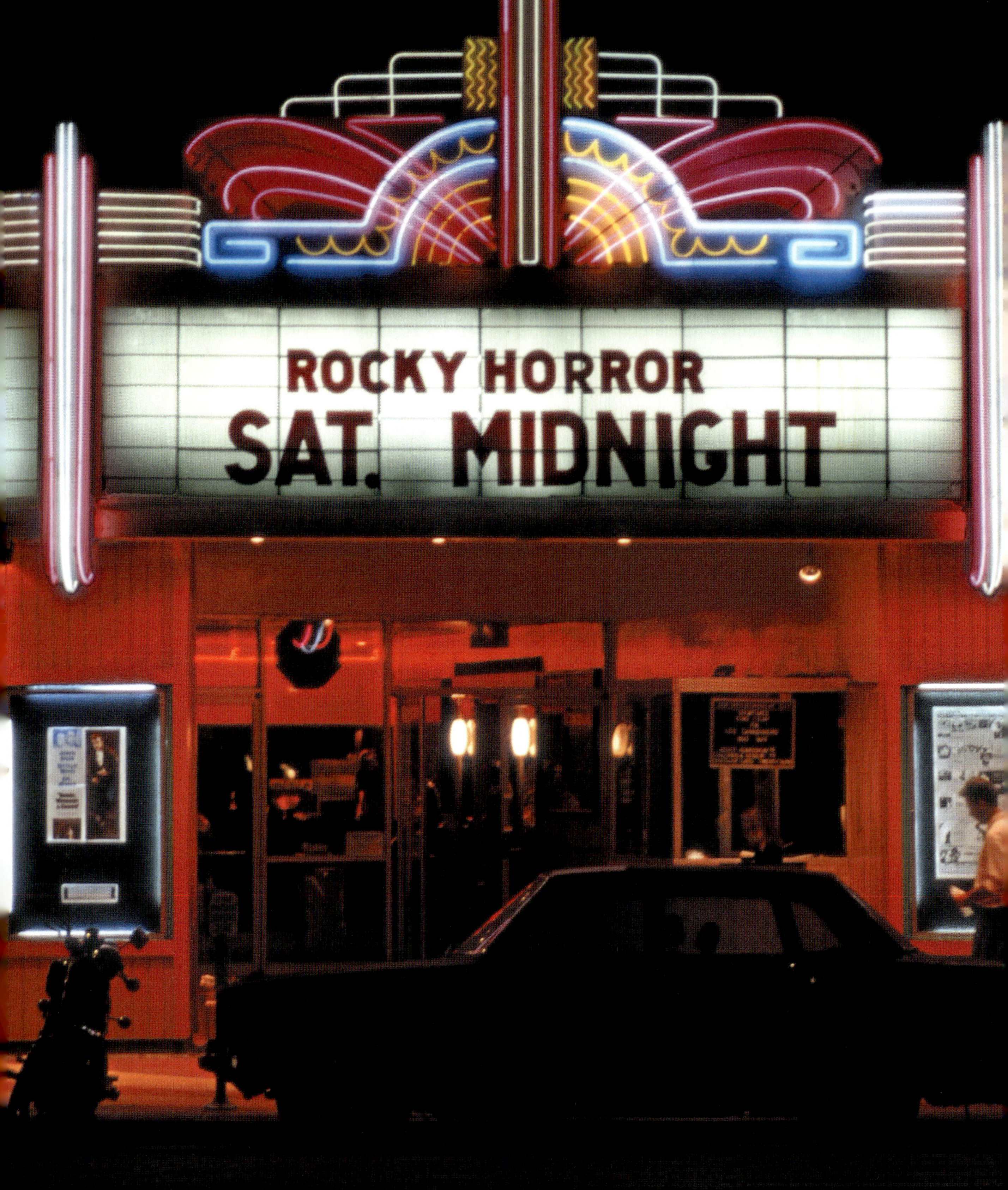
ROCKY HORROR
SAT. MIDNIGHT

IT'S NOT EASY HAVING A GOOD TIME: THE MIDNIGHT SHOW

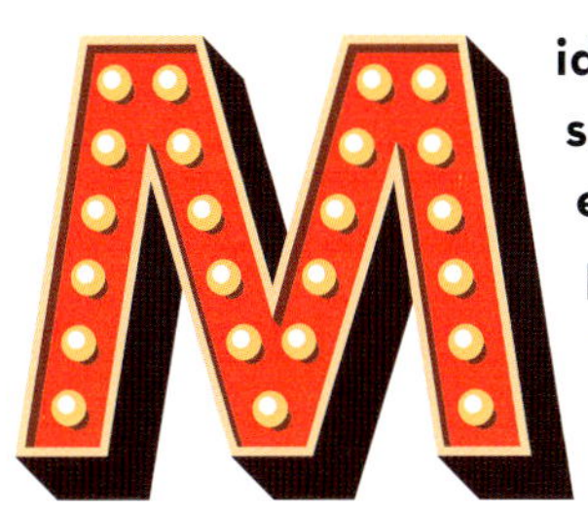

idnight movies are so thoroughly ensconced in popular culture today that it's easy to forget there was a time when they didn't exist, not even in major cities like New York and LA. In fact, the concept of showing late-night movies started only a few years prior to the release of *The Rocky Horror Picture Show*. The two phenomena were so perfectly suited to each other that it can be argued this magical combination single-handedly ensured the long-term cultural and financial importance of this essential cinematic experience—which also kept many struggling independent cinemas in business.

The nascent midnight movie phenomenon was largely rooted in orgies of violence far more explicit than had previously been seen in cinemas—the origins of the circuit were screenings of Chilean-French director Alejandro Jodorowsky's *El Topo*, which a *New York Times* critic called "deranged." Midnight screenings of *El Topo* started in December 1970, at the Elgin Theater in the Chelsea district of New York City, setting off a national trend focused on similarly shocking underground movies like *Night of the Living Dead*.

But things changed when the Elgin added John Waters's *Pink Flamingos* at midnight on Fridays and Saturdays starting in 1972. Audiences began to return for repeated viewings and to recite lines, setting up perfectly for the ultimate participatory experience that was just about to explode

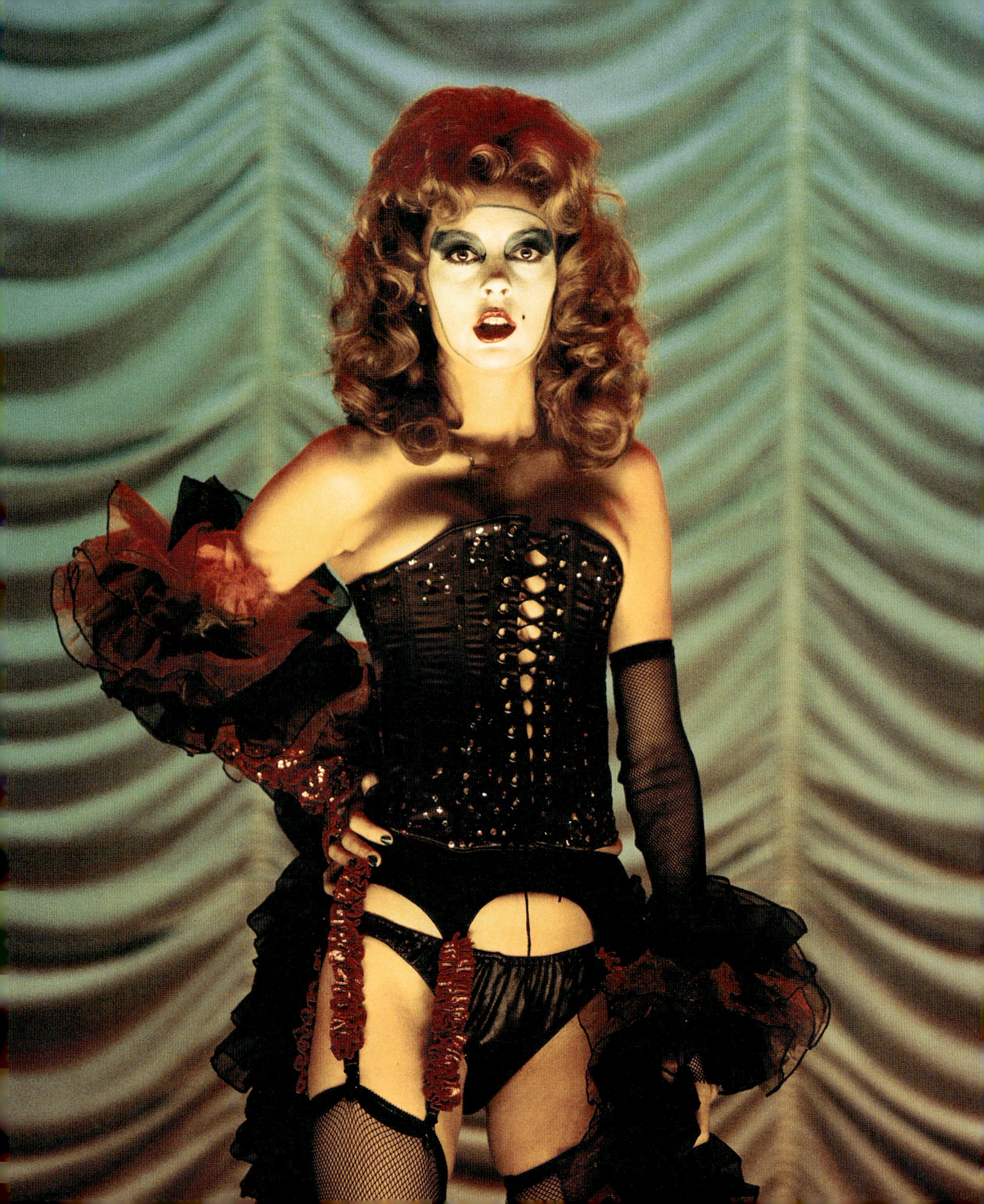

onto the scene thanks to Richard O'Brien's highly musical, theatrical vision. Unlike Waters's picture, which used cherry-picked (but actually unlicensed) pop songs from the past as a soundtrack, *Rocky Horror*'s very foundation was music, and original music at that. This made Sharman and O'Brien's picture fundamentally different, and would lend itself to fostering a new relationship with the audience. But first, the film needed to find that audience.

The Rocky Horror Picture Show officially opened in Los Angeles on September 26, 1975, despite what the *New York Times* described as a "disastrous test screening in Santa Barbara." The initial critical response was likewise abysmal. *Time* magazine wrote that "it is not easy to see why this campy trash was a long-running hit in London and a smash success in Los Angeles, except that transvestism has always fascinated the British and the L.A. scene is almost as kinky." The *San Francisco Chronicle* deemed *Rocky Horror* "lacking both charm and dramatic impact." *Newsweek* called it "tasteless, plotless, pointless."

As Susan Sarandon recalled to *EW* in 2022, "I don't think anybody knew what to make of it, and that was the end of it. I never even knew it had opened."

Tim Deegan, a young Fox publicist who was working with Adler, told the *New York Times* in 2015, "it was doomed from the start." But Deegan, intrigued by midnight screenings of *Pink Flamingos*, saw this route as a possible alternative path to success. "The thing about the midnight show was there was an ambience," Deegan later told the *Los Angeles Times*. "It didn't matter what I was going to see, I would be with my friends. It's a whole different world."

Despite reluctance from studio executives at Fox, who had already given up on the film, Deegan was able to get *Rocky Horror* into a midnight slot at the Waverly Theater in Greenwich Village in New York City, where

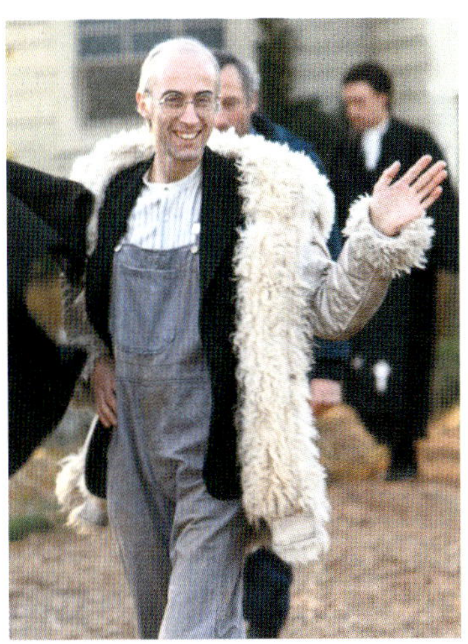

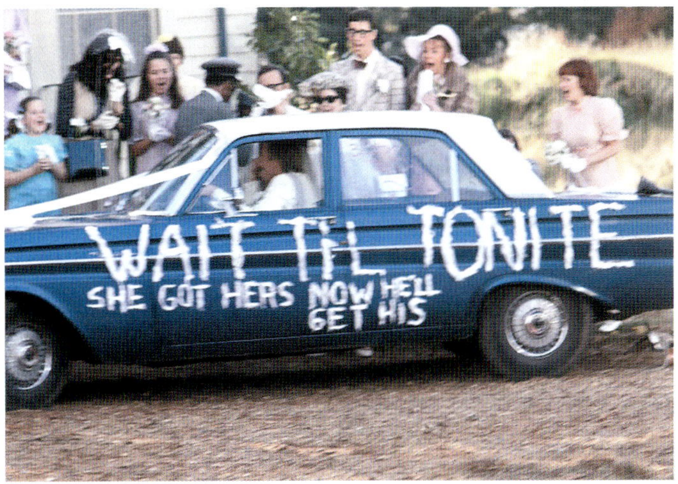

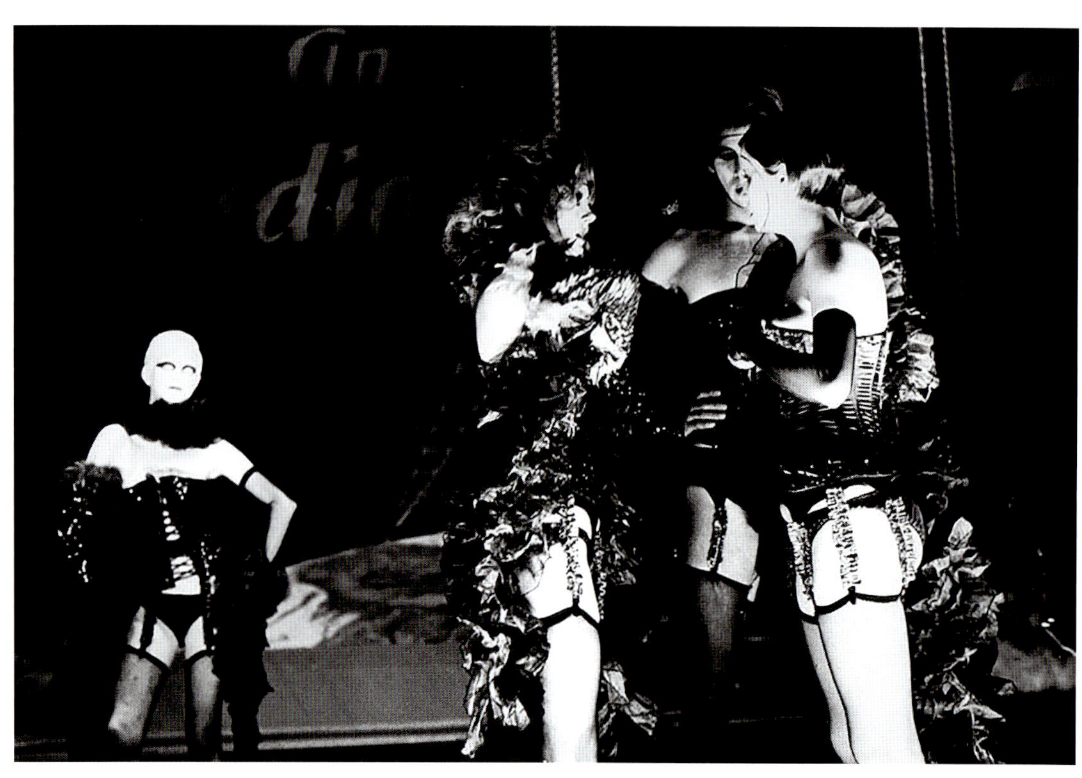

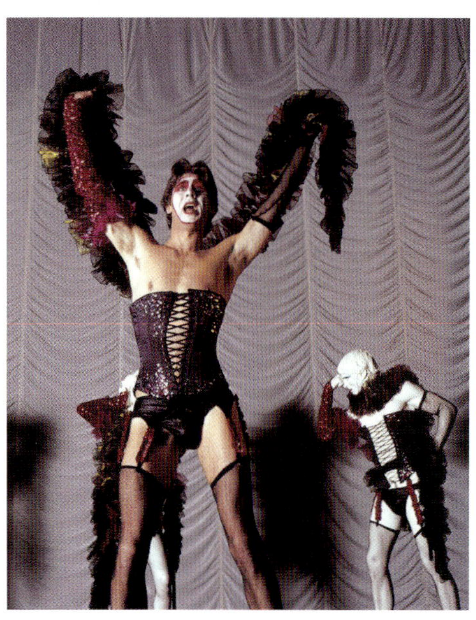

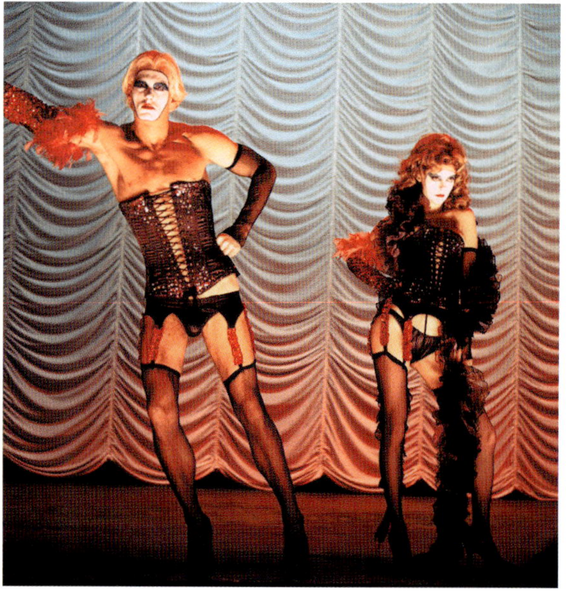

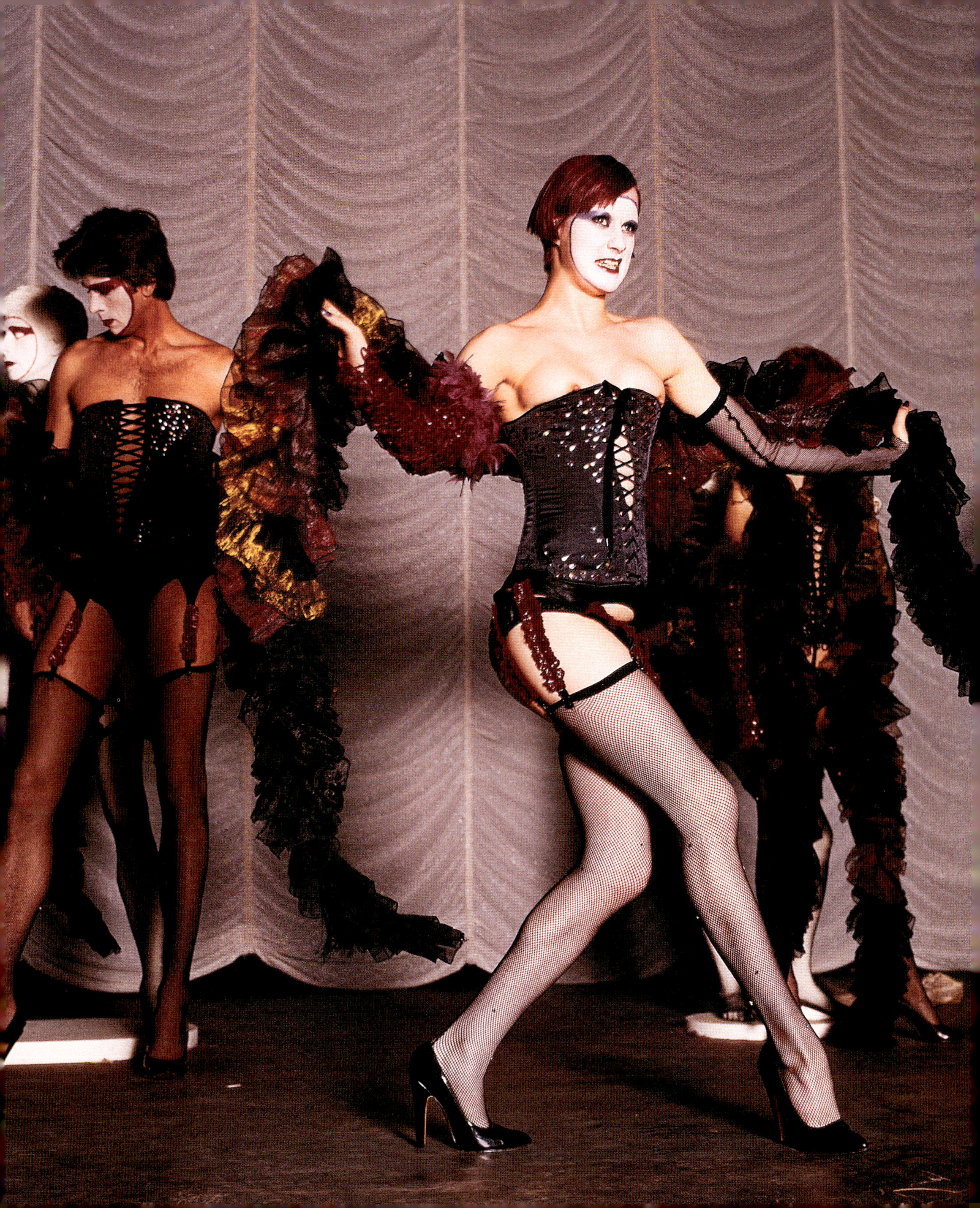

it premiered on April Fools' Day, 1976. Deegan spent sixty-four dollars on a small ad in the *Village Voice*, but didn't want to hype the film, as he hoped it would catch on by word of mouth.

And this is exactly what would happen at the Waverly, as the film's challenge—"don't dream it, be it"—was taken up by late-night audiences, who, bit by bit, turned screenings into a novel sort of participatory performance art.

Perhaps *Chicago Sun-Times* film critic Roger Ebert had been correct all along in his initial assessment: "*The Rocky Horror Picture Show* would be more fun, I suspect, if it weren't a picture show. It belongs on a stage, with the performers and audience joining in a collective send-up. . . . It invites the kind of laughter and audience participation that makes sense only if the performers are there on the stage, creating mutual karma."

Only Ebert failed to realize you could have it both ways—through ever more elaborate audience participation and live shadowcast performances at screenings of the film.

Tim Curry claims that David Bowie's wife, Angie, was an early participant in reacting aloud to the screen. "I remember when Bowie came and he brought this huge entourage, and she was with him, and when Richard O'Brien was about to kill me, she shouted 'No! No! Don't do it!' So I guess she was one of the first people to do that," he told NPR.

Such ad-libs directed at the screen continued to be encouraged and to evolve. But ritualized set pieces—throwing rice, toast, playing cards; deploying newspapers, bells, and squirt guns; snapping rubber gloves in unison—also came to be repeated at every performance. And eventually amateur or even professional casts accompanied the film live, in real time, thus doubling the experience, stage and screen—a synchronized swim in the deep end of subculture, and an experience so unique and multifaceted it soon took the world by storm.

Sal Piro first saw the film in early 1977 at the Waverly, and quickly became a superfan. "Image followed image and the impact on me was tremendous," he said in his 1990 book *Creatures of the Night: The Rocky Horror Picture Show Experience*. "I began living the movie as it unreeled."

By spring of 1977, Piro—who would eventually see more than 1,300 *Rocky Horror* screenings—founded the Rocky Horror Picture Show Fan Club, and was elected president, a position he held for over four decades until his death in 2023. Piro and the club are credited with helping the film—and in particular the in-person participatory experience—spread from the Waverly to the world.

Susan Sarandon's first exposure to the phenomenon came at its birthplace, the Waverly, thanks to another actress: "Molly Ringwald took me to a screening pretty early on. That was the first time I saw it, the whole ritual. It's given a home to so many people, especially those who need to be accepted for who they are."

Director Jim Sharman feels that the audiences at midnight screenings "found the combo of the film and the music, the masquerade and the party atmosphere, allowed them to deal with difficult things in their lives, especially their sexuality, in a

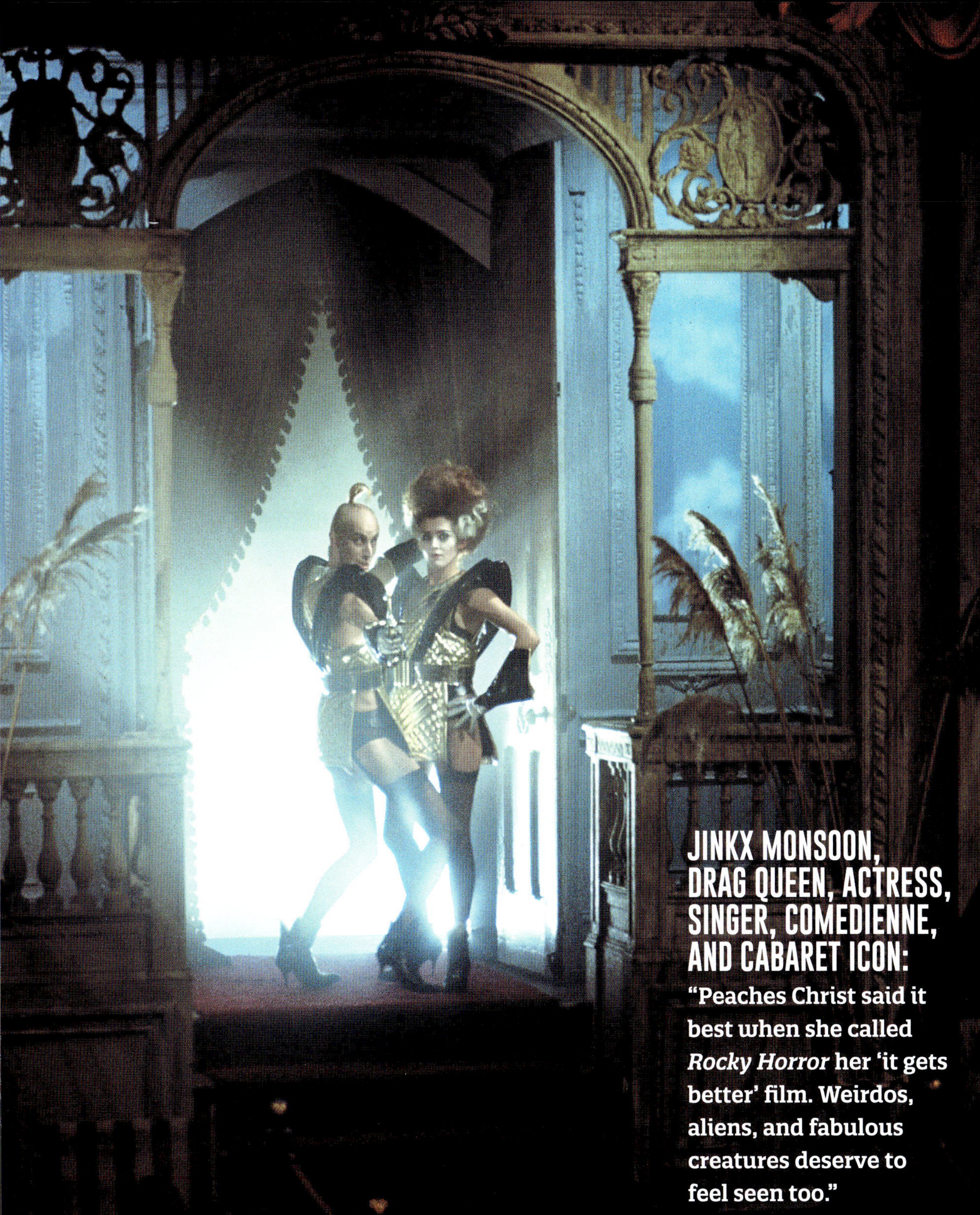

JINKX MONSOON, DRAG QUEEN, ACTRESS, SINGER, COMEDIENNE, AND CABARET ICON:

"Peaches Christ said it best when she called *Rocky Horror* her 'it gets better' film. Weirdos, aliens, and fabulous creatures deserve to feel seen too."

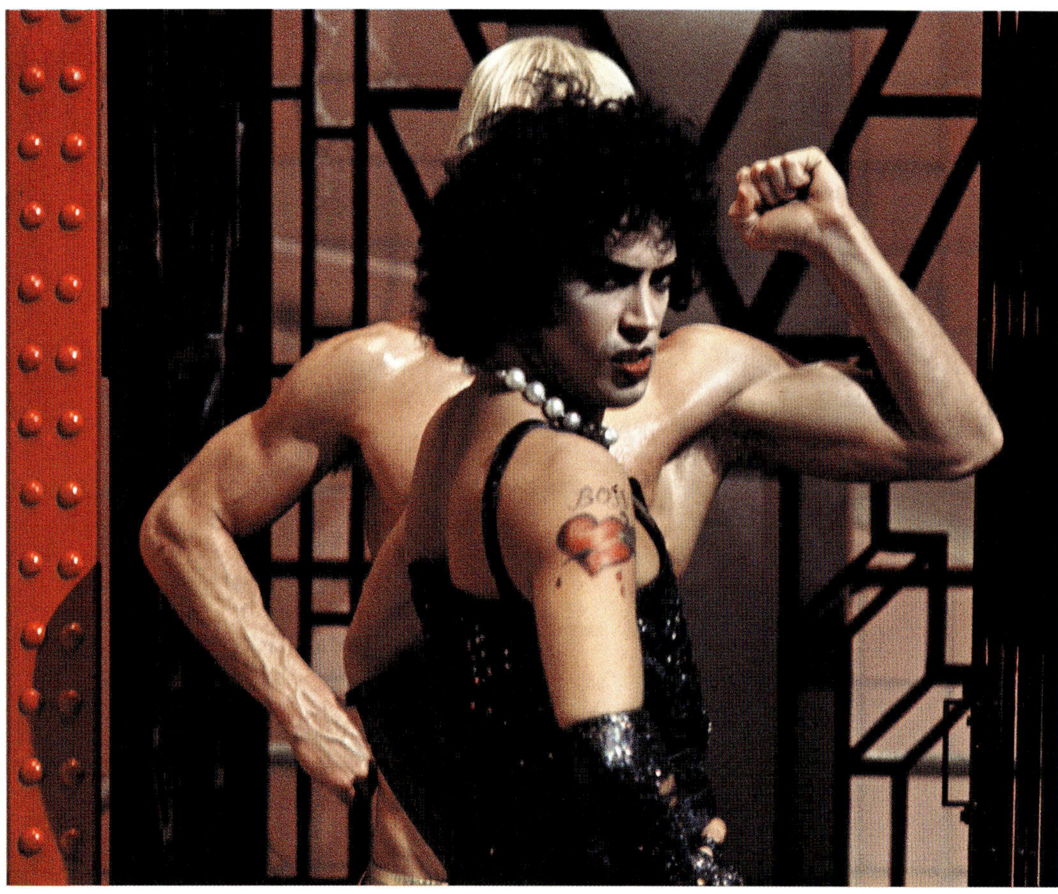

light, liberating way. The mainstream audience only saw the surface, and they turned away; but the late-night audience picked up on what was under that surface—and it spoke to them."

The evolution of audience participation made sense to Sharman for another reason too, as he explained to RockyHorror.com, the movie's official fan site. "With the original stage version we had converted cinemas into theaters, so there was a certain crazy logic in the fact that the film would end up turning cinemas into theaters, which is more or less what happened. There were aspects built into the film that helped trigger this response, including a few considered moments where characters acknowledge the audience's presence, which is rare in a film."

Rocky Horror empowered everyone to partake in this enjoyment at whatever level suited them—the participatory aspect of the phenomenon let people dabble in performance within a welcoming community. In a way, that allowed them to experiment with how and to what extent they wished to participate. This type of safe space proved to be a key

GOTTMIK, DRAG PERFORMER AND MAKEUP ARTIST: "Growing up, I always knew I was different. But I was raised in the Arizona Catholic school system, so I had nothing to look up to or to inspire me to try to figure it out. I remember seeing *The Rocky Horror Picture Show* at my friend Natalie's house when I was a freshman in high school; I can confidently say that watching *The Rocky Horror Picture Show* for the first time changed my life. It opened my world up just enough to ignite something inside and to begin to own my uniqueness and start finding my truth.

The Rocky Horror Picture Show is so line-blurring when it comes to gender and sexuality, in such an effortless way, that it makes you think everyone from Transsexual Transylvania are the 'normal' ones and Brad and Janet are the 'weirdos.' It was the first time I realized that life was all about perspective and that I could do and be anything I wanted to be.

I also remember seeing the show for the first time in person, in Phoenix. I was possessed by the participatory aspect. I had never seen anything like it, and it really did feel like my first safe space to just scream into the void and lose myself in the show.

In my own shows, I love to get everyone clapping and jumping and I love to get down into the audience and interact with people because you never know what those moments will mean to people (or to yourself as a performer). Works of iconic art like *The Rocky Horror Picture Show* were truly the only looks into gender queer, free-flowing sexuality that me and many others had, and seeing yourself in someone else's artistry makes you feel safe and seen in a way that inspires you to push your own boundaries and become the person/artist you always knew you would be."

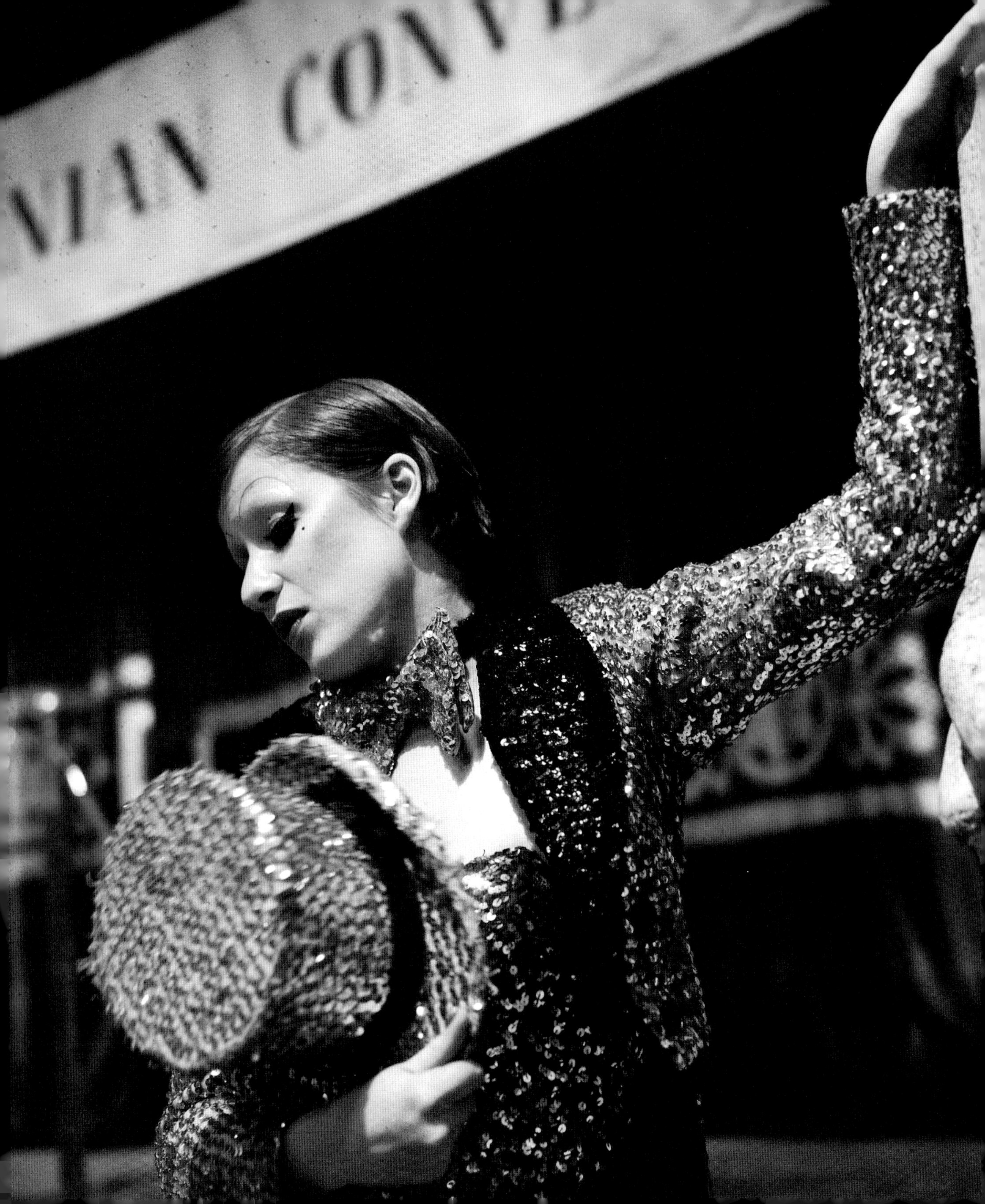

to both personal and artistic development and inspired and fostered generation after generation of performers and artists.

Musician and author Richard Barone first witnessed the audience phenomenon in the mid-1980s, at a midnight screening in Greenwich Village together with Fred Schneider of the B-52s. "We had both just returned home from a tour, and Fred was interested in seeing what all the fuss was about. Everything we had heard was true. Everyone in the theater was in costume, reciting lines perfectly, yelling at the screen, and singing every line of every song. We were pelted with rice, sprayed with water, and hit with rolls of toilet paper. We loved it! As a performer, it was significant to see how entertainment could inspire this level of active engagement. My first thought was, 'How can *I* do something like this?' But the answer, of course, is: you can't. Because it is magic. It has to happen all by itself." Long before the internet made it easier to form communities and share information far and wide, live shadowcast productions had mushroomed not only across the US, the UK, and Canada, but also in Japan, Germany, Ireland, Croatia, Spain, France, Italy, Switzerland, Israel, Vietnam, and Australia.

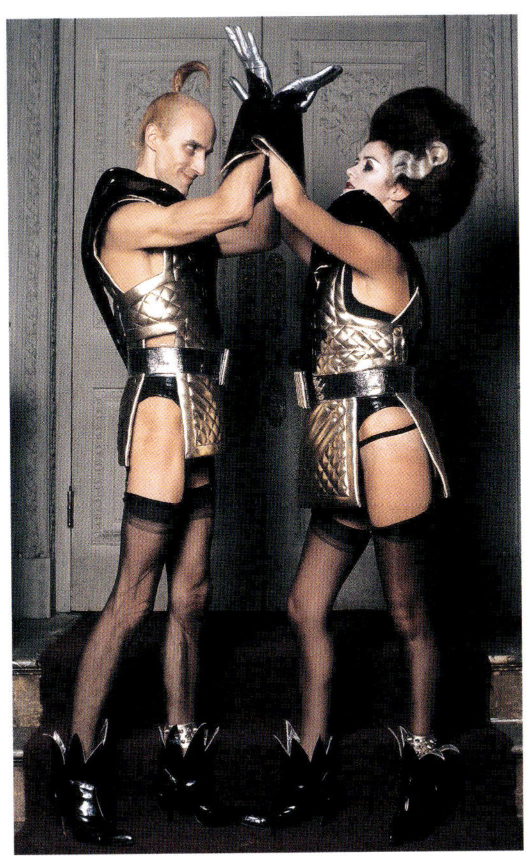

"People felt they discovered it themselves," O'Brien suggested to the blog *Cocklenuggets*, "and I think that's an element of anything that becomes a cult. When you or I discover something, you think it's just *you* that's discovered it, you go 'oh, I've got to introduce others to this.' It becomes our personal journey. It's an individual experience. Millions of people have seen *Rocky Horror* now, but it's still a cult experience. That's the paradox."

Earl Orrin, who created Chocolate Covered Rocky Horror in 2015, first saw the film in College Park, Maryland. "It immediately felt like I stumbled upon a secret society in the middle of the woods in the middle of the night. The fans! I was interested in their boldness, bravery, and fearlessness."

Since then, Orrin's production has become a leading light in the Black Arts District of Baltimore—and a mutual support system. "Our cast is no stranger to the struggles facing minorities and often we experience these hardships. We depend and lean on each other during hard times. And we are not afraid to express ourselves to one another no matter how hard the conversations may be. We genuinely want the best for each other, and encourage and support each other."

At this point, the film made for $1 million and left for dead after its initial theatrical release has earned approximately $200 million. But more important is the place it has carved out as a social phenomenon. "Even though everyone comes from different walks of life, people who find their way there tend to be social outcasts who form this camaraderie," says current official fan club president Larry Viezel. "For a lot of people, *Rocky Horror* is like their home, it's their connection to everybody—all their friends. I know of a lot of people whose lives were saved by this movie. Especially for those in the LGBT community, it's a place where they could be themselves and find people who were their family."

Kristian Lavercombe, who has performed in more than two thousand shows as Riff Raff, Frank-N-Furter, and Brad, would agree. As Lavercombe told the BBC in 2022, "It's always been ahead of its time. And I think now it's preaching a sentiment that is very popular, which is: to be yourself."

Richard O'Brien suggested something similar to *Newsweek* in 2015: "It celebrates difference. People who feel marginalized, alone, and confused; somehow, it gathers them together and allows them to coexist."

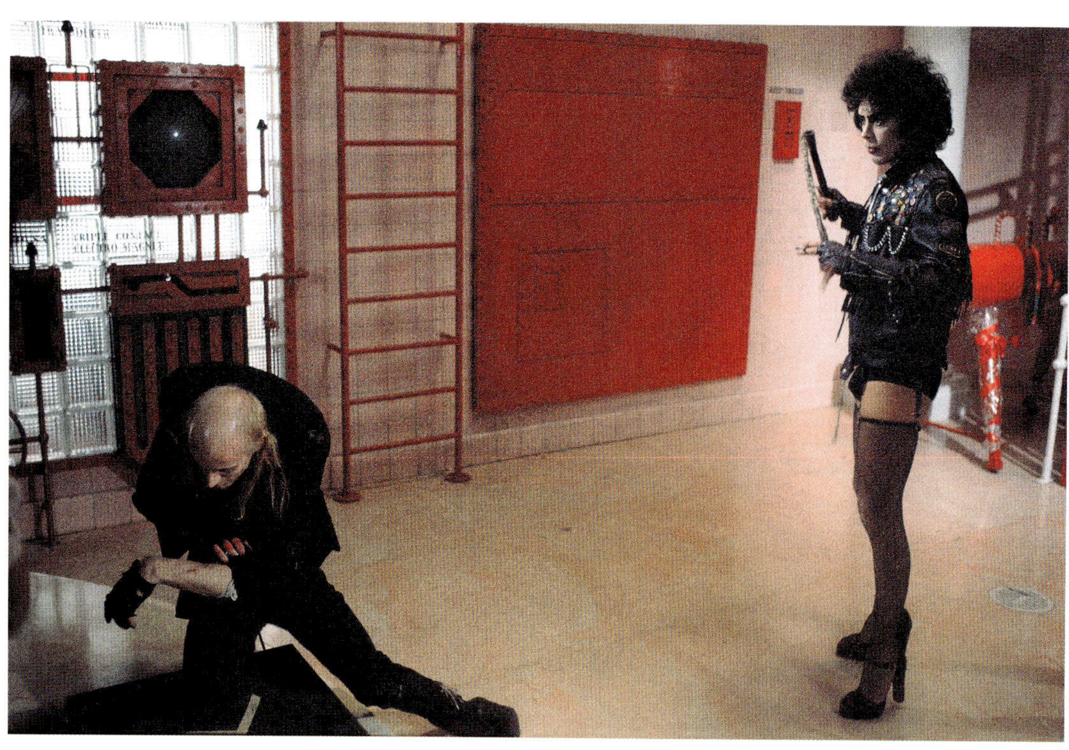

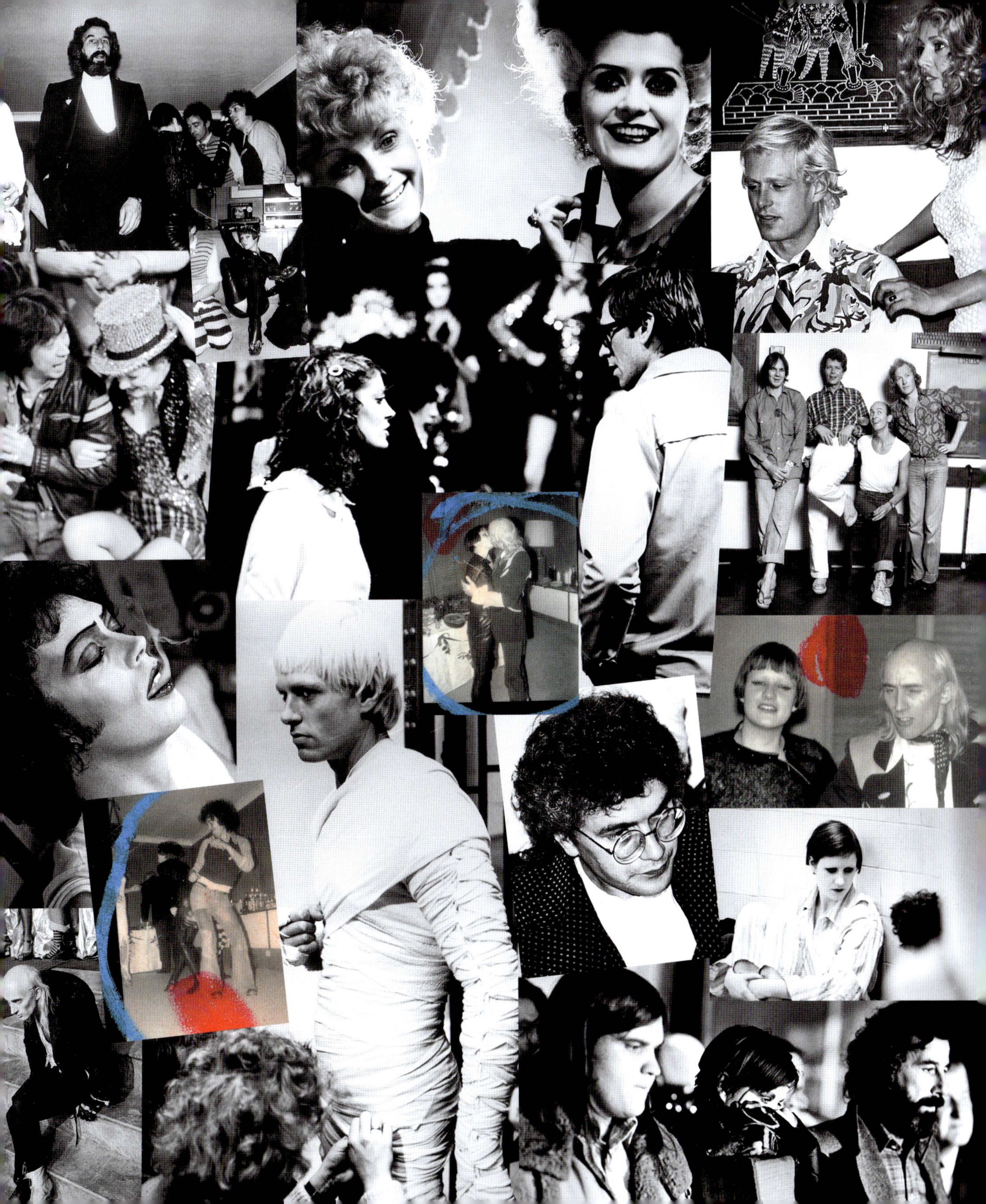

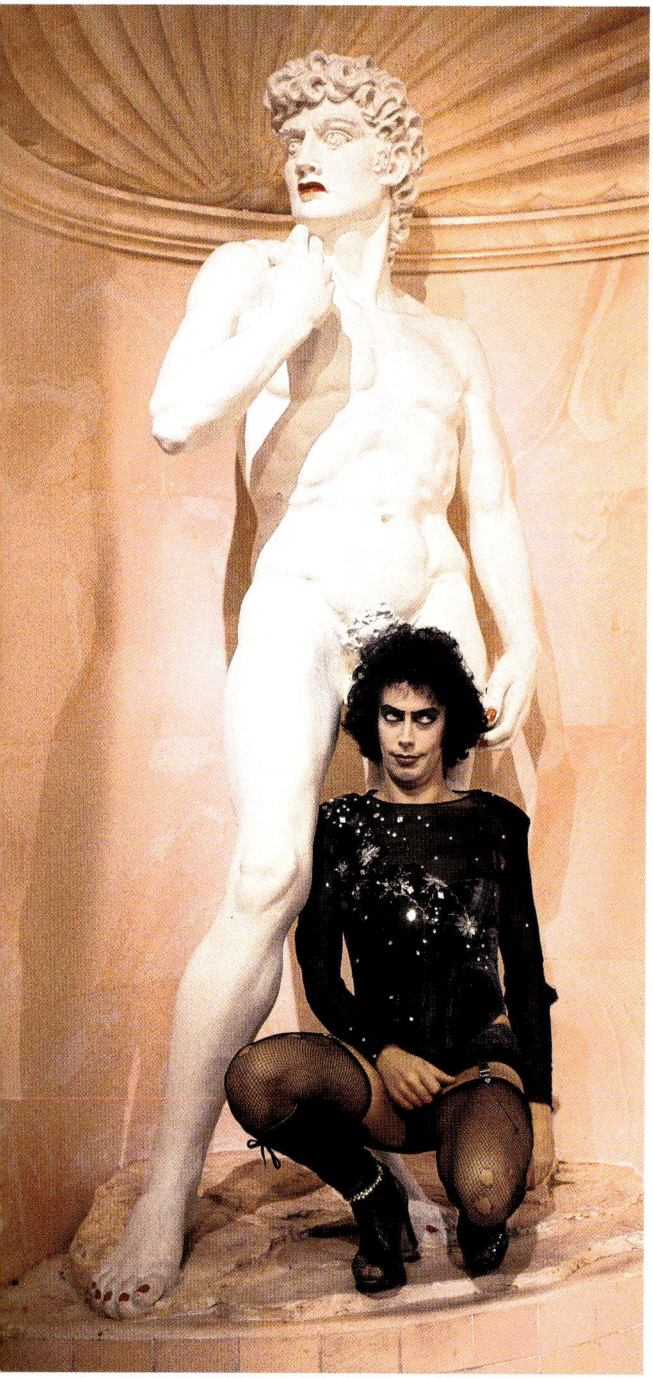

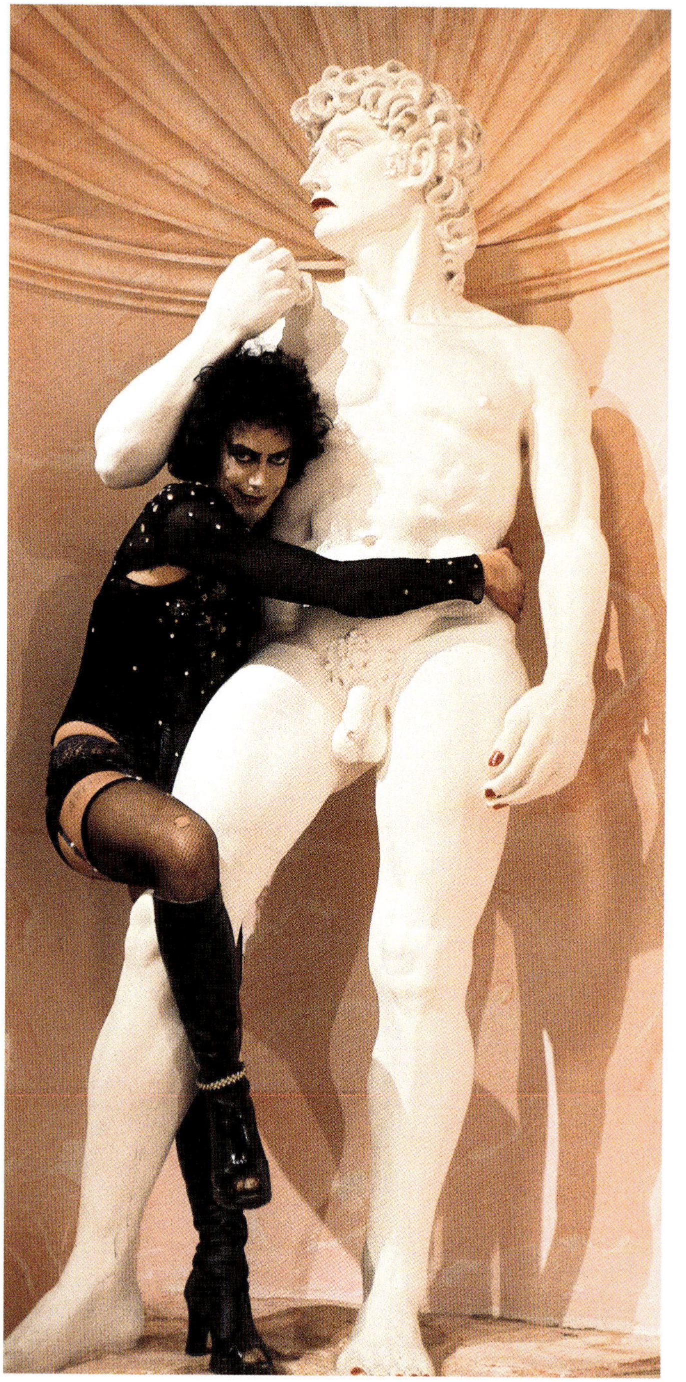

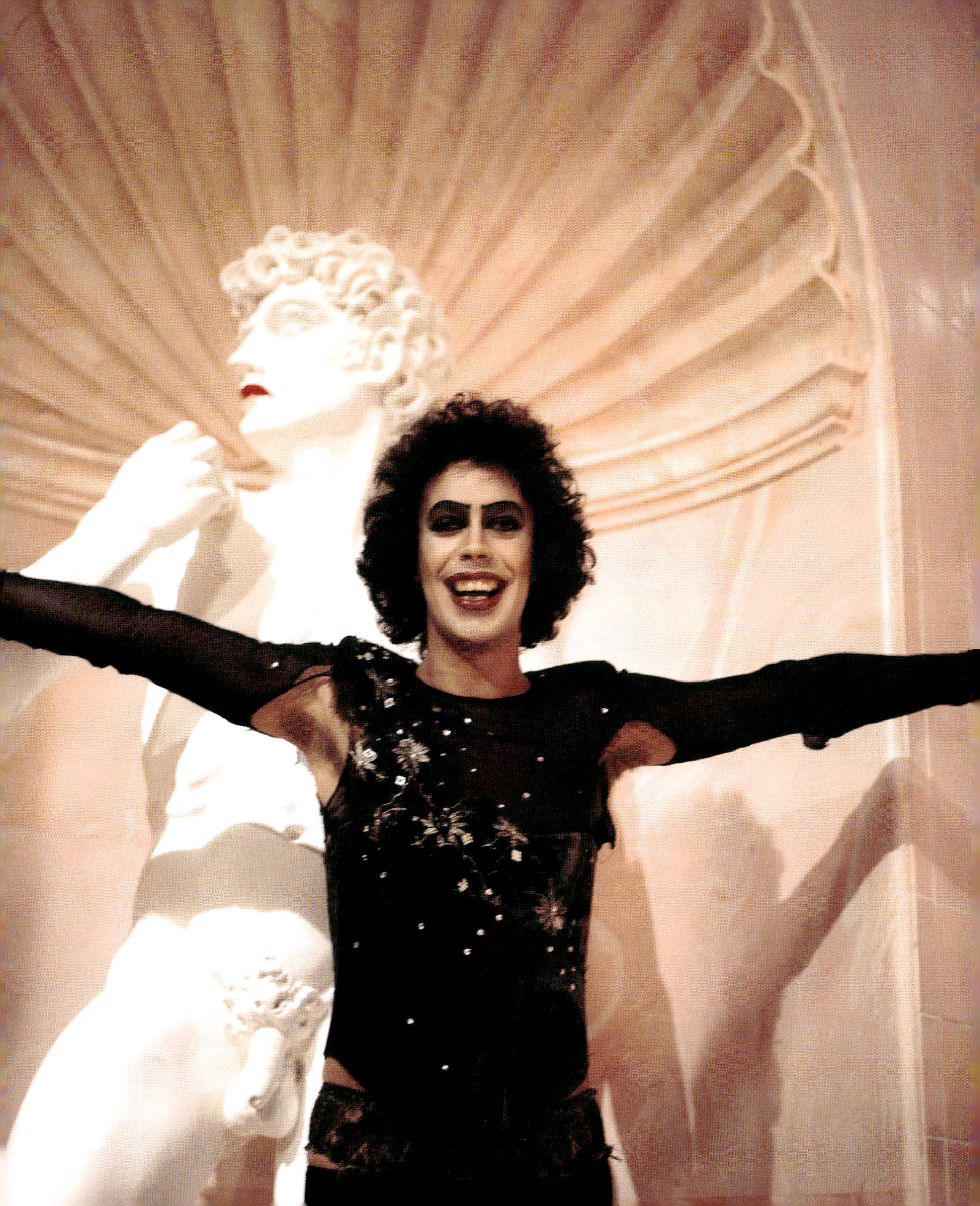

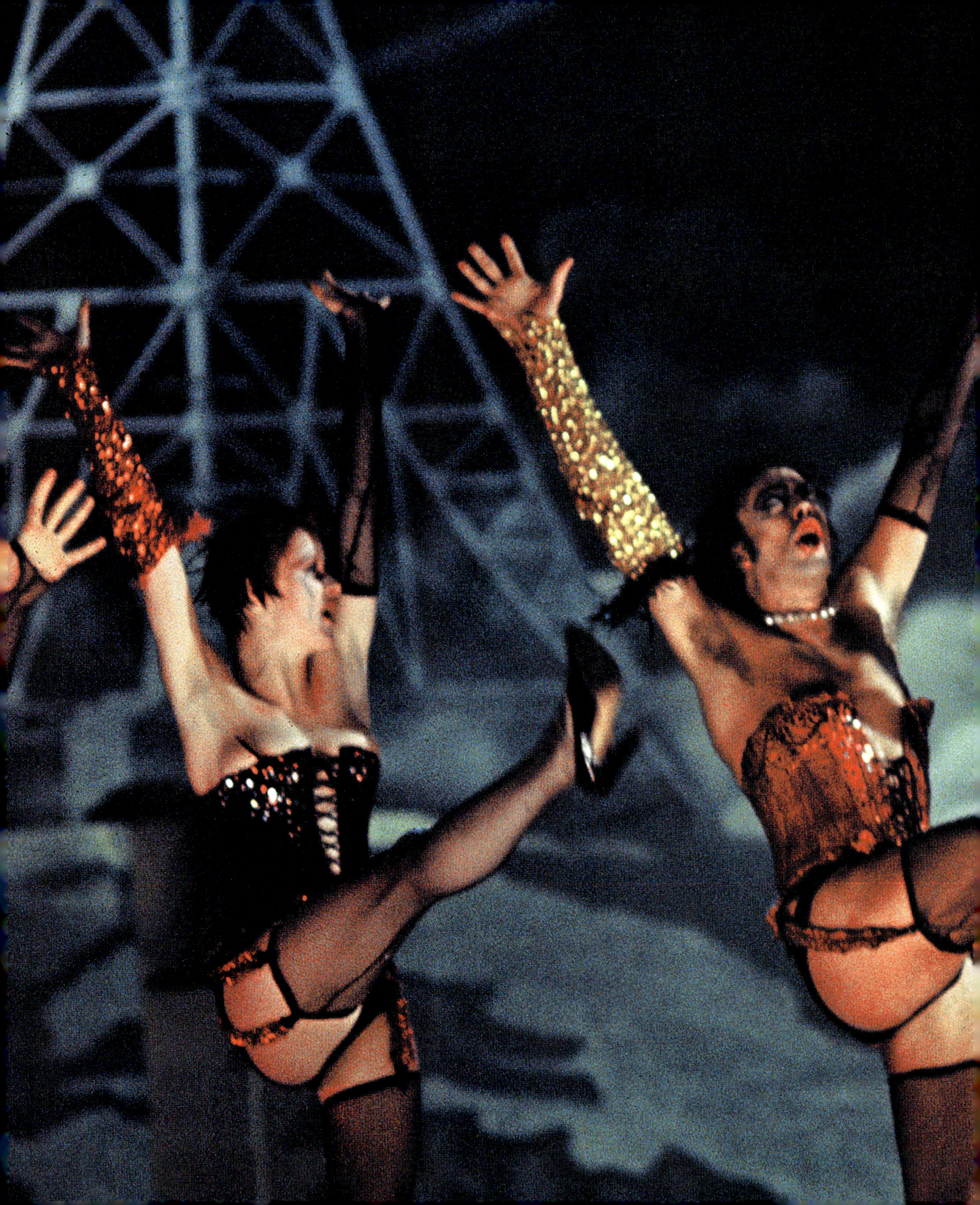

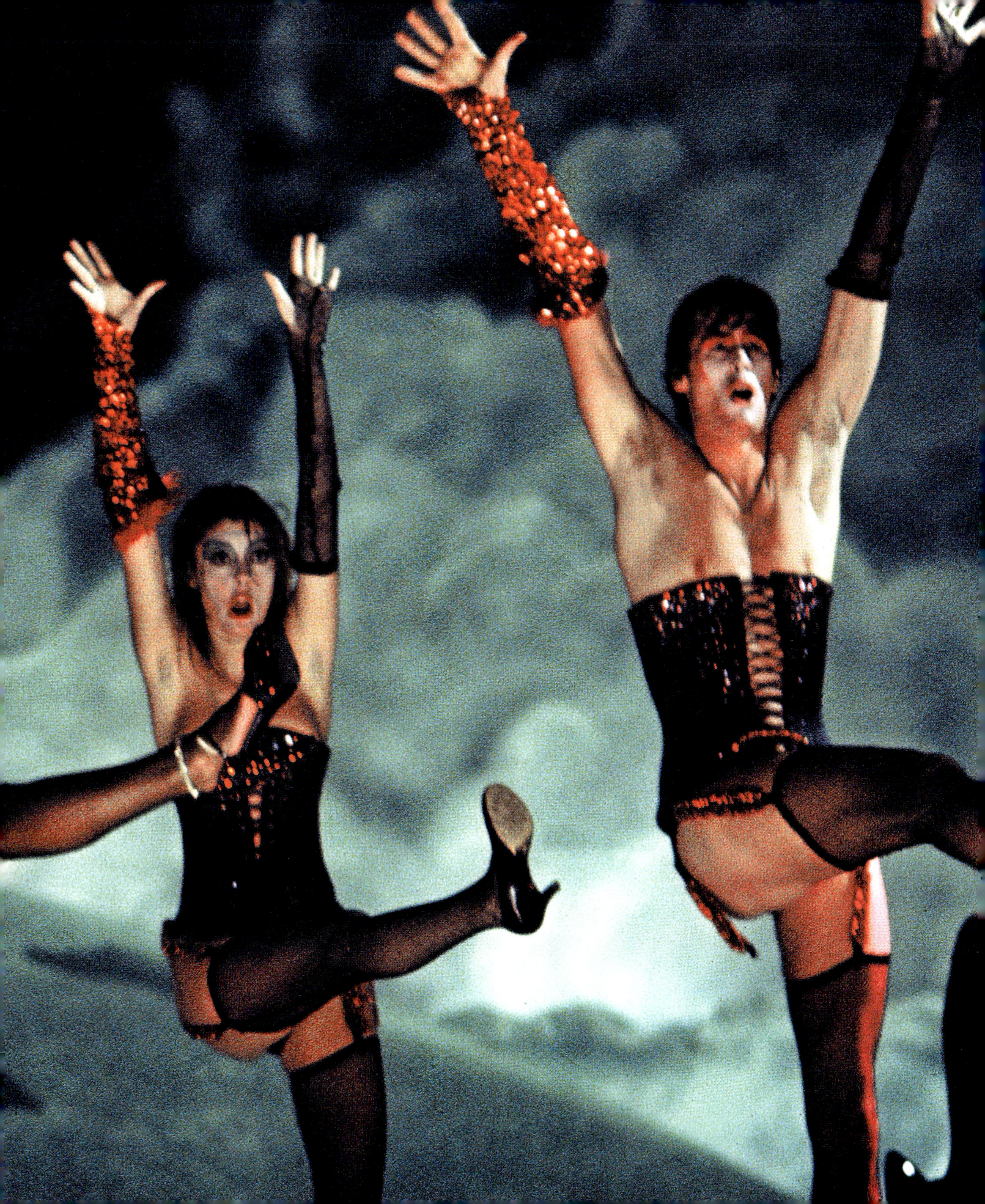

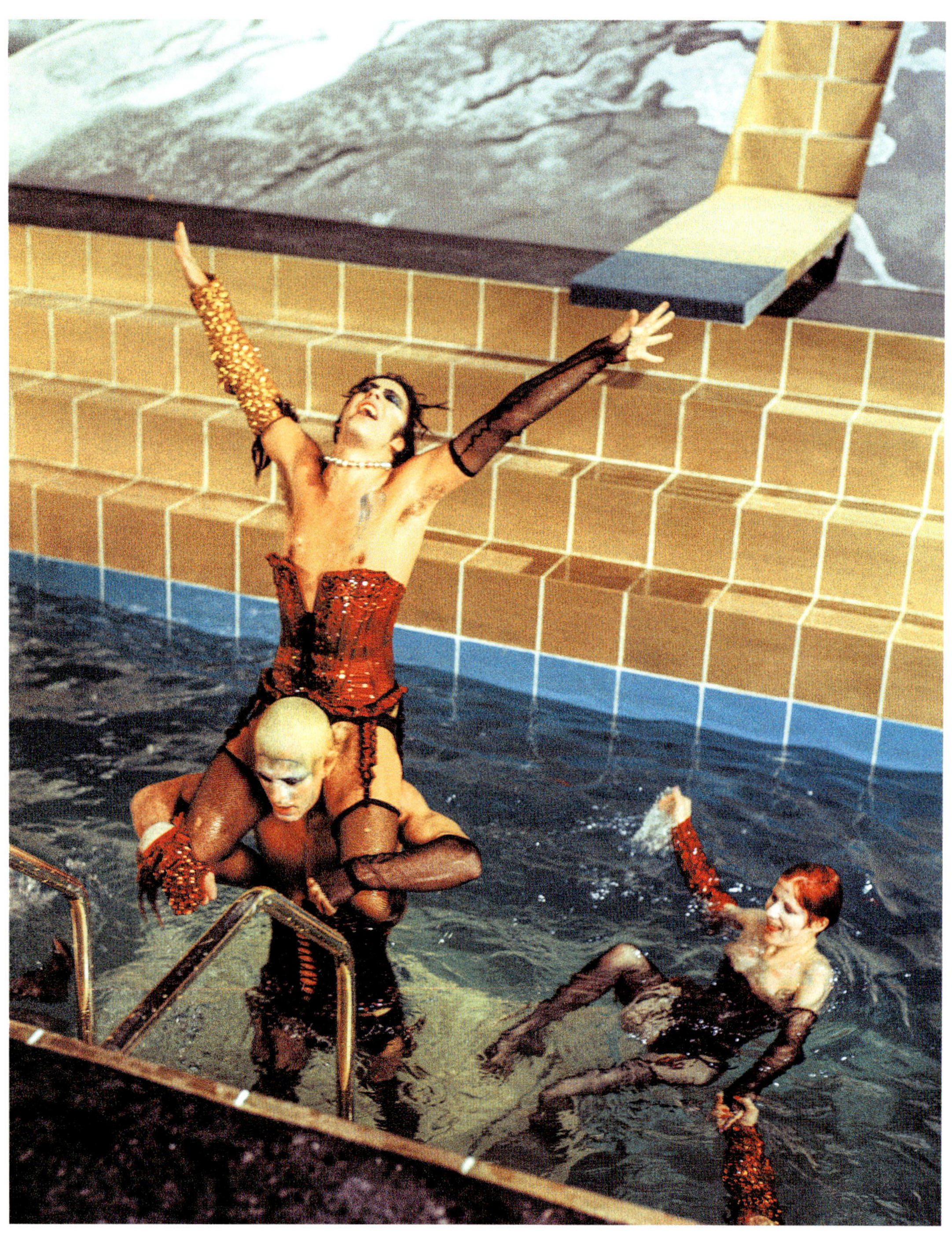

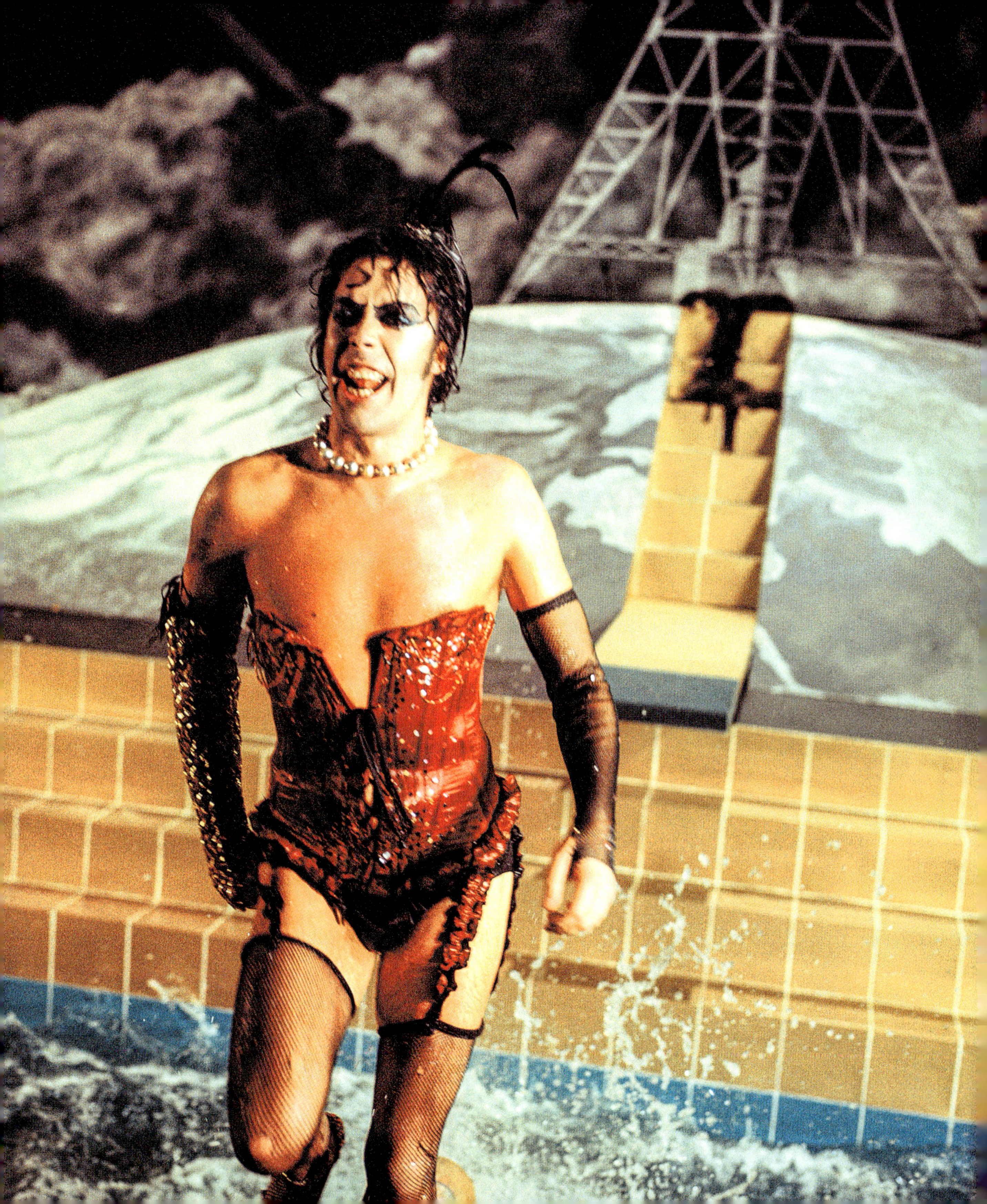

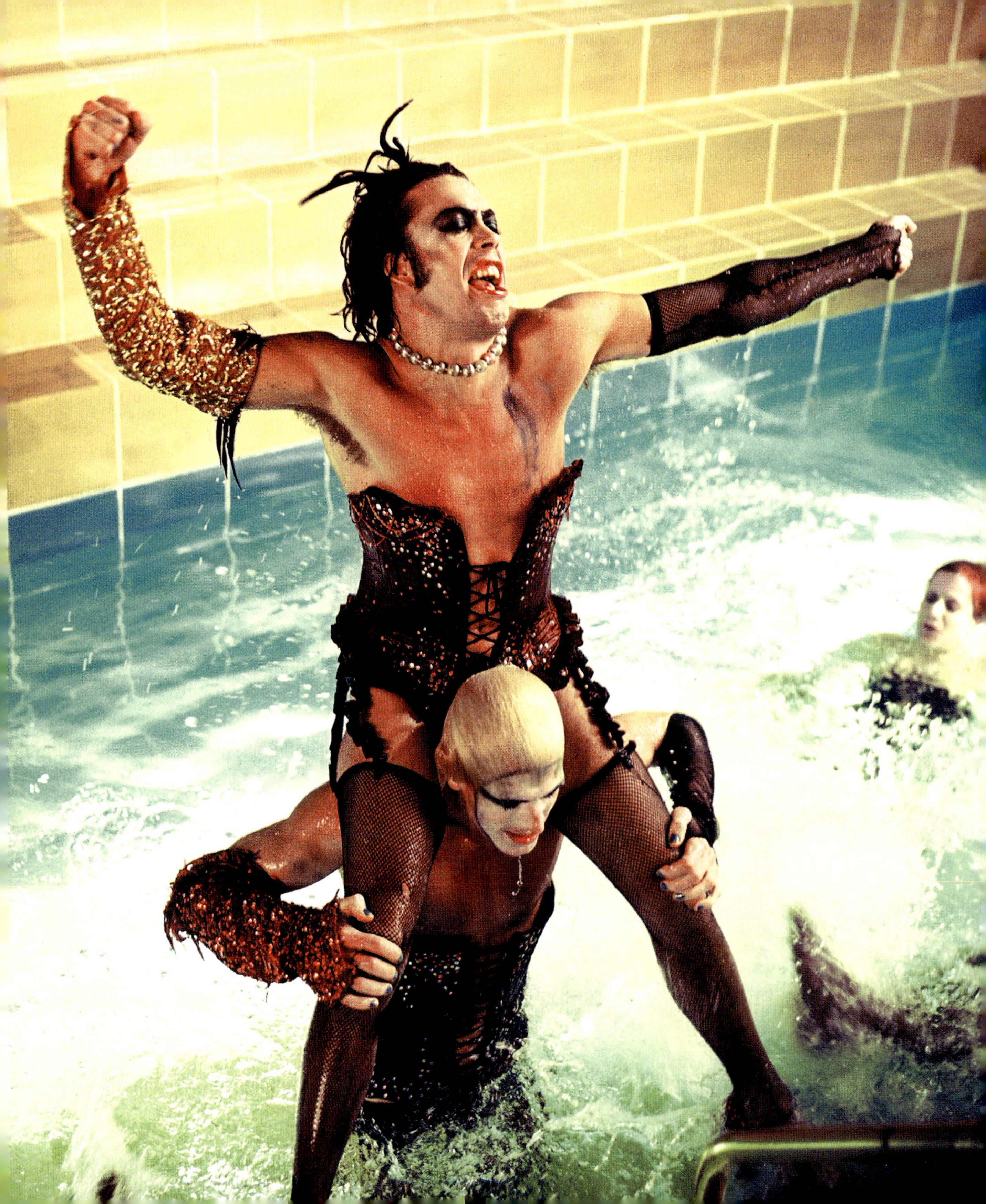

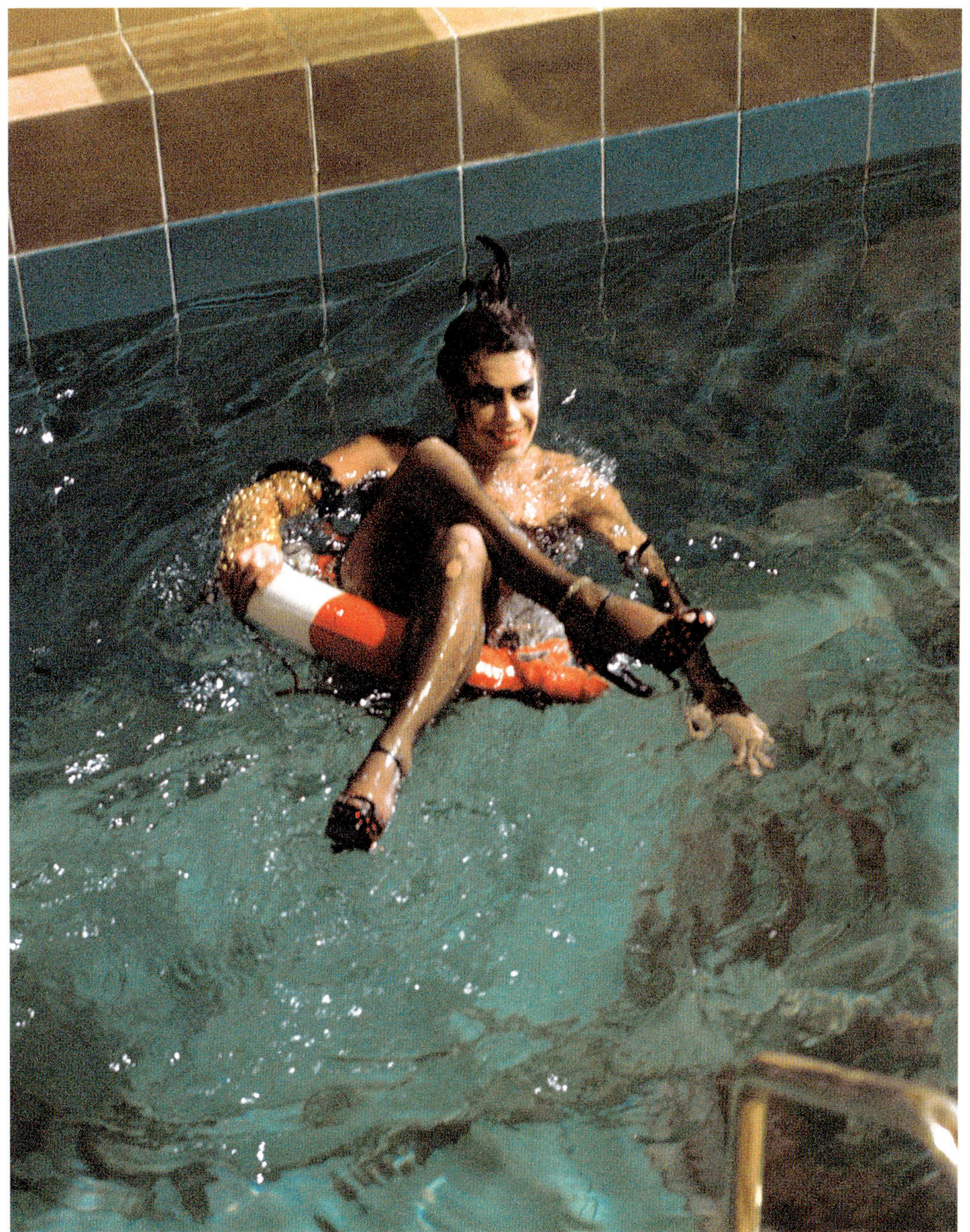

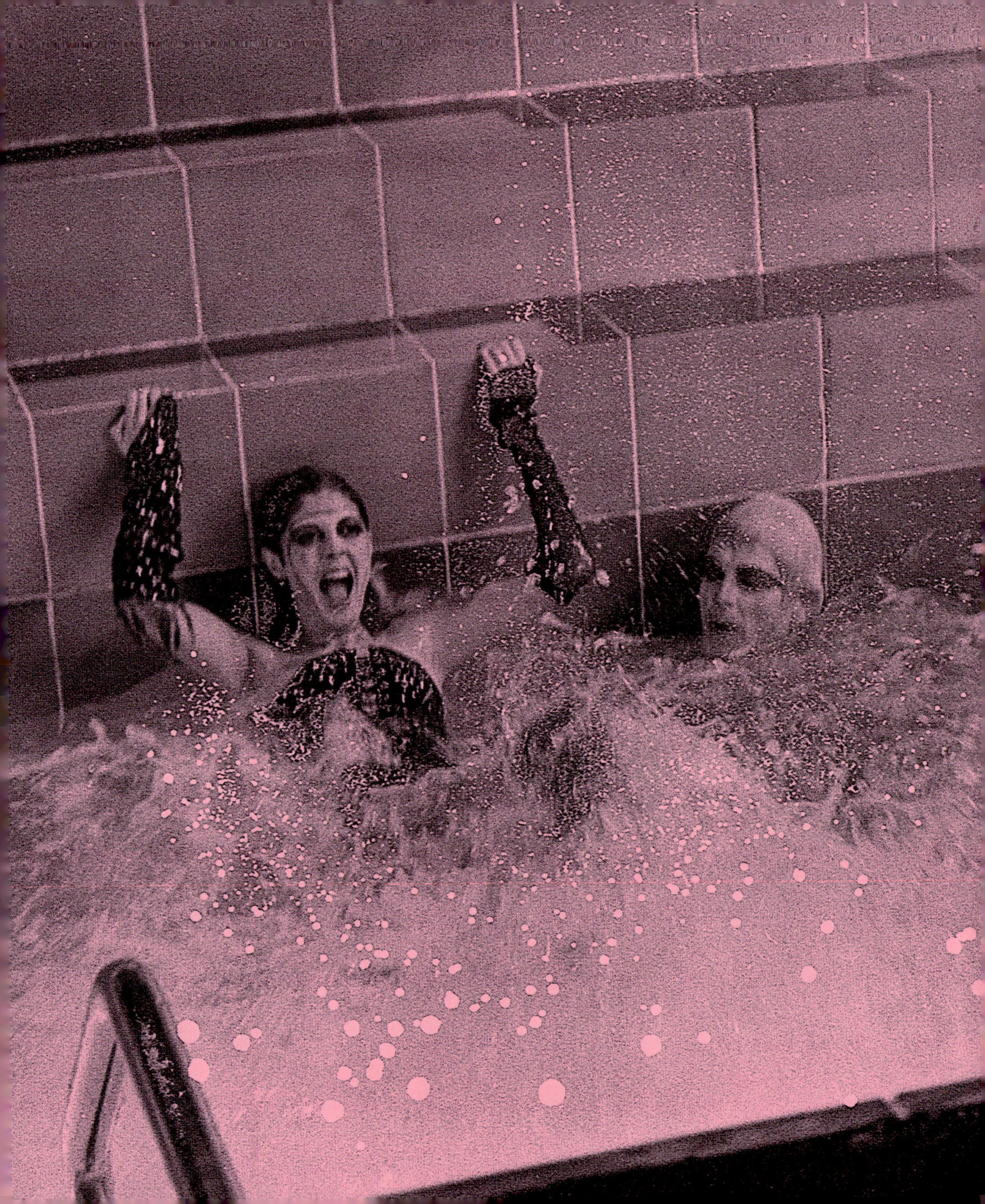

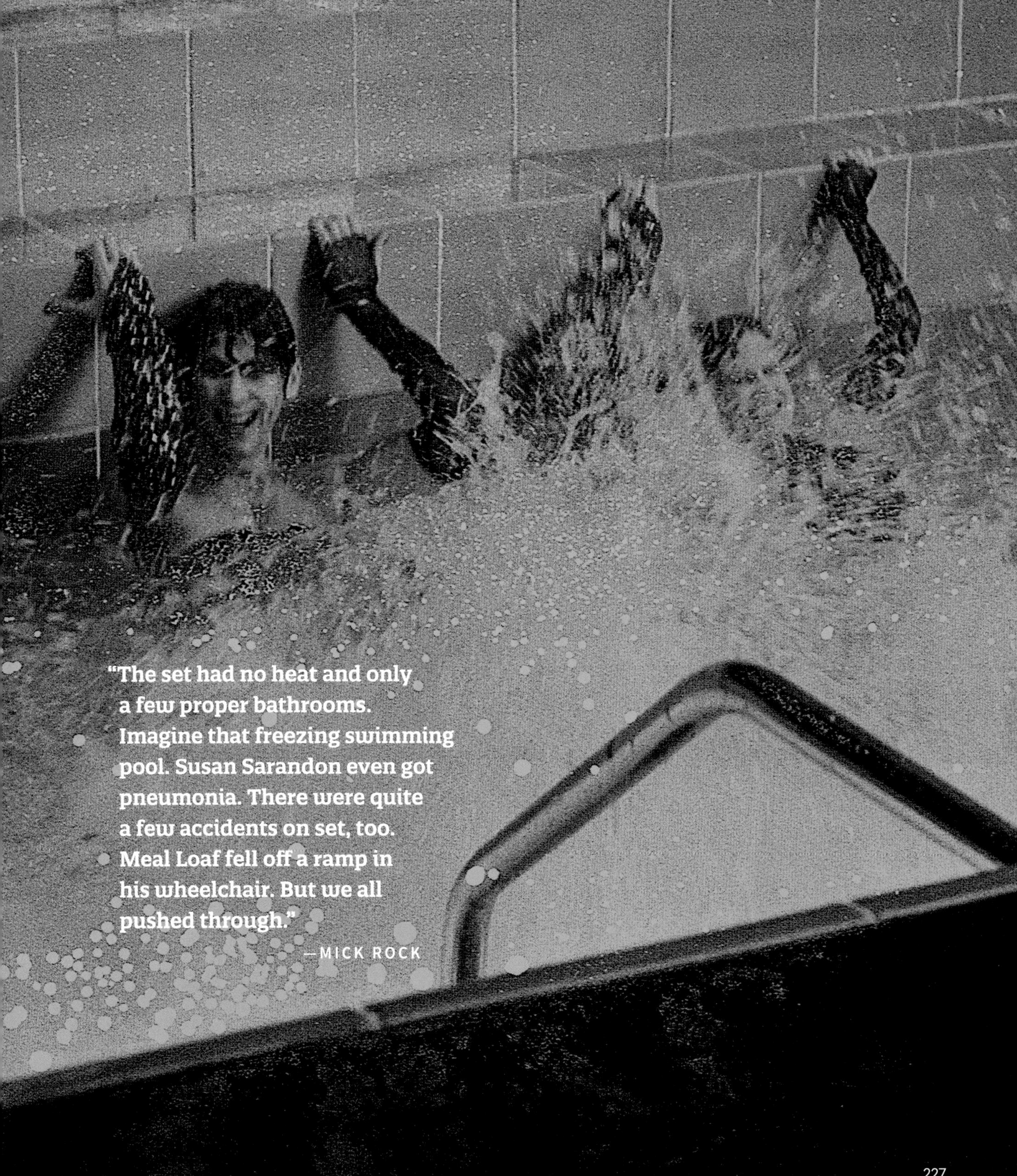

"The set had no heat and only a few proper bathrooms. Imagine that freezing swimming pool. Susan Sarandon even got pneumonia. There were quite a few accidents on set, too. Meal Loaf fell off a ramp in his wheelchair. But we all pushed through."

—MICK ROCK

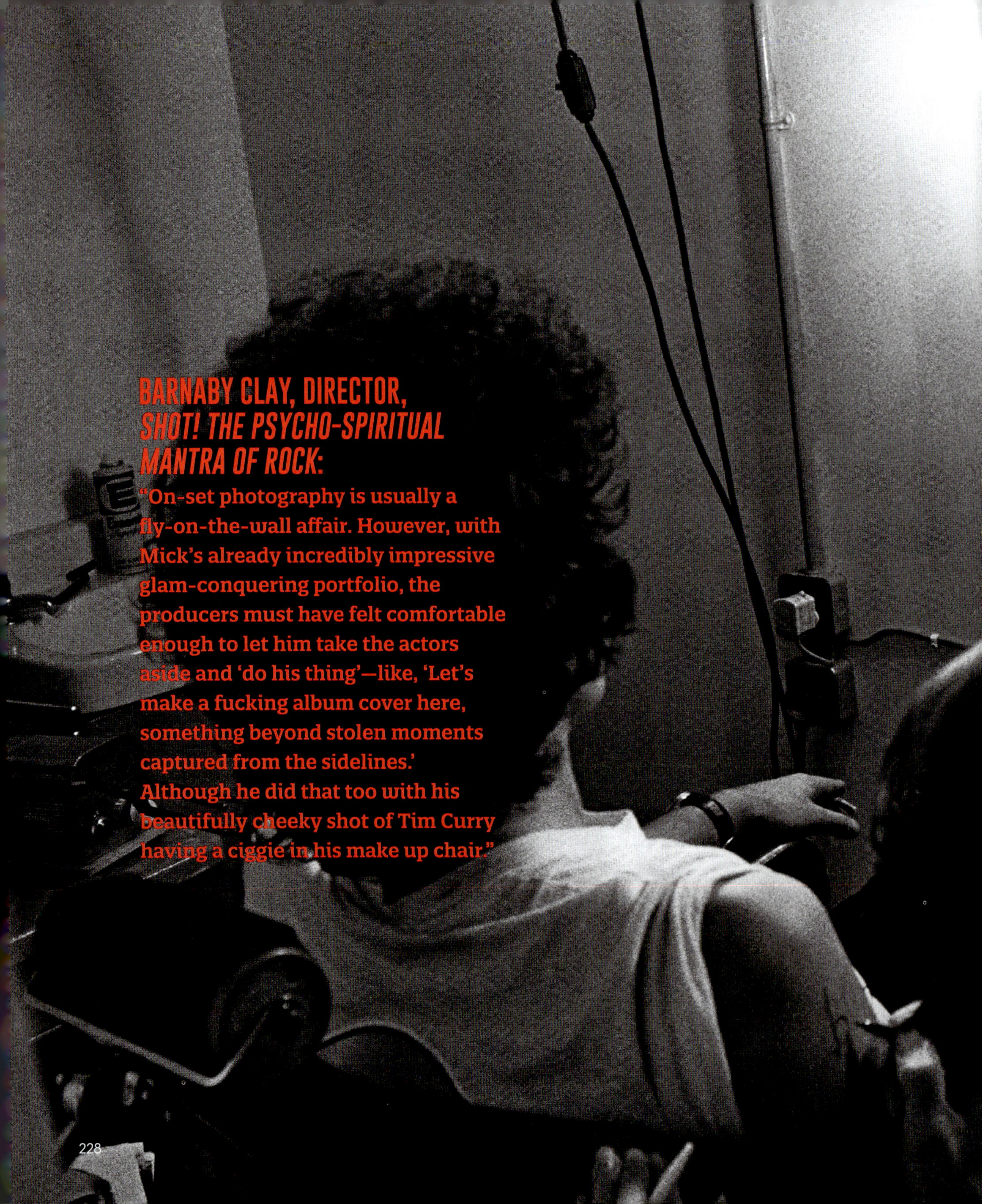

BARNABY CLAY, DIRECTOR, *SHOT! THE PSYCHO-SPIRITUAL MANTRA OF ROCK*:

"On-set photography is usually a fly-on-the-wall affair. However, with Mick's already incredibly impressive glam-conquering portfolio, the producers must have felt comfortable enough to let him take the actors aside and 'do his thing'—like, 'Let's make a fucking album cover here, something beyond stolen moments captured from the sidelines.' Although he did that too with his beautifully cheeky shot of Tim Curry having a ciggie in his make up chair."

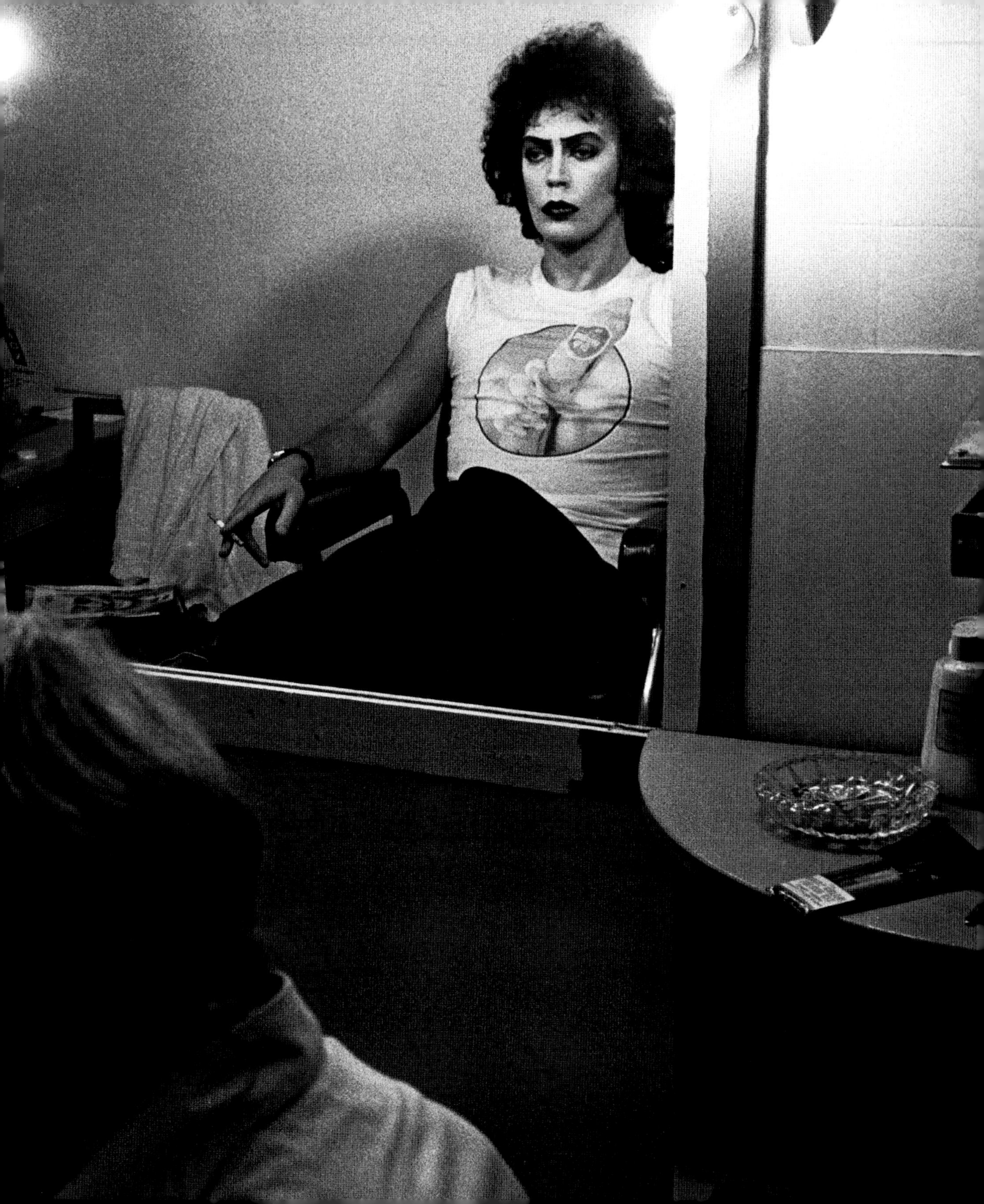

THE ROCKY HORROR PICTURE SHOW TIMELINE

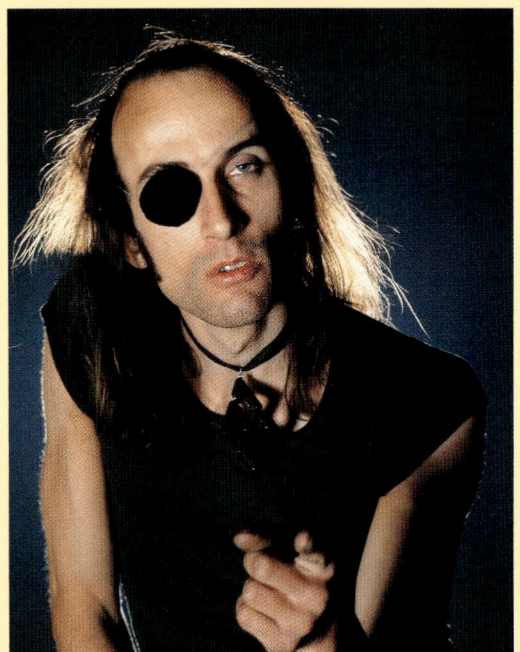

1859: Oakley Court, the Victorian country manor used as the exterior of Dr. Frank-N-Furter's home, is built by Sir Richard Hall-Say in Water Oakley, west of London.

1949: Hammer Film Productions purchases Oakley Court, which makes appearances in Hammer horror movies.

Summer 1972: Richard O'Brien is cast in *Jesus Christ Superstar*, directed by Jim Sharman. The next year, Sharman casts O'Brien in Sam Shepard's *The Unseen Hand* at the Theatre Upstairs, at London's Royal Court Theatre.

December 1972: O'Brien composes "Science Fiction/Double Feature" to perform at the EMI Records office Christmas party.

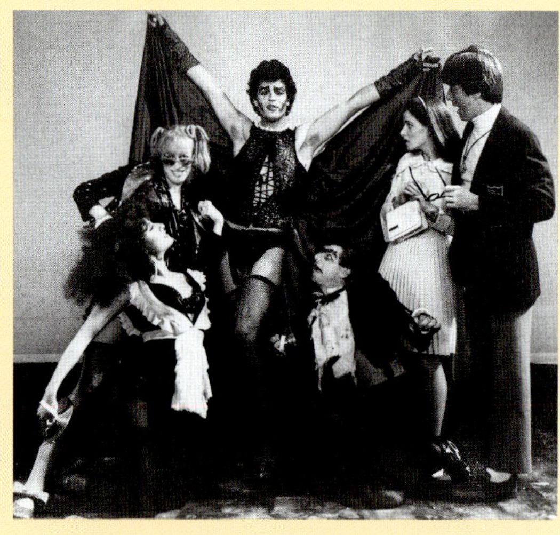

June 19, 1973: *The Rocky Horror Show* makes its stage premiere, also at the Theatre Upstairs, with a capacity of fewer than seventy seats.

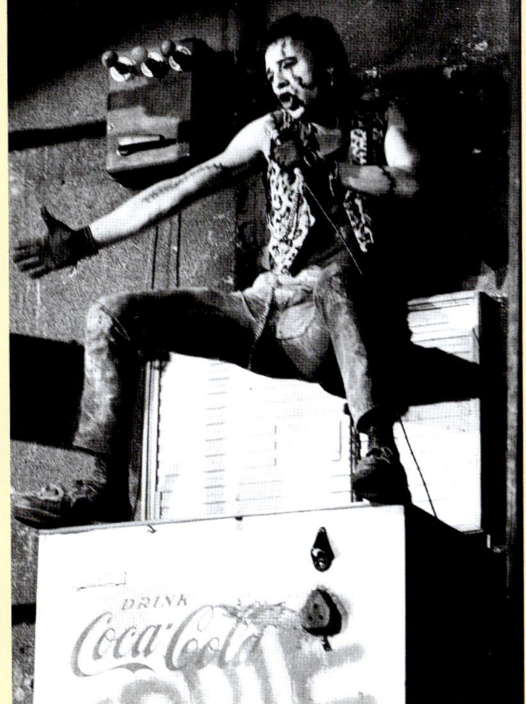

June 23, 1973: *The Guardian*'s critic Michael Billington says, "This show won me over entirely because it achieves the rare feat of being witty and erotic at the same time."

August 14, 1973: *The Rocky Horror Show* transfers from the Theatre Upstairs to the much larger Chelsea Classic Cinema, with a 230-seat capacity.

November 3, 1973: *The Rocky Horror Show* transfers again, to the King's Road Theatre, another converted cinema, with a 500-seat capacity.

March 24, 1974: The *Rocky Horror* stage production premieres in North America, when Lou Adler installs it at the Roxy, his club on the Sunset Strip in LA, with Tim Curry reprising his role as Frank-N-Furter for US audiences.

October 21–December 19, 1974: *The Rocky Horror Picture Show* is filmed at Oakley Court and Bray Studios, in the town of Water Oakley in England.

March 10, 1975: *Rocky Horror* premieres on Broadway, at the Belasco Theatre.

April 6, 1975: *Rocky Horror* closes on Broadway after just thirty-six performances.

September 26, 1975: *The Rocky Horror Picture Show* premieres—and, like the Broadway production, flops.

Autumn 1975: *The Rocky Horror Picture Show* is banned in South Africa.

April 1, 1976: *Rocky Horror* is first shown as a midnight movie at the Waverly, in Manhattan.

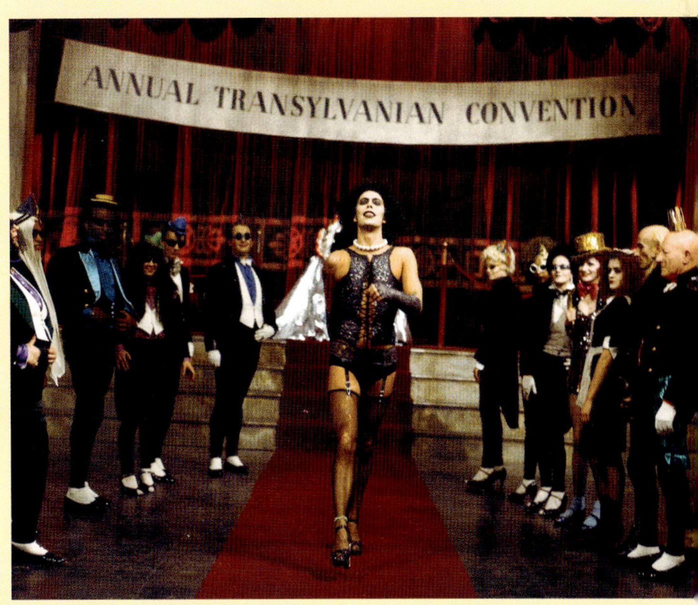

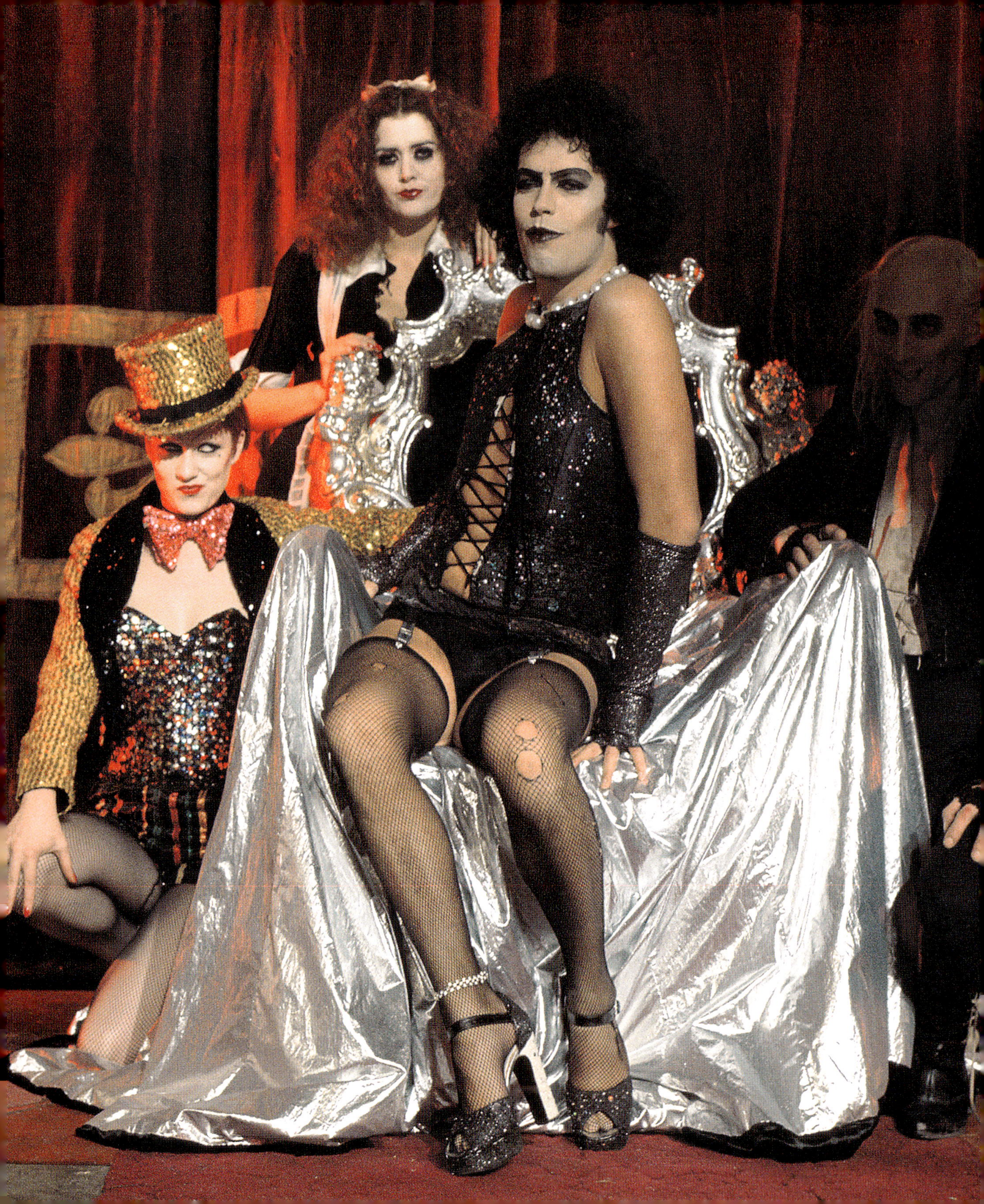

Spring 1977: *The Rocky Horror Picture Show* Fan Club is founded; Sal Piro is elected president.

September 13, 1980: The original London run of *The Rocky Horror Show* ends after 2,960 performances.

June 19, 1981: Barry Bostwick presents a framed pair of the white undies he wore on the *Rocky Horror* set to the Tiffany Theater, which had become globally famous for its midnight shows on the Sunset Strip in LA.

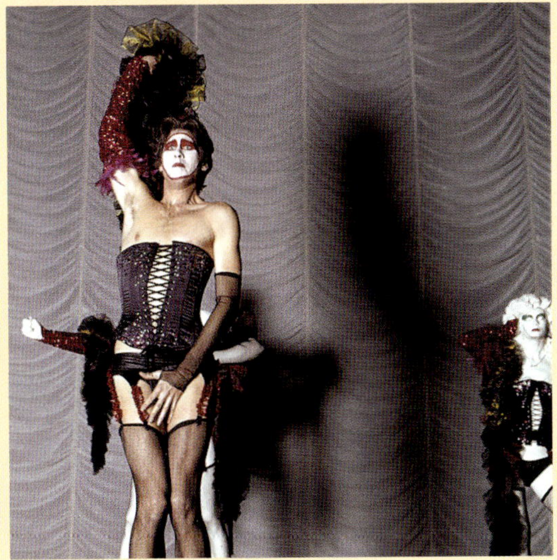

November 7, 1981: Oakley Court opens as a hotel after a two-year conversion, perhaps fulfilling Frank-N-Furter's wish: "I want to come again and stay."

October 30, 1981: *Shock Treatment*, Richard O'Brien's ill-fated semi-sequel to *Rocky Horror*, is released in cinemas.

March 13, 1983: *Rocky Horror* is the final film shown at LA's Tiffany Theater, where countless celebrities had attended its legendary screenings, and where real motorcycles had on occasion been driven through the aisles during "Hot Patootie."

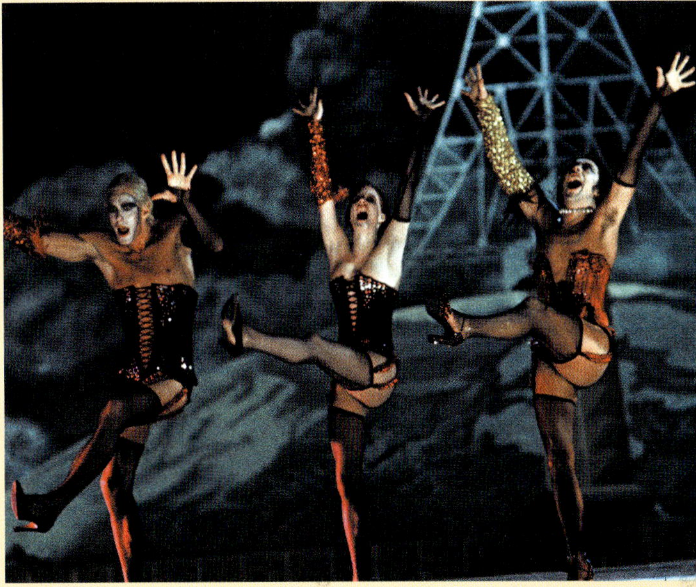

1985: Fox partners with Sal Piro's fan club, making it the official club; membership will top fifty thousand.

December 9, 1985: *Time* magazine, which had eviscerated the film at the time of its release, reassesses it a decade later, calling it "a cross-generational phenomenon, an evocation of '50s monster movies wrapped in the anything-goes spirit of the '60s that found a niche in the '70s and has blossomed in the '80s into a rite of passage for millions of American teenagers."

April 14, 1986: In Vienna to promote British Week, Princess Diana and Prince Charles attend a performance of *Love for Love*, in which Tim Curry is playing Tattle, and afterward, backstage, Di tells Curry that *Rocky Horror* "quite completed my education."

November 8, 1990: *The Rocky Horror Picture Show* is released on home video in the United States.

1994: Peter Hinwood sells the gold hot pants he wore in the title role of Rocky—for $1,000.

December 20, 2005: *The Rocky Horror Picture Show* is added to the Library of Congress's National Film Registry, alongside *Cool Hand Luke, The French Connection,* and *A Raisin the Sun*.

May 3, 2006: *The Rocky Horror Tribute Show* is staged at London's Royal Court Theatre—the main theater beneath the original production's birthplace—to benefit Amnesty International.

July 22, 2006: Richard O'Brien's *The Rocky Horror Show* company performs the "Time Warp" open air in London's Trafalgar Square.

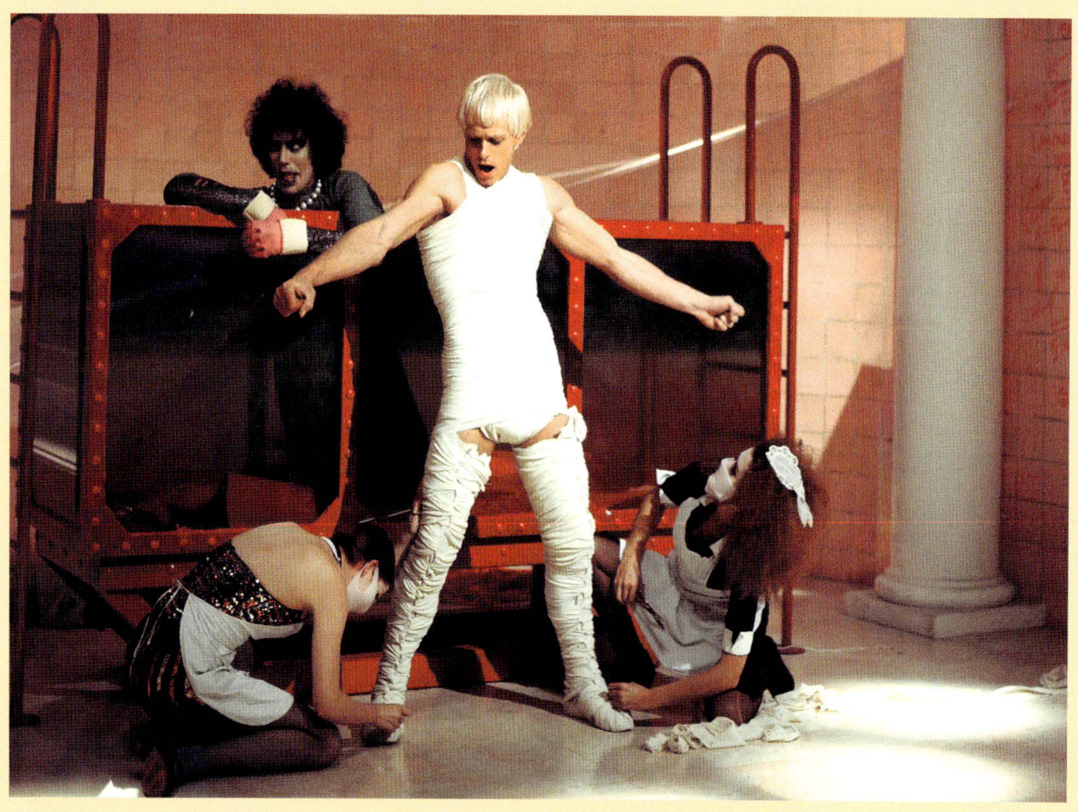

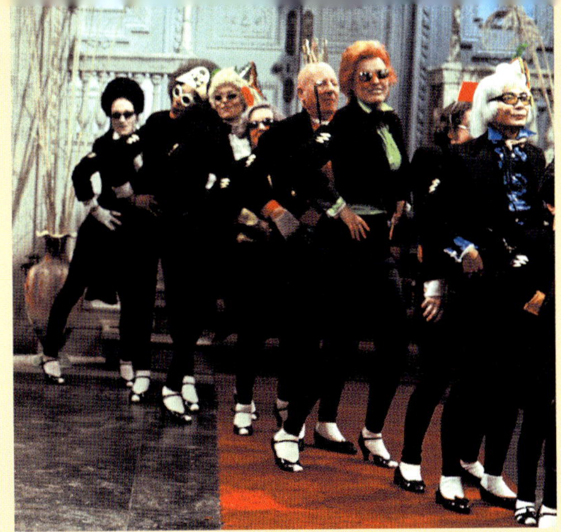

October 31, 2010: Sal Piro leads 8,239 participants in a "Time Warp" dance-along, setting an official Guinness World Record.

February 13, 2015: Chocolate Covered Rocky Horror, an African American live shadowcast directed by Earl Orrin, debuts at Joe's Movement Emporium outside Washington, DC, before moving to Baltimore in 2017.

October 20, 2016: *The Rocky Horror Picture Show: Let's Do the Time Warp Again* premieres on Fox TV, revisiting the original script with a new cast headlined by Laverne Cox.

January 22, 2023: Fan club president Sal Piro dies after more than forty-five years at the helm. "He was a very honest guy," Lou Adler told the *New York Times*. "You believed in him. He didn't have ulterior motives. The fan club wasn't a business or a means to something else, but to make it the very best for the fans—because he was one of them."

September 26, 2025: Fans worldwide celebrate the movie's fiftieth Transylversary.

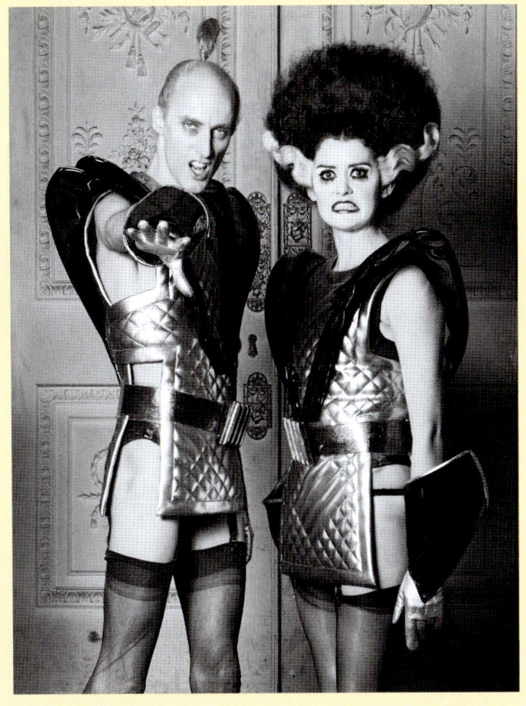

"*Rocky Horror* is as pure as 'cult' gets, because it was all word of mouth. It's the fans that made it happen, not the hype. It's very colorful, very energetic. There are lots of different elements to it. It's a bit cartoony, a bit sci-fi, a bit horror, a bit drag, a bit 1950s, a bit glam, a bit punk, and totally rock 'n' roll. It's got all these different elements that Richard collaged together. It's a brilliant piece of art whichever way you want to color it." —MICK ROCK

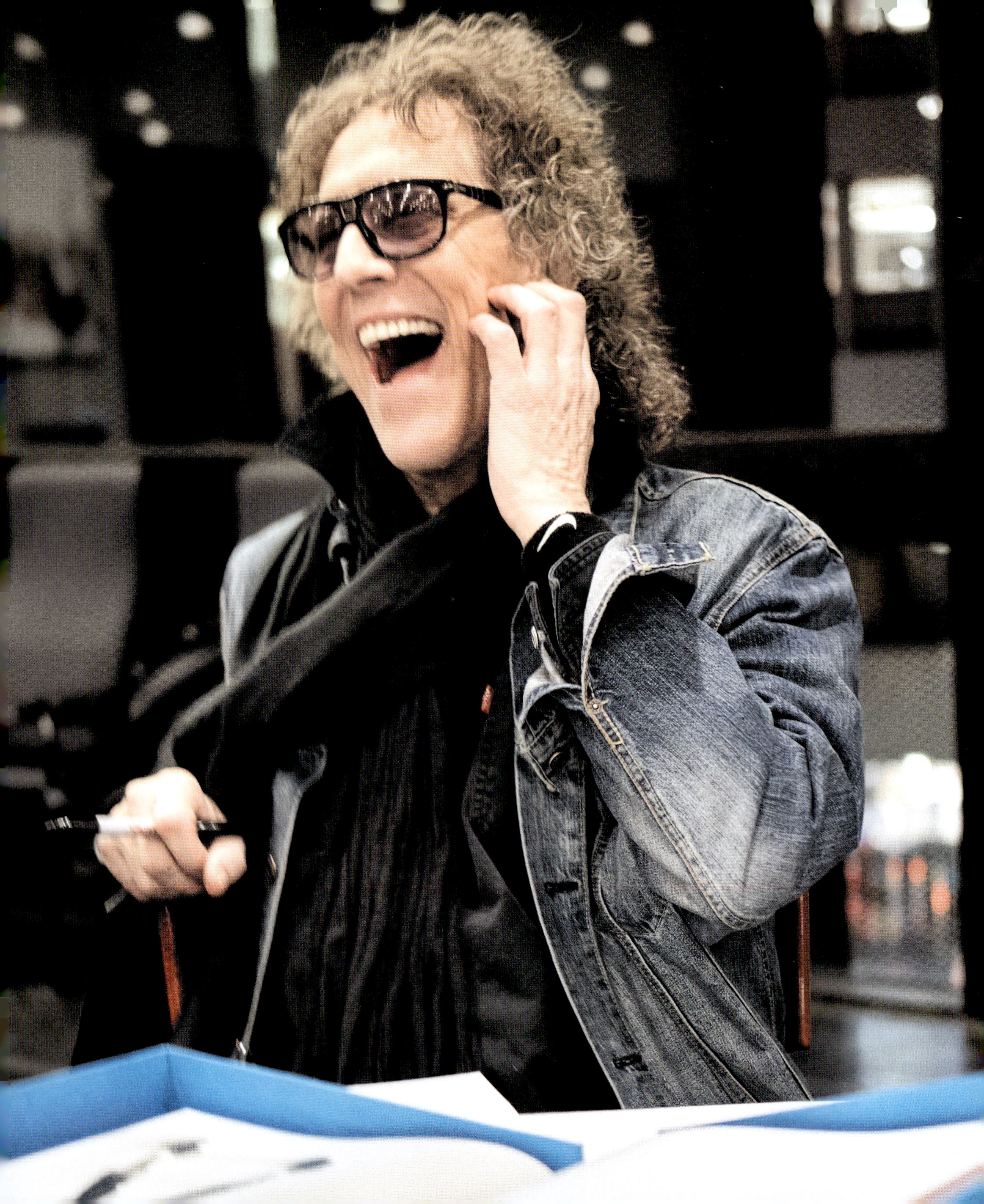

AFTERWORD BY PATI ROCK

"I have very fond memories of working with him, even though it was extraordinarily complicated at times, and he was one of the people who was by far the hardest to work with."

Those are words from one of Mick's many publishers—he published a total of twenty books during his career. I was bemused by his recollection of working with my husband, but hardly surprised, because that was how much Mick cared. Enough to be a huge pain in the ass. His images are personal touchstones, and the selections, the printing, every word was considered.

I wasn't there in 1974 when Mick was roaming the *Rocky Horror* set snapping photos of the creators and creatives, but I can surely speak about his commitment, his drive, and his single-mindedness in creating his books. Mick was not only a visual artist, he was also an exceptional writer, and he envisioned his books completely, which must have made it very difficult for any book designers involved. Difficult but also exhilarating. I was lucky to be by his side when he/we built his very first sample books. My memory of those projects is one of the many aspects of our relationship that I loved.

Mick had always been drawn to the characters and expressions of our culture: the pirate, the poet, the vain, the outsider, and the dramatic. Without a road map, he built his astounding career documenting the many people who mattered during the '70s, '80s, '90s, and '00s—including, of course, the artists here, who make up *The Rocky Horror Picture Show*.

But unlike with all his previous books, we have added Mick to the mix. More than the man who shot the '70s, he was a man who blended in with the times, the music, the style, and the artists themselves. Mick epitomized the photographer-as-friend during a time when, as he described it, "Material control and acquisition were completely subsidiary to sensory exploration and creativity."

His access was insider, his outlook uncritical, his talent part of something new happening in the world of rock photography.

It is with that blueprint, for me, that I present this truly complete collection of Mick's photos of *The Rocky Horror Picture Show*.

I love you, Mick. This one's for you.

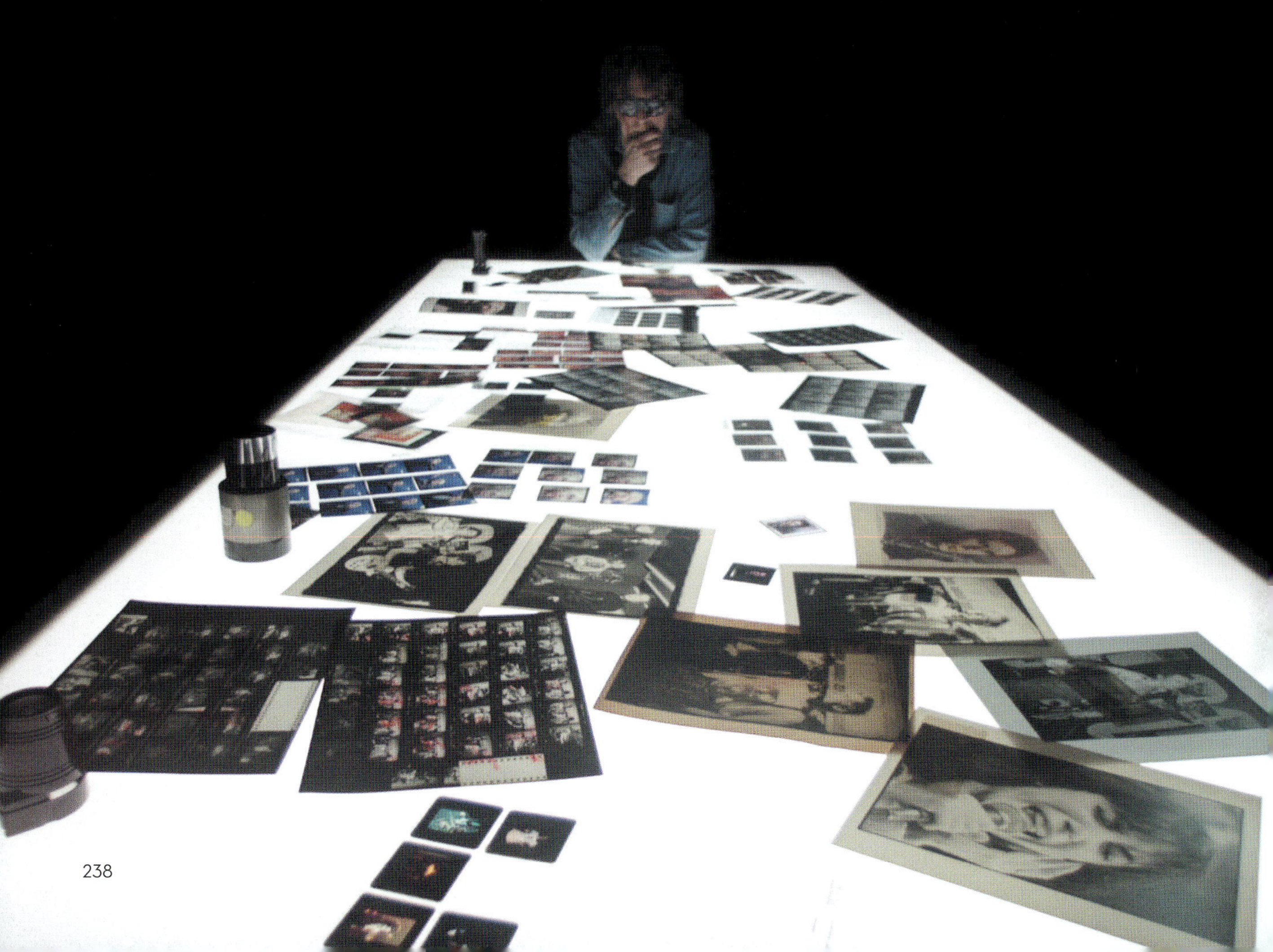

"There are more than a few people in this world who believe that ownership of a camera makes them a photographer and, when they get lucky once or twice through no discernible talented activity of their own, they become convinced of their genius. Mick's work reveals these people to be the dilettantes they really are. 'Art,' as a concept, is a delightful addition to our human experience, but how much more rewarding it is when underpinned with 'craft'—for then the artist becomes both architect and master-builder."

—RICHARD O'BRIEN

BETSEY JOHNSON, FASHION DESIGNER: "My favorite pics of me and my daughter Lulu are Mick's. He was such a fun, smart, and sexy guy. He was David Bowie, too."

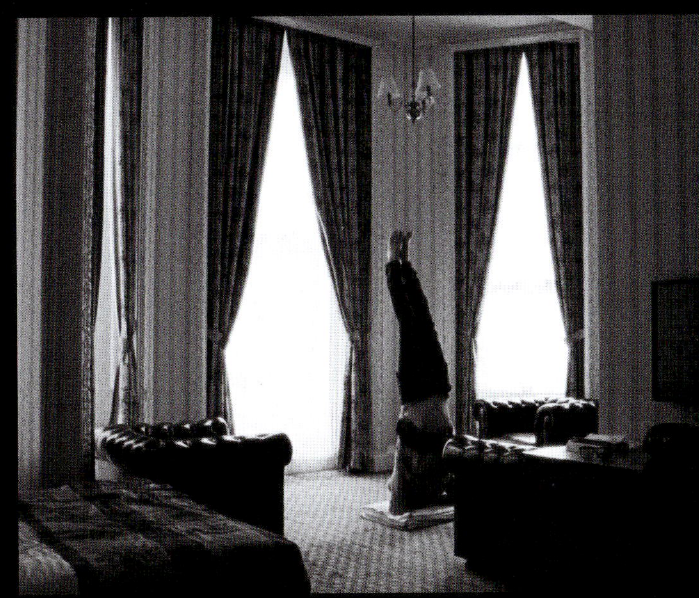

SIMON DOONAN, AUTHOR, FASHION COMMENTATOR, AND ON-AIR TALENT: "Every Mick Rock shot is infused with a jolt of Mick's own edgy charisma. Yes, he shoots fascinating people, but he makes them even more intriguing."

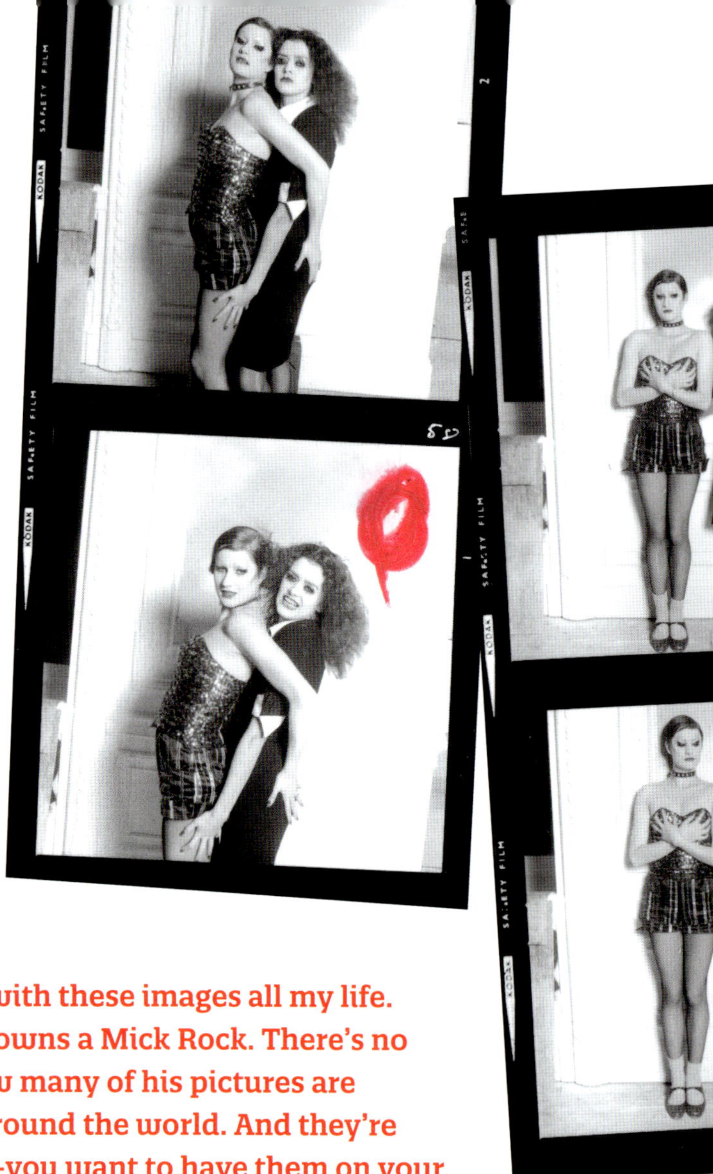

“I’ve lived with these images all my life. Every fan owns a Mick Rock. There’s no telling how many of his pictures are hanging around the world. And they’re beautiful—you want to have them on your walls. I truly believe that without Mick, there wouldn’t be *Rocky Horror*. It’s a hard thing to say, because I can’t take away from Jim Sharman’s genius or the work of others involved, like costumer Sue Blane, but without those still photos, what would we have had? If it hadn’t been captured, who would bloody know about it?”

—PATRICIA QUINN

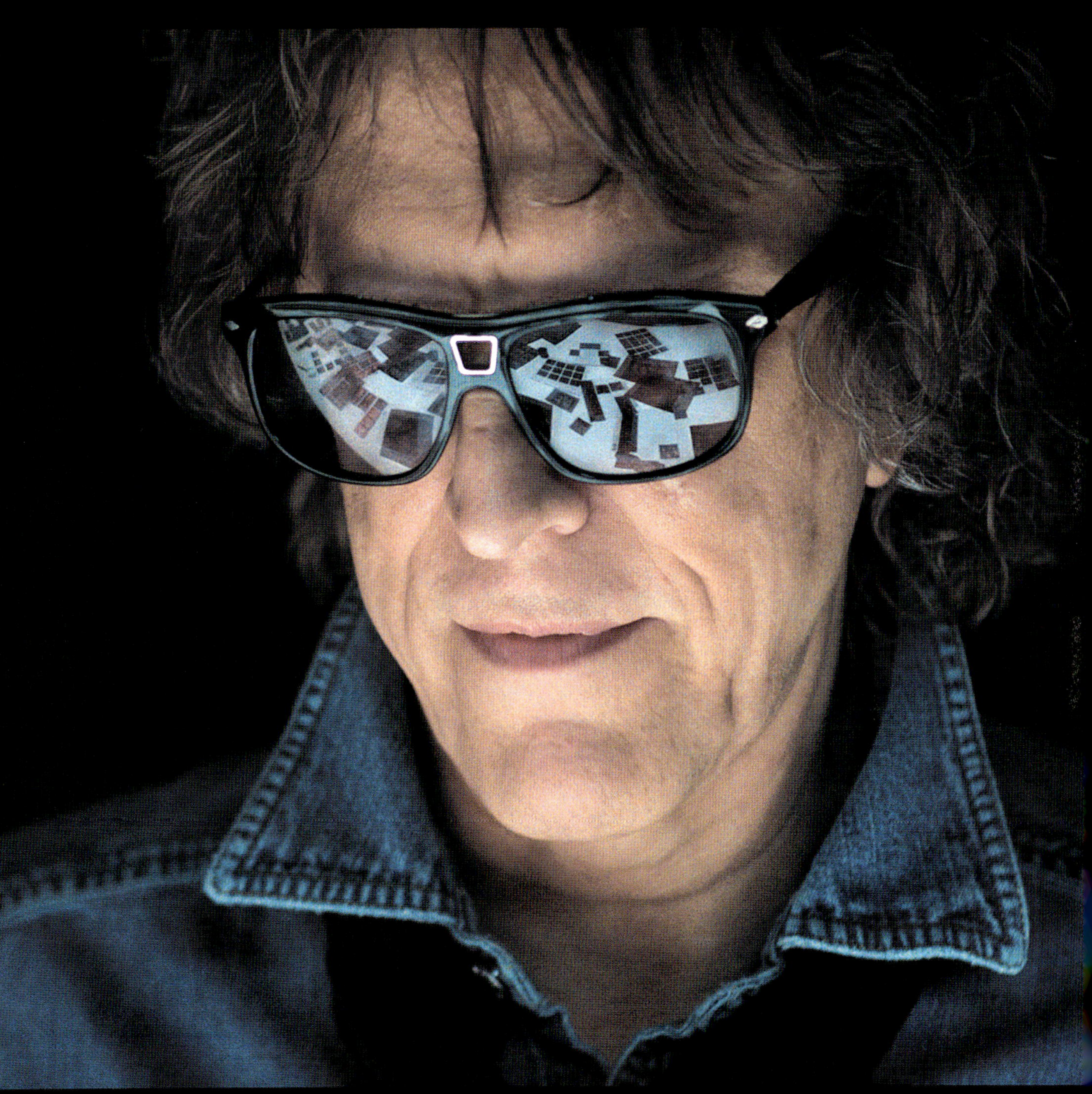

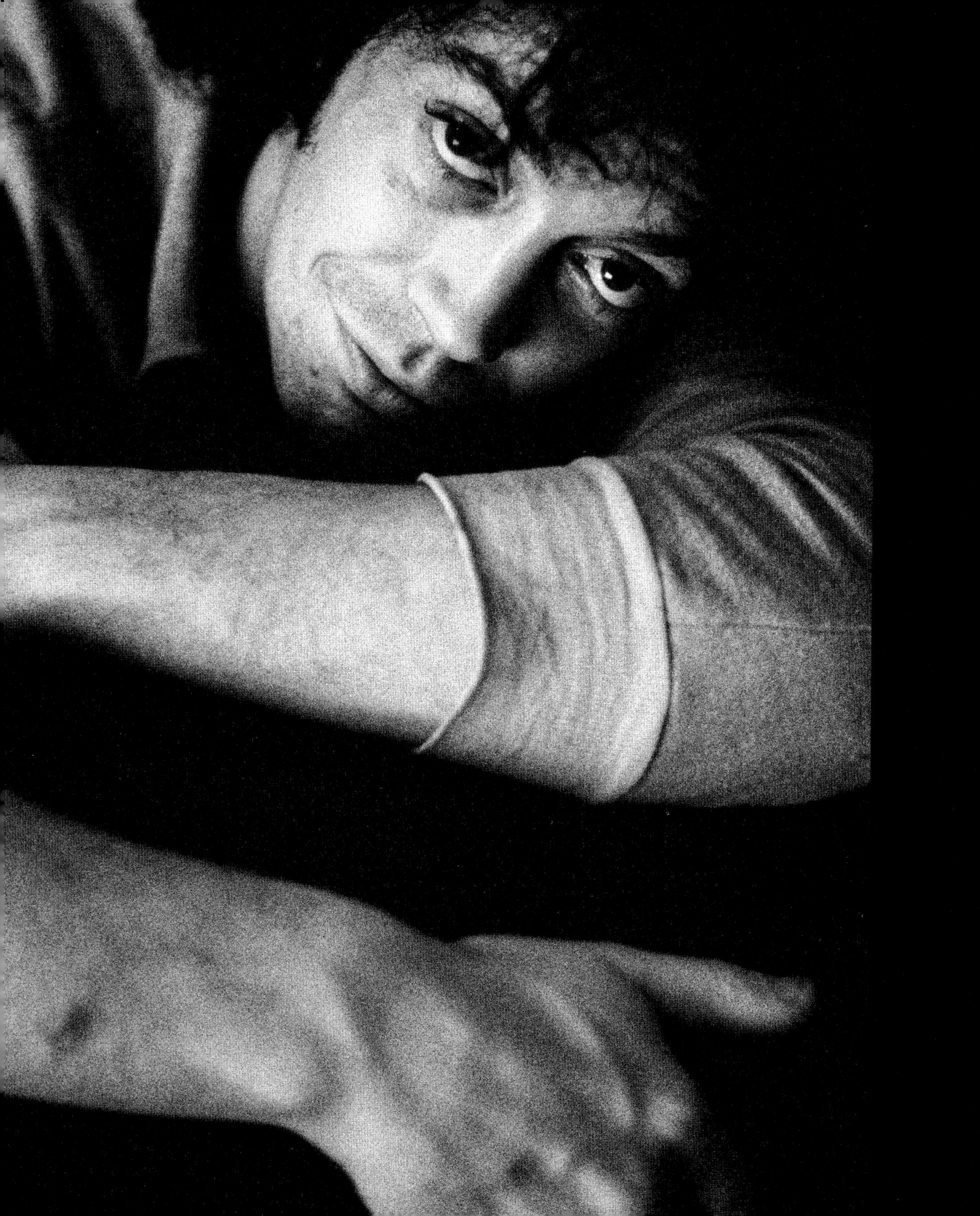

RICHARD BARONE, MUSICIAN, PRODUCER, AND FRONT MAN FOR THE BONGOS: "Mick Rock was a genius—not only at capturing but at revealing images. His photos looked beyond the surface and into their subjects' souls. So many of his shots seem to have a backstory: a whole movie in one still shot. Like a coach bringing out the hidden potential of an athlete, Mick could bring out the true, unique, and singular beauty of his subjects. He would do this with his own body language, his constant commenting, his humor or intensity, and dramatic lighting—all driven by his own acute intelligence and artist's eye. He was a master of conjuring up a kind of sexual tension and suggestion and, like a Vulcan mind meld on *Star Trek*, seemed to be able to tap into the subject's subconscious. His resulting images created eternal afterimages that remained in the viewer's mind and made his subjects immortal. After his gorgeously bisexual shots of David [Bowie], Lou Reed, and Iggy Pop in the early to mid-1970s, it's no wonder that Mick would be chosen as the official photographer for *Rocky Horror*!"

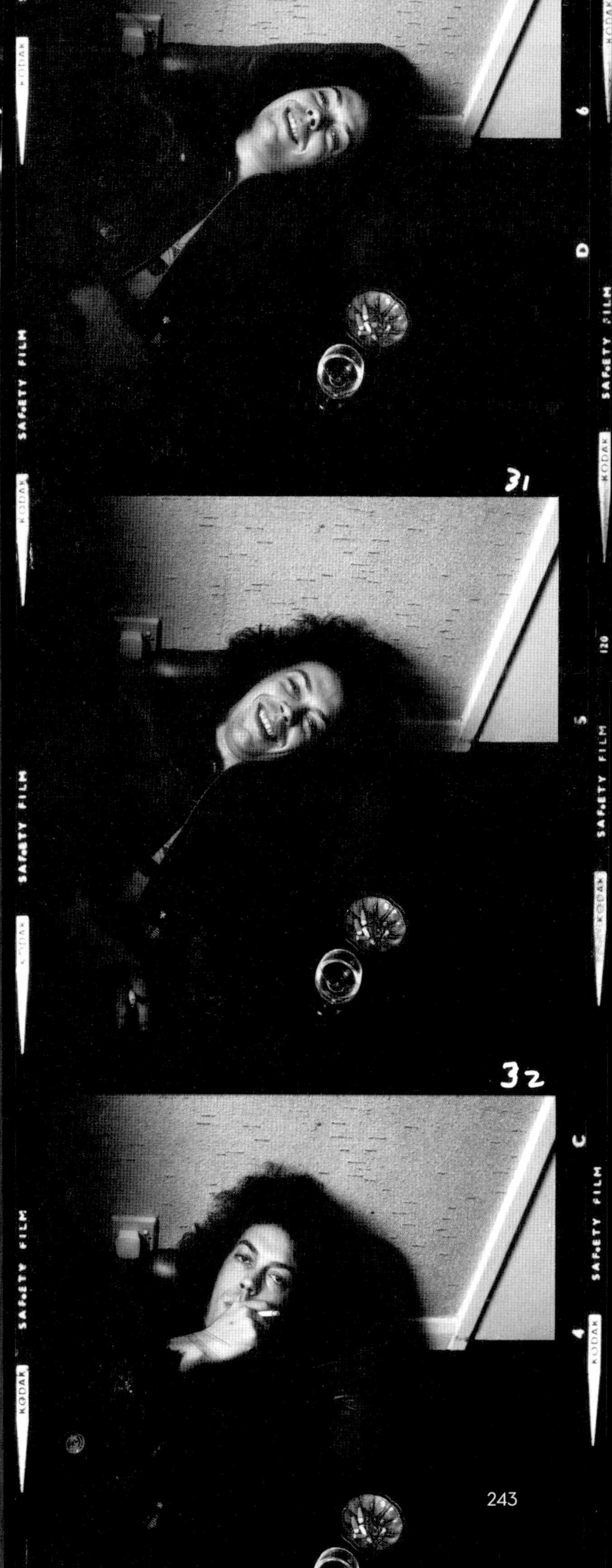

JOAN JETT, MUSICIAN:

"Mick was so involved on a creative level with *Rocky Horror* that later—when he shot the cover of my album *I Love Rock 'n' Roll*—I trusted him. Mick wanted to put me in a pink jacket with a blue bandana around my neck. I was not usually into color, but I trusted what he was doing and where he was going with it. It actually felt like *Rocky Horror* to me, with all the color. He seemed to really get who I was."

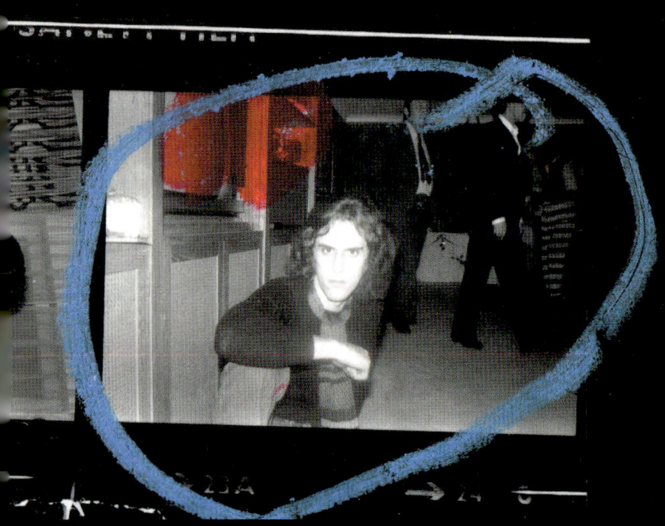

KAREN O, THE YEAH YEAH YEAHS:

"Looking back, it feels like that early Yeah Yeah Yeahs shoot with Mick for *Vanity Fair* was the only photo shoot that counts for me. I was transported—by the ferryman, as I call him. It was as if we were being ushered by Mick to the isle of rock gods and goddesses. The bulb would flash and Mick's eyes would roll back in his head and his tongue would touch the roof of his mouth. If someone told me that flash of his was stealing my soul I'd believe it and say let him take it. I miss Mick, he is one of the greatest and no can touch him. It's no coincidence that he happened to be the one in the golden age snapping the golden giants."

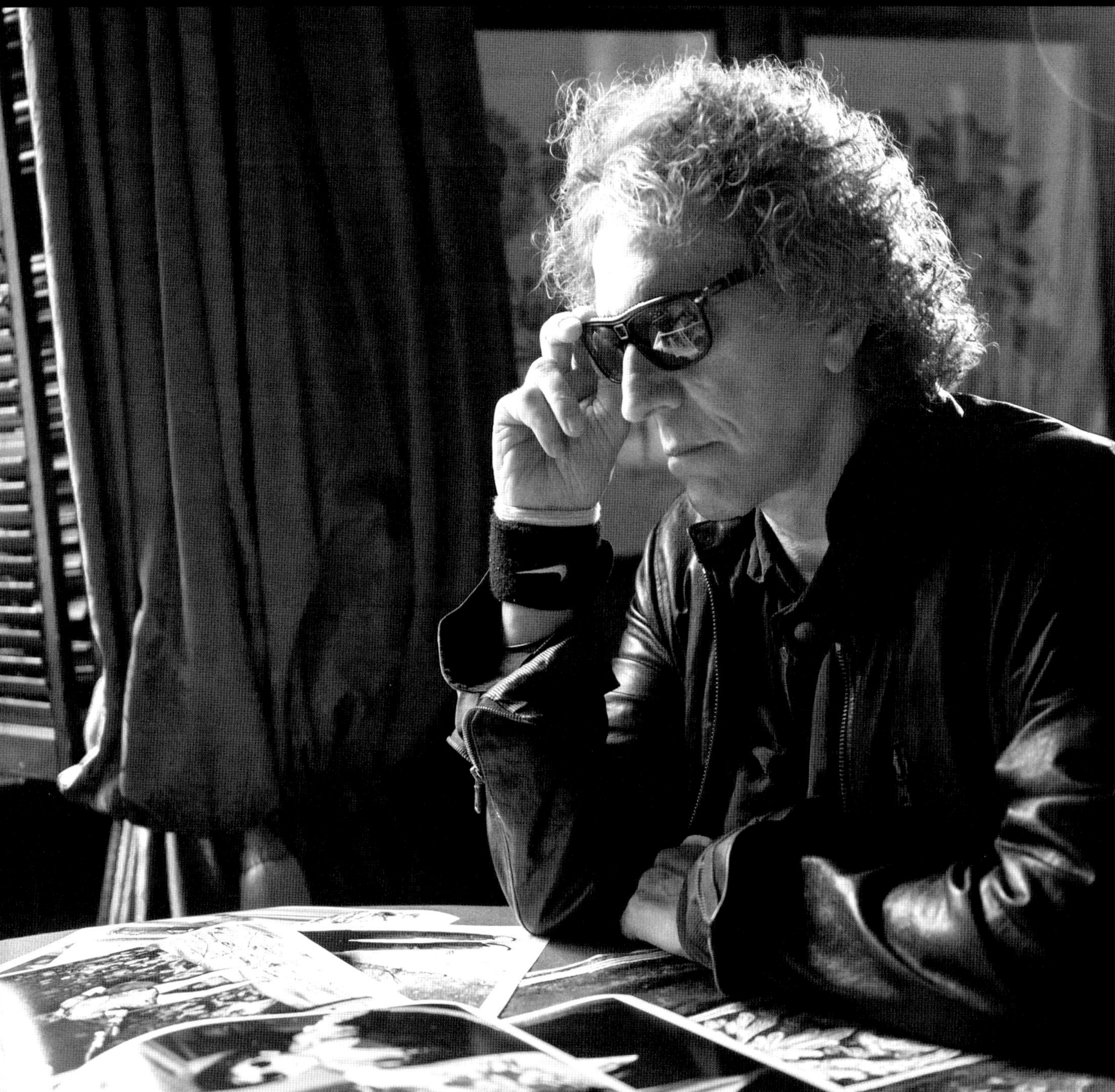

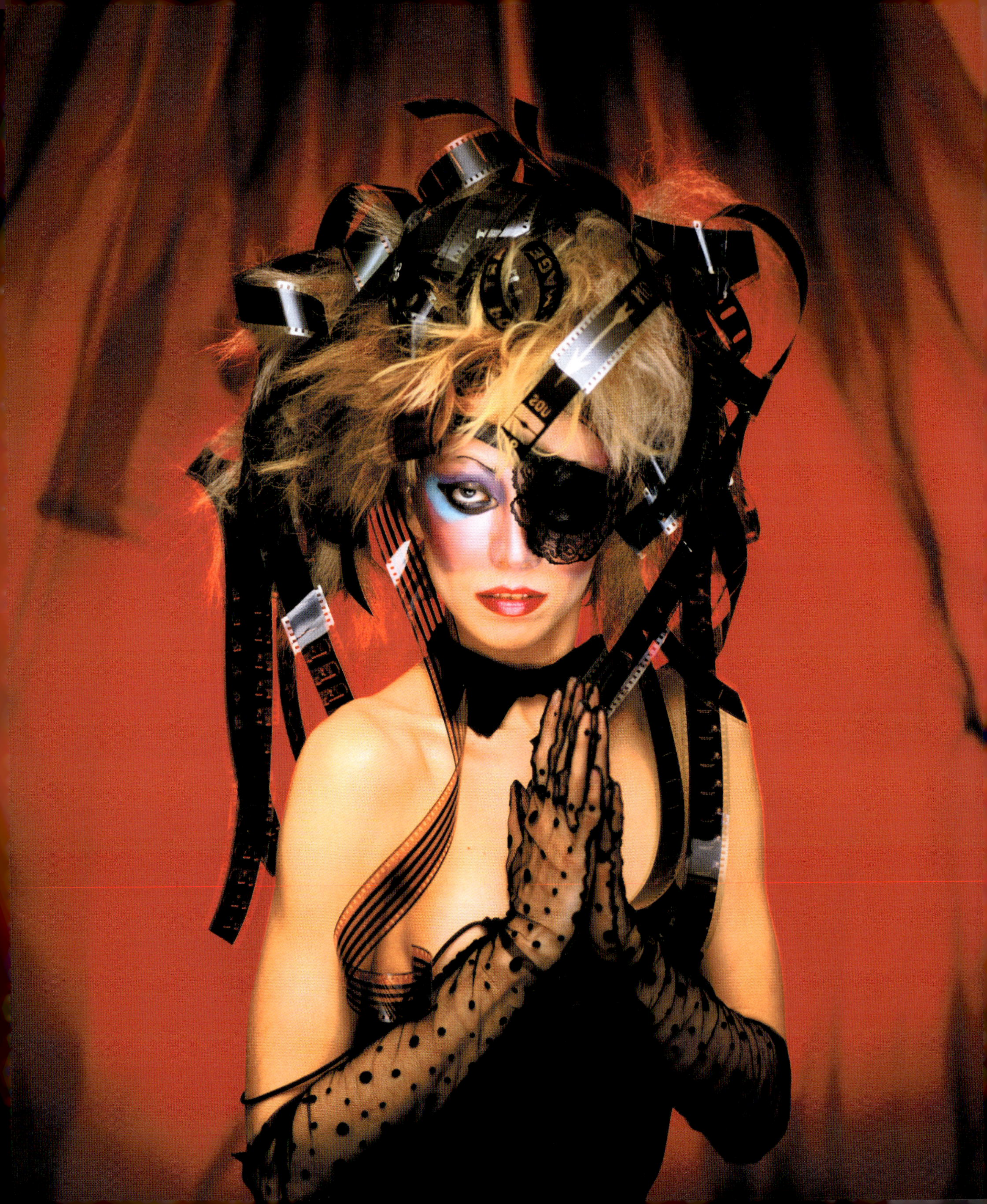

ACKNOWLEDGMENTS

First and foremost, I would like to thank Richard O'Brien for his enduring *Rocky Horror* and for his generosity and kindness.

And thank you to my HarperPop editor, Carrie Thornton, for her enthusiasm and support, as well as Carrie Napolitano, Liate Stehlik, Ben Steinberg, Libby Burton, Heidi Richter, Allison Carney, Martin Wilson, and Kasey Feather.

MAJOR THANKS TO:

Tim Mohr – Thankfully, the universe brought me Tim Mohr to craft the story around Mick's photos. Rest in peace, Tim—and tell Mick all about the book!

Peter McGuigan – for managing the whole shebang, as well as Joanna Rasheed and the Ultra Literary team.

Indelible Editions' Carol Bobolts and Dinah Dunn – for your guidance and patience

Lucky Singh – for being my guardian angel

Ashley Austin – Ninja Queen of Team Rock

SPECIAL THANKS TO:

Nell Campbell, Lady Patricia Quinn Stephens, Barry Bostwick, Tim Curry, Jim Sharman, and Sue Blane for sharing your sweet memories.

FOREVER GRATEFUL TO THESE CONTRIBUTORS:

Lou Adler, Richard Barone, Dianne Brill, Reeve Carney, Barnaby Clay, Simon Doonan, Shepard Fairey, Gottmilk, Pam Hogg, Eugene Hütz, Joan Jett, Betsey Johnson, Courtney Love, Juliette Lewis, Trixie Mattel, Duff McKagan, Jinkx Monsoon, Mark Mothersbaugh, Karen O, Julie Panebianco, Peaches, Cassandra Peterson, Arianne Phillips, Norman Reedus, Luke Spiller, Anna Sui, John Varvatos, and Andrew Watt.

A portion of the proceeds from the sale of this book will be donated to Exploring the Arts (ETA), dedicated to increasing equitable access to arts education in historically underserved schools on behalf of Richard O'Brien. www.exploringthearts.org

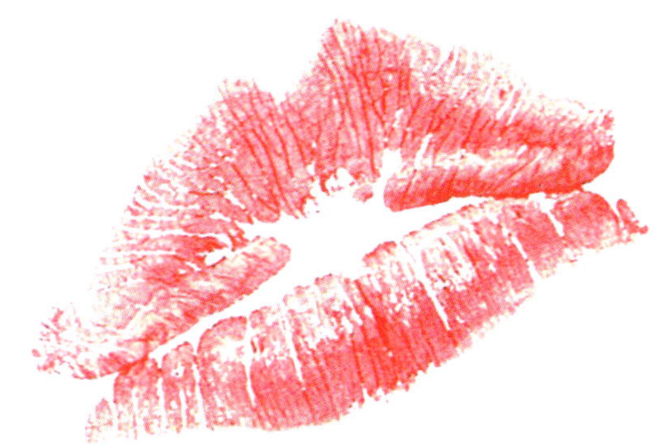

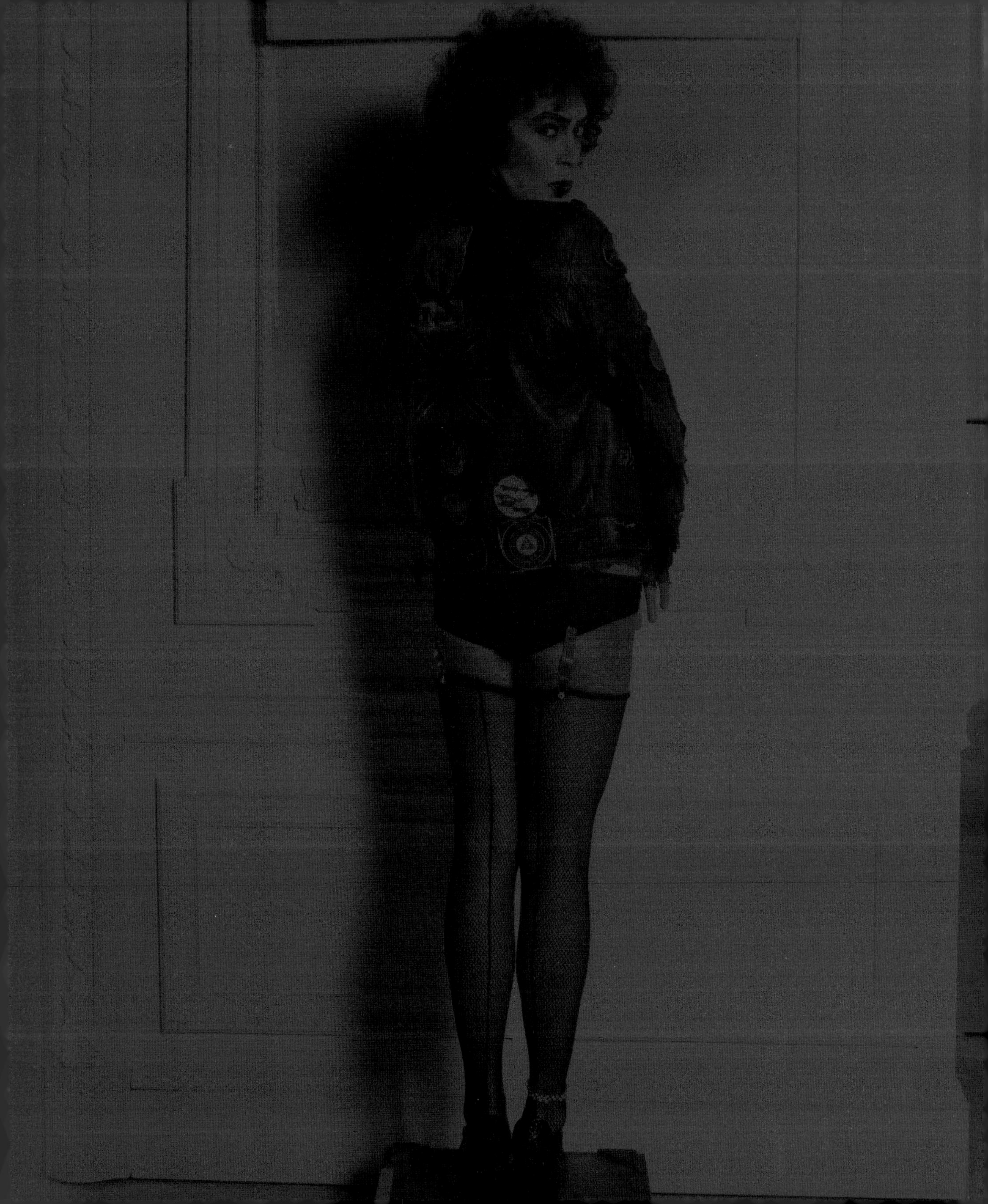